EXAMPLES & EXPLANATIONS

Dispute Resolution

Dispute Resolution

Fifth Edition

Michael L. Moffitt
Philip H. Knight Chair in Law and Professor
The University of Oregon School of Law

Andrea Kupfer Schneider
Professor of Law
Director, Institute for Women's Leadership
Director, Law School Dispute Resolution Program
Marquette University

Sarah Rudolph Cole
Michael E. Moritz Chair in Alternative Dispute Resolution
Moritz College of Law
Ohio State University

ASPEN PUBLISHING

To contact Customer Service, e-mail customer.service@aspenpublishing.com, call 1-800-950-5259, or mail correspondence to:

Aspen Publishing
Attn: Order Department
1 Wall Street
Burlington, MA 01803

Printed in the United States of America.

1 2 3 4 5 6 7 8 9 0

ISBN 979-8-8861-4215-0

Library of Congress Cataloging-in-Publication Data application is in process.

ABOUT ASPEN PUBLISHING

Aspen Publishing is a leading provider of legal education content and digital learning solutions in the United States and globally. Our innovative products and platforms—designed based on best practices in learning science—engage students and enhance outcomes. From textbooks and audiobooks authored by renowned experts to digital platforms and products like LEAF, Connected eBooks, Connected Quizzing, PracticePerfect, and JD-Next, we empower the next generation of legal professionals with innovative, trusted, and accessible resources.

The Aspen Casebook Series, affectionately known as the "red and black" casebooks among law faculty and students, includes hundreds of highly regarded textbooks across more than 80 disciplines. These range from foundational courses like Torts and Contracts to emerging electives such as Sustainability and the Law of Policing. Our study aids, including the popular *Examples & Explanations* series, help law students master complex topics with clarity and confidence.

Aspen's expertise extends to undergraduate education with our Paralegal, Criminal Justice, and Business Law series, offering the same hallmark quality to a broader audience. JD-Next, our groundbreaking online law school prep course and admissions test, provides a realistic preview of law school, equips students with essential skills for academic success, and evaluates their readiness for legal studies.

Aspen Publishing Is Proud to Be a UWorld Company

Since 2003, UWorld has been a global leader in developing high-quality learning tools for students preparing for high-stakes exams. With a commitment to excellence, UWorld has helped millions of students in undergraduate, graduate, and professional programs in fields such as medicine, nursing, finance, and law achieve their academic and career goals.

Founded by Chandra S. Pemmasani, M.D., during his medical residency, UWorld began focusing on medical education and has since expanded into various academic fields, including law. In 2020, UWorld launched its Legal vertical, starting with its comprehensive Multistate Bar Exam (MBE®) Question Bank, followed by the acquisition of Themis Bar Review, which integrated resources to provide a complete bar exam preparation experience. In 2024, UWorld expanded its offerings by acquiring Aspen Publishing, enhancing its suite of legal education products.

Today, UWorld offers an unparalleled range of study materials that blend active learning methods with expert content, ensuring students and educators can access the most effective resources. From bar preparation to law school success, UWorld is committed to supporting the next generation of legal professionals. Learn more at uworld.com.

To Roger Fisher, who gave us our passion for this field.
To Nancy Rogers, who mentored us and nurtured our intellectual growth.
To Bruce Patton, who taught us to teach.
To Bob Mnookin, who made teaching possible for us.
To Frank Sander, who taught us to take responsibility for the future of the field.

Michael, Andrea, and Sarah

Summary of Contents

Contents *xi*
Preface *xix*
Acknowledgments *xxiii*

Chapter 1 An Introduction to Negotiation 1
Chapter 2 Decision Making in Negotiation 23
Chapter 3 The Law of Negotiation 47
Chapter 4 Identifying Interests & Priorities Through Interviewing 89
Chapter 5 Attorneys, Clients, and Dispute Resolution 105
Chapter 6 An Introduction to Mediation 129
Chapter 7 Keeping Secrets: Confidentiality in Mediation 163
Chapter 8 An Introduction to Arbitration 187
Chapter 9 Must This Dispute Go to Arbitration? 219
Chapter 10 Federal Preemption and the Law(s) of Arbitration 265
Chapter 11 Dispute Resolution Within the Court System 283

Appendix 1: The Uniform Mediation Act *309*
Appendix 2: The Model Standards of Conduct for Mediators *317*
Appendix 3: The Federal Arbitration Act *325*
Table of Authorities *335*
Index *339*

Contents

Preface xix
Acknowledgments xxiii

Chapter 1 An Introduction to Negotiation 1

§1.1 Introduction 1
§1.2 Interests 2
§1.3 BATNA 3
§1.4 Bottom Lines (and Reservation Values) 4
§1.5 ZOPA 6
§1.6 Options and the Opportunity for Value Creation 6
§1.6.1 Shared Interests 7
§1.6.2 Economies of Scale 8
§1.6.3 Differences (in Risk Preference, Predictions, Time Frame, Resources and Capabilities, and Priorities) 9
§1.7 Models of Negotiation 10

Chapter 2 Decision Making in Negotiation 23

§2.1 Introduction 23
§2.2 Psychological Dynamics in Negotiation 24
§2.2.1 Endowment Effects 24
§2.2.2 Loss Aversion 24
§2.2.3 Anchoring 25
§2.2.4 Overconfidence Bias 25
§2.2.5 Zero-Sum Bias or Mythical Fixed-Pie Bias 25
§2.2.6 Reactive Devaluation 26
§2.3 Decision Analysis 26
§2.3.1 Building a Decision Tree 27
§2.3.2 The Limits of Decision Analysis 30
§2.4 Time and the Value of Money 31

Chapter 3 The Law of Negotiation 47

§3.1 Introduction 47
§3.2 Why "Good Faith" Is Not (Necessarily) the Answer 48
§3.3 Fraud 51

§3.3.1 When a Lie Isn't a Lie 51
§3.3.1.1 Knowing 52
§3.3.1.2 Misrepresentation 53
§3.3.2 When It Might Be a Lie but Isn't Punishable 53
§3.3.2.1 Materiality 53
§3.3.2.2 Puffery, Dissembling, and Misdirection 55
§3.3.3 Detrimental Reliance 57
§3.3.4 When a Lie Is a Lie and Is Punishable: Fraud 58
§3.3.5 When Silence Won't Save You 59
§3.3.5.1 Omission 60
§3.3.5.2 Duty to Correct 62
§3.3.5.3 When Silence Is Required (a Note on Client Confidentiality) 64
§3.3.6 What Happens to Liars? 64
§3.4 Misbehavior Beyond Lying 65
§3.5 Protecting the Confidentiality of the Parties' Terms of Agreement 68
§3.5.1 Hiding Settlement Terms from the Government 69
§3.5.2 Hiding Settlement Terms from Interested Parties in Related Disputes 71
§3.5.3 Hiding Settlement Terms from the Media, the Public, and Other Busybodies 72

Chapter 4 Identifying Interests & Priorities Through Interviewing 89

§4.1 Introduction 89
§4.2 Interests 90
§4.3 Attorney Client Relationship 91
§4.4 Interviewing Skills 93
§4.4.1 Welcoming the Client/Breaking the Ice 93
§4.4.2 Asking Good Questions 94
§4.4.3 Active Listening 95
§4.4.4 Facilitators & Hindrances to Gathering Information 96

Chapter 5 Attorneys, Clients, and Dispute Resolution 105

§5.1 Introduction 105
§5.2 The Duty to Advise a Client of ADR Options 106
§5.2.1 I Don't Have to Say a Thing 107

§5.2.2 I Should Advise My Client About ADR 108
§5.2.3 I Must Advise My Client About ADR 108
§5.2.4 I Must Advise My Client and Discuss with Opposing Party or Counsel 110
§5.2.5 Sanctions 110
§5.3 Duty to Communicate Settlement Offers 112
§5.3.1 Do I Have to Tell My Client About Every Offer? 112
§5.3.2 Does It Matter If the Other Side's Offer Is Terrible? 113
§5.3.3 Does This Mean That the Client Can't Give Me Discretion? 114
§5.3.4 Do I Have to Convey My Client's Settlement Offer If I Think the Offer Is Unwise? 115
§5.4 Client Confidences 116
§5.4.1 Can a Lawyer Sit Quietly in a Negotiation While a Client Commits Fraud? 117
§5.4.2 Can a Lawyer Help a Client Deceive an Arbitrator? 118
§5.4.3 Can a Lawyer Help a Client Deceive a Mediator? 119
§5.4.4 Can a Lawyer Disclose Confidential Information in a Mediation, Since Mediation Is a Confidential Process? 120

Chapter 6 An Introduction to Mediation 129

§6.1 Introduction: Definition(s) of Mediation 129
§6.2 Mediators' Approaches or Styles 130
§6.2.1 Facilitative Mediation 131
§6.2.2 Evaluative Mediation 132
§6.2.3 Riskin's Grid: The Potential Relationship Between Facilitative and Evaluative Mediation 133
§6.2.4 Transformative Mediation 135
§6.2.5 Facilitative, Evaluative, and Transformative Basic Logic 136
§6.3 Basic Principles of Mediation 137
§6.3.1 Impartiality (or Neutrality) 138
§6.3.2 Self-Determination 139
§6.3.3 Informed Consent 141
§6.4 Quality Control in Mediation 142
§6.4.1 Certification or Credentialing 143
§6.4.2 Ethics Codes 144
§6.4.3 Private Liability 145

§6.4.3.1 Immunity 146
§6.4.3.2 Standards of Care 147
§6.4.3.3 Causation and Damages 148

Chapter 7 Keeping Secrets: Confidentiality in Mediation 163

§7.1 Introduction 163
§7.2 Evidentiary Exclusions 165
§7.3 Protective Orders: Using the Court to Keep It Secret 167
§7.4 Contracts: I Promise Not to Talk 167
§7.5 Privilege: This Relationship Is Special 169
§7.5.1 Who Holds a Mediation Privilege? 170
§7.5.2 What If I Don't Want the Privilege (or Want to Waive It)? 172
§7.5.3 Are There Any Exceptions to Privileges? 173

Chapter 8 An Introduction to Arbitration 187

§8.1 Introduction 187
§8.1.1 Arbitration Is Not Litigation 189
§8.1.2 Arbitration Is a Contractual Substitute for Litigation 190
§8.1.3 Arbitration Is Not Mediation 191
§8.1.4 Comparing Litigation, Arbitration, and Mediation 193
§8.2 A Brief History of the Law of Arbitration 193
§8.3 Making Them Play: How Courts Compel Participation in Arbitration 195
§8.3.1 Motions to Stay the Litigation 196
§8.3.2 Motions to Compel Arbitration 197
§8.3.3 Defaults in Arbitration 197
§8.3.4 The Preclusive Effects of Arbitral Awards 198
§8.4 Getting Your Way: How Courts Handle Reviews of Arbitrators' Decisions 200
§8.4.1 Challenging Arbitral Awards Under the FAA 200
§8.4.2 Challenging Arbitral Awards on Nonstatutory Grounds 204
§8.5 Making Them Pay: How Courts Enforce Arbitral Awards 205
§8.5.1 Disputes at Home: Entering Arbitral Awards as Judgments 206
§8.5.2 Disputes Without Borders: International Arbitral Awards 207

Chapter 9 Must This Dispute Go to Arbitration? 219

§9.1 Introduction 219
§9.2 What Part of the Arbitration Agreement Is Being Challenged? The Doctrine of Separability 220
§9.3 Who Decides Contractual Challenges? 221
§9.3.1 Challenges to the Container Agreement 221
§9.3.2 Challenges to the Arbitration Clause Specifically 223
§9.3.3 Challenges to the Delegation Clause Specifically 223
§9.4 Objection #1: "What Contract? I Never Agreed to Arbitrate Anything." 224
§9.4.1 Mutual Assent 225
§9.4.2 Consideration 226
§9.4.3 Capacity, Authority, and Legality 227
§9.5 Objection #2: "Yes, I Signed a Contract with an Arbitration Clause, but the Contract Isn't Enforceable" 228
§9.5.1 Fraud 229
§9.5.2 "Public Policy" Objections 230
§9.5.3 Duress 232
§9.5.4 Unconscionability 232
§9.6 Objection #3: "The Arbitration Clause Itself Is Unenforceable" 235
§9.7 Objection #4: "This Particular Dispute Does Not Fall Within the Scope of the Arbitration Clause" 237
§9.7.1 Standards for Deciding If a Dispute Is Substantively Arbitrable 239
§9.7.2 Who Decides Whether a Dispute Is Substantively Arbitrable? 240
§9.8 Objection #5: "They Didn't Do What the Arbitration Agreement Requires Them to Do" 241
§9.8.1 Standards for Deciding If Conditions Precedent to Arbitration Have Been Satisfied 242
§9.8.2 Who Decides Whether a Dispute Is Procedurally Arbitrable? 243
§9.9 The Special Case of Class-wide Claims 243
§9.10 Pulling It All Together and a Preview of the Preemption Doctrine 246

Chapter 10 Federal Preemption and the Law(s) of Arbitration 265

§10.1 Introduction 265
§10.2 Some Background on the Preemption Doctrine 266
§10.3 Federal Arbitration Law as Substantive Law 267

§10.4 Five Categories of State Laws Related to Arbitration 268
§10.4.1 State Laws Affecting All Contracts 269
§10.4.2 State Laws Enforcing Arbitration Clauses 269
§10.4.3 State Laws Enforcing Arbitration Clauses, but Only with Some Modifications or Restrictions 270
§10.4.4 State Laws Disfavoring Arbitration Clauses and Some Other Subset of Contracts 271
§10.4.5 State Laws Disfavoring Only Arbitration Clauses 272
§10.5 What If the Parties Specifically Choose to Have State Law Govern the Question? 273
§10.5.1 If the Parties Specify State Law Only as to Substance 274
§10.5.2 If the Parties Specify State Law as to Arbitration 274
§10.5.3 If the Parties' Choice of Law Provision Is Ambiguous About the Scope of Its Coverage 275
§10.6 Conflicts Between Federal Law and the FAA 277

Chapter 11 Dispute Resolution Within the Court System 283

§11.1 Introduction 283
§11.2 Why a Court Has the Authority to Order ADR 284
§11.2.1 Rule 16 of the Federal Rules of Civil Procedure 284
§11.2.2 Federal Statutes and Local Rules 285
§11.2.3 The Court's Inherent Powers 285
§11.2.4 State ADR Systems 286
§11.3 What a Court Cannot Compel the Parties to Do 286
§11.3.1 A Court Can't Make Me Settle! 287
§11.3.2 A Court Can't Make Me Make an Offer! 287
§11.3.3 A Court Can't Force the Terms of an Offer (but Can Sometimes Punish Me If I Turn Down a Good Offer)! 288
§11.4 What a Court Can Compel the Parties to Do 289
§11.4.1 A Court Can Compel a Particular (Nonbinding) Form of ADR 289
§11.4.1.1 Mediation 290
§11.4.1.2 Nonbinding Arbitration 290
§11.4.1.3 Early Neutral Evaluation 291
§11.4.1.4 Summary Jury Trials 291

§11.4.2 A Court Can (but Doesn't Always) Compel Good-Faith Participation 292
§11.4.2.1 What Constitutes Good-Faith Participation? 293
§11.4.2.2 What Happens to Those Who Cross the Line? 297
§11.5 Enforcing Mediated Settlement Agreements 297

Appendix 1: The Uniform Mediation Act 309
Appendix 2: The Model Standards of Conduct for Mediators 317
Appendix 3: The Federal Arbitration Act 325
Table of Authorities 335
Index 339

Preface

No matter what kind of law you choose to practice, we are confident that the topics covered in this book will play a central role. Litigators in modern times resolve far more cases through consensual processes than through trial. Transactional lawyers negotiate the terms of deals. Family lawyers and their clients routinely attempt to mediate agreements before turning to a court to impose the terms of a parenting plan or a division of marital assets. Defense attorneys and prosecutors spend considerable energy negotiating plea agreements. Estate planners and probate attorneys anticipate (and sometimes clean up after) disputes that arise following the death of a family member or business partner. Regulatory agencies often engage in negotiated rulemaking. Court administrators routinely direct cases away from traditional litigation paths, in favor of voluntary alternative dispute resolution mechanisms. Arbitration clauses are commonplace in commercial contracts, employee handbooks, and consumer agreements. And so on. In short, alternative dispute resolution is everywhere in the practice of law.

Despite its importance, the law of alternative dispute resolution often finds itself scattered throughout a range of courses. Your Contracts class will teach you about the law of fraud and unconscionability. Your Ethics class will teach you about your duty to advise your client about settlement opportunities and the boundaries of deception. Your Trial Practice class will teach you about the integration of settlement talks into the cadence of modern litigation. And entire law school courses (like Negotiation or Mediation or Arbitration) focus on specific alternative dispute resolution processes. Each of these is important. But none of these courses fully paints the legal landscape within which alternative dispute resolution occurs.

This book aims to provide a comprehensive view of that legal landscape, and we are delighted to offer it in the Examples and Explanations format. Much of alternative dispute resolution is about *practice*— the application of principles and ideas to concrete circumstances. In what circumstances can negotiators find opportunities for creative settlement? What are the boundaries of legally acceptable behavior by negotiators? What factors influence negotiators' decisions? What constraints and opportunities does mediation present? Under what circumstances are alternative dispute resolution conversations confidential? To what extent can disputants be diverted from traditional litigation processes? What powers does a court have to enforce or avoid alternative dispute resolution mechanisms and their outcomes? How does the Supreme Court continue to define and modify the enforcement of arbitration clauses? What ethical obligations inform attorneys in alternative dispute resolution contexts?

Understanding the practice of alternative dispute resolution requires an understanding of the legal contexts in which these processes take place. This book, therefore, offers:

1. Clear, readable, and up-to-date overviews of important and complex legal doctrines and analytic frameworks, including:
   - Legal ethics relating to alternative dispute resolution, including those rules governing the role of lawyers in alternative dispute resolution
   - The psychology of negotiators' decision making, the economics of deal structures, and the decision analytic approach to alternative dispute resolution
   - The Uniform Mediation Act and state confidentiality laws
   - The Federal Arbitration Act, federal preemption, contractual challenges to arbitration, and the evolving federal policy favoring arbitration
   - The three primary ADR processes and their relationships to each other and to the courts
   - Court-mandated alternative dispute resolution and its requirements, forms, and limits
2. Practice applying legal concepts and analytic frameworks to specific alternative dispute resolution circumstances
3. A logical organization that traces the coverage in most survey courses on alternative dispute resolution
4. Liberal use of visual aids, diagrams, charts, and conceptual illustrations

Thousands of law students have read and commented on drafts and the first four editions of *Dispute Resolution: Examples and Explanations*. In a range of courses, including Dispute Resolution, Negotiation, Mediation, Arbitration, and even Civil Procedure, we have offered these materials as a mechanism to enhance our students' understanding of the law. Our students have taught us how to explain the law of alternative dispute resolution, how it works, and why it sometimes doesn't. It is no exaggeration to say that our students helped to write this book. For that reason, we are confident it is tailored to students' interests and needs.

We hope that this book will help you prepare effectively both for the Bar exam and for practice. Many states are moving toward practice-focused bar exams, and the NextGen Bar Exam, in particular, will focus on client counseling, advising, negotiation and alternative dispute resolution— all topics covered in depth in this text. More importantly, the NextGen bar intends to assess not simply whether a future lawyer understands the law, but also how to apply it in practice. In particular, the exam will require a future lawyer to successfully identify lawyering strategies within the lawyer-client relationship, including identifying a client's goals, interests and constraints. Our focus on interviewing, negotiation, mediation, arbitration and counseling clients will provide users with an excellent foundation not only in alternative dispute resolution courses, but also when they prepare for and take the NextGen Bar.

Alternative Dispute resolution is a permanent and increasingly important component of legal education and law practice. We hope that you find this book helpful as you study its contours.

Michael Moffitt
Andrea Kupfer Schneider
Sarah Rudolph Cole
September 2024

Acknowledgments

We would like to express our appreciation to our generous colleagues in the field of alternative dispute resolution, many of whom provided formal and informal assistance in the creation of this book. We specifically want to thank our coauthors in other writing endeavors, including Cynthia Alkon, Kristen Blankley, Bob Bordone, Liz Borgwardt, Jennifer Brown, Noam Ebner, Brian Farkas, Roger Fisher, Brian Ganson, Erik Girvan, Art Hinshaw, Chris Honeyman, Russell Korobkin, Lela Love, Carrie Menkel-Meadow, Jamie Henikoff Moffitt, Scott Peppet, Sharon Press, Jennifer Reynolds, Nancy Rogers, Jean Sternlight, and Nancy Welsh. Collaborating with them shaped and enriched our understanding of alternative dispute resolution.

We are grateful for the support we have received from our law schools and our faculty colleagues. They have provided not only financial and research support but also the academic leadership and encouragement that sustained our enthusiasm for this project.

Almost 70 research assistants helped to conceive, craft, and edit the first, second, third, and fourth editions of this book. Through a genuine collaboration and mutual learning experience, we came better to understand this book's potential. For their contributions, we thank Adam Anderson, Tiffany Baack, Neal Bartlett, Jessica Bloomfield, Brian Brockman, David Cadaret (who is now a law professor!), Aileen Carlos, Noah Chamberlain, Taylor Chase, Matthew Clabots, Jilian Clearman, Austin Crockett, Blake Dava, Michael Emer, Matthew Faust, Jonathan Fritz, Madison Gagne, Emilia Gardner, Matthew Garner, Kathleen Goodrich, Katherine Grant, Jeremy Guth, Starla Hargita, Piper Harris, Benjamin Heller, Morgan Henson, Matthew Hodges, Meredith Holley, Tiffany Keb, Matthew Kee, Dighan Kelly, Skylar Kogelschatz, Jessica Kumke, Samuel Leyba, Benedict Linsenmeyer, Courtney Lords, Avery Mayne, Alexa Miller, Travis Miller, Jonah Morningstar, Kathleen Murray, Erin Naipo, Hal Neth, Erika Norman, Jessika Palmer, Laura Panchot, Ron Phillips, Amanda Pirt, Tiffany Ray, Austin Richardson, Dominic Rosso, Stephanie Rubstello, Andrew Sadjak, Benjamin Scott, Sean Slisbury, Jonathan Scharrer (also a law professor!), Adam Schurle, Sara Scoles, Caitlyn Christine Slawson, Austin Smith, Joel Smith, Rachel Sowray, Bill Spiry, Margaret Spring, Brittany Steele, Jason Tashea, Paul Tassin, Andrea Thompson, Nick Toman, James Tschudy, Michael Tuchalski, and Michael Watson.

Finally, we thank the thousands of students on whom we have imposed various versions of these materials over the last decade. We look forward to continuing to learn from our students in the years to come.

Acknowledgments

The authors would like to thank the rights holders for their permission to reproduce the following material:

Dispute Resolution

CHAPTER 1

An Introduction to Negotiation

§1.1 INTRODUCTION

Most disputants, in most disputes, turn first to some form of negotiation to try to resolve their disputes. Understanding negotiation is, therefore, foundational to understanding almost all forms of consensual dispute resolution. When one attorney calls opposing counsel and tries to secure a commitment on a revised lease term, both attorneys are negotiating. When an insurance adjuster offers a financial settlement in exchange for a release, the adjuster and the policyholder are negotiating. When attorneys try to settle a case before trial, they are negotiating. When disputing parties appear before a mediator, they are negotiating (with the assistance of a third party). Disputants routinely communicate with each other, in one form or another, in an effort to persuade the other to take a particular course of action. In other words, they negotiate.

Not all disputes are resolved through negotiation, of course. Most of the court opinions you have read in law school casebooks are the product of disputes that were resolved through litigation. And as you will study in the arbitration sections of this book, an increasing number of disputes are resolved by the pronouncement of a privately hired arbitrator. Still, even in these circumstances, the disputants had an opportunity to resolve some or all of the issues through negotiation. Negotiation is so prevalent today that few disputants arrive at court (or at an arbitration) without having previously attempted to negotiate a settlement.

Though most recognize the prevalence and importance of negotiation in the practice of law, the negotiation process itself is the subject of ongoing examination. Scholars and practitioners alike continue to search for the best ways to describe the dynamics between two or more disputants who seek to persuade each other to some course of action. Compared with some aspects of legal practice, negotiation is relatively unstructured. There are few "rules"—at least not in the same way that there are rules of pleadings, of evidence, or even of professional responsibility. At the same time, some consensus has emerged about how to describe the structures underlying legal negotiation.

In this chapter, we outline some of the basic vocabulary, frameworks, and concepts central to negotiation.

§1.2 INTERESTS

Every negotiator enters a negotiation with a set of **interests**—the concerns, fears, desires, and dreams that motivate them at the negotiation table. A party will be happy with a negotiated outcome based, in large measure, on how well it satisfies that party's interests. Interests are the primary currency of negotiation—the things that guide negotiators' decisions—but they are often unspoken or masked. One key to understanding negotiators' actions, therefore, lies in understanding the interests underlying their negotiation strategies.

Negotiators are sometimes unaware of the relevant interests in a negotiation because they focus too heavily on one or both sides' negotiation **positions** (*what* they say they want), rather than on each side's interests (*why* they want what they want). A plaintiff might demand "a million dollars" to settle their claim against their former employer. The client's position is perfectly clear: One million dollars from their former employer will settle their claim. Without knowing more about the plaintiff, however, we cannot know for certain what their underlying interests might be. Having financial security for retirement? Having a face-saving story to tell their family? Removing roadblocks to their future career development? Restoring their reputation among their former colleagues? Covering short-term expenses? Punishing the company for what the client perceived to be despicable treatment?

If this plaintiff's attorney fails to ask enough questions to understand the client's true motivations—the client's interests—the attorney will be constrained to seek only one type of settlement: one that produces a million dollars. As a result, the attorney will be negotiating without some very important information. (Is it possible to satisfy the client with a settlement that includes different terms? Is the client indifferent to the payment form? Does the client care about the scope of the release? Is the client operating within important time constraints?) For similar reasons, even counsel for the defendant would do well to inquire about the plaintiff's underlying interests, despite the fact that the plaintiff's demand suggests only one outcome would satisfy them.

This distinction between positions and interests is not the only articulation of this dynamic—the difference between what people say they want and what might actually satisfy their wishes. Some authors describe differences between needs, wants, or objective values, for example. However one thinks about these terms, the idea is that negotiation involves an effort by each side to satisfy its interests as well as it can.

§1.3 BATNA

BATNA, an acronym and concept originally developed in the book *Getting to Yes*,[1] stands for **best alternative to a negotiated agreement**. The idea underlying BATNAs is that every negotiator has *some* alternative to reaching an agreement with the other side. It may be attractive, or it may be awful. (Don't let the "best" part fool you.) A negotiator's BATNA is the thing they would do if the present negotiations broke down and produced no agreement. What steps would the negotiator take to try to satisfy their interests? The answer is that they would pursue their BATNA (which might also be taking no affirmative steps at this point).

One benefit of understanding your BATNA in a negotiation is that it serves as a reality check for you on what the other side has offered. In short, a negotiator should never settle for something that is worse than their BATNA. If you knew you could buy your favorite car elsewhere for $20,000, it would make little sense to buy your second favorite car for $21,000 unless there is something important at stake beyond the quality of the car and its price tag. Using the same logic, it would not be sensible to enter an agreement if it satisfies your interests *less well* than some other course of action you could take.

The term **alternatives**, in the language of modern negotiation theory, refers to actions that one negotiator can take without the consent of the other(s). If a party walks away from the negotiation table (either literally or figuratively), they walk to whichever alternative they believe to be most attractive.

The initial step in determining a BATNA, therefore, is to assess the full range of possible alternatives to an agreement. In many disputes, one conspicuous alternative is pursuing legal actions of one form or another. You do not need the consent of the other party to file a lawsuit. But negotiators typically

1. Roger Fisher, William Ury & Bruce Patton, *Getting to Yes*, 3d ed. (2011).

have multiple alternatives. Could you pursue another potential business partner? Could you go over the head of the opposing negotiator? Could you go public with the dispute? Could you just let it drop? Without knowing the full range of alternatives, a negotiator cannot accurately assess his or her BATNA.

After identifying the range of possible alternatives, the second step in calculating a BATNA is to compare the relative merits, risks, and opportunities of each course of action. The alternative that presents the most attractive package, on balance, is your BATNA. If one alternative is finding another business partner, you would need to assess potential risks and gains from that decision. If an alternative is litigation, then obviously you will need to conduct considerable research to assess how attractive it would be to go to court. What substantive law(s) likely control this set of circumstances? What is the likelihood of success at trial? How much will discovery, trial, and possible appeals cost? How long will it take? What will be the effects of the publicity associated with the trial? And so on. Often, doing nothing (or dropping the case) is an alternative as well, and it comes with its own risks and benefits.

§1.4 BOTTOM LINES (AND RESERVATION VALUES)

According to some visions of negotiation, each negotiator has a bottom line—a limit beyond which he or she will not or cannot go. Economists typically refer to these limits as each party's **reservation value**.

A party's reservation value is a function of his or her BATNA, but the two are not the same thing. A negotiator's BATNA is typically an action—go to court, buy another house, accept the other employment offer, etc. But one action is not easily compared with another action without translating these actions into the same currency, whether this is money or something else. As a result, a negotiator might reasonably seek to translate the value of his or her BATNA into strictly economic terms so that it can be compared with a similarly translated offer during the negotiation.

In other words, a negotiator's reservation value is what the other party would have to offer to make the negotiator indifferent between accepting the offer and walking to his or her BATNA. If you are the plaintiff in a lawsuit and the defendant offers you $50,000 to settle the claim, should you accept? The answer depends, of course, on your interests and on your expectations of what would happen if you went to court.

Imagine that you are holding an offer to work for Company A for $75,000 per year. You are about to enter discussions with Company B about the prospect of working for Company B. What is your reservation value in those negotiations? If you found the two companies completely identical, your reservation value would probably be very near to $75,000. If you preferred the line of work, the job responsibilities, and the people at Company B, your reservation value in those negotiations would probably be less than $75,000, because you'd be willing to sacrifice some money in order to secure the benefits Company B would provide. How much less would you be willing to take? That depends on the strength of your interests, your financial situation, etc. For purposes of illustration, assume that you decided that you would be willing to give up $5,000 in salary to take the job with Company B. Your reservation value, therefore, would be around $70,000 as you entered negotiations with Company B. In short, if they offer more than $70,000, you'll take it.

To continue with this example, Company B also enters this negotiation with both a BATNA and a reservation value. Assume that Company B has also interviewed a more experienced job applicant—a person they consider slightly better qualified for the job. (Sorry!) The more experienced applicant is Company B's BATNA in its negotiations with you. Assume that the more experienced person has also made it clear that she will not accept the job for less than $110,000. In determining its reservation value, Company B would have to determine how much *more* valuable the experienced applicant would be as compared with you. How much more would they be willing to pay to get her instead of you? For purposes of illustration, assume that the company thinks she is worth $20,000 per year more. Their reservation value entering negotiations with you would be around $90,000. If they can get you for less than $90,000, Company B would prefer to hire you. Otherwise, they'll hire the more experienced applicant.

Negotiators sometimes face far more complex decisions, and then the process of identifying a reservation value is correspondingly more complex. Consider, for example, an unhappy consumer who is trying to decide whether they should file a lawsuit against the manufacturer of a piece of allegedly defective computer equipment. Perhaps the company has offered a modest rebate to settle the consumer's complaint. How would the consumer go about assessing whether to accept the offered coupon? Even if they viewed the decision in only monetary terms, they would have to consider the costs of drafting a complaint, the costs of filing fees, the prospects of winning at various stages in the litigation, the costs of litigating, the likelihood of recovering various amounts at trial, and the prospect of appeals. The consumer would also have to consider *when* each of these expenses would be incurred, and possible judgments would be awarded. The list of variables is long enough to cause many decision makers (particularly those who are making decisions about large sums of money) to seek mechanisms for organizing and understanding the various factors, rather than merely "eyeballing" the case or going with their instincts. In Chapter 2, we describe a more detailed set of mathematical processes for making assessments like these. For purposes of this chapter, the important concept is that the consumer, like any negotiator, would have *some* reservation value. There will almost always be *something* the manufacturer could offer the consumer that would make the consumer indifferent between suing and settling.

§1.5 ZOPA

ZOPA, or **zone of possible agreement**, refers to the space between the two negotiators' reservation values—the points at which a mutually satisfactory agreement is theoretically possible. Some scholars refer to this as a **bargaining zone**.

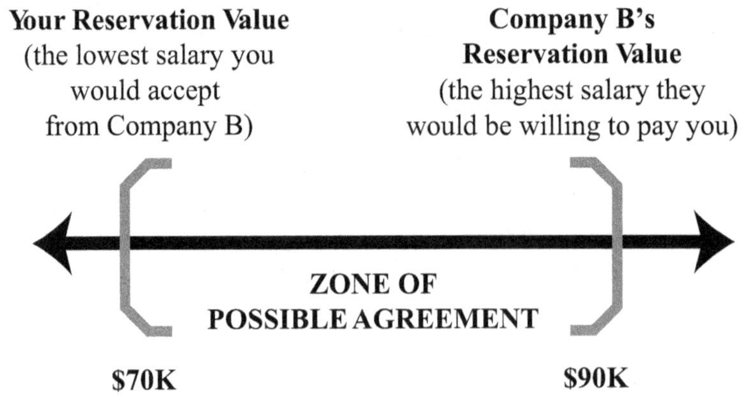

In the employment situation described above, your reservation value was $70,000 and Company B's was $90,000. This produces a ZOPA spanning $20,000. Economists would look at this situation and say that you and Company B should reach a deal, because by doing so you can each do better for yourselves than you could by walking to your respective BATNAs.

Of course, the world does not always pay perfect attention to economic analysis. There are many reasons why negotiators might not arrive at a deal, even when one is theoretically possible. Maybe the negotiators don't have adequate time to find a possible deal. Maybe one or both of them lack appropriate decision-making authority. Maybe one or both of them engage in gamesmanship or other strategic behaviors that result in a failed negotiation. (We discuss some of the decision-making factors driving negotiators in Chapter 2.) As a matter of theory, though, the existence of a ZOPA signals that a deal should be possible.

§1.6 OPTIONS AND THE OPPORTUNITY FOR VALUE CREATION

The benefit of the framework involving reservation values and ZOPAs is that these concepts provide for ready comparisons. They are simple. Unfortunately, their simplicity also presents an important limitation. In the real world of negotiations, parties will rarely be comparing one strictly monetary offer with another strictly monetary offer.

Virtually all modern negotiation theories suggest that negotiators should *avoid* negotiating based on positional haggling or behaving as though money were the only thing at issue. Instead, negotiators should "focus on interests, not on positions," and in doing so, should develop multiple options for satisfying those interests.

In the language of negotiation scholarship, **option** is the label given to an element of a possible deal between the parties. A lump-sum cash payment is an option. An annuity is an option. A confidentiality clause is an option. And so are a joint press statement, a contingent payment, a late fee, a dispute resolution clause, and a choice of law provision. (Notice the distinction between words that hold apparently similar definitions: **Alternatives** are those actions one side can take on its own, and **options** are possible pieces of a deal both sides might consider putting into an agreement.)

If they are well structured, options are vehicles for "expanding the pie"—for presenting deal packages that are more attractive to both sides than the mere exchange of dollars. Economists describe a limited set of circumstances in which negotiators can "create value." Wise negotiators recognize these circumstances and capitalize on them to satisfy their interests as well as possible in an agreement. Below, we survey seven categories of circumstances in which negotiators have an opportunity to craft value-creating options that go beyond a simple zero-sum exchange of dollars.

§1.6.1 Shared Interests

In some circumstances, both negotiators will have some interests in common. If negotiators can identify these shared interests (called **noncompetitive similarities** by economists), they can structure deal terms that make both sides better off. In a negotiation between a star soccer player and her team, for example, you risk falling into the trap of assuming that all of the relevant interests are opposed. (The player wants to be paid more; the team wants to pay the player less.) Even if those interests exist, they are not the only possible interests. For example, both the player and the team want the team to play well. Both the player and the team also want full stadiums, good press coverage, and a successful season. In this case, they might build incentives into the contract, establish agreements on media appearances and a social media strategy, or structure payments in ways that permit the team flexibility in hiring other star players. This way, both parties gain from expanding their deal package to include mutually attractive options.

Opportunities to capitalize on shared interests are often most conspicuous in negotiations between prospective business partners exploring possible deals, but even parties to a dispute sometimes hold shared interests.

For example, divorcing parents clearly differ in their visions of the future. Both, however, likely have a noncompetitive similar interest in providing for their children's health and education. They may disagree about the details of how best to accomplish this, but each is made better off if their agreement satisfies these shared interests. Similarly, labor and management often have conspicuously divergent interests in negotiating the terms of a future contract, but both share an interest in the long-term financial health of the company and the community in which it is located. A newspaper and a person accusing the paper of publishing an inaccurate statement will likely disagree about whether the statement constituted libel, but they may have a shared interest in correcting an inaccurate statement. A supplier and buyer in a dispute over a delivery of widgets may disagree as to the liability of one or the other but may share an interest in resolving the dispute quickly and amicably enough to continue their otherwise mutually profitable business.

§1.6.2 Economies of Scale

Negotiators also sometimes create value in an agreement by capitalizing on **economies of scale**. In virtually all circumstances, the more of something you buy, the cheaper each unit will be (hence the bargains at stores that sell goods in bulk). The more of something you produce, the more cheaply you can produce each unit (this is one of the reasons it can cost you more to make your own dinner than to eat out at a high-volume restaurant). Economies of scale also suggest carpooling (you don't both need to buy gas) and sharing an apartment (you don't each need a separate refrigerator).

Negotiators often have redundant expenditures—even in the contexts of disputes—and these redundancies lead to the possibility of economies of scale. An easy example is that there is no reason for each litigant to pay separately to have a deposition recorded and transcribed. The parties could easily split those costs, and each would wind up with the same product for less than it would have had to pay independently. In some cases, disputants might even agree mutually to hire a single expert to perform an analysis relevant to the dispute. For example, two disputants could split the cost of a single land surveyor to resolve a property boundary dispute or a single financial advisor to review tax consequences of different deal structures. Sometimes, of course, each party may have strategic reasons to think that the extra cost of having its own expert outweighs the potential for savings from economies of scale. Still, the basic concept underneath economies of scale is that negotiators can create value (or at least prevent the loss of value) by sharing redundant expenses.

§1.6.3 Differences (in Risk Preference, Predictions, Time Frame, Resources and Capabilities, and Priorities)

It is no surprise that negotiators often differ. Indeed, the reason they enter negotiations is typically precisely because they have some differences. What may be less intuitive is that these differences between negotiators can be an important source of value-creating trades.

Differences in Risk Preference Not everyone holds the same attitude toward risk. Some people can't stand to roll the dice; some can't stay away from the gambling table. In a negotiation between parties with different risk tolerances, the party who is more risk averse should be willing to pay a premium for the more risk-tolerant party to assume more risk in a deal. For example, in a deal between business venture partners, the more risk-tolerant party should be willing to offer the other party more of a guaranteed revenue stream in exchange for receiving a greater percentage of any "upside" in the business.

Differences in Prediction Mark Twain once wrote, "It is difference of opinion that makes the horses race." And people buy and sell stock every day based on differing opinions: sellers believe the stock price will drop while buyers believe that the price will rise. Similarly, if two negotiators disagree about the future, they can reach a deal that amounts to a "bet" on what will happen in the future. In this case, both parties will be happier with the agreement than they would have been with a straight exchange of dollars. For example, assume a landowner believes that the environmental damage caused by the defendant has only begun to be unearthed, and the defendant insists that everything has already been discovered and remediated. If the defendant believes that no further environmental damage will be discovered on the landowner's property, it can promise to pay the landowner an enormous sum of money in the event of future hazard in exchange for a smaller payment today. If each is confident of its prediction, each prefers this outcome to a split-the-difference cash payment.

Differences in Time Frame A dollar today has a different value than a dollar tomorrow. In virtually all circumstances, each of us would prefer a dollar today to a dollar tomorrow. But negotiators may differ in the *extent* to which they prefer a dollar today. (In economic terms, the parties may have different **discount rates**.) If negotiators recognize that they have differences in time frames and cash flow needs, they can craft deals to maximize their differing interests in ways that capitalize on these differences. This explains why parties sometimes pay settlements over time, and why they sometimes announce settlements immediately after the end of a company's fiscal year.

Differences in Resources and Capabilities Negotiating parties may also come to the table with different skills, different endowments, and different assets. Rather than creating dissension, these differences can also help facilitate a deal. Many joint ventures or partnership deals are predicated on the fact that one party has more time (or greater skills) to carry out the deal, while the other party is willing to finance but cannot spend (or has no interest in spending) the time to oversee the investment. Two friends, for example, who jointly invest in a rental property may divide their responsibilities by who has more abilities in home repair, who has more time to visit and oversee the property, who has more knowledge of the real estate market, or who has more cash on hand to buy the property when it comes on the market. The allocation of these responsibilities will be most efficient if they recognize and capitalize on those differences.

Differences in Priorities Virtually no negotiation of any importance is really about only one issue. Instead, negotiations usually involve multiple issues. Any time multiple issues are on the table, the parties will likely attach different values to those issues. Recognizing these differences in priorities, negotiators can trade off one issue for another (often called **logrolling** in the negotiation literature). If the prospective employee cares more about salary and job training, and the employer cares relatively more about benefits and vacation, they should structure a deal in which the employee gets more of what he wants on the issues of greater importance to him in exchange for the employer getting a more favorable deal on the other terms.

§1.7 MODELS OF NEGOTIATION

None of the frameworks, vocabulary, or concepts we describe above actually tell a negotiator what to say or do in a particular setting. Should I make the first offer? How should I respond to what the other party suggested? Should I make this proposal or that one? Should I include other people in the conversation? Should we talk here or there? Now or later? Negotiation is filled with tactical or **strategic decisions**, and it is far beyond the scope of this book to suggest specific answers to these complex questions. (They may look like simple questions, but if you take a course on Negotiation, you will start to see that they have layers and layers underneath.)

Some have suggested that there are two basic models of negotiation advice. On the one hand, there is advice to help negotiators figure out how to explore their interests, how to make sure that communication is clear and efficient, how to maintain relationships, how to persuade based on objective criteria, and how to solve problems creatively. Advice along these lines has taken on many different labels, though the most common are "principled negotiation," "integrative negotiation," "mutual gains negotiation," and "problem-solving negotiation." On the other hand, a different type of advice focuses on how to secure an advantage over the other side, how to get a bigger slice of the pie, how to claim value that has been created, and how to manipulate the other negotiator's decision. Advice along these lines has been called "competitive bargaining," "distributive negotiation," or "hard bargaining."

We are not convinced that the lines between these two models of negotiation are as clear as the labels suggest. Principled negotiators who create an enormously efficient and creative agreement must still eventually figure out how to allocate costs or benefits—an activity that involves dividing the figurative pie. And even the most steadfastly competitive bargainer would not be so foolish as to forgo a potentially beneficial trade merely because it somehow also benefits the other side. Negotiators may come into negotiations with a particular default or instinct about how best to persuade the other party. But negotiation is a dynamic, evolving process, and the most skilled negotiators would never limit themselves to merely one approach.

Examples

The Apartment of Jack's Dreams

Jack is hoping to find a new apartment to rent with his friends Chrissy and Janet. He knows of four apartments currently available, any of which would at least minimally satisfy their interests. The first is on Santa Monica Boulevard, and it is a bit smaller than Jack was hoping to find for the three of them. They negotiated with the landlord at Santa Monica Boulevard, and the best rate they could get was $3,400 per month. The second apartment is on Wilshire Boulevard. It is beautiful, but at $5,000 per month, they have all decided that they cannot afford it. The third apartment is in a neighborhood near the Third Street Promenade, far from where they were hoping to live, and it would cost them $3,200 per month. Of these three, the Santa Monica Boulevard property presents the most attractive combination of price, size, and location, though it is not ideal. The fourth apartment, on Main Street, is large, convenient, and located in an attractive neighborhood. The Main Street apartment is owned by Mr. and Mrs. Roper, who listed its rental price at $4,000 per month. Jack thinks the combination of the extra space and the better neighborhood makes the Main Street apartment worth at least several hundred dollars per month more to them than the apartments on Santa Monica Boulevard or near the Third Street Promenade.

1. **Jack's BATNA.** As Jack considers beginning a negotiation with Mr. Roper over the Main Street apartment, what is his BATNA?
2. **Jack's reservation value.** What would you estimate Jack's reservation value to be in a negotiation with Mr. Roper?

The Ropers own a number of apartments, including the one on Main Street. The current tenants of the Main Street apartment have been paying $3,200 per month, and they are leaving at the end of this coming month. The Ropers are planning to move into the apartment themselves in 12 months, but they are hoping to rent the apartment to new tenants from now until they are ready to move in. The Ropers have advertised the apartment, and they are asking for $4,000 per month. So far, only a man named Furley has shown interest in the apartment, and he was unwilling to pay more than $3,200 per month, so the Ropers have turned him down. As far as the Ropers know, Furley has not yet found an apartment, so it might be possible for them to go back and strike a deal with him for $3,200 per month. The Ropers' expenses, including rent, utilities, taxes, upkeep, and the like, take virtually all of the $3,200 per month, leaving them with no profit and no cushion in the event of unforeseen expenses. They think there is about a 50-50 chance they would be able to find a renter immediately if they dropped the rent to $3,600 per month, and they are absolutely confident that if they didn't get someone this month, they could find someone by next month at that price. They would like to get more than that, but they also don't want to let the apartment stand unoccupied (and therefore receive no rent) in the coming months. They knew there was only a small chance that anyone would agree to pay $4,000 per month for the apartment, but they thought it was worth asking for that amount.

3. **The Ropers' BATNA.** Assuming the Ropers are preparing to negotiate with Jack about the possibility of Jack and his friends renting their Main Street apartment, what is the Ropers' BATNA?
4. **The Ropers' reservation value.** What would you estimate the Ropers' reservation value to be in a negotiation with Jack?
5. **A ZOPA for Jack and the Ropers?** Based on your responses above, in a negotiation between the Ropers and Jack about renting this apartment, do you think a ZOPA exists? If yes, what would you estimate that zone to be?

Wounded in the Workplace

Alexa, an engineer at Madison's Motorcycles, suffered a workplace injury when a rack holding motorcycles collapsed, and a falling bike shattered her leg. Alexa's surgery bills are likely to be about $50,000, and she lost four months of work (at roughly $10,000/month). Although Alexa has been physically cleared to work, the mental health professional with whom she is working has indicated that her ongoing reactions to the trauma and stress make returning to work unlikely for some time yet. Alexa's lawyer's preliminary investigation found that the rack was faulty and should have been replaced at least a year prior by Madison's Motorcycles. Through her lawyer,

Alexa has sued Madison's Motorcycles for $250,000 in damages for lost wages, medical bills, emotional distress, and negligence. Privately, Alexa's lawyer has advised her that given these facts, her likely expected value of going to trial is about $150,000, but it would cost $20,000 in additional unrecoverable legal fees. Madison's Motorcycles is figuring out their litigation strategy with their lawyer and their insurance company. The insurance company's lawyer told Madison's Motorcycles that if they go to trial, the expected verdict would be a judgment of $150,000 and would cost them $40,000 in unrecoverable legal fees. Any litigation would likely take approximately two years if it proceeds to trial.

6. **Alexa's BATNA.** As Alexa considers beginning a negotiation with Madison's Motorcycles over the damages, what are her alternatives to settlement. Based on what you have read above, what do you believe is her BATNA?

7. **Alexa's reservation value.** What would you estimate Alexa's reservation value to be in a negotiation with Madison's Motorcycles?

8. **Madison's Motorcycles BATNA.** As Madison's Motorcycles considers beginning a negotiation with Alexa over the damages, what are their alternatives to settlement? What is the company's BATNA?

9. **Madison's Motorcycles reservation value.** What would you estimate Madison's Motorcycles' reservation value to be in a negotiation with Alexa?

10. **A ZOPA?** Given your answers above, do you think there is a Zone of Possible Agreement between Alexa and Madison's Motorcycles? What would that be?

Merchandise Mayhem

Athlete Alliance is a small but growing sportswear company. Its niche is non-mainstream sports, and it already has several dozen athletes under contract. According to these contracts, Athlete Alliance owns the intellectual property rights to the athletes' personal brands, including logos and branded merchandise. Athlete Alliance has a small production facility for creating branded merchandise, and it has a powerful and popular Internet site through which it does most of its sales. As the popularity of Athlete Alliance's website has grown, Athlete Alliance has struggled to keep up with demand. It has long recognized that this pent-up demand risks creating a market for counterfeit merchandise. The Athlete Alliance board of directors has been making plans to make a public stock offering in the near future to raise capital to expand, but the company's sales over the past several months lagged without any obvious explanation—until an Athlete Alliance employee noticed an Athlete Alliance athlete's branded merchandise for sale in a StrideZone retail store at the local shopping mall. The Athlete Alliance employee was quickly able to recognize the StrideZone merchandise as counterfeit. StrideZone is one of the largest sports apparel retailers in the nation, though industry insiders are somewhat concerned that the company has not been working directly with as many new athletes as it may need to sustain its growth. StrideZone has enormous production facilities, a robust distribution network, and a growing chain of retail operations. Athlete Alliance filed a lawsuit against StrideZone, alleging that StrideZone had been unlawfully producing, distributing, and selling branded merchandise by athletes under contract with Athlete Alliance.

11. **Options to explore.** Beyond the question of a possible exchange of dollars, what potential value-creating options should StrideZone and Athlete Alliance at least explore in settlement conversations, based on the facts above?

Teachers in Turmoil

The school board and the teachers union have been unable to reach an agreement regarding the terms of the teachers' contract for the coming years. Each has threatened to take action if a settlement is not reached soon.

The union has publicly announced that its priorities are (1) receiving an adequate compensation package, and (2) caring for members who are approaching retirement. Consistent with the teachers' second priority, the union has demanded that the district insert a clause in the contract that prevents the school district from transferring any teachers involuntarily once they have 15 years of service. The union considers this transfer limitation even more important than its normal opposition to any contract provisions that would allow the district to treat some teachers differently than others.

The school board has stated publicly that its priorities are (1) not agreeing to a compensation package that would threaten the financial well-being of the district or cause cutbacks in levels of service, and (2) attracting talented, entry-level teachers to the district. Related to the second of these, the board proposed that the district should have the discretion to award certain new teachers the equivalent of a signing bonus. It opposes the idea of a transfer limitation, but it considers the signing bonus an even more important issue.

Regarding compensation, the board and the union disagree fundamentally about the district's economic outlook. The board believes that the state legislature will *cut* funding for local schools again this year, making even less available to pay for teacher contracts. The union insists that the state legislature will *increase* funding in the coming year, thus providing the backdrop for the board to approve significant increases in teacher compensation.

Beyond salaries, the two parties disagree about how the district ought to handle insurance premiums for teachers' health insurance. In years past, the district has guaranteed that it will contribute a certain percentage of teachers' insurance costs. This year, over the union's objections, the district is proposing that it provide a flat-sum insurance contribution for each member. The board has explained that it "needs" to implement such a system because it is fearful that health insurance costs will skyrocket, moving the district's percentage-based insurance contribution commitments beyond its ability to pay.

12. **Options to explore.** Beyond the question of how many dollars the district will pay the teachers, what value-creating opportunities should the board and the union explore in their negotiations?

Explanations

The Apartment of Jack's Dreams

1. **Jack's BATNA.** Jack's BATNA is whatever he considers the best course of action in the event he can reach no satisfactory arrangement with the Ropers over the Main Street apartment. The facts suggest that Jack has at least three alternatives to finalizing a deal with the Ropers (the apartments on Santa Monica, Wilshire, and Third Street). He may have even more—for example, it may be that he, Chrissy, and Janet could stay in their current apartment, find another roommate and look for a larger apartment, or buy a home rather than rent an apartment. With the facts we are given, however, it appears that the course of action Jack thinks is most attractive (putting aside the prospect of the Main Street apartment) would be to rent the Santa Monica Boulevard property for $3,400 per month. Renting the Santa Monica property at that rate, therefore, is Jack's BATNA.

2. **Jack's reservation value.** At what price point would Jack be indifferent between renting the Main Street apartment and the Santa Monica Boulevard apartment? We know that Jack can get the Santa Monica Boulevard apartment for $3,400, and we know that he would prefer to rent the Main Street apartment. The question is *how much more* does Jack value the Main Street apartment over the Santa Monica Boulevard apartment? The facts suggest that Jack thinks the Main Street place is worth "several hundred dollars" extra, because of its size and location. We could, therefore, reasonably estimate his reservation value at $3,700 ($3,400 for the Santa Monica Boulevard apartment plus $300 for the added attractiveness of the Main Street features).

3. **The Ropers' BATNA.** The Ropers' BATNA is whatever they judge to be the best course of action in the event they can reach no satisfactory arrangement with Jack, Chrissy, and Janet.

In this case, the Ropers have at least two obvious alternatives: (1) try to rent to Furley for $3,200 per month over the coming year, or (2) wait and hope to find another renter who is willing to pay more. If we assume that the Ropers' estimates are correct, there is a 50 percent chance they would get a renter at $3,600 this month, and a 50 percent chance that the apartment would stand empty for one month before they get a renter at that price.

To determine the Ropers' BATNA, therefore, requires us to decide whether the Ropers would prefer the certainty of Furley at $3,200 or the expected value of the wait-and-see approach. The math involved is not complex. The Ropers could simply lay out the revenue streams each alternative would provide them and then make a comparison. For example:

Month	Expected Income from Furley	Expected Income from Wait-and-See
1	$ 3,200	$ 1,800
2	$ 3,200	$ 3,600
3	$ 3,200	$ 3,600
4	$ 3,200	$ 3,600
5	$ 3,200	$ 3,600
6	$ 3,200	$ 3,600
7	$ 3,200	$ 3,600
8	$ 3,200	$ 3,600
9	$ 3,200	$ 3,600
10	$ 3,200	$ 3,600
11	$ 3,200	$ 3,600
12	$ 3,200	$ 3,600
TOTAL	**$38,400**	**$41,400**

The calculations for the alternative of going with Furley are straightforward. The Ropers are assuming that they would receive $3,200 from him each month, so the Ropers' expected revenue with Furley over the coming year would be $38,400. (That's 12 months × $3,200 per month.)

Calculating the expected value of the wait-and-see approach is only a little more complicated. The facts tell us to assume that if the Ropers drop the asking price to $3,600 per month, there is a 50 percent chance of an immediate renter and a 50 percent chance of someone coming along one month later. The Ropers' expected rental return for the first month under this strategy, therefore, is $1,800. Of course, the Ropers will not receive $1,800 in rent this coming month. They'll either receive their $3,600 asking price, or they'll receive $0 because the apartment will be standing empty. But there is a 50-50 chance of each of those; therefore,

$3,600 × ½ = $1,800 expected for the coming month. The Ropers then assume that they would be able to rent the place for the remaining 11 months at $3,600 per month. The Ropers' expected revenue with the wait-and-see approach, therefore, would be $41,400. (That's 1 month at $1,800 + 11 months at $3,600 per month.)

If the Ropers make their decision based entirely on their expected rental revenue, it looks like their BATNA is to drop the asking price and wait for another renter. But of course, the Ropers may base their decision on something other than the cold calculations described above. Perhaps they are extraordinarily risk averse, perhaps they have an immediate need for cash, or perhaps they like Furley enough to forgo the extra dollars expected. Assessing the course of action that represents a party's BATNA requires an understanding of all of that party's interests—not merely his or her *financial* interests. Nevertheless, in this case, because we have no additional information about the Ropers, we would judge that their BATNA is to wait for another renter because doing so maximizes their expected return on their investment.

4. **The Ropers' reservation value.** The Ropers' reservation rule is the price point at which they are indifferent between renting to Jack and walking away to their BATNA. In the answer above, we determined that their BATNA is to drop the asking price and wait to see if they can find another renter—a course of action that yields an expected rental return in the coming year of $41,400. If the Ropers are otherwise indifferent between renting to Jack and renting to a currently unknown renter, the Ropers' reservation value would be the rate at which the two would yield identical total expected rental payments over the coming year. The math involved is this:

$$\text{rate} \times 12 \text{ months} = \$41{,}400$$
$$\text{rate} = \$41{,}400/12 \text{ months} = \$3{,}450/\text{month}$$

According to this calculation, the Ropers' reservation value in their negotiations with Jack would be $3,450. They would prefer to walk to their BATNA rather than accept less than $3,450 from Jack, and they would prefer to rent to Jack if he is willing to pay anything above $3,450.

Of course, these calculations, like the BATNA calculations above, make a fair number of assumptions about probabilities, about the Ropers' preferences, about their risk profile, and so on. (See Chapter 2 for more on the mechanics and limitations of a decision-analytic approach to understanding negotiation.) As a simple means of estimating, however, the $3,450 figure captures the idea that there is *some* price point at which the Ropers would say no to Jack in favor of seeking someone else.

5. **A ZOPA for Jack and the Ropers.** If we juxtapose Jack's reservation value and the Ropers' reservation value, we see that the two have a zone of possible agreement.

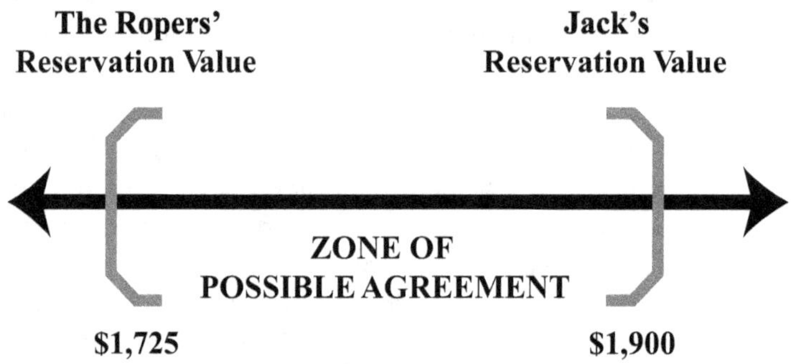

The Ropers would prefer to rent for anything above $3,450, and Jack would prefer to pay anything under $3,700. The ZOPA, therefore, is between $3,450 and $3,700.

Of course, this simple analysis ignores the possibility that the Ropers and Jack might discover value-creating trades during the negotiation process. Perhaps they will discover that Jack has little furniture and the Ropers need a place to keep some of their furniture for the coming months. Perhaps they will find that Jack has flexibility at the end of the coming year and would be willing to let the Ropers move in earlier if their plans change. Perhaps the Ropers will recognize that they will enjoy spending time with Jack, Chrissy, and Janet, and the Ropers will consider extending the lease. Maybe they will find that the Ropers do not have a short-term need for cash and Jack would be willing to pay a higher rate in the future in exchange for a lower rate now. (For more on value-creating, non-zero-sum settlement options, see the examples below.)

Wounded in the Workplace

6. **Alexa's BATNA.** Alexa's alternative to settlement would include things like litigating, launching a publicity campaign of some sort, or doing nothing (and simply proceeding with life). Each of these does not require the consent of Madison's Motorcycles, and therefore constitutes an **alternative** in the negotiation vernacular. Alexa's BATNA, the course of action she would deem most attractive in the event of non-settlement, would probably be litigating. The lawsuit has a net positive expected value, which means it is better than doing nothing, at least in economic terms. And unless there is something we don't know about Alexa or her situation, it is likely that she would opt to proceed with litigation in the event the case cannot be settled.

7. **Alexa's reservation price.** Alexa's lawyer (who we assume is well-informed and well-intended) has advised that going to trial is expected to yield $150,000, and would cost $20,000 in unrecoverable attorney fees. Alexa's reservation value, therefore, is probably in the neighborhood of $130,000 ($150k – $20k). This number does not take into account the value of time (either in terms of the costs of money or the value of her time). This number does not account for the potential that Alexa has a cash flow need to have money sooner. We go into greater detail about these kinds of analyses in Chapter 2. For now, we would assume that Alexa's reservation value—the point at which she is indifferent between settling and going to trial—is roughly equal to the discounted expected value of going to trial: $130,000.

8. **Madison's Motorcyles BATNA.** Madison's Motorcycles has only a few conspicuous alternatives to settlement in this case, since Alexa has already filed a lawsuit. They can defend against the suit. They can default (which is the legal equivalent of doing nothing). In a different fact pattern, they could potentially bring a counterclaim against Alexa if they believed that she was, in some way, responsible. But under these facts, Madison's Motorcycles appears to have limited alternatives. Their BATNA, the thing they would actually prefer to do in the event there is no settlement, is almost certainly to defend against the litigation. If they default, they would presumably owe Alexa the full $250,000 she is demanding. If they go to trial, they anticipate a $150,000 judgment and an additional $40,000 in lawyer fees. The litigation costs are, therefore, less than the default costs, so their BATNA is likely to continue with litigation.

9. **Madison's Motorcycles reservation price.** As explained immediately above, Madison's Motorcycles expects the case to cost $190,000 to litigate ($40,000 in attorney fees and $150,000 in eventual payout). In a simplified world, therefore, they would be indifferent between settling for $190,000 and litigating. In the real world, they may have other considerations that move their reservation value higher or lower. Perhaps they want to avoid bad publicity? Perhaps they want to maintain a good relationship with Alexa? Perhaps they don't want to be seen as settling plaintiffs' claims? Perhaps there is something about the arrangement with their insurer that changes their calculations. But on the facts presented, their reservation value is likely around $190,000.

10. **A ZOPA?** If our simplified calculations above are correct, a Zone of Possible Agreement exists in this case. Both parties should (in theory) prefer a settlement anywhere between $130,000 and $190,000 over the prospect of resolving the case through litigation.

Merchandise Mayhem

11. **Options to explore.** Without additional facts, it is not possible to assess whether one or both of the parties would be better off pursuing litigation. At a minimum, however, the disputants (or their lawyers) should at least explore four different, potentially value-creating categories of options.

First, they should consider whether there are ways the two companies could capitalize on their differences in **resources** and **capabilities**. StrideZone has production facilities, distribution networks, and retail outlets. Athlete Alliance has athletes under contract and an Internet presence. The two could consider a joint venture to better capitalize on the resources each company brings to the table.

Second, they should explore whether they can capture value by achieving **economies of scale**. Athlete Alliance's facility for producing brands is much smaller than StrideZone's, and it is likely that Athlete Alliance has to spend more per branded item than it would cost StrideZone to produce an identical branded item. Even if the two did not enter a formal joint venture, perhaps Athlete Alliance would be willing to pay StrideZone to produce Athlete Alliance branded merchandise—at a price both companies would consider favorable. If they can arrange their business appropriately, it may not make sense for *both* companies to have their capital tied up in separate, expensive production facilities.

Third, the companies may have different **time frames** that are important to them. If Athlete Alliance is considering a public stock offering, it is reasonable to assume that they would not want to have expensive and uncertain litigation on the books. In fact, they probably need to show some real prospects for immediate growth. StrideZone may have a longer time horizon for its business planning. Perhaps the two could explore an arrangement that provides Athlete Alliance the greater share of initial opportunities or profits in exchange for terms that are more favorable to StrideZone's longer-term plans. Alternatively, if Athlete Alliance's interest in doing the public offering is to try to raise some capital in the short term, maybe StrideZone would be willing to front dollars for Athlete Alliance's endeavors in exchange for either a fixed return or a share of the profits.

Fourth, StrideZone is in need of new athletes, and Athlete Alliance has apparently had success in signing athletes. A joint venture might, therefore, be in order. But it may also be that each side places a different **relative valuation** on the athletes, on the various rights currently being bundled together, or on the stock of the to-be-public Athlete Alliance. If the parties can identify which of these they value differently, they may be able to craft a trade.

Teachers in Turmoil

12. **Options to explore.** At least three categories of options suggest themselves beyond the question of how many dollars the teachers will receive.

First, the parties have a difference in **relative** valuations or **priorities**. The union cares more about the transfer limitation than about the signing bonus. The district cares more about the signing bonus than about the transfer limitation. The two might be satisfied with a straight trade (the union gets the transfer limitation, and the district gets discretion to award signing bonuses). Or it may be that one side cares deeply about *both* issues, while the other side cares relatively less. For example, if the union cares relatively less about these two issues, it might trade both for a more favorable salary.

Second, the parties' differing **predictions** about the future funding levels may present an opportunity for them to strike a contingent agreement that both sides will view as favorable (at least in the short term). If the union is convinced that the funding will go up, and the district is convinced that funding will drop, both should be willing to explore the following deal: If the funding drops, teachers' compensation will be set very low—at a level very favorable to the district; if the funding increases, teachers will receive a very large salary increase—one far larger than the district would normally provide. If the union truly believes its prediction, they should be willing to live with the low-pay provision, because they expect that funding will increase, triggering the favorable raise. And the district, because it expects the opposite state funding decision, should view the contingent arrangement as favorable. An alternative way of structuring the deal would be simply to tie the salary increase to a percentage of the state budget. Note that proposing either of these kinds of arrangements has the additional benefit of helping to uncover false predictions from one or both sides. Only if they are truly confident of the prediction will they be willing to go along with a contingent arrangement with harsh consequences.

Third, the question of health insurance premiums may present a situation in which the parties have differing **risk preferences**. It may be that the district is so fearful of the prospect of out-of-control insurance costs that it would be willing to pay the union the equivalent of a premium to have the union bear the risks involved. The union might be able to get more dollars from the district in a "flat contribution" arrangement than it could get trying to negotiate a particular percentage of premium coverage. In this way, assuming the union is more tolerant of risk, both sides may benefit from capitalizing on that difference.

CHAPTER 2

Decision Making in Negotiation

§2.1 INTRODUCTION

Negotiation invites (or even requires) people to make complex decisions. Some aspects of negotiation are undeniably psychological, emotional, and deeply interpersonal. No understanding of negotiation is complete if it ignores the human experience of the disputants. Furthermore, real-world negotiators' interests often extend far beyond the simple maximization of dollars. At the same time, negotiations often involve decisions with important financial implications. As a negotiation's stakes increase, the complexity of those implications also often increases. A tourist haggling over the correct price for a trinket in a market understandably uses a less sophisticated decision-making process than a litigant assessing the implications of settling a multimillion-dollar lawsuit.

In this chapter, we examine two aspects of negotiators' decision-making processes. In the first section of this chapter, we describe several of the best-understood psychological dynamics affecting negotiators. In the second section of this chapter, we describe a set of concepts commonly associated with analyzing relatively complex financial decisions in dispute-resolution processes, including the basic mechanisms involved in decision analysis and the effects of time on valuing different outcomes. Each of these topics could occupy an entire book if examined in depth. We aim here to provide a sufficient foundation so that you can begin to assess potential dynamics in negotiators' decision making.

§2.2 PSYCHOLOGICAL DYNAMICS IN NEGOTIATION

Virtually everyone agrees that negotiations in the real world involve more than just cold, economically rational calculations. Negotiators are real people, with all the beautiful features and problematic baggage associated with real people. Negotiators have partial information, and their decision-making processes sometimes suffer from cognitive biases and failures. Negotiators also have wisdom, intuition, and creativity. No accurate picture of negotiation would discount the importance of psychological dynamics involved in negotiation. Some textbooks spend considerable time surveying different cognitive and psychological dynamics underlying negotiators' decisions. Below, we describe six such heuristics, biases, or dynamics, most of which are drawn from the literature of behavioral economics and cognitive psychology. These are certainly not the only such effects for negotiators, but we think they are the dynamics most likely to appear in basic courses on dispute resolution.

§2.2.1 Endowment Effects

Most of us tend to overvalue things we already have. When experimenters randomly gave a coffee mug to half of the students in a class and then asked everyone in the class how much one of those coffee mugs is worth, the students who had received a mug named a higher value than those who did not have a mug. The **endowment effect**—the dynamic driving these differences in opinion—counsels caution about placing too much stock in one's subjective valuations in these contexts. A homeowner tends to value his home more than a potential buyer. When a plaintiff says she believes her lawsuit is worth $1 million and a defendant says he believes the lawsuit is worth only $100,000, it is possible that the difference is the product of strategy or partial information. It is also possible that the plaintiff's valuation is skewed because she holds the rights associated with the lawsuit and is overvaluing that endowment.

§2.2.2 Loss Aversion

Most of us seek to avoid accepting a certain loss, and we are even willing to accept the risk of greater loss to avoid agreeing to lose something now. **Loss aversion** means that a defendant faced with the choice of agreeing to pay $1 million today or going to trial and facing a 10 percent chance of paying $10 million will usually choose to go to trial. The defendant is averse to agreeing to a certain loss. Often, we are willing to accept mathematically unwise risks to avoid accepting a loss. For example, many would refuse to pay $1 million today, even if doing so means that we will have a 10 percent chance of paying more than $10 million.

Similarly, most of us are unwilling to risk certain gains. That is, most of us faced with the choice of $50 cash or a one-third chance of $150 cash will gratefully accept the $50 cash. We are averse to the prospect of giving up a certain gain of the $50. Many of us would choose to cling to the certain gain (for example, $40), even in exchange for a risk with a mathematically higher value.

§2.2.3 Anchoring

Many of us focus unwittingly on the first numbers we hear. As our brains become **anchored** to those numbers, we move away from our initial conceptions only reluctantly—particularly when those conceptions can be articulated in numerical terms. A first offer, a home listing price, or even an automobile sticker price can become the focus of a negotiation, whether or not that number is actually fair or relevant. Negotiators can use this phenomenon proactively to anchor their counterparts but run the risk of the effects of anchoring on themselves.

§2.2.4 Overconfidence Bias

Most negotiators significantly overestimate the accuracy of their predictions—particularly when they attempt to predict their own future performance. A negotiator believes he is "very likely" to get more than $1 million in the next round of negotiations. A litigator believes they have a "90 percent chance" of winning if the case is taken to trial. In most contexts, with most negotiators, estimates like these are typically inflated. The **overconfidence** bias suggests that these negotiators are not merely saying something they know to be puffery. Instead, it suggests that their confidence is at a level unwarranted by objective facts. The result of the overconfidence bias is that negotiators risk holding inappropriately self-serving, rosy visions of the future, making a settlement harder to reach.

§2.2.5 Zero-Sum Bias or Mythical Fixed-Pie Bias

Many negotiators—even sophisticated negotiators—reliably overestimate the degree to which negotiations present zero-sum, win-lose situations. Perhaps this is because images of competitive contexts (such as sporting events) are so vivid, or perhaps it is because they have an antagonistic history with their negotiation counterpart. The **zero-sum bias** does not merely describe negotiators' tendencies to act in competitive ways. Such actions may be the product of a strategy, rather than any assessment about the nature of the negotiation. Instead, the well-documented zero-sum bias results in negotiators assuming or believing that a given negotiation is purely distributive far more often than it actually is. This bias causes many to miss opportunities for value-creating settlements.

§2.2.6 Reactive Devaluation

Many of us form opinions about a proposal's merits based on the proposal's source. (Think about the current political discourse in the United States for easy examples.) This leads to the risk of **reactive devaluation**—the devaluing of a proposal because of its source, rather than because of its merits. A negotiator who is told that an idea comes from a neutral party tends to think more highly of that idea than if the negotiator is told that the idea comes from someone they view as an adversary. At some level, this might make intuitive sense. ("After all, if *they* like this idea, I must be missing something.") Especially when coupled with the zero-sum bias, described above, reactive devaluation can lead negotiators to miss settlement opportunities that would have otherwise been mutually attractive.

§2.3 DECISION ANALYSIS

Some disputants use a process involving mathematical calculations that attaches a particular value to a course of action (for example, taking a case to trial.) In making these calculations, these negotiators employ a graphically based process of laying out current and future decisions, along with their probable outcomes. This method of calculation has the generic label: **decision analysis**.

Decision analysis helps compare decisions over time, in circumstances in which the future may hold a variety of possible outcomes, each of which has a different likelihood of occurring. For example, you might want to place a bet on your favorite team to win the Super Bowl at the end of the NFL season. Your choice right before the Super Bowl—your team will win or your team will lose—is a much simpler choice than at the beginning of the season. Right before the Super Bowl, you only need to assess the likelihood of this single victory. At the beginning of the season, you need to calculate the likelihood that your team will win enough games to make the playoffs *and* the likelihood of them making it through the playoffs *before* you can make the final assessment about how likely they are to win the Super Bowl.

Calculating how you will do at trial is similarly complex. Although one might view a prediction to win or lose at trial as a simple either/or choice, in fact there are multiple steps along the way to trial victory. Decision analysis helps to put those choices into perspective so that you can make wise decisions about whether to accept a settlement offer (or put one forward). Consider the following example of a simple lawsuit: You sustained certain injuries in an accident at a retail store. You believe you were entirely without fault, you bring suit against the store, and based on your lawyer's advice, you are seeking $50,000 in damages. The store's insurer has offered you $10,000 to settle the case. Should you accept it?

The answer, of course, depends on many variables. Perhaps your decision will hinge entirely on nonfinancial considerations. Perhaps you want to "teach the store a lesson." Perhaps you want an opportunity to air your frustrations in a public forum. Alternatively, perhaps you have such a pressing and immediate need for cash that you feel you cannot afford to do anything but accept the offer. Or perhaps you have reason to want to stay out of the public spotlight. In any of these events, you might not have any need to engage in any calculations. For many litigants, however, the settlement decision might hinge on their expectations about the risks and opportunities presented by litigation. Decision trees aid in making that kind of assessment.

§2.3.1 Building a Decision Tree

Decision trees are graphic constructs that can facilitate the math involved when there are multiple variables or future events with various payouts and probabilities. You certainly do not need to construct decision trees to arrive at mathematical assessments of these decisions. But the step-by-step nature of decision trees helps many people to visualize the implications of and connections between what might otherwise appear to be an impossibly complex set of factors.

Certain standard conventions apply in constructing decision trees. For example, time moves from left to right as you follow the various paths the future might take. At every branch in the tree, something happens. If you face a decision (for example, "Shall I accept this settlement offer or not?"), you place a square (called a "decision node"). If you face an uncertain outcome that is beyond your control (for example, "Will the jury find in my favor or not?"), you place a circle (called a "chance node"). At the point where each branch of the tree has reached its logical end (the end for purposes of your analysis), you place a triangle (called a "terminal node"). And where, along the way, you incur costs, you place a funny-looking little gate (appropriately called a "cost gate"). Once the tree is constructed, you can then insert the payouts that each of the eventualities would provide, and the probabilities associated with each of the chance nodes. The last step is using the decision tree to help you do the math that produces an expected value for the litigation.

Decision Tree Graphics	
Decision node	□
Chance node	○
Terminal node	◁
Cost gate	

Returning to the accident case, then, the question to ask is, "Shall I accept this settlement offer or not?" In constructing the decision tree, the first thing to do is lay out the choice graphically.

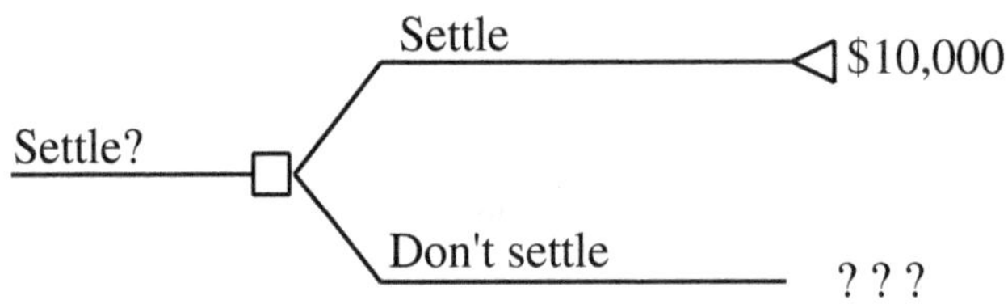

It is clear what happens if you accept the settlement, but we need more information about what happens if you go to trial. For purposes of illustration, we will assume that the litigation would be highly simplistic. Assume the defendant has filed a summary judgment motion against you. If you lose on that motion, you are done. If you win, you proceed to trial, and you believe you have an 80 percent chance of defeating the defendant's summary judgment motion. In either event, assume that it will cost you $5,000 in unrecoverable attorneys' fees to defend against the summary judgment motion. At trial, you believe you have a 50-50 chance of winning. If you win, you'll recover $50,000, and if you lose, you'll recover nothing. Assume as well that going to trial will cost you another $5,000 in unrecoverable attorneys' fees. The completed decision tree would then look like this:

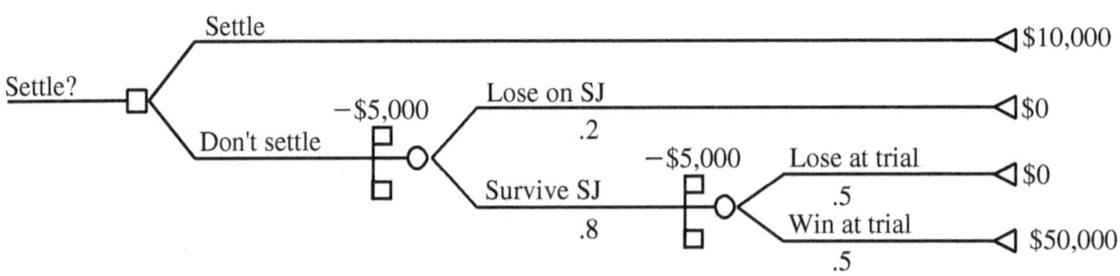

Once the tree is constructed, you can do some basic math to help you to understand the expected value of taking this case to trial. "Rolling the tree back" involves taking the expected payout (at the far right side of the tree) and multiplying it by the probability of that branch occurring. Below you'll see how the math at each stage works out.

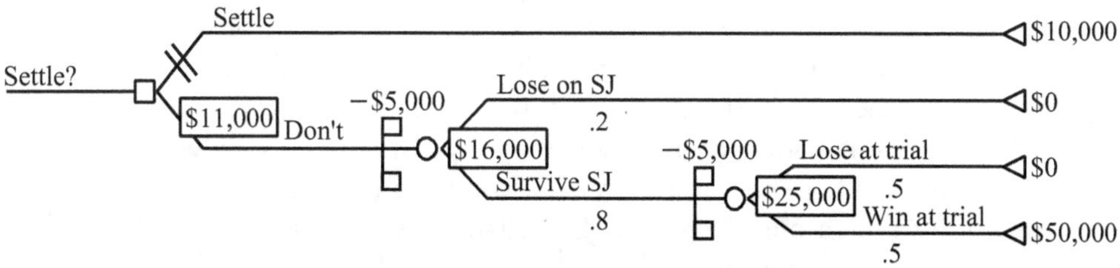

To understand how the tree arrives at the figures in the boxes, begin reading from the right-hand side of the tree. The payout of a branch is multiplied by the probability of that branch occurring. For example, "win at trial" has a payout of $50,000, which is then multiplied by 0.5. That produces $25,000. "Lose at trial" has a payout of $0, which is then multiplied by 0.5, which produces $0. The $25,000 and the $0 are added together to produce the $25,000 that appears in the box just to the right of the chance node related to trial.

The same logic applies then to the rest of the process of rolling the tree back. The $25,000 has to roll back through the cost gate, and after subtracting $5,000 becomes $20,000. That figure is then multiplied by the probability for "survive SJ." Because $20,000 × 0.8 = $16,000, and because $0 × 0.2 = $0, the value $16,000 ($16,000 + $0) appears in the box related to surviving summary judgment. We then roll that back through one more cost gate ($16,000 – $5,000) and arrive at the expected value of not settling: $11,000.

The last step in using a decision tree, of course, is to figure out the meaning associated with the number(s) your analysis produces. In our case, we are particularly interested in the final values the tree assigns to the two branches stemming from the decision node. The tree suggests that the expected value of settling is $10,000, while the expected value of not settling is $11,000. Graphically, therefore, the path leading to the less favorable outcome is marked with little bars, indicating that the decision tree does not recommend making that choice.

Few clients would base their decisions entirely on such numbers, of course, particularly when the two choices produce very similar figures. The expected value is only that—an expectation. It is no certainty. Perhaps if you have reliable information, and perhaps if you had a thousand of these cases to litigate, you would notice that *on average* each case returns about $11,000. But that doesn't necessarily tell you whether to roll the dice on litigating this case. And in no actual circumstance will you, in fact, receive $11,000. Below we discuss general limits of this analysis.

§2.3.2 The Limits of Decision Analysis

Decision analysis is used every day by sophisticated businesses to make important decisions. As a tool, it has gained extraordinary acceptance as a component in business practices. But there are limits on the contributions that mathematical decision analysis (even when it is conducted properly) can provide to decision makers. Below, we outline four of the most significant limitations. Even though limitations exist, a negotiator should nevertheless conduct an analysis of a deal's implications. But the existence of these concerns suggests that a negotiator should put a decision tree's conclusions in perspective.

Garbage In, Garbage Out Even if you do the modeling and the arithmetic correctly, unreliable estimates about the likelihood of various outcomes should make you cautious about a decision tree's conclusions. Insurance companies and other repeat players have enough experience with different scenarios that they often have relatively high confidence in the quality of their predictions (note, however, the danger of overconfidence as outlined above.) Similarly, although often less formally, experienced attorneys develop a "sense" of cases, based on their years of practice. This is not to suggest that decision trees have no value without perfect information. None of us *ever* has perfect information, yet we have to make decisions all the time, and we should try to make them the best way we can. Still, the more unreliable the data put into the equations, the more cautiously you should consider the equations' conclusions.

Anchoring Risks As we described above, the anchoring effect tends to cause our brains to cling to the first numbers to which they are exposed. Because decision trees reduce complex decisions to a single number (and often even a single choice), there is some risk that decision makers will lock on to that final number unhelpfully. In the case of something like a piece of complex litigation, the landscape shifts frequently. Ideally, decision makers would update their assessments along the way, but the anchoring effects make doing so difficult.

Ignoring Value Creation Opportunities and Nonmonetary Interests Decision trees ask, rather narrowly, about dollars and probabilities. As you know from Chapter 1, negotiations almost always involve more complex interests than just money. Even when both sides care principally about money, there are many ways to structure agreements beyond a simple, one-time lump-sum payment.

Those who use decision trees must take care not to forget the availability of these efficient, value-maximizing strategies.

Ignoring the Impact of Time These simple versions of decision trees (yes, there are more complex versions for those of you who adore math) do not consider things like the question "When would I get this money?" In a more complex model, you would also include the time value of money—figuring out how much that $10,000 offer today would earn you in interest during the time you would otherwise be waiting for a final outcome in the courts. (See the section immediately below for more on the effects of time on these calculations.)

Despite these various caveats, a decision tree may provide decision makers with some insight into the magnitude of the trade-offs they are considering. A key lesson for you or your client in the scenario we described above, for example, is that despite the ability to win $50,000 at trial, the expected value of all that time and effort is merely $1,000 more than you could receive tomorrow. For most people who focus on what they might win at trial, discovering the actual calculated expected value is an eye-opening experience and can help move parties from a particular anchor.

§2.4 TIME AND THE VALUE OF MONEY

As a basic proposition, in almost all circumstances, everyone would prefer to receive a dollar today instead of receiving a dollar a year from now. Maybe we want the dollar now because we are afraid the other side will not pay up a year from now. Or maybe we want the dollar today because we have an immediate need for cash. Or maybe we just want the dollar today because we could invest it and expect to have more than a dollar by the time next year rolls around.

Consider a basic scenario in which you are a plaintiff in a lawsuit, and the defendant has offered you $100,000 to settle the case. You have done your research and have concluded that you have a 50-50 chance of winning the case at trial. Assume also, for simplicity's sake, that you know you will recover $200,000 if you win and nothing if you lose. Finally, assume away (for simplicity's sake) the impact of any attorneys' fees. You probably do not even need a decision tree to tell you that your expected return on going to court equals $100,000.

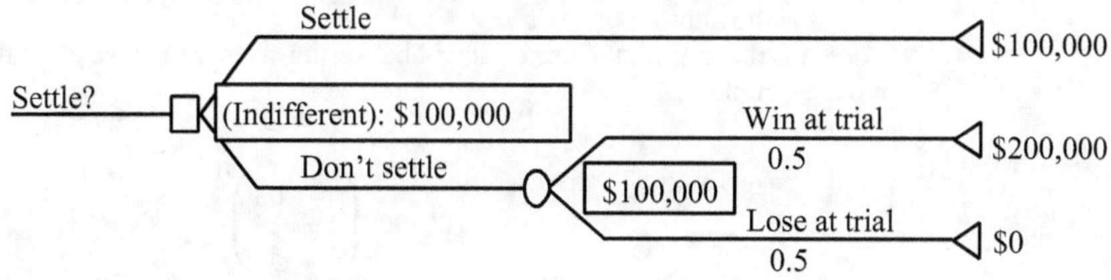

From the perspective of a decision tree, therefore, you might appear to be indifferent between settling for $100,000 or litigating (with its expected return of $100,000). But what if the court's docket is such that you should not expect to complete the trial and receive any award until two years from today? In theory, you should be able to earn some sort of return on any money you invest. Assume for purposes of this section (though not necessarily for purposes of your own financial planning) that you could make a 5 percent annual return on any money you invest. Comparing the two choices then looks more like this:

	Expected Value of Settling	Expected Value of Litigating
Today	$100,000	
One year from today	$105,000	
Two years from today	$110,250	$100,000

This is not a book on finance, of course. But even the most basic concepts of interest make clear that *when* you receive or pay a particular sum of money can have a large impact on how valuable or costly that money is.[1]

In the real world, of course, the circumstances are even more complex. If we add back in attorneys' fees, for example, it would not only make the math more complicated, it would also invite us to examine the effects of time on those expenditures as well. (You could have done something else with those attorneys' fee dollars during the two years this will take to litigate, for example.)

We might also look at the **cash-flow** implications of the decision to press forward with litigation. Even though you expect to win $100,000 with this litigation, what if the attorneys' fees will cost you $20,000 and

1. The mathematical formula for calculating the effects of compound interest is:

$$A = P\left(1 + \frac{r}{n}\right)^{nt}$$

where P is the initial principal amount
r is the interest rate
n is the number of times per year the interest is compounded
t is the number of years
A is the amount the principal will be worth t years from now, given that interest rate.

So, in our example:

$$110,250 = 100,000\left(1 + \frac{.05}{1}\right)^{(1\ 2)}$$

you do not have that kind of cash available? Unless the attorneys agree to take your case on a contingent-fee basis, your decision will probably not only be driven by the eventual expected payout. Instead, it will also be based on what you can afford to pursue right now.

Each side in a dispute would prefer money today rather than money next year. The plaintiff would rather have its money today so that it can invest the money and enjoy the benefits of the interest on that money. The defendant would rather keep its money today, so that it can continue to earn interest on the money. (Or in some cases, the defendant would rather pay later, because paying the plaintiff would require the defendant to tie up its capital or to borrow money and pay a bank some interest rate on that money.) Sometimes, the two sides will have utterly equal opportunities for investing and borrowing money, in which case, the time factor is less significant. In most circumstances, however, one side or the other places more value on having the money immediately and so is willing to pay a premium (in effect) to have the money now.

Recall from Chapter 1 that differences between the parties can lead to value creation and more options. The basic principle of different interests with respect to money and timing underlies the increasingly common use of **structured settlements** to resolve claims. Structured settlements typically involve one or more financial instruments (such as annuities) to provide payment over time. Depending on the parties' financial circumstances, such arrangements may create more total benefit for each party than a simple one-time lump-sum payment, because their structure and terms include calculations based on what each party would have done with the money in the interim periods. For example, if the defendant (the party making the payments) expects greater returns on the money than the plaintiff (the party receiving the payments), it may be more efficient to have the defendant hold on to more of the money for longer, in exchange for paying out a greater total to the plaintiff over time.

EXAMPLES

Examples

The Apartment of Jack's Nightmares

Jack, Janet, and Chrissy entered into a one-year rental agreement with the Ropers. During Jack's first week in the new apartment, he became violently ill. Based on some initial medical testing, Jack came to believe exposure to a toxin caused his poor health. Jack called the Ropers and accused them of exposing him to "deadly chemicals and other toxins" in the apartment, and Jack told them that he considered the rental agreement to be void. The next day, Jack, Janet, and Chrissy moved out of the apartment.

Two days after moving out, Jack filed a lawsuit against the Ropers, alleging that they knowingly exposed him to unsafe living conditions.

In his complaint, Jack demanded $10,000 for medical and moving expenses, plus pain and suffering compensation of $50,000. The Ropers denied that the apartment contains any toxins, denied all liability, and filed a counterclaim for the approximately $18,000 Jack still owed them in rent for the coming year. Neither side has yet engaged in any discovery in the case.

Jack and his attorney (Jack's good friend, who gave him a discounted fee for her services) made the following estimates about their prospects in litigation: Jack's case will hinge almost exclusively on the question of whether the apartment contains toxins capable of causing an illness like Jack's. To determine this, Jack will need to hire an expert to conduct tests on the apartment. Jack's attorney gave him the following summary of the likelihood of various outcomes at trial: "If your expert finds toxins, we're a lock to win our claim for $60,000, and there's no way the Ropers' counterclaim will succeed. If, on the other hand, the expert finds no toxins, you're out of luck—the Ropers' claim will succeed and yours will fail." In either event, Jack would owe the expert $10,000 and he would owe $5,000 to his attorney. Jack has admitted to his attorney that he might have been exposed to toxins elsewhere, and they therefore estimate that there is only a 50 percent chance that the expert's report will show the presence of toxins in the apartment.

1. **Jack's reservation value.** Based on the information above, what do you think Jack's reservation value would be in a negotiation with the Ropers over settling these claims?

Jack's attorney returns to him the next day and says, "I've done some more research, and I have some good news and some bad news. The bad news is that there's a chance you won't be able to receive the pain and suffering award, even if you win your claim. I'd say there's about a 60 percent chance I can get you the full award amount if you win. Otherwise, you would just receive the $10,000 of actual damages. The good news is this: Even if you lose your claim and the Ropers win theirs, there is a 90 percent chance that they would only be able to recover about $3,000 from you, because they almost certainly have a duty to mitigate their losses by renting to someone else. That leaves only a 10 percent chance they can recover the full amount they are demanding in their counterclaim."

2. **Jack's revised reservation value.** How does this new information affect your estimate of Jack's reservation value in his negotiations with the Ropers?

3. **Assessing Jack's assessment.** Which, if any, of the psychological dynamics described in this chapter suggest that Jack ought to treat the answer to question 2 with some caution?

The Ropers' Choices

The Ropers have hired an attorney who has agreed to handle the preliminary aspects of this case for no charge, but if the case proceeds to trial, it will cost the Ropers $10,000 in legal expenses. The Ropers and their attorney have privately assessed the risks and opportunities present in the litigation with Jack. The Ropers believe that there is only a 25 percent chance that Jack's expert will find toxins in the apartment. Their attorney would be even more confident than that, but she recently heard about another local landlord—one whom the Ropers consider very trustworthy—who found toxins present in a unit similar to the one they rented to Jack. If Jack's expert finds toxins, Jack will surely win his claim, and the Ropers will lose their counterclaim. In the event he wins, Jack has a 50 percent chance of recovering the full amount he has claimed and a 50 percent chance he will receive only the actual damages of $10,000. If Jack's expert finds no toxins, the Ropers and their attorney are absolutely confident that they will recover the full $18,000 of the counterclaim.

4. **The Ropers' reservation value.** Based on this information, what do you estimate the Ropers' reservation value to be in their negotiations with Jack over these claims?

5. **The Ropers' view of settlement.** Which, if any, of the psychological dynamics described in this chapter suggest that the Ropers' actual willingness to settle this claim may differ from the decision-analytic answer to question 4?

After reviewing their attorney's analysis of the risks and opportunities present in litigation, the Ropers say to their attorney, "Things look really bad for us if Jack's expert finds toxins. If that happens, don't you think we should hire our own expert to check the results of that analysis?" An expert would cost $10,000, and the results of the tests for toxins are 90 percent likely to come back the same. If the Ropers' expert confirms the presence of toxins, the same set of probabilities as described above would apply: a 50 percent chance of full recovery for Jack and a 50 percent chance of only actual damages for Jack. If, however, the Ropers' expert finds no toxins, the fact finder would have to choose to believe one expert or the other. There is no reason why one would be more credible than the other, making it a 50-50 chance that the fact finder would side with the Ropers. If the fact finder believes the Ropers' expert, they would expect to recover the full $18,000 they claimed. If the fact finder sides with Jack's expert, Jack would again have a 50 percent chance of receiving full damages and a 50 percent chance of receiving only actual damages.

6. **The Ropers' own expert.** Based on this information, if you were the Ropers' attorney, how would you respond to their question about whether they should plan to hire a competing expert in the event Jack's expert finds toxins in the apartment?

Pay Me Now, Pay Me Later

Assume that Jack and the Ropers have each learned some new information, leading them to revise their expectations about the likely outcome of litigating their dispute. Assume that both sides have decided to proceed without attorneys, eliminating those possible expenses.

After rerunning his numbers, Jack has concluded that his expected benefit from litigating is $14,000. Unfortunately, Jack has not managed his finances well up to this point, and he is carrying tens of thousands of dollars of credit card debt right now, on which he is paying an annual interest rate of 19 percent.

After rerunning their numbers, the Ropers have concluded that the expected result of litigating would be that they would owe Jack $12,000. The Ropers' real estate business has more than enough funds to cover any judgment against them. At the moment, they have their company's reserves invested in an account that yields 6 percent interest per year.

7. **ZOPA?** Based on each party's expected trial outcome, if the trial were to take place immediately, does it appear that the Ropers and Jack have a zone of possible agreement?

8. **Time cures all?** Assume that the current backlog of cases in the local courts means that any judgment in this case would not occur until two years from today. What effect, if any, would this two-year court delay have on the ZOPA analysis from the question immediately above?

9. **Have I got a deal for you!** The Ropers learn during the course of the negotiations that Jack has not yet found a long-term solution to his housing problem. During a break in the negotiations, the Ropers tell their attorney, "Look, we've got other buildings with other apartments sitting vacant. Why don't we offer to have him stay in one of those in lieu of us giving him a cash payment? It's economically rational and we can capitalize on our differences. We'd have to work out the details of course, but I think this has real promise. What do you think?" To which, if any, of the psychological dynamics described above would you refer as you formulate a response to them?

Honeymoon Hangup

Newlyweds Archie and Veronica arrived at the airport, eager to begin their honeymoon. They had been saving for this trip for more than a year, and their families gifted them the extra dollars needed to make their dream trip possible. Just before the flight was to board, an apologetic airline representative announced over the public address system, "We regret to inform you that this flight has been canceled due to mechanical failure. All travelers should form a line to discuss their travel options with an airline customer service agent."

10. **Uncle Fred's flight.** Standing in line, Archie tells Veronica, "This happened to my Uncle Fred one time when flying a different airline, and he got them to pay 150% of the cost of the original tickets, as compensation." What psychological dynamic(s) might be brought to bear by Archie's observation?

11. **Airport honeymoon?** The customer service agent began with an apology and an offer, "We can book you on a flight a couple days from now. We cannot guarantee that the seats will be together, but we can get you to your destination at least. If you take this option, you will receive no additional compensation beyond covering your hotel here in the airport over the next two days. That's what I'm permitted to offer. You could always decline and try calling the main office to see if you can get something better, but these tickets and this offer will no longer be available." What psychological dynamic(s) might be implicated by the customer service agent's offer?

12. **Honeymoon delayed is honeymoon denied?** Sensing the couple's frustration, the agent finally says, "Well, instead of all of this, I could offer you a credit with the airlines for the full amount of your ticket, to be accompanied by a 40% discount on any single upgraded fare ticket purchase using that credit, good for any of our flights, provided the travel is completed within the next 24 months." What psychological dynamic(s) might be implicated by the customer service agent's offer?

Explanations

EXPLANATIONS

The Apartment of Jack's Nightmares

1. **Jack's reservation value.** One way to analyze Jack's reservation value would be to construct a decision tree to reflect the various costs, opportunities, and risks involved in the litigation Jack faces. The facts tell us that going to litigation will cost Jack $15,000, regardless of the outcome. According to the facts, the entire litigation hinges on whether the expert finds toxins, so the decision tree should include a chance node—one branch showing a victory for Jack, and the other showing a loss for Jack. If Jack wins, he stands to gain $60,000. If he loses, he would wind up owing the Ropers $18,000.

   The facts tell us that Jack estimates the odds at 50-50. Of course, Jack might have reason to doubt the precision of such an estimate. To say that something is 50 percent likely to happen (as opposed to 45 percent or 60 percent likely) has questionable reliability. Still, because these are the figures we are given, we should use them at least for a basis of getting a sense of the magnitude of Jack's decision. The tree below shows how one might lay out the probabilities and set up the basic arithmetic involved in estimating Jack's expected payout if he pursues the litigation.

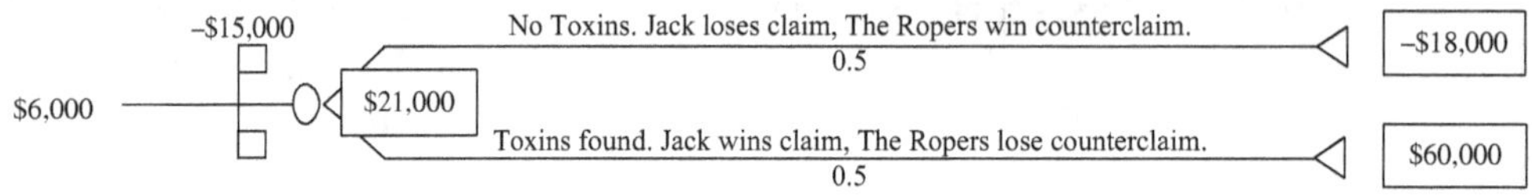

According to this decision tree, Jack's expected benefit from pursuing litigation is $6,000. (That is, (– $18,000) × 0.5 + ($60,000 × 0.5) – $15,000.) One might imagine, therefore, that Jack's reservation value in a negotiation with the Ropers would be $6,000. If we knew more about Jack, we might be able to judge the accuracy of this estimate. How risk averse is Jack? How important is it to him to see the Ropers "punished" by the justice system? How badly does Jack need the money now (recalling that he would not see any dollars from litigation for some time)? How confident is Jack in his estimates of the probabilities and the payoffs involved? Based on the information we have been given, though, we might reasonably assume that Jack would be willing to settle for anything above $6,000, but might prefer to litigate if the Ropers' offer is below that figure.

Note that we are assuming that Jack's reservation value is a function of his BATNA, translated into dollars. Jack's actual medical and moving expenses in this case may already be greater than this amount. By stating that this is Jack's reservation value, we are not saying that this is an amount that Jack would feel happy about, an amount that would make Jack "whole," or an amount that is based on some vision of fairness. A reservation value estimates the point at which a party would be indifferent between two courses of action—in this case settling or litigating. If we assume that Jack is economically rational (an assumption that is surely worthy of testing), and that his primary motivator is net expected dollars (again, an assumption worth testing), his reservation value should not be far from $6,000.

2. **Jack's revised reservation value.** Jack's revised reservation value should consider these two new variables—the probability that recovery would be less than complete for either Jack or the Ropers in the event of a victory at trial. Modifying the decision tree described above yields the following:

   The Ropers win full counterclaim amount.

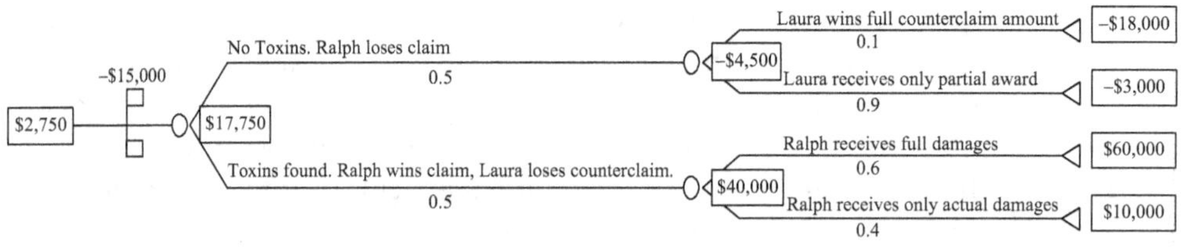

So, according to this analysis, Jack's reservation value would drop to under $3,000.

To make the math explicit:

0.1 × (–$18,000) = –$1,800
0.9 × (–$3,000) = –$2,700
(–$1,800) + (–$2,700) = –$4,500

$17,750 – $15,000 = $2,750

0.5 × (–$4,500) = –$2,750
0.5 × $40,000 = $20,000
$20,000 + (–$2,750) = $17,750

0.6 × $60,000 = $36,000
0.4 × $10,000 = $4,000
$36,000 + $4,000 = $40,000

3. **Assessing Jack's assessment.** At least two of the psychological dynamics described above suggest caution. First, we would caution Jack about the risks of anchoring associated with the number the analysis in question 2 produces. Taking in new information and revising expectations is both difficult and important. Still, it is difficult to estimate probabilities with great reliability. To say that something is unlikely to happen may be correct. To distinguish something that is 10 percent likely to happen from something that is 15 percent likely to happen is questionable at best. Further, this analysis does not consider Jack's personal preference for or tolerance of risk. And it does not consider any value Jack places on his own time. (How many hours will Jack spend in litigation that he might have spent doing something else?) In sum, what this analysis can tell us is that Jack's expected net benefit from going to trial is only modestly above zero. Second, Jack might want to consider the possibility that his attorney's estimates are optimistically overconfident. Like most people, attorneys tend to overestimate their likelihood of success in future, uncertain conditions like litigation. This is not to suggest that Jack should ignore the attorney's revised assessments, of course. But there is reason to treat them as something other than infallible.

The Ropers' Choices

4. **The Ropers' reservation value.** The point at which they would be indifferent to continuing with litigation and settling would be in the neighborhood of $5,250. That is, if they were basing their decision purely on expected economic opportunities and costs, they would be willing to pay slightly over $5,000 to settle this case. To arrive at this figure, the

decision tree below sets out the attorneys' fees, the probability that Jack's expert will find toxins, and the various expected payouts and probabilities at trial.

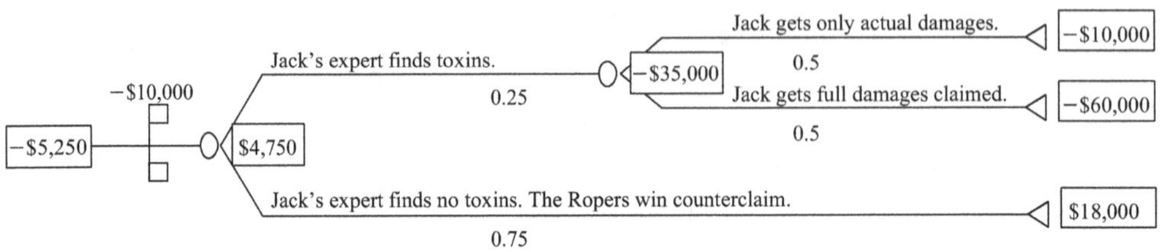

Note that the value of this calculation depends on the quality of the estimates the Ropers and their attorney generated. However, based on the facts provided, this is the best estimate we can produce. (Of interest here also is the fact that the Ropers' expected net benefit/liability from litigation is positive before we factor in the attorneys' fees. That is, if they could get the same odds at trial without hiring a lawyer, they might prefer to go to trial.)

5. **The Ropers' view of settlement.** At least two psychological dynamics may affect the Ropers' willingness to settle for an amount different from the number produced in question 4. First, the Ropers may (like most people) experience loss aversion in this context. Settling with Jack may feel tantamount to accepting a certain loss. After all, settling would mean agreeing to incur an expense of more than $5,000. Many of us would prefer to roll the dice rather than accept that kind of loss—even if the expected outcome of rolling the dice is not better than the proposed settlement. Second, anchoring may be affecting the Ropers. In this case, several numbers have presented themselves. If the Ropers fixated on Jack's initial demand of $60,000, then a roughly $5,000 settlement will look different than if the Ropers fixated on the $18,000 they hoped to recover from Jack.

6. **The Ropers' expert.** The Ropers' instinct to hire an expert to verify the findings of toxicity is understandable, since everything essentially rides on this one finding. The transaction costs of hiring an expert, however, make it financially unwise for them to invest the extra money—at least from the perspective of its effects on the expected outcome of this litigation. According to the decision tree below, hiring their own expert only improves their expected outcome in litigation by a few thousand dollars, while the expert costs $10,000.

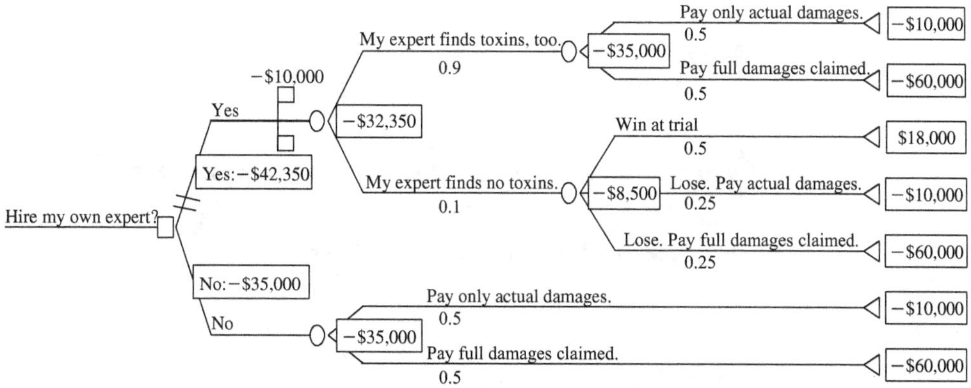

The Ropers' choice boils down to this: Hiring their own expert brings down their expected loss at trial from $35,000 to $32,350. But the expert would cost $10,000, far outweighing the expected benefits the expert would bring.

As always with decision trees, this analysis is sensitive to the probability estimates created by the Ropers and their attorney. The tree also does not consider any interests the Ropers may have beyond the net expected payouts in this piece of litigation. Perhaps the Ropers are willing to incur the additional expenses of having an expert because they have several other units that would be susceptible to the same kind of claim. Perhaps they place a premium on their reputation—and would therefore either pay for a confidentiality agreement (see Chapters 3 and 7 for more on confidentiality agreements) or would be willing to take on greater risk at trial rather than admit liability. And so on. Based on the information provided, however, if Jack's expert finds toxins in the apartment, the Ropers should not bother to hire a competing expert.

Pay Me Now, Pay Me Later

7. **ZOPA?** No. If we look only at what each expects to happen at trial, and if the trial and judgment occur immediately, there appears to be no zone of possible agreement. Jack would want more than he expects to receive by going to trial ($14,000), and the Ropers would want to pay less than they expect to pay by going to trial ($12,000).

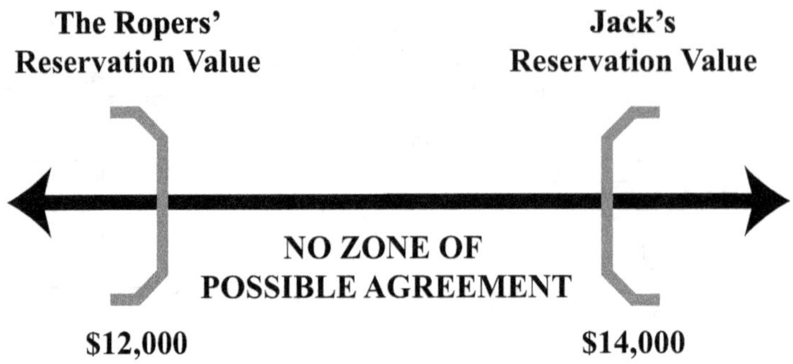

8. **Time cures all?** This is a classic situation in which the parties both prefer money today, but differ in the rates at which they prefer money sooner rather than later. Because Jack is paying such a high interest rate on his debt right now—far higher than the interest rate the Ropers are receiving—the most efficient agreement between the two would be one in which the Ropers pay Jack quickly. Jack will, in effect, be willing to take a discount from the Ropers (or depending on your perspective, pay a premium to the Ropers) in exchange for getting the money now.

   To illustrate this proposition mathematically, consider how each party would assess a lump-sum settlement today of $10,000. Jack would, theoretically at least, be able to use that money to pay off some of his credit card debt. Since he is paying 19 percent interest on his debt, if he were to pay $10,000 of his debt today, it would save him from having to pay $11,900 a year from today. So, today, the $10,000 would be worth $10,000 to Jack. But to Jack, receiving that $10,000 today would be the equivalent of receiving $11,900 a year from today ($10,000 × 1.19 = $11,900). And that, in turn, is the equivalent of Jack receiving $14,161 two years from today ($11,900 × 1.19 = $14,161). The miracles of compound interest! The Ropers would, of course, prefer to keep their money, so that they can continue to earn the 6 percent interest on it. If they were to keep their $10,000 and invest it this year, it would be worth $10,600 to them a year from today ($10,000 × 1.06 = $10,600). And a year later, it would be worth $11,236 to them ($10,600 × 1.06 = $11,236).

   Now compare each party's expectation of what trial would yield two years from now with how each party values $10,000 today.

   What does all of this mean for a ZOPA analysis for the Ropers and Jack if we are looking two years down the road? Absent the time consideration, these two parties had no apparent ZOPA. But by factoring in the effects of interest over time, these two parties could arrive at a settlement (for example, a flat $10,000 payment today) that each would find more financially attractive than going to court and getting an outcome two years from now.[1]

Jack's Choice		The Ropers' Choice	
Amount of expected award two years from now	$14,000	Amount of expected liability two years from now	$12,000
Value two years from now of an immediate $10,000 lump-sum payment	$14,161	Cost two years from now of an immediate $10,000 lump-sum payment	$11,236

The dollar figures in this case are not terribly large, of course. It is not clear that either party would necessarily make a decision about settlement based on just a few hundred dollars difference in expected cost of benefit. But the principle is there. And if you consider the potential implications of these analyses in cases that involve millions (rather than thousands) of dollars, you can imagine why this becomes important.

9. **Have I got a deal for you!** The Ropers' basic idea is certainly worth pursuing from a value creation perspective. Recall from Chapter 1 that negotiators can often capitalize on differences in resources (like having an apartment) and on different relative valuations. (Having an apartment is probably worth more to Jack than it would cost the Ropers to provide an apartment.)

   The question asks what psychological dynamics risk complicating the Ropers' idea of making this offer. At least three are potentially implicated. First, the Ropers risk overvaluing their own apartment. The

---

1. To calculate how each party's reservation value shifts under the effects of time and interest (and therefore, to calculate the contour of any possible ZOPA), the relevant formula would be:

$$PV = \frac{FV}{(1+r)^n}$$

PV = present value
FV = future value
r = interest rate
n = number of periods
Applying this formula to the figures in this case suggests that a trial one year away still produces no ZOPA. (The Ropers' maximum would be $11,321, and Jack's minimum would be $11,765.) If a trial is two years away, however, a ZOPA emerges. The Ropers' maximum is $10,680, and Jack's minimum is $9,886. Any number between $9,886 and $10,680 should, at least theoretically, be more attractive to each party than continued litigation.

endowment effect suggests that because the Ropers own the apartment, they are likely to consider any given apartment to be more valuable than might be objective. They can overcome the risk of this bias by collecting good, comparative, objective data. In fact, they have likely done so in the process of setting rental rates for their apartments. Second, the Ropers will need to fight against the likelihood that Jack suffers from zero-sum bias. The proposal is one that has the potential of making both parties better off than they would be with a simple exchange of dollars. If Jack is caught in conceiving of this as a mythical fixed pie, he may not perceive the possibility that this is something other than a trick. Third, Jack may devalue the offer simply because of its source, through reactive devaluation. If Jack has come to distrust the Ropers, he may not attach as much value to their offer as he might rationally. This suggests that the Ropers might consider using one or more intermediaries, like the attorneys, to be the source of a "trial balloon" idea, or something that would, in Jack's mind at least, disassociate the Ropers from the idea.

10. **Uncle Fred's flight.** By naming the outcome his Uncle Fred obtained, there is some risk that Archie will be creating conditions in which the **anchoring effect** will take hold. It may be hard for either of them to assess the airlines' offers without using Uncle Fred's experience as the reference point—the number against which to judge the offer. In some ways, it is unproblematic, even helpful, to have some comparison, some experience, some reference point. The risk would be that they would give this number greater weight than it deserves in their calculations.

    Similarly, there may be some risk of the **endowment effect** here. Archie and Veronica have tickets (albeit tickets that will not actually allow them to arrive at their honeymoon as scheduled). People are not reliably good at assessing the value of things they possess. Here, they may overvalue the tickets (as compared with an objective valuation) simply because they are theirs.

11. **Airport honeymoon**? As described above, Archie and Veronica may observe in themselves or each other, the endowment effect—the likelihood of overestimating the value of the ticket they currently hold. They might, therefore, be at risk of passing up an offer that is objectively attractive.

    This scenario may also implicate the concept of loss aversion. Archie and Veronica might reasonably be comparing their options here (delayed flight and airport hotel, or *maybe* something better from the main office) against their original plans. In that case, each of these looks like a loss. And people are reluctant to accept a certain loss, even in the face of the prospect of losing even more by rolling the dice. They might, therefore, be disinclined to accept the offer, even if they have no good reason to believe they'll get better (or even as good a deal) from the main office.

12. **Honeymoon delayed is honeymoon denied?** The agent has presented an option that *might* be attractive, under the circumstances. Archie and Veronica may, however, be at risk of either zero-sum bias or reactive devaluation. They may assume that anything the airline is offering that would be good for the airline must be bad for travelers, and vice versa. It is true that there are distributive aspects to this (and almost every) negotiation. But this could be an example of a time when one side can offer something that is of greater value to the other side without incurring additional costs. In other words, this could be an example of a value-creating offer. But if Archie and Veronica have a fixed-pie mindset, they are at risk of missing it. Similarly, they may, at this stage, view the airline with such hostility that they simply discount the attractiveness of anything that was the airlines' idea.

CHAPTER 3

The Law of Negotiation

§3.1 INTRODUCTION

This chapter focuses on three sets of legal issues that often form the boundaries of negotiators' conduct: good faith, fraud, and confidentiality.

With each topic, we describe the line between sanctionable negotiation behavior and negotiation behavior that is not. We are not talking about the line between what is effective and what is not (that is a question of strategy). We are not talking about the line between what is acceptable and what is not (that is a question of reputation and community norms). We are not talking about the line between what is ethical and what is not (that is a question of personal norms and philosophy). We are simply asking the question, "If I engage in this kind of behavior, can I get into trouble under the law?"

Please do not misunderstand us to be suggesting that the question of "what is legal" is the only (or even the most important) question relevant to a negotiator. In fact, our experience suggests the opposite. Reputations matter, in both the short and long term. Further, deception and other forms of "misbehavior" in negotiation often prove to be both costly and ineffective. This book is not written as a best practices guide. But you should understand that the ABA's Model Rules of Professional Conduct and the cases discussed in this chapter represent an ethical floor—something below which you should never fall. In fact, most lawyers wisely operate well above that level.[1]

1. We quote the text of several sets of rules of professional conduct and their comments in this chapter and Chapter 5. When we reproduce particular rules, we are quoting the Delaware

Legal boundaries, for the most part, are drawn from two sources: The Model Rules of Professional Conduct outline a variety of ethical duties for lawyers, including duties related to negotiations, and the common law of contracts and torts creates boundaries on legally tolerable bargaining behavior.

§3.2 WHY "GOOD FAITH" IS NOT (NECESSARILY) THE ANSWER

This chapter examines the boundaries between what bargaining behavior risks causing a lawyer to be sanctioned and what is permissible. If all negotiators operated under a system akin to the familiar Golden Rule ("Do unto others as you would have them do unto you"), we might expect to see few instances of misbehavior. But the reality is that negotiators have no common understanding of what constitutes a negotiator's duty. Even for attorney-negotiators, the boundaries of what is tolerable are nuanced and ambiguous.

At the outset, we want to address the question of **good faith** in the context of negotiations. The concept of good faith in bargaining does not serve as a guarantee against misbehavior for two reasons. First, it is not clear what boundaries result from the determination that negotiators must act in good faith. Second, it is not clear that a duty to act in good faith applies in a wide range of negotiation contexts.

If an obligation to negotiate in good faith applies, it is not always clear what this obligation requires. Even statutes requiring good-faith negotiation in the relatively narrow context of court-annexed ADR programs rarely define good faith. Given this lack of clarity, one commentator suggests that "perhaps [good faith] is like obscenity: You know it when you see it."[2]

In the broader context of voluntary negotiation, good-faith obligations present a constraint only against the most horrible negotiation behavior, leaving a vast gray area unpunished. Nevertheless, some examples of actions punished under this admittedly loose good-faith standard exist. Courts have found parties in violation of a good-faith obligation for delaying negotiation, for failing to seek approval for agreements, for breaching an agreement of exclusivity by making a deal with a competitor during negotiations, and for improperly delaying investments.

Lawyers' Rules of Professional Conduct. However, these rules and comments are identical to the ABA Model Rules and comments except where we have noted the text differences.

2. Kimberlee K. Kovach, *Good Faith in Mediation—Requested, Recommended, or Required? A New Ethic*, 38 S. Tex. L. Rev. 575, 600 (1997).

The definition of good faith may also depend on the type of dispute the parties are trying to resolve. In the context of labor-management negotiations, for example, each side is under an obligation to refrain from engaging in a wide set of behaviors that would otherwise be permissible. In most negotiations, either side is free to walk away from the table, or even to refuse to enter negotiations. But in the context of collective bargaining, such behavior risks being treated as an unlawful violation of the statutory duty to bargain in good faith. Similarly, even though negotiators in a broad range of contexts commonly present take-it-or-leave-it offers, such behavior in the context of a labor negotiation could be considered an unfair labor practice because it violates the duty to bargain in good faith (as explained in the well-known case *NLRB v. General Electric Co.*, 418 F.2d 736 (2d Cir. 1969), outlawing "Boulwarism"—a particular form of take-it-or-leave-it negotiating named after General Electric vice president Lemuel Boulware).

Even if we could define good faith, it is not always clear that there is a duty to negotiate in good faith. Although the Uniform Commercial Code and the Restatement (Second) of Contracts both refer to a duty of good faith in performance and enforcement of contracts, neither specifically mentions a duty to negotiate in good faith. Consistent with this approach, courts frequently reject a general good-faith requirement that would apply to every party in every negotiation. The best-known pair of cases demonstrating the complexity of good faith as a standard for negotiators is *Hoffman v. Red Owl Stores*, 26 Wis. 2d 683 (1965), and *Gray v. Eskimo Pie Corp.*, 244 F. Supp. 785 (D. Del. 1965), both of which were decided in the same year and turn on the question of detrimental reliance (discussed later in this chapter).

In *Red Owl*, Joseph Hoffman operated a bakery, but wanted instead to own a Red Owl franchise for a grocery store. Red Owl Stores expressed interest in the project, and when Hoffman indicated that he had only $18,000 available to invest in the project, the Red Owl representative assured him that he would not need more than that. Hoffman sold his bakery, bought and sold an interim grocery store, moved his family, and purchased fixtures in anticipation of opening a Red Owl store. Red Owl then told him that he would need more capital after all. The Wisconsin Supreme Court upheld a jury verdict in favor of Hoffman against Red Owl, citing the injury resulting from Hoffman's reliance on Red Owl's promises.

A more recent case gives us another example. In *Tour Costa Rica v. Country Walkers, Inc.*, 758 A.2d 795 (Vt. 2000), Country Walkers promised a two-year exclusive deal to receive walking tours from Tour Costa Rica. Given their limited resources, Tour Costa Rica shut down their ongoing operations to focus on designing, arranging, and preparing for Country Walkers' tour needs. However, a few weeks before tours were to begin, Country Walkers informed Tour Costa Rica that it would be using another company for their tours, leaving Tour Costa Rica without the promised business or whatever other business they could have developed if they had not relied on the promise from Country Walkers. When asked about the two-year exclusive promise, the owner of Country Walkers replied, "If I did and I certainly may have promised you a two-year commitment, I apologize for not honoring it." The Supreme Court of Vermont upheld a jury verdict awarding Tour Costa Rica $22,500 in damages on a promissory estoppel claim.

Compare this to *Eskimo Pie*, in which negotiations between two prospective business partners went awry but the court rejected a claim based on reliance damages. In *Eskimo Pie*, the Grays approached Eskimo Pie Corporation about a new idea for marketing a donut-shaped ice cream pie. (The Grays called it a "Snonut.") Eskimo Pie expressed initial interest, but then dragged out negotiations for more than two years, citing excuses ranging from its president being out of town, to a corporate reorganization, to an insistence that negotiations take place face-to-face (but never being available for such meetings.) During these negotiations, the Grays did not approach any other companies about marketing their idea. Eskimo Pie eventually declined the Grays' offer to do business on the ice cream pie idea. Shortly after that, the Grays discovered that Eskimo Pie had been testing the idea internally the whole time and had begun production of a Snonut-like product. The court in *Eskimo Pie* dismissed the Grays' complaint, acknowledging the possibility that Eskimo Pie may have acted in bad faith, but finding that the Grays had not adequately demonstrated any reasonable, detrimental reliance on any assertions from Eskimo Pie.

In *Red Owl*, *Country Walkers*, and *Eskimo Pie*, one party engaged in behavior that would violate the Golden Rule, and perhaps even the concept of "good faith." Only the plaintiffs in *Red Owl* and *Country Walkers* demonstrated that they had reasonably and detrimentally relied on the behavior in question, however, and as a result, they were the only ones to recover.

As we discussed, modern courts typically recognize a good-faith obligation only in specific, relatively limited contexts. For example, many courts recognize a limited obligation to bargain in good faith when the parties in question have already established a preliminary agreement. If the parties sign a letter of intent to lease space in a shopping center, a court will likely find that the parties are obligated to negotiate the details of the lease in good faith. (Knowing this, many parties now explicitly write into their letters of intent that there is no duty of good faith attached.) Similarly, if one party makes a preliminary agreement to lend the other money, a court will probably find that the parties are obligated to negotiate the amount of money and repayment schedule in good faith. Some negotiations occur under a court order, and that order frequently carries with it an obligation to act in good faith. (For more on court-affiliated ADR, see Chapter 11.) Other contexts may include a statutory duty to bargain in good faith, such as in the labor-management negotiations mentioned above, which occur in a wide range of settings. But generally, good faith does not constrain the behavior of many negotiators, in many contexts.

The problem with good-faith requirements, therefore, is twofold. First, even if a duty to act in good faith exists, the scope of the duty is not typically clear enough to prevent all ambiguity. Second, it is not necessarily clear (even in a given jurisdiction) whether negotiators have a duty to act in good faith. We are not suggesting that good faith is irrelevant—far from it. But your inquiry into the boundaries of punishable behavior cannot end with an inquiry into good faith.

§3.3 FRAUD

Many people have drawn analogies between negotiations and poker. These analogies are imperfect at best. The poker imagery likely ignores those aspects of negotiation that involve value creation, relationship building, and problem solving. (See Chapter 1, on negotiation, for more on these.) Nevertheless, in at least one limited way, the analogy to poker may be on point, because in both negotiations and poker, people sometimes perceive a competitive advantage if they are able to deceive the other side effectively. In some sense, it almost does not matter how often this advantage actually exists in negotiation. The *perception* that deception (and other misbehavior) creates an advantage is so strong that understanding the boundaries of deception is an important part of understanding negotiation.

§3.3.1 When a Lie Isn't a Lie

Negotiators face several tensions as they sit across the table from their counterparts. Among the most significant of these is the perceived tension between the desire to disclose information (to promote efficient communication and better outcomes) and the desire to withhold information (to prevent being exploited by the other side.) Some believe that this tension is so pervasive and so significant that they simply label this as **the negotiator's dilemma**. Taken to its extreme, a negotiator might perceive pressure to mislead the other side to gain a strategic advantage with respect to the distributional aspects of the negotiation. This leads to the simple-sounding question: Are negotiators permitted to lie?

No legal duty directly revolves around the term "lying." The law speaks, instead, about fraud, misrepresentation, deception, and other legal concepts. So, it is important to understand what behaviors are permissible and what behaviors are not. The boundaries of permissible behavior are clearly not the only things that matter in negotiators' decision making. There are plenty of good reasons why people might not do everything they are technically

> **Elements of Fraud**
>
> 1. Knowingly
> 2. Misrepresents
> 3. A material fact
> 4. Causing reasonable detrimental reliance

permitted to do. But, in theory, people will be particularly hesitant to do things they are definitely not allowed to do.

To describe the boundary between what is permitted and what is not, we start with two fundamental concepts: the mental state of the speaker (did they have the intention to deceive?), and the falsity of what is being said (was it a misrepresentation?).

§3.3.1.1 Knowing

Liars know they are liars. Embedded in the concept of lying is the idea that the speaker intends to deceive, which only occurs if the speaker knows their statement is untrue. Take a simple example: The plaintiff's lawyer tells defense counsel that the plaintiff has suffered severe injury, requiring extensive hospitalization. If the plaintiff's lawyer knows that the plaintiff has not suffered severe injury and was never hospitalized, we would be comfortable saying that the lawyer is lying.

Now, what if the plaintiff's lawyer believes that the plaintiff has suffered severe injury, tells the defense counsel that the plaintiff has suffered severe injury, and it turns out that the plaintiff has not suffered severe injury? Would we say that the plaintiff's lawyer is lying? Probably not. Though the statement turned out to be untrue, the plaintiff's lawyer did not know it was untrue at the time she said it. *Knowledge* matters. As you will see below, there is a difference in how tort law and contract law treat the question of knowledge. In short, knowledge is required for recovery in tort, but it may not be necessary to avoid a contract's terms.

Of course, the term *knowledge* is not self-defining, and there are many legal twists, clarifications, and complications that can arise. For example, some parties might try to get cute by advancing an argument along the lines of, "Well, really now, who can *know* anything, anyway? In this postmodern world, the concept of knowledge is outdated." We cannot speak to the kind of success such an argument would meet in a philosophy class. But negotiators charged with defending themselves against an accusation that they lied should certainly hope to have something more to stand on than this. Courts virtually never treat a knowledge requirement as "100 percent absolutely certain."

Similarly, courts will be more likely to frown on assertions of lack of knowledge if the accused person is responsible for their own lack of knowledge. This concept can be labeled "contrived ignorance." For example, imagine a corporate executive who specifically informs his accounting and finance department *not to tell him* any bad news related to a particular business initiative. The executive then tells the media and investors all kinds of wonderful things about the initiative. If the executive's comments were inaccurate, has the executive lied? The executive may not *know* that what he was saying was untrue, but he was the reason he did not know it to be untrue. In most contexts, the law would not look favorably on the executive's behavior, despite his lack of knowledge. Even with somewhat less intentional shielding from information, certain conduct can constitute "constructive fraud" through negligent misrepresentation.

§3.3.1.2 Misrepresentation

Falsity is another component of figuring out what constitutes a lie. Short of revealing something like state secrets or trade secrets, the law doesn't generally punish people who say things that turn out to be true. Or more accurately, if we get upset at a truth-teller, it is not because what they said is untrue, but for some other reason, i.e., what they said was impolite, breached confidentiality, or caused injury. Embedded in the concept of lying is the idea that the statement in question was a misrepresentation of the truth.

§3.3.2 When It Might Be a Lie but Isn't Punishable

Not all knowingly false statements are treated the same. Some are treated as fraud. (See the next section for more on fraud.) But legal and professional institutions are apparently indifferent to a number of different categories of knowingly false statements. Again, we remind you that there may be reasons—reputation, for example—why a person might prefer not to lie, even if lying is not punishable. Still, it is important to understand the limits of legal sanctioning. Three concepts—materiality, puffery, and detrimental reliance—will help to clarify the boundaries of what might cause a lawyer to be sanctioned.

§3.3.2.1 Materiality

Both the common law of fraud and the ABA's Model Rules of Professional Conduct draw a distinction between misrepresentations about **material** facts and misrepresentations about facts that are not material. Only misrepresentations about material facts will land a speaker in hot water.

Most courts find that a misrepresentation is material if it would influence a reasonable person's decision or course of action or if the maker of the representation knows that the recipient is likely to view the fact as important. Some examples may help to illustrate the boundary. A client walks into your office one day, opens his wallet, points proudly to a picture of his new granddaughter, and asks, "Isn't this an adorable little girl?" What do you say if, in fact, you hold an opinion about the cuteness of the granddaughter that would be likely to disappoint your client? This is the concept of the "white lie." Many (though not all) lawyers would immediately respond with a statement affirming the cuteness of the baby, in spite of their actual opinion. They have knowingly misrepresented their assessment, but the misrepresentation is not material because it is not a misrepresentation concerning the particular business that the lawyer and the client are about to transact. (Of course, telling someone their granddaughter is not absolutely adorable may very well affect the relationship.)

Moreover, an issue does not become material simply because it is somehow related to the negotiations. Imagine that the owner of a car is negotiating with a buyer. The owner tells the buyer that she took the car to a specific garage for the car's most recent maintenance inspections, forgetting that she actually took it to a different, more reputable garage. The buyer makes an offer on the car. This misrepresentation is probably not material, because it would not have changed a reasonable buyer's decision to make an offer.

On the other hand, in some circumstances, a fact will plainly be material to the negotiations at hand. For example, in *James v. Lifeline Mobile Medics*, 341 Ill. App. 3d 451, 792 N.E.2d 461 (2003), when the parties were negotiating a settlement after the plaintiff received a court judgment in its favor, defendant's counsel argued that, if they did not settle, defendant would have to declare bankruptcy. When plaintiff learned the truth (that defendant had plenty of money to pay), they moved to set the settlement aside. The court held that the defendant counsel's deliberate misrepresentations concerning his client's financial situation for the purpose of inducing the plaintiff to accept a lower settlement amount were sufficiently material to provide the basis for a fraud claim. Defendant lawyer's statements concerning his client's financial circumstances and bankruptcy intentions constituted "misrepresentations that [went] beyond the usual hyperbole of accepted negotiation techniques."

In negotiations over a joint venture, each party might make representations about its production capacity, its client base, or its existing assets. Any of these representations would be considered material to the negotiations because a prospective business partner would contemplate a joint venture precisely because of these issues. A misrepresentation of any of these material issues, therefore, would create a risk of fraud. The Uniform Commercial Code also provides guidance on the materiality of any description of goods that might be the subject of negotiation. UCC §2-313 provides that a seller can make an express warranty in several ways, including:

> (a) Any affirmation of fact or promise made by the seller to the buyer which relates to the goods and becomes part of the basis of the bargain creates an express warranty that the goods shall conform to the affirmation or promise.
>
> (b) Any description of the goods which is made part of the basis of the bargain creates an express warranty that the goods shall conform to the description.

An express warranty (which can be oral and need not even be explicitly "incorporated" into the agreement) is a term of the contract, and it is part of the "basis of the bargain."

§3.3.2.2 Puffery, Dissembling, and Misdirection

One vision of negotiation largely mirrors the kind of haggling one might expect to find in a quintessential flea market: Both sides make outrageous initial demands, concede only reluctantly, vigorously oppose any assertions made by the other side, and perhaps eventually reach an agreement at a point somewhere between the initial offers. As you know from Chapter 1, we think this vision is neither accurate (because it is far too simplistic to capture the reality of most legal negotiations) nor advisable (because it risks too much inefficiency and too many suboptimal results). Still, the image of haggling remains, and it has had some effect on how legal ethicists conceive of the duties that attach to negotiators.

The haggling vision of negotiation appears most prominently in the concept of **puffery** in negotiations. Puffery refers to statements in which the "puffer" is exaggerating the value or quality of the good or service in question. As we outline above, if a speaker knowingly misrepresents a material fact, and the listener detrimentally and reasonably relies on those misstatements, the speaker has engaged in fraud. But what if the listener knew better (or should know better) than to rely on the statements in question? Or what if the statements in question were not really about material facts? These are the contexts in which the law distinguishes fraud from puffery. The comment to Model Rule 4.1 explains that under generally accepted conventions of negotiation, certain types of statements are not material fact and, therefore, not to be relied upon in a negotiation.

> **Rule 4.1**
>
> **Truthfulness in Statements to Others**
>
> In the course of representing a client a lawyer shall not knowingly:
>
> (a) make a false statement of material fact or law to a third person;

> **Rule 4.1, Comment 2**
>
> This Rule refers to statements of fact. Whether a particular statement should be regarded as one of fact can depend on the circumstances. Under generally accepted conventions in negotiation, certain types of statements ordinarily are not taken as statements of material fact. Estimates of price or value placed on the subject of a transaction and a party's intentions as to an acceptable settlement of a claim are ordinarily in this category, and so is the existence of an undisclosed principal except where nondisclosure of the principal would constitute fraud . . . .

The drafters of the Model Rules do not explain how they concluded that one convention or another is "generally accepted," and it is also not clear why general acceptance should be considered synonymous with "ethical." Nevertheless, this comment to the Model Rules declares various forms of puffery to be tolerable, in part because the rules deem the subjects of puffery not to be material facts.

Under Rule 4.1, an attorney can misrepresent the value of a deal or purchase because it is understood to be puffery. Statements like, "This property will surely be home to the best shopping mall ever," or "This company has produced the finest cars in Europe," are commonly taken to be sales talk and not considered material facts.

Similarly, under legal ethics rules, an attorney is permitted to misrepresent his client's settlement intentions. For example, imagine that a defendant instructs his attorney to agree to "any deal that costs me less than $200,000," and the plaintiff subsequently asks defense counsel, "Would your client be willing to settle this for $150,000?" What options does the attorney hold for the defendant? The attorney could say yes and try to finalize that deal. The attorney could evade the question. Or the attorney could say no and hold out for an even better deal. Of course, the latter strategy has some risks—both tactical and reputational—associated with it. But as a matter of legal ethics, the attorney has not run afoul of Rule 4.1's prohibition against making fraudulent statements, because the statements would be considered "mere puffery" and are in the general realm of a party's intentions, as outlined under Comment 2. Under the common law of fraud, none of these options would be actionable—including a knowingly false statement about the client's willingness to settle for a particular price.

There are, however, some ways in which Rule 4.1 and the common law of fraud do restrict negotiators' assertions about the limits of their willingness to agree to particular terms. Imagine an attorney for a landlord who is negotiating with a current tenant at the end of the tenant's lease. If the landlord's attorney says to the tenant, "The landlord has no intention to renew your lease unless you agree to a $500 per month increase in the rent," the landlord's attorney cannot be found to have committed fraud or violated Rule 4.1—even if the attorney knew the landlord would consider renewing the lease for far less. Now imagine that the landlord's attorney says to the tenant, "You had better renew this lease, along with a $500 per month increase, because the landlord already has a prospective tenant who is ready to sign on those terms. We're going to close with them tomorrow if you don't agree today," when, in fact, there is no prospective tenant. Unlike the first (vague) assertion about what the landlord was willing to do, the second (specific) assertion about the landlord's best alternative to a negotiated agreement (or BATNA; see Chapter 1) does create the risk that the attorney has committed fraud, and courts have rescinded lease contracts in cases like this. Similarly, a specific assertion about the lawyer's authority to settle can get a lawyer in trouble. As the ABA Ethics Committee has written:

> For example, even though a client's Board of Directors has authorized a higher settlement figure, a lawyer may state in a negotiation that the client does not wish to settle for more than $50. However, it would not be permissible for the lawyer to state that the Board of Directors had formally disapproved any settlement in excess of $50, when authority had in fact been granted to settle for a larger sum.[3]

What justifies the distinction between lies about what a client is willing to do and lies about what competing offers a client has? Though they are not specific about their logic, most courts seem to explain this distinction with reference to the listener's expectations and whether it would be reasonable to rely on the negotiator's statements. Perhaps the listener has comparatively less reason to trust a general assertion about settlement intentions and comparatively more reason to trust a specific assertion about a fact relevant to the speaker's settlement intentions. If this is true, then that suggests that the law is at least partially driven by a belief that a negotiator should know when to trust what the other negotiator is saying. This leads us to the concept of detrimental reliance.

§3.3.3 Detrimental Reliance

What if a speaker told a lie, but the listener never relied on the speaker's lie? This is not an idle philosophical question along the lines of "if a tree fell in the woods and nobody was around to hear it . . . ." Instead, this question raises the concept of **detrimental reliance**. Without detrimental reliance, it is quite unlikely that the speaker's lie will be punished.

3. ABA Formal Ethics Op. 06-439 p. 3.

In general, a party cannot recover damages for fraud unless they rely on a false statement to their detriment. For example, if a father falsely tells his daughter that he will pay for college if she quits her job, but the daughter remains in her job, the daughter is not relying on his promise and has done nothing to her own detriment. Similarly, if the father's promise leads the daughter to quit her job, but her employer (in a moment of generosity) continues paying her salary, the daughter may not have incurred a detriment. Only in a case where the father makes the promise, the daughter quits her job, the daughter stops receiving her paycheck, and then the father refuses to pay for college would there be an argument that the daughter suffered a detriment from reliance on her father's promise. Without reliance that causes harm to the listener, no action in fraud will stand.

In most jurisdictions, a party must show not only that she relied on a statement to her detriment, but also that her reliance was reasonable or justified. Reliance on a statement is usually reasonable or justified if the statement appears reasonable on its face and the listener has no reason to doubt its truth (as in the case of puffery, where the listener should know better than to rely on it.) Imagine an aggressive salesman in a clothing store who tells a shopper looking for new professional attire, "If you buy this suit, your salary is guaranteed to double in a year!" Even if the shopper buys the suit but fails to secure the promised salary increase, a court would be extremely unlikely to consider the shopper's reliance on the absurd (puffed) assertion to be justified.

In contrast, if the daughter whose father promised payment for college has no reason to doubt that he will pay, her reliance on his promise would be reasonable. However, if the daughter knows that her father has neither the capacity nor the intention to pay for college, her reliance on his statement might not be reasonable. If there is no detrimental reliance, or if the reliance is not reasonable, a speaker is unlikely to face any legal consequences for their misrepresentation. In the lease example above, the tenant can only recover if he reasonably relied on the threat of another tenant and agreed to the lease increase.

§3.3.4 When a Lie Is a Lie and Is Punishable: Fraud

As outlined above, certain lying statements (nonmaterial, puffery, or ones upon which no one has relied) may not be fraud. But even statements that fall within one of the categories listed above (and are, therefore, not the subject of official prohibitions) may damage a negotiator's reputation or ability to successfully persuade a counterpart.

Some lies run not only those risks, but also the risk of legal or professional sanctions. The biggest category of these lies is given the label **fraud**. All negotiators, including lawyers, operate under the strictures of the common law prohibition against fraud. The common law tort of fraud generally involves four elements that we have already discussed. A negotiator engages in tortious fraud if she or he (1) knowingly (2) misrepresents (3) a material fact (4) causing reasonable detrimental reliance.

The common law of contracts makes it somewhat easier to avoid a contract than to recover in a tort action because the first element of fraud, knowing, is not required to void a contract. The test for avoidance under contract law hinges principally on the materiality of the misrepresentation. Even if the speaker's misrepresentation was made unknowingly, a materially false assertion that causes reasonable, detrimental reliance will suffice. It also turns out that, according to strict contract law, a party can avoid a contract even in the absence of materiality, provided the party can demonstrate misrepresentation and detrimental reliance. Cases illustrating this principle, however, are not easy to find. You are probably on safe ground to assume that successful cases of fraud are going to involve misrepresentations about something material.

In addition to the legal sanctions provided through contract or tort law, attorneys have professional ethical constraints on their behavior as well. All negotiators, therefore, must understand that the law of fraud forms an important set of boundaries on their behavior.

As you might expect, each of the elements of fraud is subject to argument, clarification, and some degree of debate. In the sections above, we have provided guidance on how courts have interpreted each of these four elements. In the sections below, we discuss when not talking can still get you into trouble.

§3.3.5 When Silence Won't Save You

Negotiators do not necessarily shield themselves from difficulty merely by keeping quiet. In most of the examples up to this point, we have described instances in which a negotiator makes an affirmative statement that the negotiator knows to be untrue. That is certainly one form of behavior that can constitute fraud. However, a negotiator's silence, in certain circumstances, can also constitute fraud.

> **Rule 4.1**
>
> **Truthfulness in Statements to Others**
>
> In the course of representing a client a lawyer shall not knowingly: . . .
>
> (b) fail to disclose a material fact when disclosure is necessary to avoid assisting a criminal or fraudulent act by a client, unless disclosure is prohibited by Rule 1.6.[4]

4. Model Rule 4.1(b) includes the phrase "to a third person" after "material fact."

§3.3.5.1 Omission

In some circumstances, a negotiator who omits information will be treated as having made a misrepresentation. The common law of fraud recognizes the possibility that a misrepresentation might be made either through an affirmative statement or through an omission. The same is reflected in Rule 4.1(b) of the Model Rules of Professional Conduct, above, and in the comment to the rule below.

> **Rule 4.1, Comment 1**
>
> A lawyer is required to be truthful when dealing with others on a client's behalf, but generally has no affirmative duty to inform an opposing party of relevant facts. A misrepresentation can occur if the lawyer incorporates or affirms a statement of another person that the lawyer knows is false. Misrepresentations can also occur by partially true but misleading statements or omissions that are the equivalent of affirmative false statements . . . .

Silence, therefore, is not always a shield against committing fraud. A lawyer must disclose information to third parties if disclosure is necessary to avoid assisting a client in committing a crime or fraud and the disclosure is not prohibited under the rules of client confidentiality (Rule 1.6). Some lawyers in years past relied on the broad confidentiality requirements of Rule 1.6 to keep even fraudulent information to themselves. However, under the current version of Model Rule 1.6, adopted in most states, a lawyer may reveal information to prevent the client from committing fraud. Because the lawyer may reveal information, disclosure under Rule 4.1 is no longer prohibited. As a result, Rule 4.1 obligates attorneys to disclose this category of information, and Rule 1.6 no longer prevents them from doing so. Because states vary widely on this provision in Rule 1.6—sometimes disclosure is permitted in criminal fraud, sometimes it is permitted in financial injuries, sometimes it is even required in Rule 1.6—it is important to confirm the exact language of Rule 1.6 in your jurisdiction.

A classic example of an omitted fact deemed a material misrepresentation arose in the case of *Kentucky Bar Ass'n v. Geisler*, 938 S.W.2d 578 (Ky. 1997). Geisler represented a pedestrian who was struck by an automobile. During Geisler's negotiations with defense counsel, Geisler's client died, but Geisler said nothing about her client's death. The attorneys eventually reached a settlement, and only following the settlement did the defendants learn that Geisler's client was dead at the time of the settlement negotiations. When she faced a Bar disciplinary action, Geisler argued that she did not have an affirmative duty to disclose the information and that the information was immaterial. The Kentucky Supreme Court was unmoved by these arguments. It found the client's death to be plainly material to the settlement of a tort claim for injuries to the client. Citing the Kentucky equivalent of Model Rule 4.1, it also pointed out that "misrepresentations can occur by failure to act." In issuing its order publicly reprimanding Geisler and ordering her to pay the costs associated with her reprimand, the Kentucky Supreme Court wrote:

> [T]his Court fails to understand why guidelines are needed for an attorney to understand that when their client dies, they are under an obligation to tell opposing counsel such information. This seems to be a matter of common ethics and just plain sense. However, because attorneys such as respondent cannot discern such matters and require written guidelines so as to figure out their ethical convictions, this Court [affirms the ABA Formal Opinion on this matter.]

There are also four specialized circumstances, as outlined by the Restatement (Second) of Contracts (and also found in the Restatement (Second) of Torts), where omission becomes misrepresentation. The first case involves the negotiator who makes a partial disclosure that is or becomes misleading in light of all the facts. For example, in a negotiation to buy a widget maker, the widget company sends over financial documents to the potential purchaser. As the negotiation progresses, if the financial statements change (for example, the cost of producing widgets triples), the widget company must disclose the change to the potential purchaser.

The second case put forth in the Restatement arises when the parties have a fiduciary relationship. Typical fiduciary relationships include trustees, corporate executives, spouses, and business partners. In each of these cases, omission of material facts will be the same as a misrepresentation of the material facts. (The two additional circumstances outlined in the Restatement involve a duty to correct, which we discuss in the next section.)

Furthermore, caselaw has required disclosure when one party has superior knowledge that is not accessible to the other side. The classic example of this is found in home purchases, where the seller has a duty to disclose that the house is riddled with termites, floods every time it rains, or has a severe cockroach infestation. A more entertaining example can be found in *Stambovsky v. Ackley*, 572 N.Y.S.2d 672 (N.Y. App. Div. 1991), in which the court held that when selling a house, a seller has a duty to inform the buyer of any ghosts that may possess the house. The court found that this defect could not be found through any inspection, noting that "a very practical problem arises with respect to the discovery of a paranormal phenomenon: 'Who you gonna' call?' as the title song to the movie *Ghostbusters* asks." Recognizing the difficulty of obtaining this information, the court found that the presence of ghosts or the reputation of having ghosts in a house is superior knowledge that a seller has a duty to disclose. And although the court found that the buyer did not have a "ghost of a chance" of success under the tort of fraudulent misrepresentation, the contract could be rescinded because of the seller's failure to disclose the information in this consumer real estate transaction. Courts in most jurisdictions do not recognize an implied warranty of fitness in commercial leases, but because states vary on this, you should check the laws of your own jurisdiction.[5]

Another example of superior knowledge can be found in *Abazari v. Rosalind Franklin University of Medicine and Science*, 40 NE 3d 264 (Ill. App. 2 Dist. 2015). An Illinois statute required postsecondary institutions to "accurately describe the degree programs offered, program objectives, length of program . . . and such other material facts . . . as are likely to affect the decision of the student to enroll." 23 Ill. Adm. Code 1030.60(a)(7) (2012). Rosalind Franklin University advertised their ability to place graduates in residency programs, convincing the plaintiff to enroll at the school. However, the university failed to secure a residency spot for the plaintiff. The court ruled that the University's half-truth advertisement promoting their ability to secure residency included a duty to disclose material facts regarding the availability and acceptance rate of postgraduate residencies. Omission of such information supported a claim of fraudulent concealment.

A final instance where omission is the equivalent of misrepresentation is when there are special codified disclosure duties such as in insurance contracts or public securities offerings. Any omission in these negotiations is the same as misrepresentation. In short, misrepresentation may occur through affirmative statements, silence, or omissions, depending on the circumstance.

§3.3.5.2 Duty to Correct

A lie sometimes takes the form of an affirmative statement intending to mislead the other side into believing something that is not true. A lie in the form of an omission has the same goal. According to Restatement (Second) of Contracts §161(b) (and the Restatement (Second) of Torts §551), nondisclosure can be equivalent to an assertion. This happens if a party "knows that disclosure of the fact would correct a mistake of the other party as to a basic assumption on which that party is making the contract and if nondisclosure of the fact amounts to a failure to act in good faith and in accordance with reasonable standards of fair dealing." So, in at least these circumstances, a negotiator will be required not merely to refrain from making statements that cause a misunderstanding, but actually to make affirmative statements to correct their counterpart's misunderstanding.

---

5. For example, since *Stambovsky*, New York enacted Section 462 NY Real Property Law (2002), which mandates a Uniform Disclosure Statement that requires forty-eight affirmative representations (!) with the goal of ensuring the revelation of superior knowledge.

You have a duty to correct a misunderstanding if *you* were the one who caused the misunderstanding. For example, imagine that a houseguest sustains a serious injury to her ankle while tripping on an unrepaired portion of the homeowner's deck. The guest calls the homeowner from the doctor's office the next day and says, "Thanks a lot. My ankle is broken." Later that day, the guest learns that the ankle is only sprained, not broken. Several days later, the homeowner approaches the guest and says, "I'm really sorry about your broken ankle. I don't have insurance that would cover this, but I've researched the typical award juries in this jurisdiction give for a broken ankle, and I'm prepared to offer that amount to you." Must the guest correct the homeowner's mistaken impression that the ankle is broken prior to negotiating a settlement with the homeowner? Yes. The guest's statement was not fraudulent at the time of the phone call because the guest did not know it was a misrepresentation of her injuries. But the only reason the homeowner believed the ankle to be broken was his reasonable reliance on the guest's phone call. The guest's nondisclosure or failure to update would be treated as if the guest were renewing his (now knowingly false) statement at the time the guest and homeowner made the deal.

You also sometimes have a duty to correct if you know your negotiation counterpart has made a factual mistake. For our purposes, mistakes can be divided into two categories: mistakes about the law and mistakes about the facts. Each category of mistake brings a unique set of standards for correction. Each attorney is charged with researching and applying the law on behalf of their client. As you might imagine, if opposing counsel misreads the applicable precedent or has misjudged the value of a claim under negotiation, the other side does not have a duty to correct that mistake.

Mistakes with respect to facts, however, may create a duty to correct in some circumstances. A simple example of a mistake of fact would be an arithmetic error in calculating the value of a set of assets. The commonly cited divorce case *Stare v. Tate*, 21 Cal. App. 3d 432 (1971), provides a clear illustration of the consequences of failing to correct opposing counsel. In *Stare*, the wife's attorney made a calculation error in valuing the marital assets, and the wife's attorney extended a settlement offer to the husband based on those miscalculations. In preparing a response to the wife's offer, the husband's attorney spotted the miscalculation immediately. According to the appellate court, "[t]here can be no reasonable doubt that the counteroffer was prepared in a way designed to minimize the danger that [the wife] or her attorney would discover the mistake." The parties' eventual settlement was based on the wife's miscalculations. After the settlement was signed and the divorce was finalized, the husband sent a note to his ex-wife gloating about the mistake she had made. As the appellate court put it, "[t]he mistake might never have come to light had not [the husband] desired to have that exquisite last word." On appeal, the court ruled in favor of the wife and vacated the previous settlement agreement on the grounds that the husband's attorney had a duty to correct the known mistake.

§3.3.5.3 When Silence Is Required (a Note on Client Confidentiality)

Given the risk that a negotiator may be required to disclose information, is it safe to assume that an attorney cannot get into trouble as long as the attorney spills all the beans? No. As an initial matter, it is likely that a negotiator who divulges absolutely everything to the other side (including not only facts, but also valuations, reservation points, etc.) would be severely disadvantaged in the distributional aspects of the negotiation. Further, in many contexts, an attorney is prohibited from divulging certain information about the attorney's client.

The legal ethical rules governing confidentiality are not specific to negotiation. That is, they do not distinguish between disclosures made during bargaining and disclosures made in other contexts. But they are very clearly relevant—sometimes central—to an attorney's decision making in the context of a negotiation.

Model Rule 1.6 provides the baseline rule governing the confidentiality of client information and requires attorneys to keep confidential any "information relating to the representation of a client unless the client gives informed consent, the disclosure is impliedly authorized in order to carry out the representation or the disclosure is permitted" under a list of narrowly constructed exceptions. Exceptions include things like complying with a court order or taking steps to prevent reasonably certain death, substantial bodily injury, or fraud. And even as to these matters, the rules in many states merely declare that a lawyer may reveal these pieces of information.

The intersection of Rules 1.6 and 4.1 risk being confusing—particularly if one just skims them. The fundamental point is that, with respect to criminal or fraudulent activity, Rule 4.1 creates a mandate ("a lawyer shall not . . ."), while Rule 1.6 grants permission ("a lawyer may reveal . . ."). As we discussed above, most ethicists now read Rule 4.1 as requiring lawyers to reveal otherwise confidential information to prevent fraudulent activity, since Rule 1.6 does not prohibit it.

§3.3.6 What Happens to Liars?

We have spent most of this chapter so far describing the boundaries of permissible behavior by negotiators. Here, we turn to the "or else what?" question. What happens if a negotiator steps over one or more of the lines described above? The law provides two basic categories of sanctions applicable to all negotiators. A third set of formal sanctions applies only to attorney-negotiators.

And a fourth category—reputational harm—applies to everyone. We describe each briefly below.

First, as you may recall from your Contracts class, if a deal is reached through fraud, it is subject to **rescission**. Contract law provides a vehicle for an aggrieved party to attack the enforceability of a deal. At a minimum, the unscrupulous negotiator risks being stripped of whatever benefit he or she sought to gain from the misbehavior in the deal.

Second, a misbehaving negotiator may be subject to **tort liability** for certain kinds of behavior. For example, it is relatively common to see tort claims in cases of alleged fraud. A negotiator who commits fraud will not only see the benefits of the contract stripped away but may very well also be responsible for economic injuries resulting from the fraud. (And in a more limited set of circumstances, a negotiator who commits fraud may even be subject to criminal sanctions.)

Third, if the misbehaving negotiator is a lawyer, they may be subject to **disciplinary actions** from the Bar. This sanction rests on top of whatever other consequences the negotiator may face. For example, if a negotiator commits fraud, the contract in question is subject to rescission, and the negotiator may face private civil liability for the resulting damages. Further, the attorney may be sanctioned for failure to adhere to Model Rule 4.1. The Bar can issue a wide range of different sanctions on attorneys for violations of their professional responsibilities, ranging from a mild censure to permanent disbarment.

Finally, although not formal or grounded in the law, risks to negotiators' **reputations** create an important set of potential consequences of misbehavior in negotiations. Good reputations are hard to establish and are relatively fragile. If you have a reputation as a successful and ethical negotiator (the two are entirely consistent), you will be better able to persuade your counterpart in a specific negotiation, because they will trust your assertions and suggestions. Further, having a reputation for effectiveness and trustworthiness will be useful in the larger picture of your interactions with your colleagues, your prospective clients, and your counterparts.[6]

§3.4 MISBEHAVIOR BEYOND LYING

We have focused primarily on the question of lying in the context of negotiation because it is such a prevalent question. But lying is not the only form of misbehavior to which some negotiators are prone, so the law includes other boundaries as well. An unscrupulous negotiator might try to intimidate or

6. See Tinsley, Cambria & Schneider, *Reputation in Negotiation*, Negotiator's Desk Reference, vol. 1 (2017).

coerce a counterpart into signing an agreement. Or a negotiator might try to sneak terrible provisions into the agreement at the last minute, hoping to catch the unsuspecting counterpart unaware. Or a negotiator might take advantage of his counterpart's desperation by demanding onerous terms on a take-it-or-leave-it basis. And so on.

A substantial portion of the common law of contracts seeks to address these forms of misbehavior. In many respects, doctrines such as coercion, unconscionability, mutual assent, and the question of how to treat contracts of adhesion arose in response to bad bargaining behaviors. The length and focus of this book do not permit a complete reexamination of your course on Contracts, but you should recognize that you are already familiar with many (if not all) of the mechanisms available to curtail the misbehavior of negotiators.

Duress, as you may likely recall, is when one side in a negotiation forces the other side to accept the bargain under coercion or threat. Clear examples of duress include physical coercion, threat of physical harm, or a threat of criminal prosecution. Another example of duress is when the threat would harm the victim (such as publicizing unpleasant matters) but would not actually help the person making the threat; rather, it is made solely for vindictive or malicious reasons. The threat of a civil action, however, is not seen as duress because civil action is an appropriate legal action to resolve a conflict.

Duress has been found in cases where there is an illegitimate use of power, such as when an employer threatened to fire the employee unless he sold his stock in the company, or when an employer threatened to fire another family member unless the employee agreed to sign a release for a work-related injury. In narrow circumstances, duress can also occur when one side threatens not to carry out an already existing contract. For example, if one party threatens not to deliver promised goods, if the remedy for breach would be insufficient, and the parties are already considered to be bound by a duty of good faith under the contract, this threat would be duress.

It is important to note that general hard bargaining and taking advantage of one's better position in a negotiation is not duress. As E. Allan Farnsworth notes in *Contracts* §4.17 (4th ed. 2004), "A party will ordinarily be held to an agreement even though that party's adversity has been taken advantage of, as long as the contract has been shaped by prevailing market forces." When, however, the contract is the result of an illegitimate use of power, this will be considered duress.

Unconscionability is another type of bargaining misbehavior to which contract law has developed a response. Courts can void a contract they deem to be unconscionable, or they can modify the terms of the contract that are particularly problematic. One of the key issues—presenting both a benefit and detriment to the enforcement of the law of unconscionability—is its lack of a clear definition. Unconscionability typically includes both procedural unfairness (an inquiry into how the negotiation was conducted) and substantive unfairness (an inquiry into the merits of the agreement's terms.) Procedural unconscionability would include, for example, the use of "sharp" bargaining practices like fine print and confusing language. Procedural unconscionability may also include a lack of understanding and unequal bargaining power. Substantive unconscionability, as the name suggests, looks at the equities of the bargain. A deal is considered substantively unconscionable if one side has reaped the full benefit of the bargain at the expense of the other.

As the court outlined in *Williams v. Walker-Thomas Furniture Co.*, 350 F.2d 445 (D.C. Cir. 1965), "Unconscionability has generally been recognized to include an absence of meaningful choice on the part of one of the parties together with contract terms which are unreasonably favorable to the other party." In this case, Walker-Thomas sold Williams a stereo on credit, knowing that Williams received only a $218 monthly government check for herself and seven children and that she already owed the store money for several other purchases. The terms of the contract permitted Walker-Thomas to repossess any of these items if Williams failed to make a payment at any time before the entire debt was paid off (rather than credit her with paying off one item, then the next, then the next, and so on). The court found this contract to be unconscionable.

The doctrine of unconscionability has been most typically used in consumer cases and in cases dealing with franchisees—cases in which the courts perceive that one party has significantly less bargaining power and sophistication. Unconscionability is generally rejected in negotiations between two equally sophisticated bargainers—probably because the parties' relative equality in sophistication makes the negotiations more equal (therefore making procedural unconscionability unlikely) and makes it far less likely to result in skewed deal terms (therefore preventing substantive unconscionability).

As we will discuss later in the arbitration chapters, parties who seek to avoid the effects of arbitration clauses in contracts often appeal to the law of unconscionability to make their case. Such arguments are rarely successful, for reasons that will become clear in later chapters. But you should know that some arbitration clauses have been stricken on the grounds that they were unconscionable. For example, in *Brower v. Gateway 2000 Inc.*, 676 N.Y.S.2d 569 (N.Y. App. Div. 1998), consumers had various complaints related to computers they had purchased from Gateway. Gateway tried to enforce a contractual provision that compelled the consumers to bring any complaints before an arbitrator in Chicago, and Gateway required that consumers follow the International Chamber of Commerce arbitration procedures. One of those procedures included a $2,000 nonrefundable registration fee, akin to a filing fee. Given that the consumers had suffered less than half that amount in damages, they argued (successfully) that the arbitration clause's nonrecoverable filing fee unconscionably deprived them of any recourse in this case.

§3.5 PROTECTING THE CONFIDENTIALITY OF THE PARTIES' TERMS OF AGREEMENT

Most disputes, although desperately important to those immediately involved, simply are not interesting to the outside world. And if the world did not even care to know that two people were in a dispute, it is unlikely that the world is going to care about the terms of an agreement those two reached to resolve their uninteresting dispute. As a matter of practice, therefore, many settlement terms remain out of the public eye for the simple reason that even if the public had access to the terms, the public would not care. But not all disputes, and not all disputants, are of such little interest to the outside world.

In many circumstances, disputants have a presumptive right to keep the terms of their settlement agreements private. If you and your neighbor get into a fight about appropriate hedge-trimming protocols and eventually resolve your fight, it is unlikely that some outside person could come in and insist upon knowing how you resolved your fight. In the context of disputes that have proceeded to litigation, the procedural rules in effect in most states have a provision permitting a plaintiff simply to dismiss their complaint voluntarily. If two disputants settle a case, therefore, part of the settlement almost always includes an agreement that the plaintiff will cease pursuing the legal claim, and the case will be dismissed. And if the only thing that appears in the court record is an indication that the plaintiff voluntarily dismissed its claim, the outside world would again have little ability to access the terms of that settlement agreement.

Outsiders have a greater opportunity for access to settlement terms when disputants file the contents of their agreement with the court. (Parties might opt to file the terms with the court, for example, to have the court enter the agreement as a judgment, thereby making it easier to enforce in the event of a breach.) You will see examples of such circumstances in some of the cases described below. In some jurisdictions, filing a settlement with the court may not threaten the confidentiality of the deal's terms. But many jurisdictions have passed "open records laws" or "sunshine laws," providing public access to court records, including settlements, unless there is some substantial interest that outweighs this presumption of openness.

A disputant may attempt to achieve a degree of secrecy by simply filing only *part* of the settlement with the court. However, the court's judgment (which is now public) must generally reflect any private side agreements, so that it is accurate. In *Janus Films, Inc. v. Miller*, 801 F.2d 578 (2d Cir. 1986), Janus Films and Miller reached a settlement after Janus sued Miller for copyright infringement. The settlement, as stated by counsel for Janus, included the defendant conceding liability and a judgment for $100,000 in addition to a separate confidential agreement regarding the terms of the judgment. It turned out that the separate side agreement basically allowed the defendant to pay considerably less than $100,000 to the plaintiff in installments over an extended period of time. When Janus crowed about its litigation success to a Hollywood trade publication, Miller protested. The court refused to set aside the parties' settlement, but it did order that the judgment of the court be revised to reflect accurately all the terms of the settlement.

Who are these people who might want to learn about settlement terms? Three major categories of outsiders might want access to the terms of certain settlement agreements: the government, interested parties in related disputes, and the media. The ability of each of these parties to break through the default assumption of privacy is different, and so we treat them in separate sections below.

§3.5.1 Hiding Settlement Terms from the Government

In certain contexts, the government has an affirmative interest in knowing about the terms of a privately negotiated agreement. Perhaps the easiest illustration of this is the set of circumstances in which the agreement itself is evidence in a civil or criminal investigation. For example, if the state is prosecuting you for dealing drugs illegally, and they want to present a signed contract for heroin between you and one of your "business associates," you will not be able to stand up in court and say, "Hey, wait a minute. That's a private deal!" In that same vein, if the government is investigating allegations of price fixing and antitrust activity, it will have an affirmative interest in knowing the terms of otherwise private agreements between otherwise private businesses. Of course, a typical drug deal does not involve a signed contract. A typical case of price fixing does not involve a written covenant to collude. But to the extent such agreements exist, the government will have unfettered access to those agreements. Additionally, the government, under state "sunshine" laws, may be able to access certain settlements it perceives as affecting public safety. For example, if the agreement implicates public health or the environment, the state agency tasked with protecting the public may be able to request production of certain terms of the settlement that would otherwise hide certain hazards. More recently, in the era of sex abuse scandals and the #MeToo era, some state governments have argued that access to these settlements should also be permitted requiring companies to publicly disclose any settlements reached through the EEOC or have forbidden settlements that punish the plaintiffs for sharing the terms of settlement.

In other contexts, the government not only wants to know about the terms of an agreement, but also takes responsibility for approving the terms of those private settlements. As we described above, the normal presumption is that private litigants have complete control and autonomy over the shape and nature of claims and their settlements. But in certain circumstances, the law reverses this presumption and requires courts to examine the terms of an agreement before it is given effect.

One example of this governmental supervision arises in the context of class action lawsuits. Once a suit is certified as a class action, the named plaintiff (now the named representative of all class members, however the class might be defined) is no longer fully free to settle the case whenever or however he or she wants. Instead, under Federal Rule of Civil Procedure 23(e) (and its state equivalents), a court must approve a proposed settlement of a certified class action before it takes effect. In some cases, the proposed settlement must also be presented to the absent class members, providing them an opportunity to "opt out" of the settlement, thus preserving their right to litigate whatever the claim in question may be. When reviewing a potential class settlement, the court is charged with safeguarding against deals that inadequately protect the interests of class members. For example, a court would refuse to endorse a so-called "sweetheart deal," in which the named plaintiff receives a large payout, but the other class members receive little or nothing. Similarly, a court guards against a settlement that protects class attorneys at the expense of class members (for example, by allocating all of the defendant's payment to plaintiff's counsel, rather than to payouts to class members). Class action litigation has been the focus of considerable legislative and judicial attention in recent years, and our purpose is not to provide a comprehensive survey of its procedural mechanics. Instead, our purpose is to point out that class actions are one instance in which the government (through the courts) takes an affirmative interest in knowing the terms of an otherwise private settlement. Bankruptcy cases are similar in that courts will oversee any settlement in order to make sure that they are fairly treating all creditors. For example, the U.S. Supreme Court in 2024 overruled a bankruptcy plan for Purdue Pharma, the makers of OxyContin, that would have shielded the principal owners (the Sackler family) from liability.

Another example comes from family law, where judges are routinely charged with reviewing the terms of agreements—particularly those affecting the welfare of children. For example, two divorcing parents may agree on the terms of asset division, child custody, and support. Before the terms of their agreement take effect, in most jurisdictions, a judge will review the terms of the proposed decree for fairness and best interests of the child before entering it as a judgment. Again, this represents an example of a time when the state examines the terms of agreements struck between private actors.

§3.5.2 Hiding Settlement Terms from Interested Parties in Related Disputes

An agreement settling a dispute is typically of little interest to anyone other than the parties. But sometimes, one dispute is so related to another that the settlement of one will be of interest in the other. In those circumstances, parties who were not part of the settlement might be very interested in learning the contents of the settlement. Imagine that multiple former employees of the same company have now brought separate lawsuits against their former employer, each alleging that she was the victim of sexual harassment while on the job. If one plaintiff settles her claim, the remaining plaintiffs would probably have a strong interest in learning the terms of the settlement—both because of what it might suggest about the possible settlement value of their cases and because it might indicate something about the nature of their claims.

Sometimes, an agreement's terms are relatively easy for an outsider to access. For example, one of the remaining plaintiffs might be able to simply call up her former colleague and ask about the terms of the settlement. If the former employee has no contrary obligations (as in, she did not sign a confidentiality agreement), she will be free to discuss the settlement.

Even if the parties who settle are now not inclined to volunteer information about the settlement, the remaining litigants may be able to compel the disclosure of the settlement through the civil discovery process if the terms of the settlement really are relevant to the remaining dispute. A subpoena can do wonders for someone's willingness to spill the beans!

Recognizing this possibility, some disputants enter into complex confidentiality agreements, and some even go to court to have the terms of their agreement filed with the court under seal. Doing so may shield the settlement terms from the outside world, but not necessarily.

The case of *Bank of America v. Hotel Rittenhouse Associates*, 800 F.2d 339 (3d Cir. 1986), provides an illustration of a case in which filing the agreement with the court eventually permitted a nonparty access to its terms—even though the settlement terms were filed under seal. In *Rittenhouse*, a bank and a developer reached a settlement in a dispute over financing for the construction of a hotel. To ensure the enforcement of the agreement, the bank and the developer filed their settlement under seal with the district court. Shortly after the settlement agreement was entered, the parties called upon the court to resolve a dispute about the terms of the settlement, which the court did.[7] Later, a concrete contractor on the project filed suit against the

7. Of course, this is not always an automatic process. In United States v. Amodeo, 44 F.3d 141, 145 (2d Cir. 1995), the Second Circuit required the requested documents for unsealing to be relevant to the function and process of the court in order for it to be designated as a judicial document and subject to the right of public access).

bank seeking direct payment for the concrete work conducted on the same project that had been the subject of the lawsuit between the bank and the developer. The concrete contractor then filed a motion to unseal the settlement between the bank and the developer, claiming that the settlement's contents would support a claim of conspiracy. The court acknowledged "the strong public interest in encouraging settlement of private litigation" but ordered the settlement terms to be unsealed. The court wrote, "Having undertaken to utilize the judicial process to interpret the settlement and to enforce it, the parties are no longer entitled to invoke the confidentiality ordinarily accorded settlement agreements. Once a settlement is filed in the district court, it becomes a judicial record, and subject to the access accorded such records."

In many circumstances, however, the existence of a seal will preclude others from discovering the settlement terms' contents. The case of *Leap Systems, Inc. v. MoneyTrax, Inc.*, 638 F.3d 216 (3d Cir. 2011), illustrates this point. Leap Systems sued its former employee, Norman Baker, and Baker's new employer, MoneyTrax, for allegedly misappropriating confidential proprietary information from Leap Systems. At the urging of the presiding judge, the three parties reached the basic terms of a settlement agreement late one night at the courthouse. At the request of the parties, who indicated they would not settle without such a step, the judge created an audio recording of the terms of the agreement, in order to facilitate the subsequent drafting of settlement language. The judge then placed the transcript of this recording under seal. Not long after the settlement, Leap Systems again sued Baker along with Baker's colleague, Todd Langford, on a similar claim. Langford believed that the terms of the earlier settlement would provide him with a defense in this lawsuit, so he sought access to the transcript of the judge's articulation of the terms of the settlement, citing *Rittenhouse* and the public's right to know. Leap Systems sought to prevent this disclosure. The appeals court upheld the confidentiality of the settlement terms, citing the judge's specific assurances that the terms would remain confidential as a policy justification outweighing the usual presumption in favor of disclosure.

§3.5.3 Hiding Settlement Terms from the Media, the Public, and Other Busybodies

In some circumstances, the public will be denied access to the terms of private agreements, even if it is keenly interested in those agreements. Imagine that two Hollywood stars get into an altercation outside of a popular nightclub, one sues the other, and the parties subsequently announce that they "have reached an undisclosed mutual agreement fully resolving the matter." The tabloids, the entertainment shows, and many fans would love to have access to the terms of the agreement. But unless the disputants submitted their agreement to be entered as an order of the court, or unless one filed a claim on the basis of the agreement, that agreement's terms are entirely private. The media can ask all they want about the terms of the agreement, but the media cannot force either party to share a copy of the settlement any more than they can force one of the stars to sit down for a tell-all interview.

Although public access to a settlement agreement between Hollywood stars is unlikely, courts are more willing to grant public access when the dispute has significant public implications. For example, the Pittsburgh Post-Gazette sought to unseal a settlement between a family and Range Resources, a Marcellus Shale gas development company. The Hallowich family claimed the fracking by Range Resources around their property sickened their family and depreciated the value of their property. The lawsuit ended with a settlement agreement that included a nondisclosure stipulation and a lifetime confidentiality clause. Two years after the case was then dismissed, a Pennsylvania court granted the newspaper's open records request. *Hallowich v. Range Resources Corporation*, 2012 Pa. Super. 234U (Pa. Super. Ct. Dec. 7, 2012). The newspaper subsequently discovered and then reported that the lifetime gag order was meant to be enforceable against the entire Hallowich family, including their two minor children, ages 7 and 10. The public uproar that ensued, which included a segment on the Colbert Report, has since caused Range to retract its original desire to enforce the confidentiality agreement against the children.

And, if one of the disputants is a public governmental entity, the typical presumption is in favor of access. For example, if the local schoolteachers' union and the local school board have a dispute, the public will probably have far greater access to the process(es) by which the dispute is resolved and to the terms of its resolution. With only some exceptions, open-meetings laws in many states provide the public with access to decision-making processes of governmental units like the school board, and any agreement to which the school board is a party is generally a matter of public record. In these cases, therefore, the public can have access to the outcome.

A final example of public access involves processes that are quasi-judicial. As a baseline matter, absent a special court order to the contrary, court proceedings and papers are public records. Anyone can access them. But what if a case starts in court but is resolved through a court-affiliated, nonlitigation alternative? In *Cincinnati Gas & Elec. Co. v. General Electric Co.*, 854 F.2d 900 (6th Cir. 1988), multiple parties were in a dispute over the construction of a nuclear power plant. At the outset of their litigation, the parties negotiated a comprehensive protective order for documents the parties classified as confidential. During litigation, the court ordered the parties into a summary jury trial that was closed to the press and public. Two months after the summary jury trial, the parties reached a settlement. When the settlement was filed with the court, the court held that the gag order regarding the summary jury trial and the sealing of all documents and transcripts related to the summary jury trial should remain in effect. Several newspapers filed a joint motion to intervene in the litigation for the purpose of challenging the closure of the summary jury trial. The newspapers argued that there was a public right to know what happened in the summary jury trial, in part because the summary jury trial is structurally similar to a civil jury trial. (See Chapter 11, on court-connected ADR processes.) The Sixth Circuit held that there was no right to observe *any* negotiations leading to the settlement of a case and that summary jury trial is another example of a process used to promote settlement. As a result, the newspaper had no access to these quasi-judicial (but ultimately private) proceedings.

Examples

The Chef's Tomato

After graduating law school and working at a firm for years, Krithika decides to pursue her first love, cooking. She goes to cooking school, trains at some great restaurants, opens her own restaurant, and even competes on a popular television cooking show. Although Krithika is a celebrated chef, her first restaurant performed poorly. She is in the process of opening a new one, about which she is excited. Acting as her own general counsel, Krithika is negotiating with Walter Hamilton Farm to supply heirloom tomatoes for her new restaurant. She received Walter Hamilton Farm's standard purveyor contract, which offers a 5% discount in exchange for her promise to have the Farm as the exclusive source for her tomatoes. Krithika asked if she could highlight the Farm's tomatoes and heirloom growing practices on her menu in exchange for a 15% discount. She explained, "After all, I am a celebrity chef and can guarantee that thousands of people will try my restaurant and then purchase any highlighted suppliers' products." After a lengthy negotiation, Walter said, "Well. . . if thousands are gonna read about me and my tomatoes, then I guess you could have a bigger discount." They settled on 9%. They shook hands and signed the updated contract.

1. **Fraud Gras?** Assume that Krithika's restaurant is successful, but not on the scale of "thousands of people." It is perhaps a little too early to tell why, but the hordes of tomato-seekers Walter had envisioned have not materialized at his farm. Does Walter have any recourse against Krithika for her declaration about the thousands of customers?

2. **Ready, set, grow!** Walter Hamilton had agreed to provide Krithika with 26,000 tomatoes every year. However, Walter Hamilton Farms has had a bad year, and Walter realizes he can only provide 11,000 tomatoes himself. Walter asks his friend, Farmer Joe, to provide the rest of the tomatoes this year in exchange for a proportional payment from Walter

plus a bonus amount for saving Walter's most lucrative contract. Farmer Joe grows the exact same kind of tomatoes using similar growing methods as Walter. Walter drops off the tomatoes each week, as usual, without mentioning anything about the change. In fact, at each drop off, he announces, "Another great delivery of Walter Hamilton Farms tomatoes!" If Krithika found out about the switch, would she have a case against Walter?

3. **Margarine of error.** Walter and Krithika agreed that the discount on the tomatoes would be 9%, which was significant given the tight margins in both farming and the restaurant industry. Assume though, when writing out the contract, Walter accidentally wrote in a 19% discount instead. Krithika noticed the disparity but kept quiet about it, knowing he would never have agreed to that price. After receiving the first shipment of beautiful heirloom tomatoes, Krithika called Walter. "This price is a little high, isn't it? I thought we agreed to a 19% discount?" Walter disagreed, and Krithika pointed him to the contract's terms. What recourse does Walter have against Krithika?

4. **Tomato, tomahto.** To her delight, Krithika's restaurant is such a huge success that she urgently needs more tomatoes than her original contract with Walter provides. Luckily, the tomato contract is up for renewal in just a couple weeks. The two agree to meet about a subsequent contract.

   Krithika: "Can you double the volume of each delivery over the next year?"

   Walter: "Well. . . I suppose. But the price of these tomatoes has skyrocketed, due to their popularity. I can still offer you a 9% discount. But the overall price has increased 150%. So you're going to be looking at a steeper overall bill, I just want to make sure you're clear about that."

   Krithika: "I can't afford that, and that's gouging. I made you! You'd be nothing without the fame I brought you."

   Walter: "Well, ma'am, I can just end this relationship right now. You've seen the last of my tomatoes, if that's your attitude. Or you can agree to the price hike in exchange for the new terms. What do you say? Do I call my guys and have them deliver tomatoes to you tomorrow, or are we done?"

Krithika, knowing she needs tomatoes tomorrow, accepted Walter's terms for renewal. After seeing the increase in the restaurant's bills, Krithika's restaurant partner Khusbu pulls her aside to ask what happened. Krithika told Khusbu everything. She felt terrible that she had saddled their great new restaurant with such a huge payment. Is there anything Krithika can do?

5. **Nomato.** After a strongly worded letter from Krithika's attorney threatening a suit, Walter agrees to reform the contract. Krithika comes back to the negotiations.

   Krithika: "I've been investigating other tomato suppliers, and I've found a much better deal elsewhere."
   Walter: "Not for the same quality as my tomatoes, I'm sure!"
   Krithika: "The other farm uses essentially the same growing techniques as you, and they have amazing reviews in restaurants around the region. They've guaranteed the quality of their produce, and they will even permit me variable pricing in the event tomato prices fall in the next year."
   Walter: "That's. . . I mean, I just don't see how that could be true."
   Krithika: "I wouldn't lie to you. They call themselves TechieVeggies, use state-of-the-art equipment, and are located just across the state line. They're offering me to take over the contract you and I have, and to double the volume of deliveries, without raising the overall price of the contract at all."
   Walter: "I can't match that. But I guess . . . I could, maybe, I guess extend a little more of a discount."

   They continued the negotiations and Walter agreed to double his deliveries for only a 50% increase in the overall price of the contract. A month later, Walter was telling a neighbor about the negotiations with Krithika, and his neighbor said, "TechieVeggies? The robo-tomato guys? They went out of business last year. Buddy, you got swindled." What options does Walter have?

6. **Brie better.** Krithika and Walter take some time to figure out a fair contract. In the meantime, Krithika buys tomatoes from a regional produce distributor, GrowInBulk. She does not update her menu to reflect the change in her tomatoes' provenance. Scott, a tomato afficionado traveled for hours to try Krithika's restaurant's signature dish. Delighted with his dinner, he left the restaurant prepared to post glowing reviews online, but then saw GrowInBulk boxes behind the restaurant. Scott is aghast that he paid so much for inferior tomatoes! A lifelong tomato fan, he documents the scene and reaches out to other tomato enthusiasts, who have lauded Krithika's restaurant as a must-try experience. What options exist for the tomato enthusiasts and Krithika's regular customers?

The Lion's Den

7. **Tusk's business pitch.** Cooper Tusk, a budding entrepreneur, law school graduate, and now general counsel to their new company, was invited to go on the show *Lion's Den* to recruit business partners. Their electric

scooters, called Edisons, have been going viral on social media, and they were confident in their ability to find business partners to buy in. Tusk was nervous about the growing manufacturing problems and interest rates on the business loans they took to launch their product, but they figured that the Lions (a group of TV personalities who sometimes invest in companies) would be excited by their existing and projected sales figures.

Tusk believed that a realistic valuation of their company was $5 million. Tusk was concerned, however, that they might find himself in an unfavorable position with the Lions, so they decided to "start high," in anticipation of the Lions' counteroffers.

On the day of the episode, the Lions watched Tusk proudly ride an Edison into the room. "Hello Lions! Introducing the future of mobile transportation, the Edison," Tusk declared. "Given the popularity and success of my product, I'm looking to find a suitable business partner to buy in at $2 million for a 10% stake." Tusk's initial proposal would value the business at $20 million, four times more than what Tusk believed was a realistic valuation. Was Tusk's initial offer permissible?

8. **Tusk's business pitch II.** The Lions, skeptical of such a high valuation, began to pepper Tusk with questions.

"Haven't electric scooters been done already? What are your sales & profit margins for this year?"

Undeterred, Tusk began to answer the questions. "There is no electric scooter on the market like the Edison. Its connectivity features and built-in Scooter Play technology make it the first of its kind! Our sales have been astronomical at $5 million this first year, and our profit margins are $700 per scooter because we make them so cheaply!"

Tusk was not aware that another scooter company, Lemon Scooters, had already created Scooter Play technology six months ago. Moreover, Tusk opted to not mention how the surprise endorsement of a particular influencer was likely a driving reason why the Edisons were going viral after months of flat sales. They also did not mention that the materials used and manufacturing processes were likely not compliant with government regulations, particularly with respect to the scooter's batteries.

Nonetheless, Tusk's smile seemed to convince one Lion, Clark Ruben, to buy in at $2 million for 20% of the business (so valuing the company at $10 million). In a post-deal interview, Ruben explained, "Being at the forefront of technology advancements is my whole brand. With Edison innovating in ways where no one has before, I had to jump on the opportunity."

For purposes of this question, assume that we are not considering the diligence requirements that would normally attach within the realm of corporate law or financing. If we focus instead exclusively on common law rules governing negotiations, if Tusk and Ruben end up in a dispute, what are the two best arguments Tusk could make that his business pitch was permissible? Conversely, what are the two strongest arguments that Ruben could make to find Tusk liable for misrepresentation?

9. **Tusk's dilemma.** Following Ruben's investment, Tusk and Ruben began to work through the details of the business agreement. Assuring Tusk, Ruben boasted, "With my track record of successfully managing previous show contestants, I'm going to make Edison the next stock-market powerhouse. You can depend on me to help with manufacturing and distribution with my connections. Even though this contract only states that I'll provide consultation, I promise you'll have my attention, resources, AND connections."

   Relieved that Ruben's help would remedy many of the problems Tusk perceived, Tusk eagerly shook hands with Ruben and signed the deal.

   During the next few weeks, Tusk began contacting their existing manufacturers and distributors to let them know Tusk would be terminating their relationship with them, in anticipation of Ruben's promised infrastructure. Tusk even temporarily shut the Edison online store with the announcement, "Great things to come. Ruben upgrades coming soon!" However, as the final Edison shipments were delivered, Ruben still had not yet followed through with the promised connections, or even with any significant consultation help.

   Panicked, Tusk frantically called Ruben and asked, "Hey Ruben, when are you going to help with Edison?"

   Ruben replied, "Edison? Oh, yeah that thing from the show. Look here pal, I can't help you with that. I've got bigger things to worry about, so unless it's a consultation thing that is for the show, don't call me again." Ruben hung up.

   What are the best arguments Tusk and Ruben might each present, if Tusk files a claim regarding Ruben's unfulfilled promises?

10. **Tusk tells all? Part 1.** Tusk and Ruben reach a settlement after Tusk filed suit, one aspect of which terminated their business relationship. The settlement also included a confidentiality clause that prohibits either party from sharing the "terms, conditions, or underlying facts related to any and all claims related to this settlement." Recently, however, Tusk has taken to a social media platform to complain about Ruben's withdrawal from their business deal. Tusk's post included a link to Ruben's profile and the message, "Ruben = con-man! His boasts? Nothing but snake oil salesman." The settlement agreement between Tusk and Ruben was never filed in court.

Tabloid platforms quickly swarmed to Tusk for more details, in hopes of finding a scoop on *Lion's Den*. What, if any, avenues might the newspaper have for obtaining the terms of the settlement between Tusk and Ruben?

11. **Tusk tells all? Part 2.** During this time, William Fence, a recent contestant of *Lion's Den* who also experienced a tumultuous business deal with Ruben, filed a lawsuit against Ruben for breach of contract. Fence later saw Tusk's rant on social media. What, if any, opportunities might Fence have for learning the details of the settlement between Tusk and Ruben? Would Fence have any opportunity to learn about the facts underlying the dispute between Tusk and Ruben?

Bananas Cabana Bonanza

12. **Trouble in paradise.** Newlyweds Archie and Veronica arrived at Bananas Cabana, and before anything else, the desk agent greeted them with complimentary drinks complete with paper umbrellas. Delighted, the two begin sipping their drinks, basking in the glow of their long-planned honeymoon. The desk agent interrupted the couple to ask for their names. When Archie replied, the agent balked.

    "Oh my gosh, did you not receive my messages?" The agent explained that she had called them several times to inform the couple that rare sea turtles had laid their eggs in the beachfront honeymoon suite they had booked. By law, the nests could not be moved. "However," the agent said, "I can upgrade you to the Super Honeymoon Suite for an extra $1,500. That is a discounted rate offered due to the circumstances, but the difference in room scale and amenities offered precludes me from providing a complimentary upgrade." Archie turned to look at Veronica and saw her tearing up. "Yes!" Archie said. "We accept that. You can put it on my card." He handed over his credit card and sent Veronica to the spa. As the agent looked at the room's rate again, the agent realized that she was actually supposed to charge Archie and Veronica $2,500. What recourse does the agent have?

13. **Trouble in paradise II.** A few days into their stay, Archie and Veronica have a reservation at the restaurant's fanciest restaurant. The menu featured a photo of a celebrity chef, complete with chef's outfit, standing at the restaurant's entrance, beaming with pride. After an incredible meal, Archie said to Veronica, "That meal was spectacular. I want to meet the celebrity chef myself." Veronica agreed. "The restaurant is basically closed anyways. Let's just sneak into the kitchen and say thank you for the best meal of our lives." Archie and Veronica opened the kitchen door to see rats sitting on the cooks' heads, piloting the cooks by their hair. Veronica screamed. She and Archie ran out the kitchen door.

Returning to the desk agent, Archie shouted "I didn't come all this way to find rats in the kitchen!" He demanded a full refund. The agent refused, noting that the meal they enjoyed was excellent. If this developed into a lawsuit, would Archie have a case that this constitutes fraud?

14. **Trouble in paradise III.** At the end of Archie and Veronica's stay, the resort offered Archie and Veronica a full refund plus a small settlement on the condition that Archie and Veronica not disclose anything about "their experiences at the resort, their experiences at the restaurant, the terms of this settlement, or any of the facts underlying the dispute leading thereto." Archie and Veronica discussed the payment and the terms with their attorney, Betty. Betty noted that the resort's offered payment is higher than she would have expected, but she also highlighted the stringency of the confidentiality clause. Archie and Veronica signed the agreement as written.

    Some months later, Archie, who is a comic artist, wrote a comic in which two of his characters had a disastrous honeymoon at a fictional luxury resort called Monkey's Paw. The similarities to their experiences at the Bananas Cabana were striking. In fact, Archie's comic about their unfortunate meal was so popular, an animated movie studio has optioned it for their next film.

    The desk agent, who was promoted to executive director after she saved the resort from ruin, was furious after she received the comic in an email from a friend. Does the resort have any recourse against Archie?

15. **Trouble in paradise IV.** The local government, after seeing Archie's comic strip, is now concerned about the restaurant and its compliance with local health and safety regulations. Given the existence of the confidentiality clause, could the health inspectors call upon Archie to testify about what he saw in the kitchen? Could the health inspectors gain access to the settlement terms?

Knead to Know Basis

16. **Cheaper by the oven.** Mia and Jerry open a bakery together. After a successful first year in business, Mia and Jerry take over the space next door to the bakery and start a connected kitchen store selling their line of branded bakeware. One day, they decide to replace the bakery's ovens with top-of-the-line, industrial ovens. As Jerry is carting out an old oven, the (new) oven timer goes off. He leaves the old oven in the middle of the expanded store and goes to grab a batch of muffins. In the meantime, Matt comes into the kitchen store and sees the oven.

When Jerry returns, Matt asks how much Jerry is selling the oven for. On the spot, Jerry says the first number in his head and names the price at $5,000 — the retail price of one of his new ovens. Matt balks at the price and turns to leave. He stops at the door, realizing that he absolutely loves the oven. "I'm remodeling my kitchen, and this would be perfect. I'll take it!" Later, Matt looks up the price of the oven, realizing that it's a much older model and that it certainly is not worth $5,000. Put aside any potential considerations regarding the UCC or any relevant statute of frauds, would Matt have any recourse under the common law?

17. **The cake is a lie.** Mia was getting ready to close the bakery after a slow day when a customer, Dighan, walked in. She asked Mia, "Do you guys make any Genoise sponge cakes?" Mia, having never heard of such a thing, replied "Absolutely we do. One of our bakers even specializes in baked goods from Genovia."

    "Fantastic!" exclaimed Dighan, "I'll take five. Can you have them ready in two weeks?" Mia agreed and asked for one moment to go and get the bakery's order forms.

    While in the back, she searched online to find a recipe for Genoise-style cakes. Seeing that it didn't look too hard, she brought back the order form to Dighan. "Since this is a special request, demanding more complex ingredients and treatment than our usual cakes, it will cost three times more than the prices listed on our menu. After all, premium quality comes at a premium price." Dighan agreed immediately, delighted she had found a specialized baker so easily.

    Dighan later discusses her "find" with a friend who is a baker and learns that, in fact, Genovia sponge cake has the exact same ingredients and virtually the same preparation costs as any other high-quality cake. What are the best arguments Dighan would have in a potential action against Mia for fraud? What are the best responses Mia would have to such a claim?

18. **The cake is a lie II.** Over the next two weeks, Mia struggled to make a Genoise sponge cake. She continually deflated her eggs, or the cakes collapsed completely after baking. Running out of time and surrounded by cake disasters, Mia made her standard cake recipe and decorated it to Dighan's specifications. The result looked exactly like a Genoise sponge cake. Delighted when she picked them up, Dighan talked about how much her guests from Genovia would appreciate a taste from home. When they cut into the cakes, however, it was immediately clear that they were simply regular cakes. What options does Dighan have?

Explanations

1. **Fraud gras?** Walter could try claiming that Krithika's statement was fraudulent and that he was counting on the prediction as the basis of his agreement. But if there is no specific guarantee of client attendance in their contracts, courts will likely hold that Krithika's statements were **puffery**, for example predictions of future market behavior, rather than promises of what one of the contracting parties would do or deliver. See, for example, *In Great Am. Food Chain, Inc. v. Andreottola*, 2016 U.S. Dist. LEXIS 27658, where the court found that statements about the defendant's future ability to manage and operate restaurants were non-actionable puffery.

2. **Ready, set, grow!** If we assume that the contract does not have a specific provision permitting or prohibiting substitution, Krithika's complaint against Walter would likely depend on whether the exact origin of the tomatoes is considered material. Walter might argue that the substituted tomatoes are indistinguishable from a dietary and culinary perspective, and that they share the same geographic, genetic, and farming heritage. In essence, he would argue, "What's the harm?" Even if the tomatoes were indistinguishable from Walter's, and unobjectionable from a cooking perspective, Krithika could argue that the assertion was material and that she has suffered injury because she can no longer truthfully advertise that her tomatoes are sole-sourced, which was the point of her contract.

3. **Margarine of error.** Given that Walter and Krithika negotiated and agreed on 9%, Walter likely does have recourse. The Restatements on both Contracts and Torts requires a party to correct the mistake of the other party "as to a basic assumption on which that party is making the contract and if nondisclosure of the fact amounts to a failure to act in good faith. . ." This is also similar to *Stare v. Tate*, in which the husband knew of his wife's math mistake in a proposed divorce settlement, and the court therefore vacated the agreement.

4. **Tomato, tomahto.** There are two different issues here—one is the immediate need for tomatoes that had been promised for tomorrow and the other is the terms of the renewed contract. Krithika might be able to argue duress as to the delivery of tomatoes that was to occur tomorrow. When one party threatens not to deliver promised goods, courts have sometimes found duress and Krithika could argue that the threat to withhold the remaining shipment or two of tomatoes was exactly this. As to the renewal terms for the contract, courts are clear that taking advantage of good market conditions is not an example of duress. The fact that Walter is in an economic position to demand more favorable terms on a subsequent deal does not mean that he is subjecting Krithika to duress.

5. **Nomato.** The question here is whether Krithika's claims about her alternative supplier is material misrepresentation. Without a real offer in hand, Krithika is plainly lying about her BATNA. Assertions about one's alternatives may (or may not) be actionable or the basis for voiding a contract. In general, the more specific the false assertion, the more likely it is that courts will find the lie to constitute fraud. If Krithika had said, "I can get a much better deal elsewhere," courts would almost certainly treat that as mere puffery. See, e.g., Sutton Assoc. v LexisNexis, 761 N.Y.S. 800 (Sup. Ct. Nassau Cty. 2003) (declaring proposed rate the "lowest available" and "best rate available" was mere puffery, even though other business were paying less at the time). The specificity (and falsity and materiality) of Krithika's assertion may very well constitute the kinds of assertions that would support a claim of fraud. The question for a court would be whether it was reasonable reliance, given the courts will normally charge contracting parties with constructive knowledge of their industries. A court might, therefore, say that Walter should have known about TechieVeggies (who is, after all, one of his competitors), independent of anything Krithika said.

6. **Brie better.** Krithika's menu is presently a false advertisement if she is promising one kind of tomato and delivering another. Customers and tomato enthusiasts who ate at the restaurant expecting Walter's tomatoes but getting regular ones might be entitled to damages. After all, they relied on her assertions about the tomatoes and had no easy way to verify those assertions. Still, their potential damages are likely limited. (Perhaps a refund of the cost of the meal?) Scott might argue that he should be entitled to a refund of all of the expenses associated with his trip to the restaurant, but he would likely have a hard time with that argument.

7. **Tusk's business pitch.** Anyone participating (or watching) the Lion's Den should know that something like the projected value of a company would not be an assertion about a material fact, but rather a potentially inflated or exaggerated negotiation posture. If the valuation were treated as an offer, then clearly there would be no misrepresentation. Saying what you are willing to do is not an assertion about a fact. Tusk is a law school graduate (the facts are ambiguous about whether Tusk is a practicing attorney), and so one might wonder about ABA Model Rule 4.1, Comment 2, which states "certain types of statements ordinarily are not taken as statements of fact . . . estimates of price or value placed on the subject of a transaction . . . are ordinarily of this category." In this case, to the extent that the assertion was not an offer, but rather more specifically about a valuation, the assertion would still almost certainly be treated as permissible **puffery**.

8. **Tusk's business pitch II.** Even though Tusk wasn't aware that Lemon Scooters were already beating the Edison to the technology advancement, the deal could yet be subject to recission because material **misrepresentation** in contract law doesn't require knowledge on the part of the speaker—even though fraudulent misrepresentation would require a showing of knowledge. Because Ruben's decision to buy-in was based on the mistaken belief that the technology was ground-breaking, the mistake could be deemed material. A question might be whether the assertion was specific enough to constitute a false statement. ("It has brand new technology," for example, would not likely create a specific enough statement. "No one else has this technology," by contrast, is specific enough to be problematic under these facts.) Furthermore, Tusk also runs into potential problems regarding a potential duty to disclose in context of superior knowledge. Did Tusk's **silence and omission** regarding **the** manufacturing issues and lack of government compliance constitute fraudulent misrepresentation? Silence or an omission about materials facts such as these certainly *can* create conditions of fraud, but in this context, because Tusk did not create the misunderstanding in question, a court might deem that Ruben had an opportunity to conduct greater diligence (in the form of further questions).

   Tusk has two different arguments. The first is that they did not know (and therefore could not knowingly commit fraud) about the Scooter Play technology. The second would be that their statements about the quality and popularity of the scooter are likely to be considered puffery. On the other hand, Ruben could argue that the lack of disclosure about the materials used and noncompliant manufacturing process are omissions where Tusk's superior knowledge or partial disclosure would lead to his liability. Second, the fact that Tusk does not know about the new technology does not eliminate the possibility of a court finding this material misrepresentation and a mutual mistake.

9. **Tusk's dilemma.** Tusk's best arguments would assert that Ruben's promises induced **detrimental reliance**. In an action for fraud, Tusk would argue that they relied on Ruben's promise to assist with manufacturing and distribution. Based on this promise, Tusk terminated their relationship with existing partners and even closed the online store down to prepare for the changes. Given Ruben's track record, Tusk had no reason to believe otherwise. Therefore, Tusk's reliance is reasonable and to his detriment. See *Hoffman v. Red Owl Stores*, 26 Wisc. 2d 683 (1965); *Tour Costa Rica v. Country Walkers, Inc.*, 758 A.2d 795 (VT 2000).

   Ruben's best argument would be that his promises were not specific enough to induce the kind of reliance Tusk is claiming. He would argue that Tusk's unilateral decision to change existing business arrangements was of no particular benefit to Ruben, and that even if Tusk now regrets that decision, Ruben breached no specific promise. In essence, Ruben would argue that *his* assertions were, at most, permissive **puffery** and that they are far too vague to be enforced or to be the basis of a fraud claim.

10. **Tusk tells all? Part 1.** The newspaper could try to demand access to the settlement's terms with the courts, but in this case, the settlement agreement was not filed or enforced in court, so the agreement is not a judicial record that might potentially be open for public access. Furthermore, although courts have sometimes granted public access to settlement terms when the dispute has significant public implications (for example on matters of public health), a business deal gone poorly does not likely rise to this level. See *Cincinnati Gas & Elec. Co. v. General Electric Co.*, 854 F.2d 900 (6th Cir. 1988).

11. **Tusk tells all? Part 2.** Like the newspaper in Part 1, Fence would have no immediately obvious avenue for going through the courts to try to gain access to the settlement terms. The court in the *Tusk v. Ruben* case could not turn over that which it does not have. The settlement was never filed, much less filed under seal.

    Fence could consider seeking to depose Tusk in the *Fence v. Ruben* lawsuit or could seek some of the relevant documentation through a discovery demand. Fence could argue, for example, that Tusk is able to provide relevant evidence by testifying to similar behavior in another case. Courts would likely allow testimony about the underlying behavior leading to a lawsuit, but would likely not permit this line of questioning to force the disclosure of the terms of the resulting settlement. See *Kalinauskas v. Wong*, 151 FRD 363 (D. Nev. 1993). In some circumstances, a court might consider the possibility of a protective order regarding such discovery, but this would be a fact-specific determination.

    Finally, Fence could consider just asking Tusk to provide the information. It is true that doing so would expose Tusk to the risk that disclosure would unwind his settlement with Ruben, but Fence could try.

12. **Trouble in paradise.** This is the agent's **mistake**. Once the agent makes the offer and Archie accepts it, with consideration paid by handing over his credit card, the agreement is final. Archie did not create any of the misunderstanding, did not fail to disclose anything, and acted only upon information he was entitled to rely upon (in this case, the desk agent's representation of the price that would be charged), so the agent likely has no recourse.

13. **Trouble in paradise II.** Archie's best hope in a lawsuit against the resort would be to argue that he and Veronica were induced to pay for an excellent dinner, in part, based on the provenance of the meal. Specifically, the celebrity chef's picture created at least an implication that he would

be the chef, and it was reasonable for them to assume that he would be the brains behind the meal. The resort, in response would likely (accurately) point out that they never made any promises about who the chef on that evening would be, and that it is common knowledge that chefs may have underlings conduct the business of the kitchen on many, most, or even all evenings. (Many famous chefs license the use of their likeness on restaurants around the world, and there is no way they could be at each of them all the time.) Furthermore, the resort would note that the couple greatly enjoyed their meal, and argue that the meal was worth the price, even there was any merit to the couple's disappointment about who was there on that particular evening.

14. **Trouble in paradise III.** The resort's legal prospects will hinge on the degree of similarity between the comic and the terms covered by the confidentiality clause. The clause itself is both sweeping and specific. So, if the resort is identifiable, and if the depiction matches the couple's experiences closely enough, Archie may be in violation of the confidentiality clause. Perhaps Archie will judge that the lucrative movie contract is worth it. At a minimum, the resort would be entitled to recission of the agreement, if Archie is in breach. The couple would then owe the full payment (which would surely be far less than the value of the movie option). However, the resort could also argue that it suffered damages as a result of the breach of confidentiality (for example, to its future business), and that could create far greater exposure for Archie.

15. **Trouble in paradise IV.** Some jurisdictions have Sunshine Laws that prohibit confidential settlements in contexts that implicate public health. Typically these laws envision guarding against settlements that hide things like product defects, but rat-controlled kitchens might (?) fall under this exclusion. In that case, the health inspectors could clearly seek both Archie's testimony and the terms of the settlement. Even outside of such jurisdictions, Archie would be unlikely to successfully guard against the disclosure of the underlying facts if the health inspector issued a subpoena. Most confidentiality clauses have an explicit exception for disclosures compelled by the courts. And even if no such exception is written into the contract, it is hard to imagine that the courts would enforce a clause (outside of a context creating a privilege, such as lawyer-client, doctor-patient, or counseling) that prohibits someone from testifying under oath simply because they received payment. In this way, the confidentiality clause may be treated differently in an enforcement action by the government than it would be in a subsequent private action. See *Saini v. Int'l* Game Tech., 434 F. Supp. 2d 913, 923 (D. Nev. 2006).

16. **Cheaper by the oven.** Even if the objective "value" of the oven is less than $5,000, Matt is unlikely to have any recourse. Jerry naming a price is not, in any way, fraud. At the very most, it might constitute **puffery**, since Jerry *might* be considered to have implied that the price had some relationship to the oven's objective value. But Matt simply made a mistake here. Or more accurately, Matt wishes that he had made a different decision during his negotiations with Jerry. No basis appears in these facts that would permit Matt to avoid the contract to which he agreed.

17. **The cake is a lie.** Dighan's best argument would be that Mia knowingly misrepresented a material fact (the necessity for expensive ingredients) in the negotiations over the price. Dighan would argue that it was reasonable for her to rely on Mia's assertion, given the baker's (presumed) superior knowledge. And she would argue that the misrepresentation constituted fraud. Mia would likely respond that even if the particulars about the costs associated with production were not fully accurate, the price she named was simply part of the negotiations. What someone is willing to pay or accept is not a "fact" for purposes of the law of fraud.

18. **The cake is a lie II.** By handing over the regular cakes, rather than the Genoise sponge cakes, Mia was, at a minimum, breaching the terms of her contract with Dighan. She had not necessarily committed fraud at the moment of their initial negotiations (since at the time she presumably intended to deliver Genoise sponge cakes). But by the time of pick up, Mia had an duty at that stage to correct Dighan's misunderstanding about the nature of the cakes in order to avoid both breaching the contract and potentially committing fraud.

CHAPTER 4

Identifying Interests & Priorities Through Interviewing

§4.1 INTRODUCTION

This book is primarily focused on dispute resolution processes—negotiation, mediation, and arbitration. Before you advise your client about possible approaches for how to resolve disputes or get deals done, however, you need to know more about your client. What is the client trying to accomplish? Do they want a deal as quickly as possible? Or perhaps a deal at the right price? Or do they want a deal that leads to a long-term relationship? These goals are not necessarily in tension with each other, but the lawyer will be better at negotiating (and better at making their client happy) if they understand answers to these kinds of questions. Similarly, when settling a dispute, a lawyer should consider whether their client seeks to maximize their financial gain (or minimize their loss). Or do they seek to obtain an apology from the offender? Or do they seek to settle as quickly as possible? Do they want to avoid publicity? And in all events, *why* are their preferences what they are?

These questions might seem standard in any attorney-client relationship and yet barriers to clear communication often exist between attorneys and clients. Clients are sometimes embarrassed about the events that led them to seek out a lawyer, or they assume the lawyer doesn't really need to know all the details (and, if the lawyer is billing by the hour, the client might not want to pay for any more time than they are already paying). Conversely, lawyers' questions may be the problem. Lawyers sometimes ask questions that are too narrow or too fact specific, and as a result, they miss cues about their clients' interests and priorities.

For years, the organized bar and bar examiners assumed that lawyers were innately skilled because law school taught them to "think like a lawyer," or the notion was that recent graduates would develop these skills on the job, perhaps through mentorships or observation of other lawyers or continuing legal education courses. Recently (some might say finally) the bar has recognized that these are skills that are often taught in law schools, through clinics, externships, and workshops. More crucially, these are skills that the new bar will now be testing.

This chapter is designed to outline some key concepts around identifying interests and priorities, and recognizing different kinds of questions that lawyers should be asking their clients. In outlining these materials, we discuss the kinds of questions that facilitate learning important information from clients, and we also describe some of the common hindrances to gathering information effectively.

§4.2 INTERESTS

A client walks into a lawyer's offices (or calls or emails) because they have an issue that they cannot resolve themselves. They need a lawyer's help to draft a document, facilitate a deal, figure out the next steps in resolving a lawsuit, or any number of reasons. Often it might appear as if the overall goal is obvious: "Help me divorce my spouse" or "I want to buy the apartment building at the corner to develop it" or "Make my neighbor pay for the trees they cut down on my property." But a lawyer (and their client) will be well-served to slow down and consider the concerns, fears, needs, and motivations underlying any of these pronouncements. It is the client's interests and priorities that will determine the best course of action—to negotiate or to litigate, to accept a settlement, how to structure the deal, whether to include a parenting coordinator, what to explore with opposing counsel, whether to consult others, and so forth.

A client's interests should determine potential strategies and which dispute resolution process makes sense. As we outlined in Chapter 1, lawyers can miss the relevant interests of a client if they focus too much on the parties' expressed **positions** (*what* they say they want), rather than on each side's **interests** (*why* they want what they want). A plaintiff might demand "a million dollars" to settle a discrimination claim against a former employer. But without knowing more about the plaintiff, the lawyer cannot know for certain what the plaintiff's underlying interests might be. Having financial security for retirement? Having a face-saving story to tell the plaintiff's family? Removing roadblocks to future career development? Restoring the plaintiff's reputation among their former colleagues? Covering short-term expenses? Punishing the company for what the plaintiff perceived to be despicable treatment? All these questions highlight potential client interests. Each suggests a potentially different approach to dispute resolution. This chapter now focuses on how to elicit those interests through the skill of interviewing.

If the plaintiff's attorney fails to ask enough questions to understand the client's true motivations, the lawyer might only ask for one type of settlement: one that produces a million dollars or pursue processes that do not match the client's long terms goals. (Imagine in this case that the plaintiff most needs a job referral or actually wants the job back—the different processes that we outline in future chapters make it more or less likely that one of these interests could be met.)

Once you have gotten a good sense of your client's interests, it is also important to help them weigh their interests and determine their priorities. Is "making them pay" a priority in which the client wants to prioritize money over all else? Or is "making them pay" actually a desire that the defendant be forced to admit their wrongdoing and promise not to harm others? For example, in deciding on a settlement offer after a medical malpractice case, a parent of a child who died as a result of medical error may be less interested in the amount of money the hospital proposes to give the family and more interested in the hospital using that money to relabel its pediatric medicine, provide more training, or, as in one case we know of, plant a grove of trees in the child's honor (strategically located between the physician parking lot and the hospital so that the doctors walked through it every day!) Even if a client's true interests are purely financial, a lawyer will still be best positioned if they understand more about what motivates that. What do they plan to do with the money? Does the timing of the money matter? What tax or financial planning issues might be relevant? As you can see, figuring out interests is already challenging—helping your client figure out their priorities will be more so.

We should also note that the process of dispute resolution may well have an impact on your client's priorities and that these priorities can shift over time. Unfortunately, parties that become more adversarial in the way that they handle the process may shift their priorities toward punishing the other. ("After the way they treated me in that deposition. . . .") On the other hand, disputes handled efficiently and respectfully can open the door to shifting in the other way. ("I now trust them to pay on a payment plan.")

§4.3 ATTORNEY CLIENT RELATIONSHIP

In your class on professional responsibility, you will likely spend some time discussing the creation of the attorney-client relationship and your obligations as a lawyer regarding competence, diligence, and communication. In the area of dispute resolution, your duties may also include the obligation to inform your client about dispute resolution processes and the variety of ways that cases can be settled. (We cover those obligations in Chapter 5.) In this chapter, as we focus on the beginning of the relationship and your ability to identify interests and gather information from your client, we think it is also helpful to consider why clients hire lawyers and what tensions might naturally exist between lawyers and their clients.

As we note above, most clients would probably save their money and avoid engaging lawyers if they could accomplish their goals by themselves. So why hire a lawyer? (We also think this is a good question for you to know the answer to as well.)

Sometimes clients engage lawyers for their substantive expertise—lawyers have particular knowledge of a field—tax, divorce, compliance, securities, etc. Sometimes, clients hire lawyers for their process expertise—how to file a patent, how to comply with consumer safety regulations, or how to successfully represent a client in a mediation process. And sometimes clients might think that a certain lawyer would have particular influence—the reason some clients hire attorneys as lobbyists, for example.

Other times, clients hire lawyers to provide some "distance" from the dispute. Divorce lawyers can (perhaps) provide some emotional detachment. A plaintiff's attorney can provide detachment from the anger and hurt over a discrimination claim. Outside counsel for the company accused of a discriminatory practice may have the external perspective necessary to permit a candid and accurate assessment of the claim. Or perhaps the client wants the detachment of an agent who will get things done and not bother them until it is time to finalize the details of the deal or settlement, like a business owner or high-level executive that does not want to or cannot spend the time to manage the dispute themselves.

There are, of course, other reasons to hire lawyers. Perhaps the client wants some tactical flexibility (the lawyer can play hardball while the client maintains the relationship) or the lawyer has a better relationship with the counterpart.

For whatever reason a client hires a lawyer, there are some built-in tensions between attorneys and clients. These tensions could be hindrances later as the lawyer interviews the client to discover their interests and priorities as well as when it comes time to finalize the terms of a deal or settlement.

These differences are understandable and also important to recognize in any principal-agent (client-attorney) relationship. First, attorneys may have different preferences than the client—the client might want to settle immediately while the attorney wants to bill more hours (or, conversely, the client might want to take a case to court while the attorney believes that is a waste of time.) Attorneys can have a different stake in the outcome—while some attorneys are paid only when successful on behalf of the client (contingency fees), other attorneys who are paid a flat fee or are paid by the hour receive compensation regardless of how the dispute resolves or the deal gets done. Attorneys likely have reputational interests in a good outcome for the client—and, yet, the client is clearly the one who has the higher stake. Finally, clients and attorneys may have additional information unavailable to the other (for example, clients often do not really know how hard the attorney is working or what strategy they are considering).

These differences then show up in terms of monitoring (how does the client really know what is going on); the incentive structure (where fees can weigh on either party in terms of calculating settlement decisions in particular); and a strategy problem (how do you agree and execute a strategy together and also manage any negotiation strategy between the two attorneys). Many of these topics fall beyond the immediate scope of this book, but we name them here because they may be part of what a client is thinking during an interview with their lawyer.

§4.4 INTERVIEWING SKILLS

This next section turns to the primary interaction between the lawyer and client—the interview. The interview's purpose is to gather information about the client, the facts of the situation, and the all-important interests outlined above. Without knowing what your client wants, it is difficult to make sure that a proposed course of action meets their needs or to advise them about which process makes the most sense for them. Moreover, this interaction is also the opportunity to build rapport with your client, so that they are comfortable sharing information with you at the outset and then more willing to trust your advice throughout the relationship.

§4.4.1 Welcoming the Client/Breaking the Ice

Starting off the relationship between you and your client is much like any other relationship—most of us are more comfortable with some kind of relaxed chit chat to start things off. And, while the weather, sports, or traffic are mundane, those topics are also useful for safely establishing a connection. If you and the client have other connections (family, the referral, neighbors, soccer team), it can be helpful to reestablish that bridge. You might ask if they would like some water or coffee. All of this is designed to make someone comfortable and build rapport so that they will trust you and share the information you need in order to proceed on their behalf. Some clients will be so stressed they want to "dive in" right away to the problem. Others will signal when they are ready to talk business. So, there is no need to force small talk when the client does not need or want that. You will, over time and with experience, develop your own routine for helping clients get comfortable and ready to talk.

§4.4.2 Asking Good Questions

Consider the multiple goals you have as you begin to ask your client questions. You need the facts and other important information. You seek to develop a sense of their interests and priorities for the situation. And you are continuing to try to build rapport and a relationship with them so that you can proceed in the dispute resolution process with their trust and approval. Not surprisingly, some types of questions are better at accomplishing some of these goals, while others are better for other purposes.

Although it might seem logical to start with the narrow questions of fact, "did you see the red light?" "how fast were you going?", in almost all circumstances, you and your client will be better served by open-ended questions—those without yes/no answers. You may not know the answers they will offer, and you may not even know the potential implications of their offers ahead of time. An invitation to tell the story ("tell me what happened," "let's start at the beginning—what brought you here today," "I've read the other side's letter—tell me how you view this situation") provides several advantages. The client will tell the story, at least this first time, in their own order and in their own words. They have likely been telling themselves the story of what happened before they walked in your office, so it makes sense to start there and let them share first. This also allows them to share the details about which they are most confident and that are the most important to them—giving you yet more insight into their interests. In addition, it invites them to share their emotions—sadness, fear, anger—at whatever level is initially comfortable.

In terms of finding out the facts or other information you may need, you can ask more narrow and focused questions after the client has had the opportunity to explain things more broadly. With either type of question, it is helpful to continue to encourage the client with facial expressions, nodding, body language, and verbal cues like "I see" or "yes," etc. The lawyer should also allow the client to finish their answers fully and refrain from interrupting as interruptions can interfere with the client's memory and recollections of the situation. Even urging, "Is there anything else you think I should understand?" provides an open-ended invitation for the client to discuss their perceptions of the past, their emotions, their thinking about the current situation, or their interests or concerns about the future—all of which is helpful for you to know, if you are to serve them effectively.

To be clear, there is a moment when you, as a lawyer, will need to harvest specific information from your client. To the extent it does not emerge from their telling of the story (perhaps they forgot, or did not realize it was important, or are ashamed of the answer or afraid of its implications) you will need to make sure that you have foundational facts in order to provide accurate and helpful counsel. "At what point did you first discover the defect in the repair job?" "Was anyone else in the room when your boss said this to you?" "Can you tell me more about exactly what you remember your neighbor saying about the fence?" "Do you know if there are any medical bills or other similar records associated with your injuries?" You know from your legal expertise that a client's prospects in litigation often hinge on specific facts, and so it might be tempting to start by seeking information about each of the elements of a claim or of an affirmative defense. Our advice is to wait. You will have time to collect this information later in the interview, and you will be in a better position to do so, once you and your client are on the same page about the broader questions.

§4.4.3 Active Listening

A particular type of good listening to clients (and to your counterpart in negotiation) is called active listening. This kind of listening entails more than writing notes while the client talks and also more than follow up questions. In particular, active listening involves the demonstration in a variety of ways that you have been carefully listening to the client and that you understand their perspective. Note that this accomplishes both your goals of gathering accurate information from the client as well as establishing that rapport and trust with them.

Active and reflective listening can involve a variety of follow up questions. You can reflect back on the specific content of what the client shared—"so you called them back the next day?" You can reflect more broadly on the content—"wow, that seems like a pretty challenging situation!" You can reflect their emotion as stated—"sounds like you were quite frustrated by this" and you can also reflect their emotion as you interpret it—"I can imagine that I might be confused or upset in a situation like this." All of these types of reflection are designed to both validate what the client is sharing and to confirm if your understanding is correct. Perhaps they are not exactly upset but more disappointed. Perhaps the timing of the story as you reflected it was not quite accurate. And any reflective statement can start with something more general to the effect of "what I hear you saying is . . ." or "let me be sure I understand this. . ." Active listening aims to help both the speaker and the listener—providing a mechanism for *both* to have confidence that the two are beginning to share an understanding of what is being discussed.

Active listening should be used throughout the interview for both open and closed questions. As the client is telling their story, confirming your general understanding and reflecting their emotions helps the client feel comfortable and willing to share more. As you focus on more narrow facts you might want to know, active listening is used to confirm you are accurately understanding what the client is telling you. "So, if I understand this correctly, you received positive feedback on your performance on March 8 in your review but were then fired on March 25?" And active listening is equally important for confirming your understanding of the client's interests and priorities. "What I hear you saying is that some acknowledgement of wrongdoing is the most important goal for you and that you also want to be compensated for all of your expenses in pursuing this goal?"

§4.4.4 Facilitators & Hindrances to Gathering Information

A last note in this chapter reflects the consideration that clients may not want to or believe they need to share all of the details of their particular situation. Building rapport, asking open-ended questions, and using active listening typically facilitates a successful interview. Demonstrating respect and understanding throughout the interview—by not interrupting, using encouragement, and letting them tell their story—is key.

At the same time, we want to understand where clients might be coming from and why they might be hesitant to share. Perhaps this entire situation is horrifying to them—minimizing the time in the interview with you is just part of trying to minimize the dispute. Perhaps they are embarrassed—the details are often personal and may not reflect well on the client's character or choices, even if they are "in the right." Perhaps the client does not want to share details that seem to weaken their case (not yet realizing that you need to know both the good and bad facts to help them). There might be barriers in terms of age or culture or profession where, for example, the client doesn't really understand what you are asking but does not want to appear to challenge you or appear unprepared. There is no easy fix to any of these hindrances other than continued relationship building and explanations about how information sharing is important. Helping the client understand that you will be talking to them multiple times in order to gather information can also ease the pressure of the first interview.

Examples

Mrs. Park Goes to the Beach

Assume a solo practitioner is running their own personal injury practice. One day, a woman, with one leg and one arm in casts, arrives at their Manhattan office for an intake meeting. When she arrives, the lawyer greets her and escorts her to their conference room for the intake consultation. The following transcript is provided below.

Lawyer: Can you please state your name?

Hazel: My name is Hazel Park.

Lawyer: Thank you, Ms. Park. You told me a bit about your story on the phone, but could you please run through the events from top to bottom?

Hazel: I have these casts because of the explosion caused by the Long Island Railroad, the LIRR. Didn't you hear the news about this?

Lawyer: I did, ma'am, but your recollection is extremely important.

Hazel: Well, it happened in August, when I was taking my two daughters to the beach. We were standing on the platform, waiting for our train to arrive.

Lawyer: You were waiting for the LIRR?

Hazel: Yes, we were waiting for the LIRR . . . Two men were running to catch the train and jumped into the car with open doors right in front of us. One of them dropped the package he was holding onto the platform. The package exploded, throwing me off the platform and leaving my children in shock and in pain.

Lawyer: I see. You're looking at a classic negligence case here, and I'm assuming you want to hold both the man and the train station financially responsible for your medical bills and a little more for the harm they've caused, does that sound about right?

Hazel: Well, I guess money would be nice, since these hospital bills were expensive. But I care more about —

Lawyer: Well Mrs. Park, you've come to the right person for high money verdicts! Let's start laying out our strategy for prevailing on this negligence claim. Remember, I only win if you win. Were there any other witnesses at the scene?

Hazel: I think there might have been a few more employees on the platform and maybe another passenger or two. But I'm not entirely sure.

Lawyer: No worries if you can't remember, these are great leads that I can chase down. I think I have everything I need right now to win you a case. I'll reach out to you shortly if I've missed anything.

1. **Interests?** At this point, what might be some of Mrs. Park's interests? List two possible interests for her.

2. **Questioning the questions.** Identify what type of questions the lawyer asked. Give two examples of other questions that the lawyer could ask.

3. **Listening to the client.** If the lawyer wanted to engage in more active listening/building rapport, what are two things the lawyer could have said or asked to their client?

4. **Are we on the same page?** What type of attorney-client tensions might arise in this case?

This Farm Belongs to Me!

Ada and Bobby Zimmerman were married at Bobby's childhood home on the family's farm fifty years ago. While Ada and Bobby are no longer working Zimmerman Farm themselves, they're still very proud of the farm and look forward to passing it to their grandchildren one day. Their neighbor, Timmy Buffet, often told the couple how much he'd like to buy their farm and made frequent offers. Every time, Ada or Bobby would wave him off and say they're not selling their heritage. Nevertheless, the three remained good friends.

One night, the three went out to dinner at a local tavern. During dessert, Timmy once again tried to charm the Zimmermans into selling the farm. After ordering a fancy bottle of whiskey, Timmy offered a toast. "To great friends, better neighbors, and perhaps, even better business partners."

Ada scoffed, "Partners in minding our own business!" but toasted Timmy anyway. As the conversation went on, the bottle of whiskey was drained, and Timmy kept trying to convince the Zimmermans to sell Zimmerman Farms.

"If you guys sell me the farm, I'll pay you any price you want and never bother you again!" Timmy begged.

"Yeah, okay, we'll sell for $5 million and a winery by the beach." Bobby sneered, annoyed by Timmy's barrage. Ada said to Bobby, "Take that back! No way in heck are we selling." But Timmy's eyes were wide. He shouted, "We have ourselves a deal!"

Ada and Bobby gawked as Timmy frantically wrote down the terms on a napkin. Knowing that Bobby was the sole owner of the farm, he pushed the napkin and the pen towards Bobby. Bobby signed the word "BALONEY" and pushed it back to Timmy. "Now then," Bobby said, "will you never ever ask about the farm again? I'm serious."

"No need to ask about what's mine!" Timmy said, with a grin.

The next morning, the Zimmermans peered out their screen door to see Timmy eagerly waving a photocopy of the napkin contract from the night before as he led a team of surveyors onto the property. Seeing the Zimmermans at the door, he called out to them.

"A good morning to the Zimmermans! Just so you know, I had my lawyer confirm that the napkin is binding and valid. I've moved your money to escrow, and I've already begun the process of hiring movers to take your things to the winery."

As soon as they could, the Zimmermans paid a visit to a new attorney in town. They were desperate to save the farm but still skeptical of attorneys. Truly, they didn't understand why Timmy kept coming onto their property and acting like he owned the place. He even invited himself over one morning to make coffee and breakfast, saying that he was just "testing out the kitchen." Exhausted and afraid, Ada convinced Bobby to get a lawyer.

The lawyer cheerily welcomed the Zimmermans into their office. After some introductions, the lawyer asked, "What legal magic can I assist you with today?" Bobby quietly said, "I need help with a contract dispute." Embarrassed about the situation and terrified of losing the farm, Bobby said nothing further as Ada sobbed.

5. **Talk to me!** What advice would you give to the lawyer to de-escalate the situation, and get Ada and Bobby talking to him?
6. **Appropriate questions.** What questions should the lawyer ask next? What other information does the lawyer need?
7. **Is there a contract?** Given the conflicting assumptions about whether a contract was actually formed between the Zimmermans and Buffet, what legal research will the lawyer need to perform? What factual questions should the lawyer ask? Why might it be challenging to find this information?
8. **What else is at stake?** What other nonlegal interests might the Zimmermans have? List two questions the lawyer could ask to help uncover those.

Can We Please Have a Plane?

Last year, Dr. Energy soda company created a program to generate sales. Customers could earn Dr. Dollars from the packaging of Dr. Energy products and trade the Dr. Dollars for prizes, some of which were quite expensive. Dr. Energy filmed and released a commercial promoting the Dr. Dollars program. The commercial outlined the Dr. Dollars program by showing a child collecting Dr. Dollars and, finally, trading them for a private jet complete with a personal pilot to fly him to school. As the child shook hands with the Dr. Dollars CEO to complete the exchange, the pilot said, "And I'll be flying your jet FOREVER!" The commercial ended with "This could be all yours, too, for 7,000,000 Dr. Dollars! Start earning today!"

Mia and Jerry saw the commercial and immediately started plotting to get that jet. They had realized that it would only take about $100,000 to purchase enough Dr. Energy products to earn the requisite Dr. Dollars. They gathered the money, bought $100,000 of Dr. Energy products through their bakery's commercial supplier, and counted all their Dr. Dollars. They documented all their work and submitted the prize form to Dr. Energy, requesting the jet with the personal pilot and presenting their 7,000,000 Dr. Dollars.

Their prize form was passed up to the CEO of Dr. Energy, Natalie McMann. She scoffed at the form and made her team of assistants count the Dr. Dollars. "There's no way they could have collected enough!" she shouted. When it turned out that there were 7,000,003 Dr. Dollars in the envelope, Natalie fell out of her chair. From the floor, she demanded her assistants contact the company's in-house counsel.

Upon discovering (although they weren't surprised) that Dr. Energy had no intention of providing them a $32 million jet and a full-time pilot,

Mia and Jerry paid a visit to their lawyer. They requested that their lawyer file a breach of contract suit. Meanwhile, Mia and Jerry also began a media campaign against Dr. Energy for reneging on the terms of what they described as a contract.

Although Dr. Energy was confident that the company would prevail in convincing a judge to dismiss the lawsuit (given *Leonard v. Pepsico*), their stock was quickly plummeting due to the barrage of negative social media chatter and bad press that Jerry and Mia had started. Fearing an expensive situation as the pleadings dragged on, corporate counsel convinced Natalie to go to the bargaining table with Mia and Jerry. Prior to the negotiation, Mia and Jerry met with their lawyer to discuss strategy.

9. **Well, you will lose in court but. . .:** Mia and Jerry's lawyer admires the creativity that Mia and Jerry used to take advantage of the Dr. Dollars promotion. Nonetheless, after reading *Leonard v. Pepsico*, the lawyer recognizes that a judge was likely to find similarly that no reasonable person could believe the advertisement constituted an actual offer. The lawyer, therefore, believes that Mia and Jerry will almost certainly lose if this case proceeds to court. The lawyer will need to explain the costs, risks and opportunities that litigation presents—and in this case it is mostly risks and costs. There is still the possibility that Mia and Jerry will be able to satisfy some of their interests through a negotiated settlement (recall our discussion of BATNA from Chapter 1). What questions does the lawyer need to ask Mia and Jerry in order to have a foundation from which to prepare for settlement negotiations?

10. **Here's an idea?** After developing a better understanding of the situation, the lawyer attempts some option generation with Mia and Jerry. "What if Dr. Energy offers $100,000 to pay you back for the money you spent on Dr. Energy products as long as you launch a social media campaign for the next six months promoting Dr. Energy?" Outline the potential benefits and drawbacks of an option such as this, based on what we know of Mia and Jerry's interests.

Explanations

Mrs. Park Goes to the Beach

1. **Interests?** Given that Mrs. Park is still in bandages, she likely has medical bills and could be concerned about ongoing recovery, costs, and rehabilitation. She also listed the concerns for her children, so there might be interest in counseling for them. She might also want to hold the man with the exploding packages responsible. Or she might want to hold the railroad responsible.

2. **Questioning the questions.** Although the lawyer started with an open-ended question, "could you please run through events," the lawyer quickly shifted to asking narrow questions about the facts. "You were waiting for the LIRR?" "Were there witnesses?" The lawyer could have continued with open-ended questions about the story, eliciting more information about the harm to her and her children. The lawyer could have also asked more questions about the impact of the harms since the time of the accident.

   The other category of open-ended questions that is missing here is about her interests. In fact, the lawyer assumes that she is interested in damages and cuts her off when she might tell the lawyer more. And then there is the concern that the lawyer already presumes liability without getting more details about what actually happened. You might recall from your torts classes that legal arguments like duty of care on the part of the railroad (as Justice Cardozo wrote in the majority opinion of *Palsgraf v. Long Island Rail Road*), the proximate cause of the harm to Mrs. Park (as the dissent in *Palsgraf* argued) or foreseeability as is now outlined in the Restatement Third would each need specific facts to support those arguments

3. **Listening to the client.** At the beginning, the lawyer could have welcomed Mrs. Park into the office and chatted a little bit more. Recognizing that Mrs. Park might be intimidated to be coming into a fancy office or that there could be other class differences that would make her uncomfortable, the lawyer should have spent more time making her comfortable and at ease. The lawyer could have mirrored her emotions as she was describing the situation, instead of just saying "I see." The lawyer could have let her finish her list of interests and priorities rather than cutting her off. And the lawyer could have confirmed with her that the lawyer understood her interests fully.

4. **Are we on the same page?** In a personal injury case where the attorney is only paid as a percentage of the recovery, the lawyer might be more focused on the amount of money to recover rather than meeting other nonmonetary interests Mrs. Park might have (for example, in having LIRR train its workers better or provide a safer boarding platform.) This might also impact the settlement if LIRR were to offer more creative options (lifetime free rides on LIRR for Mrs. Park and her children). Attorneys are, of course, ethically required to pursue the best outcome for the client's interests at the cost of their own pecuniary interest. For example, in *Evans v. Jeff D.*, 475 U.S. 717 (1986), the Supreme Court (in holding that attorney's fees could be waived as part of a settlement) outlined, "[p]lainly, [the attorney] had no ethical obligation to seek a statutory fee award. His ethical duty was to serve his clients loyally and competently." If a lower settlement is on the table with concessions that might appeal to the client, the lawyer must pursue that at the cost

of a higher contingent fee. But a client might not fully understand the lawyer's ethical duties and be concerned about this tension.

Differences as to timing could also arise—Mrs. Park could have a more immediate need for money and be willing to take less to get this done while the lawyer would otherwise be far more willing to extend settlement talks to gain more overall.

This Farm Belongs to Me!

5. **Talk to me!** This is all about making the clients comfortable and understanding why clients do not want to share information. The lawyer could dial down the enthusiasm and match his client's more serious tone. The lawyer could get Ada tissues. The lawyer could ask Bobby to "start at the beginning."

6. **Appropriate questions.** The lawyer needs to find out the whole story and start with open-ended questions to find out what happened. They will need to understand, at some point, the details of the alleged contract. They will also need to understand Ada and Bobby's interests and their priorities. It may also be useful for the lawyer to understand what Ada and Bobby can share about their neighbor, and about what his interests might be.

7. **Is there a contract?** The key legal question is whether the parties formed a contract. *Lucy v. Zehmer* held in similar circumstances that as long as the plaintiff (Timmy Buffet) believed there was a contract, it did not matter that the defendant (the Zimmermans) thought it was a joke. So here, the lawyer would need to know whether the parties had legal capacity (given the drinking) and whether it was reasonable for Timmy to believe they had a contract given that Zimmerman never signed his name and said it was "baloney." The lawyer will want to ask about the alcohol, the exact conversation, and witnesses. The lawyer could also ask for more information about the nature of their relationship with Timmy. Do they often say things like this to each other that are understood to just be jokes? Finally, given that the Zimmermans seemed embarrassed about all of this, they might be reluctant to admit how much they drank or give the lawyer the names of other people in the tavern that witnessed all of these exchanges.

8. **What else is at stake?** Owning the farm seems important to Ada and Bobby regardless of the economic impact. Exploring more about this, including discussion about the history of the farm in their family, would be useful. The story of this "negotiation" also seems potentially embarrassing in front of other neighbors and friends at the bar as well as their children. So, possible questions include: I'd love to learn more about the property itself. I can tell that it's special to you, and I'd love

to hear about your relationship with the land. Given that you were no longer working on the farm, tell me what keeps you there? What vision do you have for the property while the two of you are still living there? What vision do you have for it once the two of you are gone?

Can We Please Have a Plane?

9. **Well, you will lose in court but. . .:** The lawyer should find out more about their clients' motivations. The lawyer might ask, "Tell me more about why you started down this path with the Dr. Dollars. What were you hoping to achieve?" And then, "What are your priorities now, with respect to this lawsuit?" The lawyer is going to want to know whether this was a game to them, whether they were hoping for (or have real need of) a plane, or whether their goal was publicity for their business. But the lawyer is better served to ask open-ended questions, rather than ones where the lawyer is guessing about specific interests, because doing so may narrow, rather than broaden the lawyer's understanding of their client's interests.

10. **Here's an idea?** On the upside, this option would provide Mia and Jerry with some financial compensation, which is more than the lawyer's expectations about the returns they can expect from going to trial. It also provides them with a face-saving way to transition out of this situation, if they are feeling caught. There might (?) then be some opportunity for them to capitalize on their momentary fame.

    The principal drawback is that this ties Mia and Jerry into a business relationship with Dr. Energy—a company with whom they have already had tense dealings. It would be important to tie up the details of the agreement very tightly. It might also not align with Mia and Jerry's interests—either because they don't want to spend their time on a media campaign, or because their concerns are less about finances than about something else. (We don't know what their answers were to the questions above about their interests and priorities.) And as structured, the option doesn't take advantage of differences in resources (see Chapter 1) the way it might if, for example, they considered paying Mia and Jerry in Dr. Energy drinks, rather than cash.

CHAPTER 5

Attorneys, Clients, and Dispute Resolution

§5.1 INTRODUCTION

Lawyers have a set of ethical duties toward their clients, their counterparts, and the court. Because each state has a separate Bar, each state sets the specific parameters of these duties. We are saved from a 50-state survey, however, because virtually all states model their legal ethics on one of two documents — the ABA Model Rules of Professional Conduct (the Model Rules) or the ABA Model Code of Professional Responsibility (the Model Code). Because the Model Rules are, by far, the more commonly employed set of standards, this chapter focuses on the Model Rules. We will, however, indicate if the Model Code has provisions substantially different from those in the Model Rules.[1]

We will first examine the lawyer's duty to advise a client of available ADR options prior to litigation. Second, we consider the lawyer's duty to communicate offers of settlement to a client and the consequences when a lawyer fails to do so. Finally, we focus on the lawyer's duty to maintain client confidences during mediation, arbitration, and other settlement negotiations.

1. As noted in Chapter 3, when we reproduce particular rules, we are quoting the Delaware Lawyers' Rules of Professional Conduct, which happen to be almost identical to the Model Rules of Professional Responsibility.

§5.2 THE DUTY TO ADVISE A CLIENT OF ADR OPTIONS

A lawyer's core task is to counsel and represent clients effectively. In some contexts, effective counseling and representation will involve engaging in litigation. In others, clients' interests may be best served by pursuing some other legal or nonlegal process. As a result, in most circumstances, a lawyer can only meet her or his responsibility to help clients make informed decisions by providing information about the risks and opportunities presented by each of the different approaches to addressing her or his clients' problems.

Rule 1.2	(a) Subject to paragraphs (c) and (d), a lawyer shall abide by a client's decisions concerning the objectives of representation and, as required by Rule 1.4, shall consult with the client as to the means by which they are to be pursued. A lawyer may take such action on behalf of the client as is impliedly authorized to carry out the representation. A lawyer shall abide by a client's decision whether to settle a matter. . . . (c) A lawyer may limit the scope of the representation if the limitation is reasonable under the circumstances and the client gives informed consent. (d) A lawyer shall not counsel a client to engage, or assist a client, in conduct that the lawyer knows is criminal or fraudulent, but a lawyer may discuss the legal consequences of any proposed course of conduct with a client and may counsel or assist a client to make a good faith effort to determine the validity, scope, meaning or application of the law.
Rule 1.4	(a) A lawyer shall: (1) promptly inform the client of any decision or circumstance with respect to which the client's informed consent . . . is required by these Rules; (2) reasonably consult with the client about the means by which the client's objectives are to be accomplished; (3) keep the client reasonably informed about the status of the matter; (b) A lawyer shall explain a matter to the extent reasonably necessary to permit the client to make informed decisions regarding the representation.
Rule 2.1	In representing a client, a lawyer shall exercise independent professional judgment and render candid advice. In rendering advice, a lawyer may refer not only to law but to other considerations, such as moral, economic, social and political factors, that may be relevant to the client's situation. **Comment 5 (excerpt)** Similarly, when a matter is likely to involve litigation, it may be necessary under Rule 1.4 to inform the client of forms of dispute resolution that might constitute reasonable alternatives to litigation.
Rule 3.2	A lawyer shall make reasonable efforts to expedite litigation consistent with the interests of the client.

The four rules above, adopted in most states, outline lawyers' obligations to help clients understand various dispute resolution alternatives. Put roughly, Rule 1.2(a) requires a lawyer to defer to clients' decisions about the clients' objectives and to consult with clients about the means they will pursue. ("What are you trying to accomplish? Here's how I'm thinking we should try to do that. What are your thoughts?") Rule 1.4 requires a lawyer to provide enough information to clients so that the client can make an informed decision about the case. ("Here's what you need to know about the risks and opportunities of this situation.") Similar to Rule 1.4, Model Code EC 7-8 states that "[a] lawyer should advise his client of the possible effect of each legal alternative." Rule 3.2 requires a lawyer to expedite litigation, consistent with clients' interests. ("I'll make this as painless as possible.") And finally, Rule 2.1 permits a lawyer to refer not only to the law, but also to social, economic, and moral factors relevant to the case. ("As I see it, this case raises the following legal and nonlegal issues. . . .") Within this baseline framework of obligations, it is not difficult to imagine why lawyers' responsibilities often involve counseling about ADR.

Although many states model their legal ethics rules on the Model Rules or the Model Code, each state is free to (and often does) add variations, creating additional or different definitions of lawyers' duties. Furthermore, federal jurisdictions can write their own rules about advising clients about ADR separate from whatever the state ethics rules might be. Broadly speaking, a lawyer's state-created obligation to advise about ADR falls somewhere along a continuum, ranging from no explicit obligation to an unequivocal obligation to advise clients about dispute resolution alternatives.

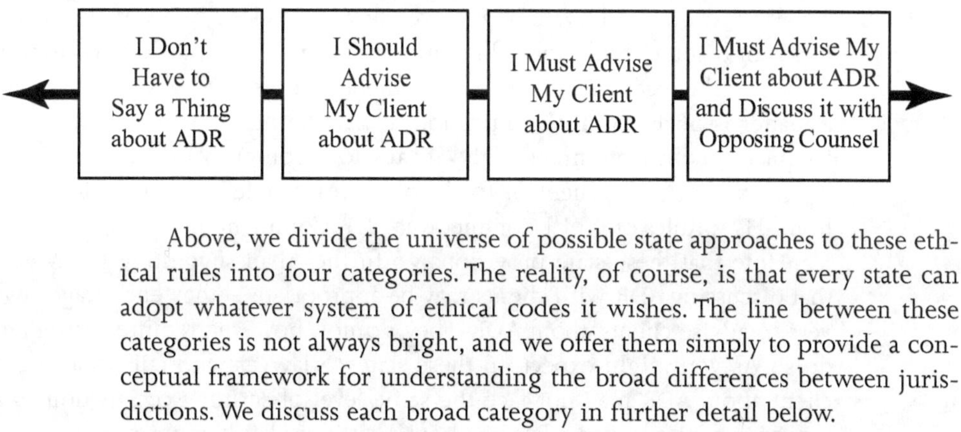

Above, we divide the universe of possible state approaches to these ethical rules into four categories. The reality, of course, is that every state can adopt whatever system of ethical codes it wishes. The line between these categories is not always bright, and we offer them simply to provide a conceptual framework for understanding the broad differences between jurisdictions. We discuss each broad category in further detail below.

§5.2.1 I Don't Have to Say a Thing

The far left end of the continuum represents an absence of any explicit duty regarding ADR. Reflecting the reality of modern legal practice, though, few states' laws are utterly silent about ADR.

A somewhat greater (though still not very significant) obligation arises when a state suggests that discussing ADR with a client may sometimes be appropriate. For example, Florida Supreme Court Rule of Professional Conduct 4-2.1 provides in a comment, "[W]hen a matter is likely to involve litigation, it **may** be necessary . . . to inform the client of forms of dispute resolution that might constitute reasonable alternatives to litigation" (emphasis added). Similarly, §A(3) of the Lawyer's Creed of Professionalism of the State Bar of Arizona provides, "*In appropriate cases*, I will counsel my client with respect to alternative methods of resolving disputes" (emphasis added). Such provisions imply that ADR counseling might be helpful, without going so far as to declare it a good idea.

§5.2.2 I Should Advise My Client About ADR

Many states have legal ethics rules with provisions that specifically suggest lawyers ought to discuss ADR with clients, as a matter of best practice. Some states accomplish this through statute. For example, the Arkansas Code states, "An attorney licensed in this state when practicing in this state is encouraged to advise his or her client about the dispute resolution process options available to him or her and to assist him or her in the selection of the technique or procedure, including litigation, deemed appropriate for dealing with the client's dispute, case, or controversy" Ark. Code Ann. §16-7-204 (2018). Other states achieve the same end through court rules. For example, Hawaii's Supreme Court Rules of Professional Conduct state, "In a matter involving or expected to involve litigation, a lawyer should advise a client of alternative forms of dispute resolution which might reasonably be pursued to attempt to resolve the legal dispute or to reach the legal objective sought." "[W]hen a matter is likely to involve litigation, it may be necessary under Rule 1.4 [requiring consultation about the means to accomplish the client's objectives] to inform the client of forms of . . . reasonable alternatives to litigation." Haw. Rules of Prof'l Conduct Rule 2.1, Comment 5.

Note that these state provisions go further than suggesting to lawyers that discussing ADR with clients may be appropriate—they encourage lawyers to advise clients about ADR. They do not, however, require lawyers to do so. As you might expect, in these states, a lawyer who fails to advise a client about ADR may not face the same level of scrutiny or sanction as a lawyer in a state where advising about ADR is explicitly required.

§5.2.3 I Must Advise My Client About ADR

An increasing number of states enact a mandatory duty for lawyers to advise clients of available ADR options. These provisions vary in their scope, but all rules in this category use terms like "must," "required," or "shall." These requirements can be found in many different places: state codes, court rules, creeds, district rules, and local rules. For example, Missouri Supreme Court Rule 17.02(b) states, "[Counsel] shall advise parties of the availability of alternative dispute resolution programs." Therefore, a lawyer in Missouri who fails to discuss ADR with a client has breached a specific obligation. Virginia places the obligation within the context of the duty to keep a client informed. Virginia Rule of Professional Conduct 1:4, Comment 1 states:

> This continuing duty to keep the client informed includes a duty to advise the client about the availability of dispute resolution processes that might be more appropriate to the client's goals than the initial process chosen. For example, information obtained during a lawyer-to-lawyer negotiation may give rise to consideration of a process, such as mediation, where the parties themselves could be more directly involved in resolving the dispute.

Similar to a number of states, Texas has a creed in its code of professional behavior which, to gain membership to the Bar, requires the candidate lawyer to promise that he or she will uphold an obligation to advise clients. The Texas Lawyer's Creed, R. II.11, states, "I will advise my client regarding the availability of mediation, arbitration, and other alternative methods of resolving and settling disputes."

Some states have codified the duty to advise in a way that removes all ambiguity regarding the scope and timing of this consultation. For example, Massachusetts Supreme Judicial Court Rule 1:18, Uniform Rules on Dispute Resolution Rule 5, states, "Attorneys shall: provide their clients with this information about court-connected dispute resolution services; discuss with their clients the advantages and disadvantages of the various methods of dispute resolution, and certify their compliance with this requirement on the civil cover sheet or its equivalent." Massachusetts is serious enough about this rule that compliance requires lawyers to sign, confirmed by a witness, a certification stating they consulted with their clients to "consider the resolution of the litigation through the use of alternative dispute resolution programs. . ." D. Mass. LR 16.1.

Even when a jurisdiction might not have an across-the-board requirement to advise, specific practice areas may have such a requirement. For example, the United States Bankruptcy Court for the Southern District of California has a rule stating, "Prior to the pre-trial status conference, counsel shall confer with the client and discuss the mediation program, and shall ask the client for authorization to participate in the mediation program." U.S. Bankr. Ct. R. S.D. Cal., LBR 7016-3.

§5.2.4 I Must Advise My Client and Discuss with Opposing Party or Counsel

At the far right end of the spectrum in the range of possible rules are states whose rules require lawyers not only to advise clients about ADR, but also to engage opposing counsel or opposing parties in discussions of ADR or settlement efforts. Some jurisdictions require ADR notification of the opposing party. For example, more than two dozen states have created foreclosure mediation programs to mitigate the damage of foreclosure. In many states in which these programs exist, the lender's attorney is statutorily required to notify the lender and borrower of the mediation program and a mediation must be scheduled before an appearance in court is permitted.

Additionally, some states require that disputants discuss ADR options together. For example, one Texas rule states that "[b]efore the initial conference in a case, counsel are required to discuss with their clients and with opposing counsel the appropriateness of ADR in the case." U.S. Dist. Ct. for S. Dist. Texas Local Rule 16.4.B.1. An Ohio rule requires that "[b]efore the initial pre-trial conference in a case, counsel shall discuss the appropriateness of ADR in the litigation with their clients and with opposing counsel." Hamilton County Municipal Rule 15.2. Similarly, the Middle District of Louisiana Rule 16.3.1M, Rule C-1(a), states, "Before the initial conference in all civil cases, counsel shall discuss the appropriateness of ADR in the litigation with their clients and with opposing counsel." Even if a state merely had an obligation for counsel to confer with opposing counsel about ADR possibilities, each lawyer would necessarily have an obligation to discuss the matter with her or his client. Requirements like these, therefore, are the strongest currently in force.

§5.2.5 Sanctions

A lawyer who fails to adhere to the Bar's standards is subject to various forms of discipline. In cases of modest transgressions, a lawyer may merely be reprimanded, censured, or fined. In more serious cases, a lawyer may be stripped of their license to practice law for some fixed amount of time or even permanently.

Since the ethical rules concerning advising clients about ADR vary from state to state and the sanctions for violating ethical rules are so fact-specific, we cannot offer a uniform description of what happens to those lawyers who do not adequately advise their clients about ADR. In cases in which a lawyer has been in trouble for failing to advise a client about ADR, the lawyer has almost always also been guilty of a number of other misdeeds, making it hard to assess the severity the Bar would attach to an independent failure to advise a client about ADR. For example, consider the case of *In re Potter*, 952 P.2d 936 (Kan. 1998). Denise Carson, a car accident victim, hired Marcus Potter to handle her case. She did not hear from him again until 16 months later, after she had filed a disciplinary complaint against him. During that time, Potter had failed to advise his client even about the fact that the other driver's insurance company was trying to engage in settlement conversations. The court reviewing the complaint against Potter concluded that the attorney violated Model Rule 1.4 when "he did not consult with [Carson] . . . about her claim or explain the settlement negotiations to her despite numerous phone calls from [Carson]." When determining Potter's sanction, the court split on either an indefinite suspension from the practice of law or a public censure. Despite Potter's history of client complaints due to lack of communication, the court decided that the correct sanction was a public censure because Carson did not suffer any demonstrable monetary harm stemming from the lack of communication with Potter.

Beyond the prospect of Bar sanctions for ethical violations, lawyers also practice under the shadow of possible malpractice suits. Some kinds of malpractice are easy to spot and easy to quantify. For example, a lawyer who fails to submit a pleading within the prescribed time limit and thereby loses the case will have a difficult time arguing that submitting an untimely pleading is an acceptable practice. But even in this straightforward situation, a client must prove that the lawyer's misconduct caused injury to the client. In essence, the lawyer's defense may be, "Sure, I lost your case at the pleadings stage, but you never would have survived summary judgment anyway, so what's the harm?" The highly speculative inquiry this demands presents a real challenge to pursuing a legal malpractice claim successfully.[2]

Now imagine how much harder it would be to prove that a lawyer's failure to tell a client about mediation caused a client harm. Who's to say the client would have agreed to mediation, even if the lawyer had provided the advice? Who's to say the client would have settled in mediation, even if the lawyer had advised mediation? As a result of these realities in the dynamics of legal malpractice claims, malpractice claims against lawyers solely on the grounds of failure to advise a client about ADR possibilities are surely rare. Indeed, we are aware of no examples of attorneys sanctioned solely for failing to satisfy this requirement.

---

2. See Michael Moffitt, *Settlement Malpractice*, 86 U. Chicago L. Rev. 1825 (2019) (available at https://www.ssrn.com/abstract=3358368).

§5.3 DUTY TO COMMUNICATE SETTLEMENT OFFERS

One important distinction in the Model Rules is between those matters about which a lawyer must *defer* to the client's wishes, and those about which the lawyer merely must consult with the client. In general terms, a lawyer must defer to the client's wishes regarding the goals of the representation. ("What I want to do here is maximize the total dollars I recover from the insurance company," versus "What I want to do is deal with my immediate need for cash, so I want to get as much as I can reasonably get quickly," versus "What I want here is to show the world what a lousy company this is.") By contrast, a lawyer is obligated ethically only to consult with clients about the means the lawyer will pursue. ("I believe you will fare best in this litigation if we join your neighbor as a codefendant, but I want to talk with you about the implications of doing that." "I think we should focus our defense on the causation question alone, not on the more speculative assertion of qualified immunity.") Similarly, ABA Model Code EC 7-7 states that "[i]n certain areas of legal representation not affecting the merits of the cause or substantially prejudicing the rights of a client, a lawyer is entitled to make decisions on his own. But otherwise the authority to make decisions is exclusively that of the client."

As a result of this distinction, courts and Bar grievance committees give considerable deference to lawyers' judgment calls about many decisions along the way during litigation. Clients typically do not have the authority to micromanage their lawyers throughout the litigation. Nevertheless, at the end of the day, the case remains the client's, and the client retains the ultimate decision-making authority about its disposition. In short, because the client gets to decide whether to accept an offer of settlement, the lawyer is obligated to communicate such offers.

§5.3.1 Do I Have to Tell My Client About Every Offer?

In short, yes. Rule 1.2(a) provides that "a lawyer shall abide by a client's decisions concerning the objectives of representation and . . . shall consult with the client as to the means by which they are to be pursued. . . . A lawyer shall abide by a client's decision whether to settle a matter." Under this rule, the decision to settle and under what terms is clearly the client's choice. Following from this, Rule 1.4(b)'s duty to inform the client sufficiently to make an informed decision about the representation necessarily requires a lawyer to inform the client about any offers of settlement from the opposing party.

As with almost all forms of lawyer misconduct, the sanction for failing to communicate a settlement offer depends on the circumstances involved.

At the most extreme, it can lead to disbarment. For example, in *In re Brown*, 453 P.2d 958 (Ariz. 1969), Francis Brown represented the plaintiff in a dog-bite case. On the eve of trial, the defendant offered to settle the case for $600, but Brown did not communicate the settlement offer to his client. The case went to trial, and Brown's client lost and had to pay costs and jury fees. As a result of this conduct (and a host of other unimpressive practices listed in a Bar complaint against him), Brown was disbarred.

Perhaps it is obvious, but these rules also require an attorney to communicate settlement offers *accurately*. In the case of *In re Ragland*, 697 N.E.2d 44 (Ind. 1998), attorney Michael Ragland represented a client who brought action against a nursing home. The nursing home made an $18,000 settlement offer, which Ragland communicated to the client. Ragland also told the client that additional funds would be available through her insurance company, but, in fact, that was not the case. The client could not recover any additional money from the insurance company or from anyone else under the terms of the agreement to which the client (mistakenly) authorized Ragland to agree. As a result of a complaint alleging this and other misconduct, Ragland was suspended from practicing law for six months. The court also reduced the fee Ragland collected from this representation. The court declared that Ragland had, in essence, accepted the $18,000 settlement without his client's consent, because the client had not made a fully informed decision.

Some jurisdictions have taken the duty to convey settlement offers even further by requiring attorneys to convey offers of settlement discussions. For example, State Bar of Michigan Standing Committee on Professional and Judicial Ethics, Opinion RI-255 (1996), has interpreted Rule 1.4 to mean that "[i]f counsel for the opposing party offers to resolve the pending dispute through alternative dispute resolution forums, a lawyer is required to convey that offer to the client." Nothing in the rule requires the attorney or the client to accept the invitation to try to settle the case, but the attorney has an obligation to convey the opportunity to the client.

§5.3.2 Does It Matter If the Other Side's Offer Is Terrible?

Nothing in the Model Rules prevents you, as a lawyer, from advising your client against accepting a terrible offer. Indeed, a lawyer who *fails* to advise a client about the potential downsides of a settlement offer may be violating their ethical obligation to provide competent counsel. Clients often rely on lawyers to assess the relative merits of different possible courses of action—frequently including a comparison of litigation and settlement. The mere fact that the other side has made an offer does not affect this obligation. What the lawyer cannot do, however, is to substitute their own judgment about the settlement offer for their client's. The lawyer can say,

"They made a terrible offer, and I advise you against accepting it." But if, at the end of the conversation, the client says, "Accept it anyway," the lawyer must defer to the client's decision.

§5.3.3 Does This Mean That the Client Can't Give Me Discretion?

Under the Model Rules, a client could certainly choose to give you the authority to accept a settlement offer that falls within certain parameters. For example, a client might tell her lawyer, "Do as well as you can, and I authorize you to accept anything better than $100,000." If, during settlement negotiations, the other side presents an offer that is better than $100,000, the lawyer need not convey the offer to her client and await a response. The lawyer could simply accept the offer based on the authority given by their client.

What the Model Rules prohibit is two scenarios: (1) a lawyer *rejecting* an offer of settlement without at least presenting that offer to their client for consideration, and (2) a lawyer accepting an offer on behalf of a client who has not authorized such an acceptance. For example, in *In re Eichholz*, 2007 WL 1223613, 2007 U.S. App. LEXIS 11201, a former client and a former employee accused attorney Benjamin Eichholz of having settled cases without the proper authority for several clients, of having failed to discuss settlement offers with other clients, and of having committed several other Model Rule violations. The court suspended Eichholz from practice for two years. Eichholz was later convicted of obstructing a Department of Labor investigation and surrendered his law license permanently. 287 Ga. 258 (Ga. 2010).

Clients sometimes give their lawyers final authority to settle cases and give them broad discretion about the terms of the settlement. The authority to settle on specific terms, however, must be clear, separate from any other *ex ante* grant of authority. For example, in *In re Lewis*, 463 S.E.2d 862 (Ga. 1995), Peggy Uselton hired attorney James Lewis to represent her in a personal injury action. At the outset of the representation, Uselton signed Lewis's standard retainer agreement, which provided that Lewis "shall have full power and authority to settle, compromise, or take such action as he might deem proper for the best interest of the client." Lewis subsequently accepted a settlement offer in the case without consulting Uselton, who thought the settlement terms were inadequate. Uselton filed a complaint with the Georgia State Bar against Lewis. The court rejected Lewis's argument that his contract with Uselton gave him unqualified authority to settle on her behalf, pointing in particular to Georgia's prohibition against an attorney obtaining a proprietary interest in a client's cause of action. The court suspended Lewis for 18 months. General blanket authority imposed as a term of initial representation, therefore, does not provide an adequate basis for a lawyer to enter a final settlement without consulting the client.

Because lawyers' ability to bind their clients to settlement terms is limited, disputants should also take steps to assure that *opposing* counsel has the authority to present or accept a potential settlement offer. The case of *Luethke v. Suhr*, 650 N.W.2d 220 (Neb. 2002), provides an example of the importance of assuring that the clients (and not just their attorneys) consent to settlement terms. Jonathan Luethke hired attorney Mary Wickencamp to file suits against several defendants for personal injuries stemming from an automobile accident. The defendants subsequently faxed a settlement offer of $16,000 to Wickencamp. She replied, "I am willing to recommend your offer to my client, but I need to meet with Jon to discuss it." The defendants agreed to keep their offer open until the next day. The next day, Wickencamp faxed back, saying, "My client will accept the offer. . . . Thanks for your cooperation in getting this done." Some months later, Wickencamp had still not returned final settlement paperwork, and she told the defendants, "I've sent them on to my client. . . . I'm on my way out of town and have a meeting with them set after I come back. Please understand it is not a problem." Months later, Wickencamp withdrew as counsel in the case, and the defendants sought to have the settlement enforced. The Nebraska Supreme Court rejected the defendants' argument that Wickencamp had authority (apparent or otherwise) to bind Luethke to the agreement, writing

> We hold, therefore, that although lawyers retain apparent authority to make procedural and tactical decisions through the existence of the attorney-client relationship, a lawyer cannot settle a client's claim without express authority from the client. In other words, where there has been nothing beyond a mere employment or retainer of the lawyer to represent the client in a cause and the lawyer has acquired no other authority to enter into a settlement (such as acquiescence in open court), if the lawyer seeks to enter a settlement, the opposing party should ascertain whether the lawyer has received actual authority from the client to take such action. A party who enters a settlement agreement without verifying the opposing counsel's actual authority to settle does so at his or her peril.

§5.3.4 Do I Have to Convey My Client's Settlement Offer If I Think the Offer Is Unwise?

With some decisions, the Bar clearly requires attorneys to defer to their clients' wishes. (For example, attorneys must defer to clients on whether to accept a settlement offer.) With other decisions, the Bar clearly does not require attorneys to defer to their clients' wishes, though attorneys certainly may choose to defer. (For example, attorneys need not defer to clients on intra-litigation decisions like when to file a particular motion.) A challenge arises when (1) the decision is sufficiently important that a client is likely to want deference from the lawyer, but (2) the decision is not explicitly described in the Model Rules as one of the matters on which a lawyer must defer to the client. That is the challenge with respect to clients' desires to *offer* settlement.

In brief, the answer to the question posed in this section is, "Probably yes—a lawyer must communicate a client's settlement offer to the other side if the client insists on making the offer." But this does not mean that the lawyer cannot try to persuade the client that making the offer is unwise (for example, because the lawyer thinks the client has misjudged the risks associated with the case, or because the lawyer thinks the offer would be more strategic if made in another form or at another time). At the end of the day, however, if the client wishes to dispose of the case in a particular way, a lawyer who does not communicate that offer is likely to have violated Rule 1.2.

One case illustrating this dynamic is *In re Panel File Number* 99-5, 607 N.W.2d 429 (Minn. 2000). A client informed its lawyer that it wished to extend a settlement offer at an upcoming conference at which opposing counsel and a magistrate judge would be present. The lawyer, who was operating under a contingent fee contract, did not communicate the client's offer at that meeting. A while later, the case settled, and the lawyer billed the client for more than $40,000, an amount not based on the original contingent fee contract. The attorney asserted that "because the settlement was against his advice, he was no longer bound by the contingent fee." The Minnesota Supreme Court, interpreting an earlier version of Minnesota's Rule 1.2, which did not explicitly require consultation before making an offer, nevertheless held that the lawyer had an obligation in this case to communicate the client's offer and rejected the lawyer's assertion about the fee arrangement.

The current Rule 1.2 (reprinted earlier in the chapter) adds a key provision stating that the decision whether to make or accept a settlement offer belongs to the client. In a jurisdiction that has adopted the most recent version of the Model Rules, this case from Minnesota would have been even easier to decide against the lawyer.

§5.4 CLIENT CONFIDENCES

In addition to the duty to discuss ADR and the duty to communicate settlement offers, a third lawyer duty is relevant to every dispute resolution process—the duty to maintain client confidences. As a matter of legal ethics and as a matter of lawyer-client privilege, confidentiality raises at least two significant questions: Under what circumstances must a lawyer keep information confidential if the client wants to keep it secret? And under what circumstances may a lawyer reveal a client's information against the client's wishes?

These two confidentiality questions produce a complex patchwork of rules and standards that can arise in a broad range of contexts. Many of these will be covered in your Professional Responsibility course, and it is not our purpose to review that course in its entirety here. Some of these obligations arise in the context of other courses as well. For example, you will likely encounter the Sarbanes-Oxley Act (which establishes the conditions under which a lawyer must whistleblow and withdraw from representing clients who commit corporate fraud related to securities) in a Business Entities course. Again, it is beyond the scope of this volume to summarize the entirety of the law on maintaining client confidences.

For our purposes, confidentiality raises a more limited number of issues that are truly particular to confidential client information and ADR. Below, we explore three such issues.

§5.4.1 Can a Lawyer Sit Quietly in a Negotiation While a Client Commits Fraud?

No. As you know from the detailed treatment in Chapter 3, fraud is the knowing misrepresentation of a material fact, causing reasonable and detrimental reliance. Rule 1.2(d) explicitly prohibits a lawyer from counseling or assisting a client in "conduct that the lawyer knows is criminal or fraudulent." In a comment to this rule, the Rules acknowledge that "[w]hen the client's course of action has already begun and is continuing, the lawyer's responsibility is especially delicate." Consider the intersection of Comment [3] to Rule 4.1(b) and Rule 1.6.

Rule 4.1(b) Comment [3]

Ordinarily, a lawyer can avoid assisting a client's crime or fraud by withdrawing from the representation. Sometimes it may be necessary for the lawyer to give notice of the fact of withdrawal and to disaffirm an opinion, document, affirmation or the like. In extreme cases, substantive law may require a lawyer to disclose information relating to the representation to avoid being deemed to have assisted the client's crime or fraud. If the lawyer can avoid assisting a client's crime or fraud only by disclosing this information, then under paragraph (b) the lawyer is required to do so, unless the disclosure is prohibited by Rule 1.6.

Because Rule 1.6 now permits lawyers to disclose information to prevent a client from committing fraud, Rule 4.1's requirements make it clear that an attorney must disclose otherwise confidential information, if doing so is necessary to prevent a client's fraud.

> **Rule 1.6**
>
> (a) A lawyer shall not reveal information relating to the representation of a client unless the client gives informed consent, the disclosure is impliedly authorized in order to carry out the representation or the disclosure is permitted by paragraph (b).
>
> (b) A lawyer may reveal information relating to the representation of a client to the extent the lawyer reasonably believes necessary:
>
> (1) to prevent reasonably certain death or substantial bodily harm;
>
> (2) to prevent the client from committing a crime or fraud that is reasonably certain to result in substantial injury to the financial interests or property of another and in furtherance of which the client has used or is using the lawyer's services;
>
> (3) to prevent, mitigate or rectify substantial injury to the financial interests or property of another that is reasonably certain to result or has resulted from the client's commission of a crime or fraud in furtherance of which the client has used the lawyer's services; . . .
>
> (6) to comply with other law or a court order.

§5.4.2 Can a Lawyer Help a Client Deceive an Arbitrator?

No. Rule 3.3 clearly requires a lawyer to be candid with a tribunal. These provisions specifically apply to contexts in which the lawyer is representing a client in court. Rule 1.0(m) also extends the definition of "tribunal" to include arbitrators. So, a lawyer cannot assist a client in deceiving an arbitrator any more than the lawyer could do so in front of a judge.

> **Rule 3.3**
>
> **Candor Toward the Tribunal**
>
> (a) A lawyer shall not knowingly:
>
> (1) make a false statement of fact or law to a tribunal or fail to correct a false statement of material fact or law previously made to the tribunal by the lawyer;

> (2) fail to disclose to the tribunal legal authority in the controlling jurisdiction known to the lawyer to be directly adverse to the position of the client and not disclosed by opposing counsel; or
>
> (3) offer evidence that the lawyer knows to be false. If a lawyer, the lawyer's client, or a witness called by the lawyer, has offered material evidence and the lawyer comes to know of its falsity, the lawyer shall take reasonable remedial measures, including, if necessary, disclosure to the tribunal. A lawyer may refuse to offer evidence, other than the testimony of a defendant in a criminal matter, that the lawyer reasonably believes is false.
>
> (b) A lawyer who represents a client in an adjudicative proceeding and who knows that a person intends to engage, is engaging or has engaged in criminal or fraudulent conduct related to the proceeding shall take reasonable remedial measures, including, if necessary, disclosure to the tribunal.
>
> (c) The duties stated in paragraphs (a) and (b) continue to the conclusion of the proceeding, and apply even if compliance requires disclosure of information otherwise protected by Rule 1.6.
>
> (d) In an ex parte proceeding, a lawyer shall inform the tribunal of all material facts known to the lawyer that will enable the tribunal to make an informed decision, whether or not the facts are adverse.

§5.4.3 Can a Lawyer Help a Client Deceive a Mediator?

The Model Rules are less protective of mediators than of judges or arbitrators. Rule 3.3 requires "candor" before a tribunal—an obligation that is something more demanding than "don't commit fraud." However, Rule 3.3 does not consider mediators as tribunals, largely because mediators do not act as adjudicative bodies. Even when mediators provide evaluative assessments of a case's merits, the mediator is not rendering a binding decision. As a result, the rules' requirement of candor to tribunals does not extend to mediators.

Lawyers' other ethical obligations continue to apply in the context of mediation. For example, Rule 4.1's prohibition against assisting a client in committing fraud does not differentiate among the targets of fraud and applies in mediation as it does in negotiation (See Chapter 3 for more on this in the context of negotiation.) Still, attorneys have greater ethical leeway in the context of mediation than they do in arbitrations or in hearings before judicial officers.

§5.4.4 Can a Lawyer Disclose Confidential Information in a Mediation, Since Mediation Is a Confidential Process?

No. The fact that conversations are taking place within a mediation, as opposed to some other forum, does not give a lawyer license to disclose that which she is otherwise not permitted to disclose. Nothing in the Model Rules provides for a special exception for mediation communications. If the client does not want the information revealed, and the information is not on the narrow list of exceptions in Rule 1.6, the lawyer must not reveal the information—even in mediation.

That would be the answer even if the Model Rules were irrelevant, for at least two reasons. First, although mediation communications are often treated as confidential, they are certainly not absolutely confidential. See Chapter 7 for more on the boundaries of mediation confidentiality. Second, even if mediation were reliably confidential, that should not matter for purposes of deciding whether to reveal a client's secret. (That would be akin to saying, "It's okay for me to tell your secret to my friend, because my friend said she wouldn't tell anybody.") You might think it useful for settlement purposes to share confidential information within the mediation—and this does happen—but the decision to disclose remains your client's decision, not yours.

The Model Rules contain no exception permitting disclosure in a confidential process like mediation. The following three bright-line rules, therefore, provide the best guidance:

1. A lawyer can divulge a client's confidential information if the client consents.
2. A lawyer can divulge a client's confidential information in the relatively narrow set of circumstances listed in Rule 1.6.
3. A lawyer must divulge a client's confidential information under Rule 4.1(b) if doing so is necessary to avoid assisting the client to commit a crime or fraud.

Examples

EXAMPLES

To Advise, or Not to Advise

Hamlet, upon learning of his father's death, arranged to move back home to be closer to his mother and to the family business, Ophelia's Fresh Fruit (OFF). When he returned, Hamlet was shocked to discover that things were rotten. His mother had remarried Hamlet's Uncle Claudius, and Claudius had taken over the position of CEO of OFF, even though Hamlet believed he was the rightful heir to the company. Hamlet marched into a local lawyer's office and declared, "I want to sue Claudius." The lawyer asked a few questions about the situation, and said, "Leave everything to me." Two years of protracted litigation later, with no resolution in sight, Hamlet is bemoaning his fate to a friend, when the friend says, "Have you tried to mediate or settle?" Hamlet confesses that he's never heard of mediation, and his friend suggests that Hamlet's lawyer may be part of the problem.

1. **Model Rules state.** Assume that Hamlet's state has enacted a version of the Model Rules of Professional Conduct. Has Hamlet's lawyer violated any professional obligations? If so, what sanctions might the lawyer face?

2. **State encourages ADR advising.** Assume that Hamlet's state has enacted a version of the Model Rules of Professional Conduct and has added a provision declaring that "in most circumstances, a lawyer should advise a client of alternative forms of dispute resolution that might reasonably be pursued to attempt to resolve the legal dispute or to reach the legal objective sought." Has Hamlet's lawyer violated any professional obligations? If so, what sanctions might the lawyer face?

3. **State requires ADR advice and consultation with opposing counsel.** Assume that Hamlet's state has enacted a version of the Model Rules of Professional Conduct. Assume that it also has a statute that says, "A lawyer has a duty to inform the client of forms of dispute resolution that might constitute reasonable alternatives to litigation." Has Hamlet's lawyer violated any professional obligations? If so, what sanctions might the lawyer face? Does Hamlet have a case for malpractice?

Kosmo's Pool

Kosmo hired a swimming pool manufacturer to install a room-sized pool in his tenth-floor apartment. After the pool was installed, Kosmo fell asleep while sitting in the pool one afternoon. Unfortunately, Kosmo's hand became lodged in the pool's drainage system, causing serious injury. Kosmo hires a lawyer, Jack Childs, to file suit against the swimming pool manufacturer.

4. **Chlorine for life.** Jack Childs and opposing counsel met to discuss the case. Jack Childs outlined Kosmo's product liability claim. The defendant explained that Kosmo was at fault by falling asleep in the pool. The two postured for a while, and then the pool manufacturer offered a lifetime supply of chlorine and other pool-cleaning chemicals to settle the case. Jack Childs laughed at the offer and rejected it without ever informing Kosmo of its terms. Has Jack Childs violated his professional obligations to Kosmo?

5. **Jack Childs's judgment.** Prior to a follow-up meeting with the lawyer for the defendant, Jack Childs meets with Kosmo and discusses the merits of the case. He explains the possible risks and the opportunities associated with the litigation, and at the end of the conversation, Kosmo tells

Jack Childs, "Do the best you can for me. I trust your judgment. If they make a good offer, take it. Otherwise, let's take this to trial." At a subsequent meeting, the pool company renews its offer of lifetime chlorine. Jack Childs again laughs and says, "No. Unacceptable. I don't even need to consult with my client on this one." The pool company says their offer is final, and Jack Childs rejects it. Has Jack Childs violated his professional responsibilities to Kosmo?

6. **Kosmo's idea of justice.** Kosmo tells Jack Childs that he believes that the best outcome in this case would be for the pool company to pay for a pool boy to come by the apartment every day to maintain the pool. Jack Childs explains that such a result would be impossible even in the best case scenario presented by litigation. Kosmo persists and argues that Jack should demand this for him. Jack Childs explains that making such a demand would probably infuriate the pool company, making them less likely to settle. Kosmo insists. Their meeting ends, and Jack Childs decides never to communicate the crazy demand. Has Jack Childs violated his professional responsibility to Kosmo?

7. **Kosmo's limit.** On the eve of trial, Kosmo and Jack Childs have a final conversation about the possibility of settling the case. Kosmo rescinds his blanket grant of authority to Jack Childs and instead specifically tells Jack that he will agree to "anything above $50,000." On the courthouse steps, the pool company offers to settle the case for "$60,000, but not a penny more." Jack Childs ponders the situation for a minute. His contingency fee arrangement with Kosmo entitles Jack to one-third of any recovery. The defendant's offer would leave Kosmo with only $40,000, so Jack Childs rejects the offer without consulting his client. Has Jack Childs violated his professional responsibility to Kosmo?

8. **Jack Childs's judgment, part two.** During a break in the trial, the defense lawyer approaches Jack Childs and offers a creative settlement in which Kosmo would receive $30,000, a certificate for a new pool in ten years, and free cleaning supplies. Jack Childs accepts the offer without consulting Kosmo. Has Jack Childs violated his professional responsibility to Kosmo?

Release the Hounds, but Not the Information

Leeza was soliciting donations door-to-door as part of a project for the Young Do-Gooders Club. When she rang the doorbell at the mansion of Monty Barns, no one answered, but she heard from within, "Release the hounds!" Moments later, a pack of snarling dogs attacked Leeza, causing severe injuries. Lionel Klutz agrees to represent Barns in the ensuing personal injury action.

9. **Monty's initial plan.** Early in the litigation, the two sides agreed to mediate. Klutz advised Barns about the process, and Barns agreed that it might be useful. "After all," Barns said, "I'm sure they'll ask me if this has ever happened before at some point. Better that it should be asked in a setting in which I'm not under oath, so that I can say this is the first time." Klutz then asked him how many times such a thing had occurred in the past, and Barns laughed and said, "Oh, dear me, I've lost count. So many solicitors, so few dogs." What might Klutz do in this situation, consistent with the Model Rules of Professional Responsibility?

10. **Monty Barns, man of his word.** In their final preparations for mediation, Barns and Klutz agree on a strategy: Barns will show deep remorse for the injuries, confess that this is not the first time the dogs have "gotten out," and offer $500,000 to settle the case. In her opening statement, Leeza's lawyer describes the horrific injuries Leeza suffered, including not only physical injuries but also a complete loss of memory about the events. Barns interrupts, "Loss of memory, eh? Then she doesn't remember taunting my poor puppies? Throwing rocks at them? Hitting them with a stick? That's what she did, you know. I'm sorry she got hurt, but it's no wonder they finally bit her. She's the one to blame here!" Leeza and her lawyer look shocked. Barns looks over at Klutz and, imperceptibly to the other parties at the mediation, winks. What might Klutz do in this situation, consistent with the Model Rules of Professional Responsibility?

11. **Not a penny more!** After a protracted pretrial process, including several failed efforts at mediation, Leeza's case is set for trial. In his last-minute preparations, Klutz asks Barns if he would consider settling the matter. Barns tells Klutz, "I'm willing to pay her $200,000, but not a penny more." On the eve of trial, the judge orders the parties to try mediation one more time. In an initial private caucus involving only the mediator, Barns, and Klutz, the mediator asks Barns, "What is the most you would be willing to pay?" Without hesitating, Barns replies, "$100,000, but not a penny more." What might Klutz do in this situation, consistent with the Model Rules of Professional Responsibility?

Explanations

To Advise, or Not to Advise

1. **Model Rules state.** Hamlet's dissatisfaction with the way his litigation is unfolding is not necessarily evidence that his lawyer has breached any duties. The Model Rule perhaps most directly relevant to this circumstance is Rule 1.4, which requires a lawyer to "reasonably consult" with clients about the means the lawyer will undertake in pursuing the client's aims. If one interprets Rule 1.4 as referring solely to the means *within*

litigation, Hamlet's lawyer is entirely safe. Another reading of Rule 1.4, however, suggests that the Model Rule contemplates that the lawyer will consult about a range of different possibilities, including those beyond litigation.

Hamlet might make a similar argument with reference to Rule 3.2, which requires lawyers to "expedite litigation consistent with the interests of the client." As above, one might read Rule 3.2 as requiring merely that a lawyer expedite *litigation* (for example, by limiting discovery). Hamlet might argue, however, that his lawyer did not expedite the litigation by failing to advise him of the possibility of a nonlitigation alternative (like mediation) that could have resolved the issue more quickly.

Finally, Hamlet might argue that the lawyer failed to discharge his duties with adequate care, thus committing legal malpractice. He *might* succeed in suggesting that any lawyer would at least counsel a client contemplating litigation about the possibility of ADR. But it would be difficult for Hamlet to prove any damages of significance stemming from this failure if everything else the lawyer has done in litigation has been proper.

At the end of the day, Hamlet's lawyer is unlikely to face serious sanctions in a state with only the Model Rules as a baseline for advising.

2. **State encourages ADR advising.** The addition of a state provision that merely says, "in most circumstances, a lawyer should . . ." does not change the analysis from question 1 significantly with respect to the legal ethics claim against Hamlet's lawyer. In his defense, Hamlet's lawyer would correctly point out that the language "should" means that the Bar does not require advice of this sort. And he would also probably argue that, even if advice about ADR is normally called for, the drafters anticipated that some circumstances (like the ones in this case,) relieve the lawyer of any strict obligation.

   The state provision suggesting advice giving might be useful to Hamlet if he were pursuing a malpractice claim against his lawyer. If the lawyer's defense is that advice about ADR is not normally given, the existence of this rule (and presumably local practices that accompany it) would make it easier for Hamlet to establish a breach of the duty of care. However, Hamlet would still face all of the challenges described in the explanation to question 1 in establishing a causal link between the lawyer's conduct and any injury Hamlet believes he has suffered.

3. **State requires ADR advice and consultation with opposing counsel.** In this case, Hamlet's lawyer had a duty to advise Hamlet about "forms of dispute resolution that might constitute reasonable alternatives to litigation." Given the nature of this dispute (an intra-family clash involving ongoing relationships and ongoing business affairs), it would be almost

impossible for Hamlet's lawyer to argue that no reasonable alternatives to litigation exist. Mediation, in particular, suggests itself as at least worthy of discussion.

Hamlet could file a complaint against his lawyer with the local Bar, and under these facts, the lawyer's conduct almost certainly constitutes a breach of the relevant rules. What sanction the Bar will impose depends on the Bar's assessment of the seriousness of the misconduct and, most likely, an assessment of the rest of the lawyer's conduct throughout the case since severe penalties usually require an array of rule breaking.

As for a malpractice claim, Hamlet would probably only be able to pursue this successfully in a state with the requirement to advise clients about ADR. Even then, Hamlet would have to show that (a) he would have pursued the mediation had his lawyer suggested it, (b) he would have settled the claim in mediation, and (c) the settlement would have been better than the result of litigation. Demonstrating that the attorney's conduct fell below the standard expected of lawyers should not be difficult. But causation and damages will require considerable speculation.

Kosmo's Pool

4. **Chlorine for life.** Jack Childs has breached his legal obligations to his client by failing to communicate the terms of a settlement offer, as required under Rules 1.2 and 1.4. It may be that the offer is facially unacceptable. It may be that the attorney is confident that the client will reject the offer. But the decision to accept or reject the settlement is the client's, not the lawyer's. As a result, Jack Childs had an obligation to communicate the offer to Kosmo prior to rejecting it.

5. **Jack Childs's judgment.** No. Rule 1.2 and Rule 1.4 require a lawyer to keep the client sufficiently informed so as to make an informed decision about the case. Jack Childs has done so here, and Kosmo granted Jack Childs discretion to assess the merits of any possible offers. Of course, if the offer had been in any way different from the first offer—in particular, if it had been a better offer—and Jack Childs had any doubts about what Kosmo would think about an offer, the best practice would be for Jack Childs to take it back. But here, Kosmo has given Jack Childs this authority, and Jack Childs can exercise that authority without concern that he might be violating his ethical obligations. This case is unlike the *In re Lewis* case because here the client's authority was clearly communicated and was informed (as opposed to being only the product of boilerplate language in a retainer agreement). Of course, it may have been better practice for Childs to return to his client since Kosmo's preferences and thinking may have evolved over time. But under the circumstances, Childs's behavior satisfies his ethical duties to Kosmo.

6. **Kosmo's idea of justice.** Probably yes. Big-picture decisions, like whether to bring a claim or settle a case, are clearly the province of the client, and a lawyer must defer as to those decisions. Minor, tactical decisions along the way, like the sequence of depositions or the framing of a legal claim, are clearly the province of the lawyer. The decision to make a particular offer appears to fall somewhere between these two extremes. Rule 1.2(a), however, provides, "A lawyer shall abide by a client's decision whether to settle a matter." If the state in question has adopted the Model Rules, Jack Childs may have violated them.

7. **Kosmo's limit.** Maybe. Jack Childs certainly did not handle the situation as well as he probably should have. On these facts alone, however, it is unlikely that the Bar would decide that he breached a Model Rule. Still, to give effect to his client's desires about the settlement of the case, Jack Childs should have clarified the scope of Kosmo's parameters. In particular, he should have clarified whether Kosmo meant $50,000 net. If Jack Childs had any doubts, Rules 1.4 and 1.2 strongly suggest that he should have consulted with Kosmo.

8. **Jack Childs's judgment. part two.** Yes. The circumstances surrounding the case have likely changed since their last meeting, and Rule 1.4(a)(1) requires the lawyer to keep clients informed about such changes. The offer does not fall neatly within Kosmo's stated parameters of cash only, suggesting strongly that Jack Childs has an obligation to communicate them to Kosmo under Rule 1.4(a)(3) and to seek his input. Model Rules 1.2 and 1.4 require a lawyer to communicate offers of settlement and to defer to clients' judgments about them. Even if Jack Childs thought the offer was worth far more than $75,000 (which would net Kosmo $50,000 after deducting Jack Childs's fee), he should have communicated it to Kosmo.

Release the Hounds, but Not the Information

9. **Monty's initial plan.** Klutz cannot, under Rule 1.2(d), assist a client in committing a fraud. In this case, Barns has not yet made any representation, so no fraud yet exists. But it is easy to imagine the conversation Barns is planning, and it is clear that Barns intends to commit fraud. Ultimately, Klutz would be unable to represent Barns in the action if Barns goes forward with his initial plan. But withdrawal is a measure of last—not first—resort here.

   Klutz's first effort should almost certainly be to try to talk Barns out of his plan. For example, Klutz could explain that he would be unable to continue to represent Barns for the reasons stated above. Klutz could explain the legal consequences of Barns's planned fraud. Klutz could also explain that, as a practical matter, it is quite unlikely that the lie would even be successful, given the ease with which discovery is conducted. Klutz could discuss the "moral, economic, social, and political factors" that counsel against lying in this context. In short, before contemplating withdrawal, Klutz should counsel Barns against his proposed course of action.

10. **Monty Barns, man of his word.** Klutz cannot assist Barns in committing fraud. The problem is that Barns has made a statement that is clearly a knowing misrepresentation of material facts, intended to cause detrimental reliance. Model Rule 1.2(d) Comment 10 describes this sort of situation as "especially delicate." And yet, the bottom line is clear: Klutz cannot assist Barns to commit fraud.

    Before considering withdrawing from the representation, Klutz should probably take steps to see whether Barns will correct his misstatement, and therefore, not commit fraud. Klutz could easily ask to take a break in the mediation, so that he could consult with Barns. In a private meeting, Klutz could explain the situation to Barns and encourage him to recant the story he just made up. If Barns agrees and recants, no fraud has occurred because fraud requires detrimental reliance (which has not occurred yet because Leeza has taken no steps based on the account Barns just provided), so Klutz could continue to represent Barns.

    If Barns refuses, however, Klutz will be required to withdraw from representing him. Before the most recent amendments to Rule 1.6, there may have been a difficult question about whether Klutz could withdraw "quietly," providing no indication of the cause of his withdrawal to Leeza and her lawyer, or "noisily." The combination of the revised Rule 1.6(b)(2) and Comment [3] to Rule 4.1(b)—both of which appear earlier in this chapter—make it clear that an attorney may be required to disclose information in order to prevent a client's own fraudulent statements, Klutz must withdraw, and must do so in a way (sufficiently "noisily") that corrects Leeza's misunderstanding.

11. **Not a penny more!** Barns's statement to the mediator may or may not be strategically wise (and you as his lawyer may want to take a break to talk to him about this), but it certainly does not constitute fraud. Indeed, it is possible that something has caused Barns to change his mind about the most he is willing to offer, and there's nothing wrong with that from an ethical perspective. As we discussed in Chapter 3, statements about reservation values almost never constitute fraud, because they are deemed "mere puffery" rather than statements about material facts. Further, Barns owes no duty of candor (a heightened standard above merely avoiding fraud) to the mediator. Klutz, therefore, is not constrained by the Model Rules here. Klutz may counsel Barns to adopt a different tactic, but nothing in the ethical rules requires Klutz to do so.

CHAPTER 6

An Introduction to Mediation

§6.1 INTRODUCTION: DEFINITION(S) OF MEDIATION

Two former business partners in a dispute with each other hire an expert to come in and try to help them work out a resolution to the problem. A middle-school child on the playground intervenes to help two fourth graders talk about the differences that led them to start fighting. A diplomat from a neutral (or at least less conspicuously involved) country is called in to convene meetings between the heads of two warring countries. A retired judge is asked to help resolve a lawsuit between disputants who are about to file costly cross-appeals. A psychologist helps a divorcing couple work through challenging issues regarding their children.

Each of these scenarios is *probably* an example of mediation. We say probably because there is no single, uniform, accepted definition of mediation. It's not that various people haven't suggested definitions. Instead, this lack of uniformity stems from the reality that mediation can mean many different things in different contexts. Some definitions are narrow and are, therefore, often underinclusive. They describe mediation so narrowly that one or more of the scenarios described above would be excluded. Other definitions are broad and are therefore often unhelpfully vague. That is, they describe mediation in such broad terms that everything seemingly fits, even processes that probably should not belong under the mediation umbrella.

The good news is that, because the field has yet to settle on an accepted definition, you surely do not need to have a precise definition in your head. Still, it might be useful to have at least some definition from which to work, even if it is one that needs refinement or further explanation. The Uniform Mediation Act (UMA) §2(1) (see Appendix 1) declares that mediation is "a process in which [an individual] facilitates communication and negotiation between parties to assist them in reaching a voluntary agreement regarding their dispute."

That doesn't really tell us very much about what a mediator actually does. What kinds of things serve to facilitate communication or negotiation? Does a mediator act like a diplomat? Like a therapist? Like a schoolyard peacemaker? Like a judge? Like a trusted sounding board? Like an expert? The UMA definition (probably appropriately) omits answers to these questions. But of course, their absence from the formal definition does not mean these questions do not matter. They are, in fact, at the heart of mediation practice.

§6.2 MEDIATORS' APPROACHES OR STYLES

As you might imagine, because mediation does not have a universally accepted definition, no description could possibly capture exactly what happens in all mediations. Commentators have attempted to describe the steps or stages that commonly appear in mediation. Some of these descriptions are helpful (despite their lack of precision or uniformity) because they provide a sense of the kinds of things that might happen in a mediation. For example, some authors have suggested that mediation typically includes stages such as the mediator's introduction, opening remarks by parties, information gathering, issue identification, option generation, bargaining and negotiation, and, finally, agreement. Other descriptions articulate one or more of these stages differently. Still others envision an entirely different "typical" sequence.

A far more important question than merely which steps a mediator might take, and in what order, is the question of the mediator's fundamental approach to the mediation. How does the mediator conceive of their role? The answers to these questions capture the greatest differences among mediators.

Scholars and researchers have developed taxonomies of styles as a means of describing and comparing approaches to mediation. The models of mediation described by those taxonomies demonstrate recurring patterns of mediation practice, many of which are often used in mediation literature as shorthand to describe different styles that combine key characteristics. The purpose of articulating these models is to highlight the relevant and recurring patterns that are found in mediation practice by stripping away all but the very essence of those patterns. Models certainly do not capture all of the subtle variations that can and do exist. Moreover, the classification schemes that appear in most textbooks are not all-inclusive, but instead serve to contrast one style against others for purposes of highlighting common differences among mediators' practices.

In the next section, we describe three of the most commonly articulated styles—**facilitative, evaluative,** and **transformative**. Your textbook probably lists a number of other styles, and the professional literature includes many other articulations of mediator styles. We highlight these three because they are among the most commonly taught and because they provide a good basis for comparing many mediators' explicit or implicit choices.

One final note before diving into the different styles of mediation: Many mediators consider themselves to be (or are considered by others as) followers of a particular style of mediation. Such an identification usually reflects a preference or tendency to generally follow a particular set of practices. That does not mean, however, that a mediator always adopts that style in each mediation session to the exclusion of every other style. One of the key benefits of mediation is its flexibility; it is common for mediators to apply different styles depending on the situation or to switch styles during a mediation. This flexibility allows the mediator to use the most effective tools available in helping the parties reach their dispute resolution goal(s)—the reason(s) they turned to a mediator in the first place.

§6.2.1 Facilitative Mediation

The historical roots of **facilitative mediation** in the United States stem primarily from the community justice centers and alternative dispute resolution clinics of the 1960s and 1970s. In these centers, volunteer mediators aimed to facilitate communication between disputants in an impartial manner. The volunteers' training focused on communication skills and processes, rather than on the law or a particular industry practice.

Facilitative mediators continue in that spirit. With impartiality or neutrality as a prominent principle informing their practice, facilitative mediators endeavor to maintain a distance from the parties' positions and the likely outcomes if the dispute goes to litigation. The facilitator's neutral position is motivated by three considerations. First, facilitative mediators believe the parties are optimally situated to determine which outcome(s) best meets their needs. Second, facilitative mediators see a neutral stance as more likely to engender the parties' trust. Finally, facilitative mediators believe that this approach maximizes the effectiveness of the mediator's interventions because the mediator is focused exclusively on the parties' contributions and perspectives, rather than being simultaneously focused on other things (like the law or the merits of various options).

An idealized vision of facilitative mediation unfolds something like this: The facilitative mediator establishes a process by which the parties can gain an understanding of both their own interests and those of their counterpart. By asking questions, understanding the parties' perspectives, and reframing issues, the mediator helps the parties to discover shared interests and opportunities for mutually beneficial solutions. The mediator may accomplish this in a combination of joint sessions and private caucuses. During the process, the facilitative mediator resists crafting or assessing options and leaves those substantive decisions to the parties.

Facilitative mediation is an umbrella term that encompasses several variations. One prominent variation, for example, labeled "understanding-based" mediation, shares facilitative mediation's focus on mediator neutrality. Understanding-based mediators, however, shun the idea of meeting privately with one of the disputants, out of concern that information emerging in private might affect the mediator's neutrality at the expense of the parties' mutual understanding of the situation. As with facilitative mediation, understanding-based mediators encourage parties to establish their own standards for assessing the merits of possible outcomes. In other words, the parties need not resolve their dispute on the basis of what a court would do.

§6.2.2 Evaluative Mediation

Modeled at least in part on judicial settlement conferences, **evaluative mediations** have a very different focus than facilitative mediations. While facilitative mediations focus on exploring parties' interests and the possibility of creative settlement options, evaluative mediations focus primarily on the parties' alternatives to settlement.

At the heart of the theory underlying evaluative mediation is the idea that the mediators seek ways to support parties' informed decision making. If, for example, the parties are having a difficult time reaching settlement because one or both of the parties is overestimating how attractive litigation would be, an evaluative mediator will help the parties more accurately assess the risks and opportunities each faces in litigation. An evaluative mediator might even suggest a specific value (typically, although not exclusively, monetary) they would attach to the case in question. Once they have more accurate assessments of the prospect of litigation, the parties may discover that settlement appears more attractive.

As you might imagine, the distinction between facilitative and evaluative mediators' functions suggests a different personal or professional profile for each kind of mediator. An evaluative mediator typically comes to the mediation with expertise in the law or the particular substantive topic of the dispute. Disputants often choose a particular evaluative mediator for their specific knowledge in a given industry. The parties want and expect an evaluative mediator to apply that expertise to their dispute and provide guidance on their respective positions based on regulations and standards of practice in the particular field.

An idealized evaluative mediation is one in which the mediator (having assured themselves that the parties have incompatible perceptions of their litigation alternatives) works with each of the parties to unpack the multifaceted prospect of not reaching settlement. By working with the parties to see the risks in their positions, the holes in their arguments, and the costs embedded in their litigation strategies, the evaluative mediator aims to make the prospect of settlement more attractive (or at least to assure that the parties' perceptions of litigation are well tested). In some cases, after enough information has been exchanged, the parties may even ask the evaluative mediator to make her own assessment or evaluation of the range (or even the precise figure) that the mediator believes represents the value of the claim in question. This *evaluative* process is how an evaluative mediator earns her title.

A variation on evaluative mediation—one often associated with evaluation, though not always—is "directive mediation." Evaluative mediators focus on the prospect of nonsettlement and each party's perception of its BATNA. (See Chapter 1 for a reminder about the concept of a BATNA.) Directive mediators, by contrast, focus on promoting a particular settlement option. While an evaluative mediator might say, "Your alternative is much worse than you think," a directive mediator might say, "The following settlement option is a great idea." The two can, of course, be done in tandem, with the mediator applying both methods to say, "Because your alternative to settlement is so terrible, I think this option would be a great idea for you."

§6.2.3 Riskin's Grid: The Potential Relationship Between Facilitative and Evaluative Mediation

Leonard Riskin proposed a graphical representation of some of the variations among mediators, with a particular focus on the distinction between facilitative and evaluative approaches. The following is drawn from his article *Understanding Mediators' Orientations, Strategies and Techniques: A Grid for the Perplexed*[1] (an excerpt of which probably appears in your textbook).

Riskin presented the idea that mediators' styles of mediation could best be understood as points along a continuum rather than as specific stylistic buckets. Riskin placed the facilitative and evaluative styles on opposite poles of a vertical axis that represent the role of the mediator (recognizing that many mediators adopt traits from both of those styles). He juxtaposed the

1. Leonard Riskin, *Understanding Mediators' Orientations, Strategies, and Techniques: A Grid for the Perplexed*, 1 Harv. Negot. L. Rev. 7, 35 (1996).

vertical axis with a horizontal axis, representing the scope of the problem to be mediated, where a narrow scope limited the mediation to the immediate dispute (legal and financial issues), and a broad scope allowed for exploring a wider range of issues and solutions (including community, social, personal, and broader business issues). He divided the axes into four quadrants, hypothesizing that a mediator's style could be characterized as an XY coordinate falling within one of four fundamental classifications.

Role of Mediator
EVALUATIVE

Problem Definition **NARROW**		Problem Definition **BROAD**
Urges/pushes parties to accept narrow (position-based) settlement **Proposes** narrow (position-based) agreement **Predicts** court or other outcomes **Assesses** strengths and weaknesses of each side's case		**Urges/pushes** parties to accept broad (interest-based) settlement **Develops and proposes** broad (interest-based) agreement **Predicts** impact (on interests) of not settling **Educates self** about parties' interests
Helps parties evaluate proposals **Helps parties** develop and exchange narrow (position-based) proposals **Asks** about consequences of not settling **Asks** about likely court or other outcomes **Asks** about strengths and weaknesses of each side's case		**Helps parties** evaluate proposals **Helps parties** develop and exchange broad (interest-based) proposals **Helps parties** develop options that respond to interests **Helps parties** understand interests

Role of Mediator
FACILITATIVE

Riskin suggested that while mediators will adopt a number of styles based on the needs of particular contexts and parties, each mediator has a dominant style that falls within one of the four quadrants as evaluative-narrow, evaluative-broad, facilitative-narrow, or facilitative-broad. An evaluative-narrow orientation indicates that a mediator will assess the merits and deficiencies of each disputant's case, will push the parties to settle, and will limit the debate to the immediate dispute. An evaluative-broad mediator may be more likely to look for the interests underlying each party's position and any shared interests beyond the immediate dispute, but will counsel the parties on the relative merits of their own positions. A facilitative-narrow orientation suggests that the mediator will ask probing questions of the parties to help them develop an understanding of their positions, and will allow the parties to create a solution targeted at resolving the dispute at hand. Facilitative-broad mediators will work with the parties to uncover underlying interests beyond the formal parameters of the particular dispute and to explore options for settlement that serve those larger interests. The grid is obviously not all-inclusive, but its basic observation that mediators differ in their approaches and their conceptions of the problems can be helpful.

§6.2.4 Transformative Mediation

Transformative mediation, associated primarily with the works of Joseph Folger and Robert Baruch Bush, has perhaps the most idealistic objectives of any of the mediator approaches discussed here. Both facilitative and evaluative mediation have as their focus the resolution of a particular dispute. In some cases, the dispute may be quite narrow; in others, it may be broad. But in the end, both approaches are simply a means of finding resolution. Transformative mediation, by contrast, focuses on the disputants themselves and on their interactions, rather than on the specifics of a particular dispute (no matter how broadly defined). In the words of Bush and Folger, transformative mediation seeks to enable "moral growth" for the participants.

Underlying transformative mediation is the idea that conflict tends to cause disputants simultaneously to act badly and to feel as though they have lost some measure of control over their circumstances and their reactions. Transformative mediation seeks to empower individuals to pull themselves out of that negative spiral and to develop an ability to recognize the perspective of someone on the other end of a conflict.

An idealized vision of transformative mediation is one in which the parties and the mediator work primarily in joint sessions. The mediator will take the participants through exercises that allow them to recognize themselves as decent, moral people with their own intrinsic strengths and capacity to be compassionate. When the individual feels empowered, confidence grows, and the individual is able to listen, trust, and respect the other party, and potentially build a more productive relationship. Therefore, empowerment gives a party the ability to recognize and appreciate the values and perspectives of its counterparts. These two components, empowerment and recognition, are central to transformative mediation.

Transformative mediators focus primarily on the self-determination aspects of mediation. In transformative mediation, the participants are the sole owners of the process. The mediator not only refrains from pushing a particular substantive outcome, but also refrains from imposing a particular mediation process or agenda on the parties. Because success in transformative mediation is measured by the effect on the parties and their ability to deal with each other more effectively, transformative mediation treats the resolution of the immediate dispute as a second-order outcome instead of the primary goal.

§6.2.5 Facilitative, Evaluative, and Transformative Basic Logic

At the risk of oversimplifying each of these categories, we offer the following table. You will see that each of these basic approaches to mediation has an internal logic. If you believe that different parties in different contexts face a range of different mediation challenges, then it starts to make sense that there should be a range of different mediation approaches.

	Facilitative	**Evaluative**	**Transformative**
Primary Goal	Settlement	Settlement	Improve the quality of parties' interactions
Likely Processes	Joint sessions and private caucuses	Primarily private caucuses	Primarily joint sessions
Mediation Challenges Targeted	• Misunderstood or unexplored interests • Too few creative options • Bad communication	• Parties' unrealistic expectations about litigation alternatives • Parties' need for a "nudge" toward reasonable options	• Parties' inability to resolve problems independently • Bad working relationships • Poor understanding between the parties
Mediator Role(s)	• Ask open questions • Keep parties' conversations on track • Set agendas	• Assess the merits of each side's case • Explore possible alternatives to settlement • Urge particular outcomes	• Highlight opportunities for "empowerment" (parties taking charge) and "recognition" (parties seeing each other's perspective)
Typical Mediator Statements	• "Can you tell me more about your perception of what happened?" • "Why are you asking for. . . ?" • "What interests you about a resolution?" • "Do you have ideas about ways to address this set of interests?"	• "As I see it, you face the following risks and opportunities in litigation. . ." • "At trial, how do you plan to deal with the problematic fact that. . .?" • "What would be wrong with a settlement like. . .?"	• "How do you think we should spend our time together today?" • "What would be useful now?" • "What would you like to understand better about what they're saying?"
Primary Mediation Principle	Impartiality or neutrality	Informed consent	Self-determination

§6.3 BASIC PRINCIPLES OF MEDIATION

Every approach to dispute resolution has a set of internal assumptions. For example, modern litigation assumes the utility of adversarial perspectives, an impartial fact finder, and the application of broadly applicable laws to specific facts. Later in the book, you will see that arbitration emphasizes slightly different, although similar, assumptions. Mediation's internal, organizing assumptions are somewhat different, but it is important to recognize their centrality to mediation practice.

Model Standards of Conduct for Mediators

I. Self-Determination

A. A mediator shall conduct a mediation based on the principle of party self-determination. Self-determination is the act of coming to a voluntary, uncoerced decision in which each party makes free and informed choices as to process and outcome. Parties may exercise self-determination at any stage of a mediation, including mediator selection, process design, participation in or withdrawal from the process, and outcomes. . . .

2. A mediator cannot personally ensure that each party has made free and informed choices to reach particular decisions, but, where appropriate, a mediator should make the parties aware of the importance of consulting other professionals to help them make informed choices.

II. Impartiality

A. A mediator shall decline a mediation if the mediator cannot conduct it in an impartial manner. Impartiality means freedom from favoritism, bias, or prejudice.

B. A mediator shall conduct a mediation in an impartial manner and avoid conduct that gives the appearance of partiality. . . .

III. Conflicts of Interest

A. A mediator shall avoid a conflict of interest or the appearance of a conflict of interest during and after a mediation. A conflict of interest can arise from involvement by a mediator with the subject matter of the dispute or from any relationship between a mediator and any mediation participant, whether past or present, personal or professional, that reasonably raises a question of a mediator's impartiality. . . .

As you might expect, given the potential inadequacy of any single definition of mediation, no single articulation of mediation's bedrock principles has gained universal acceptance. One prominent articulation of mediation's fundamental values is the Model Standards of Conduct for Mediators, jointly produced by the American Arbitration Association, the American Bar Association, and the Association for Conflict Resolution. We have produced an excerpt here in a sidebar, and the full text appears in Appendix 2.

The Model Standards articulate a broad range of different principles. For our purposes, we think four are critical to understand. In this chapter, we explore three: impartiality, self-determination, and informed consent. The fourth, confidentiality, is the focus of Chapter 7.

§6.3.1 Impartiality (or Neutrality)

The academic literature regarding mediation almost always includes mention that the mediator is a third party who is **impartial or neutral**. Some use the terms impartial and neutral interchangeably. Others see the two terms as distinct and argue for one or the other as more accurately capturing this fundamental mediation principle.

The basic idea is that mediators should not have an interest in the substance or outcome of the dispute. In some ways, this concept parallels the principle that judges must not have any interest in the dispute and must not have any relationship with any of the parties that would cast doubt on the legitimacy of the judge's decisions. Although a mediator's function is different from a judge's, the two share this principle of neutrality.

It is easier to understand the concept of impartiality (or neutrality, if that is the preferred term) through examples of circumstances in which the principle would be violated. Impartiality would be violated if a mediator secretly owned stock in one of the companies participating in the mediation. Impartiality might be compromised if the mediator had a prior or ongoing relationship with one of the parties and failed to disclose it to the other parties. Similarly, impartiality would be implicated if a mediator stood to gain or lose financially, depending on the terms of the mediated settlement agreement. In these circumstances, we would fear that personal interests motivated the mediator's conduct in the mediation rather than the mediator's professional obligations to the disputants. This concept of impartiality also operates in typical conflict-of-interest situations. In *McKenzie Construction v. St. Croix Storage Corp.*, 961 F. Supp. 857 (D.V.I. 1997), for example, after the parties mediated, the plaintiff then tried to hire the law firm where the mediator worked in the subsequent litigation. The defendant's motion to disqualify the attorney and the law firm was successful.

Why does impartiality matter? One of the driving ideas behind mediation, reflected in the definition offered above, is that mediation is a form of facilitated negotiation. If the mediator has an interest in the outcome of these facilitated negotiations, the mediator essentially becomes an additional party to the negotiations, rather than serving the facilitator function.

Impartiality or neutrality comes in at least two different forms, each of which is significant in the context of mediation, and both of which are reflected in the Model Standards of Conduct for Mediators. (See Model Standards II and III.) One form is **externally perceived partiality**. This principle asks whether the circumstances would cause others to view the mediator as biased in some way. It does not ask whether the mediator is actually biased, just whether it appears that the mediator might be. Conflict of interest rules address this concern. This externally perceived neutrality is important to the legitimacy of the mediation process and, by extension, to the legitimacy of the outcomes mediation produces. The other form is **internally perceived partiality**, sometimes called "actual bias." This asks the more direct (though more difficult to measure objectively) question of whether the mediator holds biases or has preexisting incentives that affect the way the mediator will conduct the mediation.

In its strongest articulation, the mediation principle of impartiality or neutrality encompasses both of these forms. The ideal mediation, therefore, is one in which the mediator is free from any actual or perceived biases.

§6.3.2 Self-Determination

Self-determination—the idea that parties voluntarily determine the elements of an agreement—is a hallmark of mediation in virtually all articulations of mediation's foundational principles. Party autonomy is also one of mediation's primary attractions. The most fundamental distinction between mediation and arbitration (to overstate it only mildly) is that in mediation, parties decide whether to resolve the dispute and on what terms. By contrast, in arbitration and other adjudicative processes, parties cede the decision-making power to a third party. Self-determination is at the heart of this distinction.

A process lacking in self-determination may produce a settlement, but it will not be consistent with this fundamental principle of mediation. For example, a mediator with sufficient authority could threaten the parties so credibly as to force them to settle a case. ("I will leak horrible things about you and your company to the media if you do not agree to these terms," or "I know you haven't eaten in 18 hours, but you're not leaving this room until you agree to these terms.") Similarly, a mediator might be able to extract a commitment from a party who is incapacitated in some way (for example, if a party is a minor or is intoxicated). In these situations, the mediator might be performing one aspect of the job (settling the case) but does so at the expense of one of the core principles underlying the process—self-determination.

Why does self-determination matter? The first part of the answer rests in mediation's profoundly informal nature. Mediation involves few, if any, preset rules. It routinely involves freewheeling conversation unconstrained by structures like the Rules of Evidence. There are no formal motions and no record of the proceedings. Witnesses and other evidence are rarely involved to the same degree one would expect to find in court. All of this is what makes mediation attractive, at least to some. This informality is part of mediation's strength—provided the parties are still choosing whether and how to resolve the case. If, instead, the mediator is deciding, this informality, the ex parte communications, the unstructured conversation, and the other trappings of mediation become troublesome. We would never permit a judge to render decisions in those circumstances. Without self-determination, the mediator might be doing essentially the same thing.

A second reason for self-determination is that empowering the mediation parties to select settlement terms enables them to maximize the opportunity for value-creating outcomes. In short, the parties know best what they care about, what is good for them, and what they can live with. If a mediator—even a mediator with good intentions—takes this decision-making power away, the mediator strips mediation of one of its most attractive promises.

Self-determination has at least two different forms, both of which are important in mediation and both of which appear in the Model Standards of Conduct for Mediators. (See Model Standards I and VI.) The first is that the parties should be permitted to make decisions for themselves *without improper interference from the mediator*. This does not mean the mediator cannot make suggestions or point out potential implications of different outcomes, but at the end of the day, the mediator must permit the parties to make the final decision.

The second form of self-determination is that the parties must be free to decide for themselves, *free of improper influence from others*. In its purest form, mediation involves all of the relevant parties to a dispute, and each has the unimpaired capacity to make an independent decision about the substantive outcome of the mediation. This principle of self-determination articulates part of what makes mediation in a case involving intimate partner violence so troubling, for example. Part of the very nature of the cycle of abuse can cause an abused partner to be impaired in (or even incapable of) deciding for themselves. Recognizing this risk, most court programs have established surveys and other instruments to try to determine whether a particular context is marked by intimate partner violence. Some systems exclude all such cases from mediation, while others attempt to establish protocols (for example, requirements about having advocates, requirements of separate meeting spaces, etc.) aimed at protecting the self-determination of the parties involved.

§6.3.3 Informed Consent

The third fundamental principle of mediation is that the parties' decisions must be adequately informed. At the heart of any voluntary process is the idea of meaningful choice. But for that choice to be meaningful, it must be adequately informed.

Not all processes that lead to agreement necessarily involve **informed consent**. Railroading a party into a particular process or a particular agreement is anathema to the idea of informed consent. For example, if the mediator precluded the parties from having a meaningful opportunity to review the terms of a potential settlement, informed consent would be threatened. ("I've put together a possible settlement package, involving multiple, complex pieces. You have five minutes to decide. And no, we're not waiting for your lawyer's opinion about all of this.")

Why does informed consent matter in mediation? Virtually all of the benefits mediation touts depend on the idea that the parties, at the end of the process, make good decisions. If the parties are unable to make high-quality decisions for themselves in mediation, then litigation or some other adjudicative process might be more appropriate. Mediation depends on giving parties the opportunity to make good decisions, and good decisions depend on the parties having adequate information.

Like the first two principles we mention above, informed consent involves at least two different components, both of which appear in the Model Standards of Conduct for Mediators. (See Model Standards I and VI.) The first component suggests that parties should make informed choices as to the mediation process. At a minimum, therefore, parties should understand the nature of mediation enough to consent to participating in it. (There is a stronger version of this principle that might suggest that parties should have some say in how a mediation process unfolds, but that is not a consensus view within the mediation literature.) Parties enter into mediations through a variety of mechanisms. In some contexts, the parties initiate mediation independently, and in others, court systems encourage or even require parties to attempt mediation. Even in circumstances in which mediation is mandatory, disputants are never required to settle the case. At most, disputants can be ordered to try mediation. (We discuss further what courts can and cannot order in Chapter 11.) And to try mediation, they must understand at least the fundamental aspects of the mediation process, including the role of the mediator. The second component of informed consent is that parties should be informed as to the substance of any possible agreement, such that they each understand the implications of the deal.

In its ideal form, each of the parties to a mediation understands and agrees to try mediation as a dispute resolution process. Each party understands their alternatives to settlement (recall that each party has a BATNA, as outlined in Chapter 1 on Negotiation), and each party understands the implications of any settlement reached in the mediation.

In the chart below, we summarize these important mediation principles. Recall, of course, that these are not the only three principles one might find in an articulation of mediation's goals. They are, however, the three most likely to be implicated in difficult or important ethical dilemmas in mediation practice.

Three Principles of Mediation[2]

Impartiality or Neutrality	Self-Determination	Informed Consent
External Impartiality	*Mediator Influence*	*Process Decisions*
Mediator is perceived as having no stake in the outcome.	Each party can decide free from interference by the mediator.	Each party understands and agrees to the mediation process.
Internal Impartiality	*Other Influence*	*Substantive Decisions*
Mediator does not believe they are biased for or against either party.	Each party can decide free from outside interference.	Each party understands the substantive implications of possible outcomes.

§6.4 QUALITY CONTROL IN MEDIATION

Unlike attorneys or doctors (or manicurists, for that matter), mediators do not require a license to provide their services. Doctors maintain a monopoly on providing certain medical services. Lawyers have a monopoly on providing legal advice to clients. But there are no general restrictions on who can be a mediator, and therefore, no restrictions on who can provide mediation (or mediation-like) services.

Of course, as a practical matter, not everyone can make a living as a mediator. Hanging a shingle announcing one's availability does not guarantee clients. In theory, one must be good (or at least appear good) to attract customers.

Still, the question remains: How can we be assured that those who are providing their services as mediators do so competently? Because no monopoly exists, we cannot rely on a quality-linked barrier to entry into

2. This construction of foundational mediation principles is drawn from Jamie Henikoff and Michael Moffitt, *Remodeling the Model Standards of Conduct for Mediators*, 2 Harv. Negot. L. Rev. 87 (1997).

the market. Doctors must pass Boards. Lawyers must pass the Bar. Mediators have no equivalent.

Below we examine three potential avenues for assuring the quality of mediator services—certification, ethics codes, and liability. As you will see, none of these is foolproof or sufficient to guarantee quality on its own. But these three avenues are not mutually exclusive, and for the moment at least, they represent the bulk of the formal mechanisms available to help mediation consumers know that they will receive quality services.

§6.4.1 Certification or Credentialing

Because mediation is not a practice for which a monopoly has been established, no license is required. But the basic instinct behind licensure—identifying a pool of people deemed qualified and appropriate to practice—has an important place in mediation. Certification or credentialing systems are vehicles for accomplishing these goals. There are two fundamental types of certification or credentialing systems: those linked to organizational affiliation and those linked to the institutions that receive mediation cases. We describe each briefly below.

Organizational affiliation credentials are established, as the name suggests, by organizations with which some mediators might want to be affiliated. As a quality control mechanism, for example, a professional mediators' association might require its members to meet certain standards (perhaps a certain level of experience, a certain kind of education, or even performance on a certain kind of assessment mechanism). The idea is that practicing mediators would want to be members of these organizations because they provide direct benefits in terms of conferences, resources, or referrals, or because the market of mediation consumers recognizes and values membership ("People will hire me because I can put this group's name on my website"). Of course, not all organizations' membership requirements are actual proxies for mediator quality. Some professional organizations' membership requirements begin and end with a prospective member's ability and willingness to pay annual dues. Still, recognizing that the state is not in a position to monitor the behavior of thousands of mediators, one mechanism for assuring mediator quality involves relying on private mediation organizations to do some initial screening by establishing membership standards.

Institutions that receive cases and assign them to a mediator provide another form of quality control. These institutions may, for example, conduct an initial screening review to determine who is eligible to receive their cases or require certain training. Much like organizational credentials, the basis for exclusion and inclusion is almost entirely at the discretion of the organization (including court programs). They could consider experience, professional training, or whatever else they want to determine which mediators receive the "stamp of approval." The difference is that these organizations are the source of potential cases. As a result, we might expect that it would be that much more attractive for a mediator to strive to attain whatever membership standards the organization sets.

For example, a court-affiliated mediation program could be the source of cases for mediators. Thousands of court mediation programs around the country *do* set certain standards (although there is considerable variation among the programs on just what they want to see in a mediator). If a mediator fails to meet the standards of a mediation program, the mediator cannot receive cases through that particular source. Many sources of cases are governmental (court systems, social service agencies, and the like), though some are private or quasi-private. The United States Postal Service, for example, sets standards for the large cadre of mediators it employs to deal with employee disputes.

§6.4.2 Ethics Codes

We have already described some of the provisions of the Model Standards of Conduct for Mediators, the most widely recognized mediator ethics code. Many other ethics codes exist as well. Some are specific to a particular type of mediation practice, for example, the Standards of Practice for Family and Divorce Mediation promulgated by the Association of Family and Conciliation Courts (AFCC). Others are specific to organizations. For example, the International Institute for Conflict Prevention & Resolution's Model Rule of Professional Conduct for the Lawyer as Third Party Neutral theoretically governs all of the mediators on its rosters.

An ethics code may enhance mediator quality control because it addresses mediators' *practices* rather than simply their qualifications. Well-trained, experienced mediators can make mistakes. If the only quality control mechanism were credentialing, those mistakes would not be addressed. However, interpretation and enforcement are the major challenges for mediator ethics codes, as currently formulated. Lawyers typically understand legal ethics codes better than do mediators. This is, in part, because the Bar regularly hears complaints and publishes what amount to explanations of legal ethics rules. Few equivalents exist in mediation, although some states have grievance procedures for certain mediator misconduct. Further, legal ethics have enforcement mechanisms that make it unlikely a practitioner would ignore their provisions. If you violate legal ethics, you can be disbarred. If you violate mediation ethics provisions, however, the threat is more nebulous: Perhaps you'll be kicked out of the organization that promulgated the ethical rules, but maybe not. Because a mediation monopoly does not exist, even if you are kicked out, you can continue to mediate as long as you can continue to attract clients.

Despite these challenges associated with mediation ethics codes, their provisions are important to understand. In addition to the three fundamental principles described above, which appear in some form in virtually all ethics codes, most codes also include a set of rules that roughly parallel legal ethics topics (like conflicts of interest, advertising, and the boundaries on representation). A look at the headings of the Model Standards is informative.

Model Standards of Conduct for Mediators

Table of Contents

I. Self-Determination
II. Impartiality
III. Conflicts of Interest
IV. Competence
V. Confidentiality
VI. Quality of the Process
VII. Advertising and Solicitation
VIII. Fees and Other Charges
IX. Advancement of Mediation Practice

Mediators who are also lawyers must be aware that some provisions of legal ethics codes touch on the practice of mediation. Most prominently, the ABA Model Rule of Professional Conduct 2.4(b) provides that "[a] lawyer serving as a third-party neutral shall inform unrepresented parties that the lawyer is not representing them. When the lawyer knows or reasonably should know that a party does not understand the lawyer's role in the matter, the lawyer shall explain the difference between the lawyer's role as a third-party neutral and a lawyer's role as one who represents a client." Giving bad legal advice in the course of a mediation, for example, could expose a lawyer to sanctions based on the *giving* of the advice (if to one party, but not the other), based on the *practice* of law (if the lawyer is not authorized in that jurisdiction anyway), and based on the *quality* of advice (if following the advice harms the client, the client could sue for malpractice).

§6.4.3 Private Liability

With most kinds of professional services—even those for which no professional monopoly exists—if a consumer receives a substandard product, the consumer may be able to file a civil lawsuit against the service provider.

Private liability for malpractice is a threat that hangs over the head of most service providers.[2] In theory, the same should be true of mediators. The reality in practice, however, is that most mediators operate without any significant exposure to malpractice liability. One scholar has estimated that far, far fewer than 1 percent of mediation cases ever results in a complaint, and that even fewer complaints result in a verdict against a mediator. At least three factors contribute to this dynamic: mediator immunity, vague standards of care, and lack of proof for causation and damages. In some contexts, mediation confidentiality (which we cover in Chapter 7) creates an additional roadblock.

§6.4.3.1 Immunity

Some mediators operate without any fear of private liability for their actions as mediators because they enjoy immunity. This immunity can come in one of three forms: quasi-judicial immunity, qualified immunity, and contractual waivers.

Quasi-judicial immunity is a common law form of immunity that shields mediators from suits alleging harm. Quasi-judicial immunity exists because we want judges to perform their job without the fear that one of their decisions might offend a party enough that the party would sue the judge. The theory behind extending quasi-judicial immunity to mediators is, as the name suggests, that mediators operate in a quasi-judicial capacity and therefore need the same kind of protections against lawsuits as judges. The most prominent case on this point is *Wagshal v. Foster*, 28 F.3d 1249 (D.C. Cir. 1994). In that case, the court appointed Foster to serve as a "neutral case evaluator" to try to settle Wagshal's claim. After a failed effort at settlement, Foster wrote the presiding judge a letter indicating that the case "can and should be settled if the parties are willing to act reasonably," and recommended that the judge order Wagshal, in particular, to mediate "in good faith." Wagshal subsequently settled his original claim, but then sued Foster, claiming that the letter to the judge had violated Wagshal's rights and had forced him to settle improperly. The court found that Foster's functions were sufficiently comparable to those of a judge to extend quasi-judicial immunity. Without much explanation, the court in *Wagshal* then also extended this logic to mediators as well as case evaluators. In some jurisdictions, therefore, mediators enjoy this common law immunity.

Instead of quasi-judicial immunity, some jurisdictions have established statutory **qualified immunity** for mediators. As the name suggests, qualified immunity is limited (or "qualified"), but typically, it only excludes

---

2. See Art Hinshaw, *Regulating Mediators*, 21 Harv. Negot. L. Rev. 163 (2016); Michael Moffitt, *Suing Mediators*, B.U. L. Rev. 147 (2003); Michael Moffitt, *Ten Ways to Get Sued: A Guide for Mediators*, 8 Harv. Negot. L. Rev. 81 (2003).

liability for injuries resulting from egregious acts like intentional torts. A mediator with qualified immunity, therefore, operates largely free of the threat of private liability.

Wyoming and Florida statutes provide two examples of statutory immunity for mediators. According to Wyoming Statutes Annotated §1-43-104 (2019), "mediators are immune from civil liability for any good faith act or omission within the scope of the performance of their powers and duties." Similarly, Florida Statutes §44-107(2) (2018) provides that, except in cases of bad faith or malice, "a person serving as a mediator in any non-court ordered mediation shall have immunity from liability arising from the performance of that person's duties while acting within the scope of the mediation function."

A third source of immunity can come in the form of a **contractual waiver**. ("The parties hereby waive any and all current or future claims against the mediator for alleged negligence or malpractice stemming from this mediation. . . .") Each jurisdiction handles the enforceability of such provisions differently, and it is beyond the scope of this text to survey those variations. You should know, however, that some mediator contracts include language that at least *purports* to serve the function of shielding the mediator from liability for any mediation conduct.

§6.4.3.2 Standards of Care

Most mediators' contracts contain vague commitments about exactly what the mediator will and will not be doing, so these contracts rarely serve as the basis for a complaint against a mediator. (How would one assess a claim that a mediator had not lived up to their promise to "try to help facilitate communications between the parties in order to explore the potential of voluntary settlement" or something similarly broad?) Instead, most complaints against a mediator more closely resemble tort-based malpractice claims of the sort filed against other kinds of service providers.

As with a negligence-based malpractice case against any other kind of service provider, a plaintiff alleging mediator malpractice must show that the mediator's conduct failed to meet the standard of care for professionals in that area. A doctor who mistakenly leaves a surgical instrument in a patient or a lawyer who misses filing deadlines, causing a case to be dismissed, each clearly violates this standard. But what could a mediator do that would clearly violate mediation's standards of practice?

Some mediator actions, of course, would fall below a generally accepted standard of care: a mediator who shows up intoxicated, a mediator who forgets to show up at all, or a mediator who violates the specific terms of the mediation agreement. In these kinds of cases, an aggrieved party would have little difficulty demonstrating that the mediator's conduct fell short of that which is required. Similarly, if a mediator fails to disclose a known conflict of interest and the state has adopted a version of the Uniform Mediation Act (which explicitly requires such disclosures), the mediator will have breached an established duty of care.

In some cases, the terms of a mediator's contract or agreement to mediate may create an explicit or implied standard of care or duty. The case of *Furia v. Helm*, 111 Cal. App. 4th 945 (Ct. App. 2003), demonstrates this point. The Levins were homeowners who were in a dispute with Furia, their general contractor. Helm was the attorney representing the Levins. Helm offered to serve as a mediator between the Levins and Furia. (That offer alone should be raising questions in your mind, as you read this.) Although Helm's engagement letter made it clear that he would represent the Levins in the event of an adversarial proceeding, Helm also said to Furia that he would "fairly mediate. . . , listen to all sides equally, and offer ideas and a perspective that respects the needs and interests of all concerned." Contrary to the mediation agreement described above, Helm separately sent the Levins a memo in which he assured them that he was "not going to be truly neutral during our efforts to negotiate an agreement." Not surprisingly, Furia sued Helm for malpractice, citing a conflict of interests. The court held that:

> Helm assumed obligations to Furia not because Helm was representing the Levins, but because Helm entered an express agreement with Furia to serve as a mediator in his controversy with the Levins. We reiterate that we do not here determine whether, consistent with his obligations to the Levins, Helm properly could agree to serve as a neutral mediator. The fact is that he did so agree and, having done so, he assumed certain obligations to those he agreed to serve.

Consistent with the variations in approach or style we described in §6.2, however, mediation has fewer "generally accepted" practices than one might imagine. A mediator might evaluate the merits of a legal dispute (evaluative mediation) or not (facilitative mediation). A mediator might try to move the parties toward settlement (evaluative or facilitative mediation) or not (transformative mediation). She might ask open-ended questions or specific questions, keep the parties together or meet with them separately. In short, an unhappy party will have a challenge in demonstrating that the mediator's actions were seen as unacceptable among the community of people who practice mediation, given the great variety of actions endorsed by that community.

§6.4.3.3 Causation and Damages

Proving that a mediator breached a duty of care is worthwhile (in practical terms) only if an unhappy party can demonstrate that the mediator's actions also caused compensable injury. This may not be difficult. ("The mediator never showed up to our scheduled meeting, causing me to lose the entire day and incur the following expenses.") If the mediator's conduct allegedly impacted the settlement of the case, the prospect of significant damages may arise. For example, "We didn't settle, but with a competent mediator we would have." Or, "We settled, but I now believe I could have done better, and it's the mediator's fault."

An unhappy mediation party in either of those circumstances faces the challenge of demonstrating causation and damages. How can you prove that a different mediator's action would have produced a settlement or a different settlement? How can the plaintiff avoid a finding that it was the plaintiff who signed the settlement agreement, not the mediator? How can the plaintiff establish the difference between what the other party was willing to do in the mediation that actually took place—as opposed to what the plaintiff imagines would have taken place if the mediation had unfolded the way the plaintiff now wishes? The highly speculative nature of these inquiries explains, in part, why successful malpractice actions against mediators are so uncommon. As a result, there is still not a landmark case in which a mediator was successfully sued for mediation malpractice.

Examples

The State of the Estate

Following their parents' untimely death, three brothers (Greg, Peter, and Bobby) find themselves locked in a bitter dispute over the division of the estate. During the decade prior to his parents' death, Bobby was largely estranged from the family. Greg, perpetually cash-strapped, had spent most of those years caring for his parents. Peter's acting career had delivered him some fame and even greater fortune.

Their parents' will included a provision containing an unorthodox division of the estate that may make the will vulnerable to a legal challenge. The three brothers met briefly to discuss whether they could agree on a division of the assets without resorting to litigation. During that meeting, Greg insisted that "a court would give basically all of it to me." Bobby laughed and lobbed personal insults at his older brothers. Peter chided both of them for "inventing things to fight about. Some things never change." When Peter suggested that this might be about something more than the money, Greg and Bobby rolled their eyes, and the meeting quickly ended.

Assume that mediators in their area accurately describe themselves as adopting one of the three styles or approaches (facilitative, evaluative, transformative) described above. In the context of this dispute, what potential benefits might the parties see if they select a mediator who is

1a. **facilitative** in her approach?

1b. **evaluative** in her approach?

1c. **transformative** in her approach?

1d. No approach to mediation is perfect in every case, and the selection of a mediator (or an approach to mediation) typically involves tradeoffs. Name at least one potential downside to each of the approaches listed above in this case.

The Discriminating Palate

Henri Leduc, the owner of an upscale restaurant named The Discriminating Palate, has a notorious temper and an impeccable record as an entrepreneur. Recently, he created a new maître d' position. Leduc hired an employee from outside of the restaurant rather than promoting someone from within. Cecilia Cervantes, a longtime employee at The Discriminating Palate, had applied for the position and was deeply disappointed not to have been given the promotion. Cervantes spoke with Leduc shortly after the decision was announced, and the conversation only seemed to make Cervantes angrier. She has indicated an intention to file a lawsuit against Leduc and The Discriminating Palate, alleging gender discrimination.

Pursuant to the restaurant's employee handbook, Cervantes and Leduc are obligated to "attempt" mediation first. They agreed on a mediator and submitted an initial brief outlining the facts above. At the outset of the mediation, therefore, the mediator knows only a limited amount of information about the case and the parties.

What kinds of questions might the mediator ask at the outset, if the mediator is

2a. **facilitative** in her approach?

2b. **evaluative** in her approach?

2c. **transformative** in her approach?

A Mediation Disaster, *Yes*, but What *Kind* of Disaster?

Romeo and Juliet are recent immigrants, neither of whom speaks English very well. After just under two years of marriage, they conclude that divorce is the only viable option for their troubled relationship. Each hires an attorney, and through those attorneys, they agree to try mediation.

At the mediation session, which takes place in English, Juliet's attorney indicates that she will be speaking on behalf of Juliet, and Juliet sits in a corner and begins to read a book. Meanwhile, Romeo's attorney fails to show up. After waiting for several minutes, the mediator says to Romeo, "Look, either we start now, or I'll report to the judge that you reneged on your promise to try mediation. And that's not going to look good for you." Romeo protests that he is not prepared "for to making the law arguments" but eventually agrees to follow the mediator and the others into the mediation room.

As the mediation unfolds, Juliet's attorney does virtually all of the talking. She lays out the basics of her legal case, and each time Romeo attempts to interject a point, she talks over him. The mediator, meanwhile, sits back and periodically nods at Juliet's attorney's statements.

After almost an hour of this, Romeo's attorney walks into the conference room. Upon seeing the mediator, Romeo's attorney's eyes light up and she laughs. She and the mediator rush to each other, hug, and begin talking about how "it's been too long since we've gone fishing."

At that point, both Romeo and Juliet sit back and watch the lawyers haggle, not understanding much of what is being discussed. Eventually, the mediator produces a coin from his pocket, flips it, and announces the result. One attorney shrugs, and the other looks pleased. Shortly after, the three announce that a final agreement has been reached, and the lawyers tell their clients to sign it.

3. **Problems to explore.** With reference to the basic principles of mediation, describe the potential problems with the sequence of events described above.

A Mediation Dilemma?

Two former business partners, Cagney and Lacey, have a dispute involving the noncompete clause appearing in their partnership agreement. They agree to try mediation early in the life of the dispute on the theory that it might be possible to resolve things before attorneys' fees become astronomical.

Cagney appears at the mediation with her lawyer. At the outset, Lacey speaks with the mediator privately and says, "I didn't know she was going to bring an attorney. I haven't hired one. I thought this was supposed to be informal. Should I go ahead with the mediation?" The mediator assures Lacey that she is not required to have an attorney to participate, but that she is free to consult one at any point. Lacey agrees to go ahead with the mediation session.

During the mediation session, Cagney's attorney takes an aggressive posture toward Lacey, outlining what he describes as the "airtight" nature of the noncompete clause. The lawyer also asserts that Cagney would be entitled to a vast range of different remedial options, including not only indefinite injunctive relief, but also punitive damages. Lacey appears shaken by the news, but after about an hour, seems convinced and appears on the verge of agreeing to drop the matter altogether.

The mediator, an attorney with extensive experience practicing employment law in this jurisdiction, is virtually positive that Cagney's lawyer has dramatically misstated the law in this case. The mediator knows that no court in the state has ever granted punitive damages in such a case, that no court in the state has granted an indefinite injunction in such a case, and that the liquidated damages figure claimed by Cagney would almost certainly be stricken under the relevant state standards. But Lacey appears to know none of this.

4a. **Doing nothing.** If the mediator facilitated the discussions through to conclusion, such that Lacey signed Cagney's attorney's proposed settlement, what principle(s) of mediation might be implicated?

4b. **Providing legal advice.** If the mediator met privately with Lacey and advised her that Cagney's lawyer's assessment of the case is flawed, what principle(s) of mediation might be implicated?

4c. **Recommending legal advice.** If the mediator met privately with Lacey and advised her to seek legal advice before accepting Cagney's lawyer's proposal, what principle(s) of mediation might be implicated?

The Trouble with "Working It Out"

The parties in a relatively simple slip-and-fall case mutually consent to having their dispute referred to a court-affiliated mediator. The mediator gathers the disputants into a conference room and asks them, jointly, "Why can't you work this out?" Each party carefully describes the facts underlying the dispute, highlighting the major points of their disagreement. The mediator responds by saying, "Okay, but why can't you work this out?" The parties explain further their prior efforts at settlement, indicating that they feel stuck. This repeats itself twice more, and after more than an hour, the mediator says, "As I see it, you all really should be working it out." The parties storm out of the mediation, furious at having wasted their time. They agree jointly to file a complaint against the mediator.

5. **Likely trouble?** Provide an assessment of the strengths and weaknesses of the parties' potential legal claims against the mediator.

Neighborly Love

Two neighbors, Fred and Barney, have had a multiyear feud over issues ranging from noise and yard maintenance to property boundaries and easements. One day, after a tense conversation in their shared driveway, they agreed that they should hire a mediator to try to resolve "everything." They did some research and ultimately agreed to hire Morton, a mediator whose business card and website include the slogan "Pushy But Effective Mediation."

During the mediation, to which neither party brought an attorney, Fred and Barney outlined the substance of their various grievances against each other. They made considerable progress and began drafting what they called an "omnibus settlement agreement." Barney was lobbying to include a revision to the language regarding an easement involving both properties. Fred opposed the revision to the language, and the entire mediation appeared on the brink of derailing.

Morton pulled Barney into a private caucus and said, "Listen, Barney. Give it up. The easement language you're pushing for is utterly unenforceable. There's a city ordinance directly on point, and the courts have weighed in as well. It's time to end this now." Barney expressed surprise indicating that he had drawn the language from a contract given to him by a lawyer friend. Morton said, "Look, so far, I haven't told Fred about the enforceability problem. I'll stay silent if you go back in there and tell him you'll drop the easement request if he'll give you the language you want about shrubbery. That should end the whole thing. Otherwise, I'll tell Fred about the law, and you'll get neither." Barney reluctantly agreed, and the mediation quickly produced a settlement on the terms Morton outlined.

A few days after the agreement was finalized, Barney learned from a lawyer friend of his that Morton's legal opinion was completely unfounded. No city ordinance exists, and there have been no recent court cases involving easements of the sort Barney was proposing. Barney is livid and wants to go after Morton.

6. **Exposure.** What potential avenues might Barney have for bringing a complaint against Morton? What would be the strengths and weaknesses of each of those avenues?

Explanations

The State of the Estate

1a. **Facilitative.** A mediator who adopts a facilitative approach to the mediation often focuses on promoting understanding of each side's interests and the prospect of creative problem solving as a means of resolving the dispute. Each of the brothers comes to the dispute with different resources, and each probably has different interests and priorities. As described in Chapter 1, these kinds of differences often lend themselves to crafting value-creating settlement options. A facilitative mediator, by unearthing each party's interests and by improving the parties' communication about possible options, might help them discover a more elegant solution to the problem than they might otherwise find. In some contexts, particularly given the prospect of ongoing (familial) relationships here, a facilitative mediator's focus on potential solutions beyond those within a court's authority to impose, might be helpful. A facilitative mediator may also help the parties overcome communication difficulties and improve their relationship so that future conflict is handled more effectively.

1b. **Evaluative.** If everyone agreed on how the matter would be resolved in court, the dispute might be less challenging to resolve. In this case, however, Greg believes he would get "basically all of it" in court, and the others apparently disagree. An evaluative mediator might be able to address the brothers' assessments of their alternatives to an agreement. Using the terminology from Chapter 1, the evaluative mediator would help them assess the strengths of their BATNAs. The evaluative mediator might also be able to shed light on the likelihood that Greg's case assessment is accurate. Extended litigation on the matter risks burning through the assets of the estate, and an evaluative mediator may help to hasten the parties' discovery of an acceptable settlement option.

1c. **Transformative.** None of the brothers is immune to the costs of their difficult relationship. These brothers act as though they dislike each other, and they are apparently not skilled at solving problems together. Even so, they are going to remain brothers forever. So there is some reason to think that they would benefit from improving their relationship. With her focus on giving the parties an opportunity to (re)craft their interactions and to find opportunities to demonstrate that they recognize each other's experiences, a transformative mediator might help in that relationship-mending process.

1d. **Tradeoffs.** One potential risk of adopting a **facilitative** approach in this case is the risk that the settlement discussions may be futile, so long as Greg believes he has a legal entitlement to the entire estate. Unless Greg's interests are not primary financial, there is a risk that he will view his alternatives to settlements as more attractive. A potential risk of an **evaluative** approach is that it may over-emphasize questions of legal entitlement, missing the parties' relational and other interests. Particularly for mediators with legal training, in a context where the parties are represented by counsel, there is a risk that the mediation conversations will be about the law, rather than about creative settlement options. A potential risk of **transformative** mediation is that it places so much of the decision-making in the hands of the parties that they may risk replicating problematic familial modes of interaction. The parties may, in this case, simply want to resolve the specific issue at hand, and the transformative approach may invite them into more complex dynamics than the mediator or the parties' lawyers may recognize.

The Discriminating Palate

2a. **A mediator with a facilitative approach** would be most inclined toward exploring opportunities for improving the parties' communication and finding problem-solving opportunities. To that end, a facilitative mediator would probably want to explore each party's perception of the events that led to the dispute underlying the mediation—for purposes of understanding what might motivate the disputants in their search for a settlement. Follow-up questions would most likely involve an exploration of each party's interests, their relative priorities among issues, and their ideas about possible avenues for settlement. What is most important to Cervantes? What kind of relationship would Leduc want with Cervantes in the future?

2b. **A mediator with an evaluative approach** would be most inclined toward exploring each party's perceptions of what a court might do in this case. To that end, like a facilitative mediator, an evaluative mediator would probably want to explore each party's perception of the events that led to the dispute underlying the mediation. But unlike the facilitative mediator, the evaluative mediator would likely explore these perceptions for the purpose of assessing the extent to which the facts establish a right to relief or a defense under the relevant law. Follow-up questions would most likely involve an exploration of whichever aspects of the legal case the mediator deems to be most important to assess accurately the risks and opportunities this case would present in litigation. Maybe the case will hinge on what Leduc told Cervantes. Maybe it will hinge on Cervantes's qualifications. Maybe the dispute over damages will be informed by Cervantes's experiences in the job market. In other words, the evaluative mediator will focus on whatever information she needs to collect in order to conduct a thorough assessment.

2c. **A mediator with a transformative approach** would be most inclined to invite the parties to suggest an agenda or sequence of topics for discussion in the mediation. The mediator might invite—but not force—conversation about each party's perception of the events that led to the dispute underlying the mediation. The aim of doing so, however, would not necessarily be the resolution of the narrow dispute in question. Instead, quite conceivably, the mediator's focus would be largely or entirely on the parties themselves or on their relationship. How well does Leduc recognize Cervantes's experience of their interactions? How well does she understand his? Are there ways of helping one or both of the parties to see more opportunities to make decisions for themselves about the mediation process and any eventual decisions that might emerge from that process? The mediator's role, in short, will be to help the parties to discover opportunities to expand their understanding of each other and of their own capacity to manage their differences.

A Mediation Disaster, *Yes*, but What *Kind* of Disaster?

3. **Problems to explore.** This is a debacle of a mediation, by many measures. Each of the three primary principles of mediation was potentially offended by one or more of these events.

   Impartiality. Two events during this sequence suggest at least the prospect of an impartiality problem. The first, and most glaring, is the hug exchanged between the mediator and one of the parties' attorneys. Neither the Model Standards of Conduct for Mediators nor any other mediation ethics codes of which we are aware prohibits a mediator from knowing one or more of the mediation participants, or even from having a relationship with them. The Model Standards demand, however, impartiality and freedom from conflicts of interest. As to the mediator's perception of his own bias, Model Standard II provides, "If at any time, a mediator is unable to conduct a mediation in an impartial manner, the mediator shall withdraw." It defines impartiality as "freedom from favoritism, bias, or prejudice." Because the mediator continued with the mediation, we are left to presume that the mediator believed he could mediate without any **actual partiality or bias**. The Model Standards do not stop there, however. Model Standard III provides, "A mediator shall disclose, as soon as practicable, all actual and potential conflicts of interest that are reasonably known to the mediator and could reasonably be seen as raising a question about the mediator's impartiality." (Model Standard III(C).) Here, the obvious prior relationship creates a **risk of perceived partiality or bias**. Perhaps the mediator thought the hug substituted for disclosure, but the question of the mediator's partiality is clearly appropriate. The mediator should have explained the context of the relationship between the mediator and Romeo's attorney and received Juliet's approval before continuing with the mediation.

   A second occurrence could—but probably does not—raise questions about impartiality in this case. As Juliet's attorney spoke, the mediator is said to have been "nodding." Clearly, there is some point at which a mediator might be so wholly and evidently favoring one side's arguments over the other's that the principle of impartiality would be implicated. At the same time, a mediator need not sit idly, stone-faced, unmoved, or unaffected by any of the things the parties are saying during a mediation. Here, the mediator's responses could, in context, be an example of bias, or they could be an example of good listening. We don't have enough information here to condemn the mediator for partiality.

   Informed consent. At the outset, Romeo appears not even to understand the basic nature of the mediation process to which he is being invited. To the extent he is **inadequately informed about the process**, we should be concerned about whether he could reasonably offer informed consent to participate in the mediation at all.

Because both parties have limited ability to speak the language used in the mediation, we would question the degree to which either could have **adequate information about the substance of the agreement** to consent to it knowingly. If the parties were unrepresented, then this would clearly be an issue. The presence of counsel *might* serve to cleanse the process and the agreement of any flaws, in some circumstances. But the circumstance would at least implicate the principle of informed consent.

Self-determination. The mediator's threat to Romeo regarding the commencement of the mediation at least potentially implicates Romeo's self-determination in the process. To the extent the mediator's (improper) threat served to coerce Romeo or to strip him of his ability to choose appropriately for himself, the mediator impaired his self-determination. This does not mean that every time a mediator helps a party to understand the consequences of one decision or another, the mediator is impairing self-determination. But here, particularly because the threat was improper, the mediator acted improperly at the outset.

The other event that might give the appearance of threatening party self-determination is the manner in which the parties themselves were excluded from the process. Self-determination permits a party to turn over some aspects of the dispute to their attorney to handle. Concerns emerge, however, if a party *cannot* participate, as opposed to merely chooses not to. That both parties remained inactive in the corner may (or may not) be evidence of impropriety here. The fact of the coin flipping, although unorthodox, is not *per se* evidence that the parties' self-determination was violated. Disputants can choose almost any method for resolving their differences in the unstructured, informal process that is mediation. Provided we are comfortable imagining that the attorneys were acting on their clients' behalf and that they were doing so with authority, perhaps surprisingly, the coin flip is the least of the problems in this sequence of events!

A Mediation Dilemma?

4a. **Doing nothing.** A mediator cannot always avoid ethical problems by simply staying silent. To be certain, there are more ways to get in trouble if you actually do something as a mediator. But in this circumstance, like some others, a mediator who does not intervene may be overseeing a mediation that runs afoul of one or more of mediation's fundamental principles.

In this case, Lacey appears strongly at risk of deciding without adequate information. In other words, her **informed consent** is in jeopardy. Her conversation with the mediator before the mediation began was not problematic, in the sense that the mediator gave her the choice of whether to continue and assured her that she was not required to have an attorney. Lacey understood mediation well enough that we would probably deem her consent informed as to the process. And it is not that Lacey fails to understand what Cagney's attorney's offer means. Instead, what is troubling here is that Lacey clearly misunderstands (as far as the mediator knows) what her alternatives to settling look like. In that sense, we might have concerns that her consent is not adequately informed.

There is a limit to this line of reasoning, of course. It cannot be the mediator's responsibility to assure that disputants have full and complete information both about the implications of possible deals and about their litigation alternatives. Such a level of information is almost surely unattainable, even if there were not impartiality and other constraints on what the mediator could do to achieve it. In addition, we really have no idea what is actually important to Lacey. What if the case—or the particular outcome she was seeking—was not actually very important to her? Still, particularly where one of the disputants is unrepresented, a mediator who sits silently while a party decides based on plainly erroneous assumptions cannot be said to have fully protected that party's informed decision making. Model Standard I(A)(1) provides: "Although party self-determination for process design is a fundamental principle of mediation practice, a mediator may need to balance such party self-determination with a mediator's duty to conduct a quality process in accordance with these Standards."

Unfortunately, as the analysis of each of the two subsequent options suggests, a mediator who wants help Lacey's understanding is in a difficult position. To improve the degree to which the mediation is consistent with the principle of informed consent, the mediator risks doing damage to another of mediation's important principles. In this way, the three principles articulated in this section often interact with each other.

4b. **Providing legal advice.** Neither legal ethics nor mediation ethics would permit the mediator to provide this kind of legal advice to Lacey.

Legal ethics prevent an attorney serving as a mediator from representing one of the parties. (See ABA Model Rule of Professional Conduct 2.4.) The idea behind this prohibition is that a mediator necessarily is providing a service when two or more parties have at least potentially conflicting (and often very conflicting) interests. And one of the fundamental ideas behind having a lawyer represent you is that you are hiring the lawyer to advocate for *you*, not for someone else. If the lawyer-mediator in this case were to provide legal advice to Lacey, they would be doing so at the expense of Cagney's interests—something legal ethics do not permit.

Mediation ethics also prohibit the mediator from providing legal advice to Lacey. The principle of **impartiality** is certainly implicated if a mediator begins to dispense legal advice. This is not merely a case of the lawyer providing a legal assessment of some sort to both parties (a practice we describe in the section below, and about which there is some controversy). Instead, this would be the mediator providing legal advice to one party, *but not to the other*. The Model Standards anticipate these dilemmas, and Standard VI(A)(5) provides: "The role of a mediator differs substantially from other professional roles. Mixing the role of a mediator and the role of another profession is problematic and thus, a mediator should distinguish between the roles. A mediator may provide information that the mediator is qualified by training or experience to provide, only if the mediator can do so consistent with these Standards." In light of the Model Standards' insistence that mediators conduct mediations "in an impartial manner" and the legal ethics prohibition against providing legal advice to only one of the mediator's parties, the mediator would not be permitted to do so in this case.

This is not to say that a mediator would be wholly unjustified to at least think about this as a possible course of action. After all, among the principles we described above, **informed consent** is critical. And it is easy to imagine that the mediator might worry that Lacey is about to sign an agreement without adequately understanding its implications and the alternatives she might encounter in litigation. But this particular avenue for addressing that dilemma—providing legal advice—appears barred.

4c. **Recommending seeking legal advice.** If the mediator met privately with Lacey and advised her to obtain legal advice before accepting Cagney's lawyer's proposal, the mediator would be increasing the degree to which the mediation is consistent with the principle of informed consent. Lacey would, at a minimum, be informed that there are relevant legal principles of which she should be aware. Theoretically, if she consults an attorney, she will be in a position to understand the trade-offs involved between the proposed settlement and the prospect of litigation.

This matches the Model Standards' vision of an ideal mediation—one "in which each party makes free and informed choices as to process and outcome." (Model Standard I(A).) In fact, the Model Standards specifically suggest that a mediator take actions like this: "A mediator cannot personally ensure that each party has made free and informed choices to reach particular decisions, but, where appropriate, a mediator should make the parties aware of the importance of consulting other professionals to help them make informed choices." (Model Standard I(A)(2).) This also supports the principle of self-determination, because the mediator is not forcing Lacey to do anything. Instead, the mediator is inviting Lacey to seek additional information in a way that enhances both her informed consent and self-determination.

The impartiality principle potentially complicates this approach. If the mediator had a standard policy of advising all clients to seek legal counsel before signing an agreement, impartiality would likely not be implicated. But here, the mediator is contemplating this intervention specifically because she believes Cagney's attorney is misstating the relevant law. Even if the mediator does not feel biased, Cagney and her attorney would likely be disappointed, to say the least, that the mediator was offering Lacey this suggestion. Of course, Cagney may never learn of the mediator's advice to Lacey because it may take place in private. But that practical consideration ("If they don't see me do it, it's not wrong") does not answer the question of whether the practice is consistent with mediation's fundamental principles.

The drafters of the Model Standards clearly recognized that a mediator in this circumstance would necessarily need to balance multiple considerations. As a result, instead of a requirement or even a blanket endorsement of the idea of sending parties to lawyers, the Model Standards include the caveat that mediators should do so "where appropriate," without any further explanation of when it might and might not be appropriate.

The Trouble with "Working It Out"

5. **Likely trouble?** The mediator in this case appears to have done little, if anything, to assist the parties. The strongest aspect of their claim would be to assert that the mediator failed to uphold their (possibly implied) promise to help with the mediation process. Ultimately, however, the parties' lawsuit would be unlikely to succeed for at least two reasons.

   The first reason the mediator's exposure in this case is limited has to do with the difficulty of demonstrating that the mediator's behaviors were, in fact, substandard. In this case, the disputants were clearly unhappy with the mediator. And the mediation did not produce a settlement. But neither of those facts is sufficient to establish mediator malpractice. Not all parties are happy, and not all cases settle, even when the mediator does a perfectly respectable job. Here, the parties would have to demonstrate that the mediator's actions fell below the level of competence demanded by practitioners in the area. Because competent mediators do an extraordinary variety of things, this will be a challenge. Even this mediator's persistent, vague question is not utterly indefensible. True, the approach does not fit perfectly within the orthodoxy of any of the three major approaches to mediation, but mediators do any number of creative things, and most are entirely acceptable—or at least not facially malpractice.

The second reason that the mediator is not liable stems from the mediator's position as an official court-affiliated mediator. Whatever court program administers these mediations may have some sanction available for dealing with terrible mediators, but at most, the sanction is likely limited to simply removing the offending mediator from the roster of mediators the program will call in the future. Even more significant, because the mediator was acting through the court system, the mediator likely enjoys some form of immunity from liability. The court in *Wagshal v. Foster* held that mediators were sufficiently judge-like in their function to warrant the common law extension of quasi-judicial immunity to mediators. Even if this jurisdiction does not go that far, it is very likely that court-affiliated mediators would be protected in all but the most egregious cases. As unimpressive as this mediator's performance was, it does not rise to the level of intentionally harmful behavior for which a mediator might be found liable.

Neighborly Love

6. **Exposure.** Barney has three potential avenues for complaining about Morton.

    First, because Morton provided legal advice to Barney, he may have violated his legal professional ethics by providing legal counsel to one client (Barney) to the detriment of another client (Fred). What precise sanction Morton faces depends on the particulars of the state Bar in question. These could range from a letter of reprimand to disbarment, though the most serious sanctions are quite unlikely. If Morton is not an attorney, the fact that he gave legal advice very likely violates state restrictions against the unauthorized practice of law, violations of which are typically prosecuted through the state Bar.

    Second, Morton not only gave legal advice, but also gave bad legal advice. As with any attorney who offers erroneous legal advice, Barney could bring a legal malpractice action against Morton. Barney may face some challenges in proving that Morton represented him and provided bad legal advice, and that Barney relied on that bad legal advice to his detriment. But given the clarity of Morton's assertions, and because those assertions were demonstrably false, Barney has a chance of recovering some level of damages against Morton for legal malpractice.

    Finally, Barney could raise a complaint that Morton violated mediation ethics by providing legal advice to just one party. The sanctions for violating these ethics codes are generally limited by the power of whatever organization promulgated them. So, for example, if Morton violates the ethics code of the Association for Conflict Resolution, the association might revoke Morton's membership. That, of course, might concern Morton, but it does not accomplish much for Barney. Could

Barney sue Morton successfully for mediator malpractice? As a privately contracted mediator (as opposed to a court-affiliated mediator), Morton is not likely to enjoy any form of immunity. Barney may have little problem demonstrating that Morton's conduct fell below the standard of care or practice reasonably expected of a mediator. But as with most forms of alleged mediator misconduct, Barney will have considerable challenges in proving that Morton's conduct caused a demonstrable injury. True, Morton gave bad advice, and that might be enough for Barney to avoid paying Morton's fees. But to recover anything more substantial, Barney would have to overcome hurdles such as proving that he would have succeeded in convincing Fred to agree to the easement but for Morton's advice.

CHAPTER 7

Keeping Secrets: Confidentiality in Mediation

§7.1 INTRODUCTION

Litigation is presumptively public. We hear about big cases in the media, and we study judicial decisions to learn about the law. By contrast, many of the alternatives we discuss in this book offer at least some degree of confidentiality—both about the terms of the resolution and about the process that led to the resolution. One reason some disputants find mediation attractive is that it frequently takes place outside of the public eye.

Is confidentiality in dispute resolution a good thing? It depends. The very best rationales for privacy accurately point out that some kinds of conversations can only take place out of the public eye. For example, diplomats find it easier to discuss delicate compromises in the confines of a secret conversation than when the world is watching. Similarly, confidential conversations incentivize greater information disclosure, which in turn presents greater opportunities to develop mutually beneficial, creative options. Further, certain kinds of relationships depend on candid exchanges to flourish. We protect the confidentiality of conversations between spouses, in part because we recognize the importance of that relationship and its dependence on candor. Similarly, in clergy-parishioner, doctor-patient, and lawyer-client relationships, confidentiality promotes the kind of candid exchange upon which the relationship is built; therefore, we assign communications within these relationships broad privacy protection from the outside world.

But some important public concerns weigh against the broad extension of confidentiality protections. Confidentiality prevents a fact finder from hearing information related to the dispute in question, and we generally favor judicial proceedings in which every party has access to all relevant evidence. Further, the public benefits from the transparency that normally characterizes litigation because, at least theoretically, it permits "the whole truth" to come out. In some cases, this transparency can be essential both to deter misbehavior and to prevent further harm.

These considerations—both for and against confidentiality—inform the policy trade-offs in mediation as well. In favor of confidentiality, the mediator-disputant relationship may not be as important as a marriage or a doctor-patient relationship, but society generally considers the benefits resulting from those conversations sufficiently worthwhile to safeguard. Most people think that confidentiality encourages parties to be candid with the mediator. ("Why should I tell you anything if you're just going to go tell others?") Many have suggested that mediators can function effectively only if the disputants are at least somewhat candid with the mediator. ("How am I supposed to help solve this problem if I don't even know the real issues?") Most people also believe that disputants' perceptions of a mediator's neutrality are important to the success of mediation—a perception put at risk by the prospect of the mediator as an adverse witness. ("How can the mediator be neutral if he is called to testify about what happened, since inevitably his testimony will favor one side or the other?") Finally, confidentiality protects against certain ways in which disputants might abuse the mediation process. ("Tell me everything, and then I'll decide what to use against you in a subsequent legal proceeding.")

But confidentiality in mediation is potentially troublesome for at least two reasons—one that focuses on mediation outcomes and one that focuses on the mediation process. First, if the substance of the dispute and its mediated resolution are confidential, the public may never learn about information it wants or needs. A company might want to keep disputes with its employees or consumers out of the news. A manufacturer of a defective product might want to shield its name and brand from the publicity associated with the defect. Two prominent Hollywood stars who are divorcing might want to keep the sordid details of the collapse of their marriage out of the public eye. Judging by media coverage, the last of these scenarios represents the kind of information in which the public is apparently most keenly interested. But confidentiality in the former two could actually prevent the public from learning important information that would otherwise be available through the mechanism of a trial. The addition of the mediator—particularly in court-connected mediations—may make it somewhat more difficult to maintain secrecy around a settlement's terms. In most contexts, however, mediated agreements are no different from any other privately negotiated settlement agreements when it comes to the enforceability of confidentiality provisions. For more on the basic legal frameworks surrounding so-called secret settlements, see Chapter 3.

The second potential cost associated with mediation confidentiality is the degree to which it shields misbehavior *during the mediation process* from public view and public sanction. If a litigant crosses the preestablished "line" during the course of a lawsuit (for example, in a pleading or in court), there is a clear opportunity for correction. A misbehaving witness is subject to perjury charges. An attorney risks Bar sanctions. A judge's decision is subject to reversal. A party's case is at risk of being dismissed. And so on. But in a mediation, if the broadest possible confidentiality were applied, any of the participants may be able to engage in shenanigans that threaten the legitimacy of the process. (For more on the challenges of quality control in mediation, for example, see Chapter 6.)

The combination of these considerations for and against confidentiality in dispute resolution has resulted in a complex compromise. Society has neither granted absolute confidentiality to all ADR processes nor insisted on complete transparency. Instead, a patchwork of protections may (or may not) exist in a given context.

Four basic mechanisms, each of which is jurisdiction specific, may provide confidentiality protections in the context of mediation:

1. Evidentiary exclusions ("If the only place you heard it was during our settlement efforts, you can't use it in court. Probably.")
2. Protective order ("Under penalty of contempt, you have to keep your mouth shut.")
3. Contract ("We have a deal to keep our mouths shut.")
4. Privilege ("You can't make me testify. You can't even make me produce information in discovery.")

Each of these mechanisms sometimes assures mediation parties that their conversations in mediation will remain confidential. We examine each below.

§7.2 EVIDENTIARY EXCLUSIONS

The law establishes certain confidentiality protections for negotiations between two disputants. To encourage both candor and flexibility in the negotiations, the common law and, more recently, the Federal Rules of Evidence preclude the use of these conversations against a party if the dispute does not settle and proceeds to litigation. Most of these protections attach to all negotiation efforts aimed at settlement, not just in the context of mediated conversations.

Federal Rule of Evidence (FRE) 408 prohibits one party from introducing evidence that the opposing party made a settlement offer or discussed the merits of a claim during negotiations, if the purpose of introducing this evidence is to show liability, the invalidity of the claim, or the amount being claimed. In other words, one cannot get on the stand and say, "They offered to pay me $300,000 for my injuries, so you know they are liable." Similarly, one cannot say, "They were willing to accept a measly $10,000 as payment, so their claim is clearly bogus." This protection includes conduct and other statements during the settlement talks as well as any documents prepared for settlement talks.

Rule 408. Compromise and Offers to Compromise

(a) Prohibited Uses. Evidence of the following is not admissible—on behalf of any party—either to prove or disprove the validity or amount of a disputed claim or to impeach by a prior inconsistent statement or a contradiction:

(1) furnishing, promising, or offering—or accepting, promising to accept, or offering to accept—a valuable consideration in compromising or attempting to compromise the claim; and

(2) conduct or a statement made during compromise negotiations about the claim—except when offered in a criminal case and when the negotiations related to a claim by a public office in the exercise of its regulatory, investigative, or enforcement authority.

(b) Exceptions. The court may admit this evidence for another purpose, such as proving a witness's bias or prejudice, negating a contention of undue delay, or proving an effort to obstruct a criminal investigation or prosecution.

An offer of settlement does not necessarily say anything about the offering party's perspective on the merits of the underlying claim. A plaintiff may have an immediate need for cash and might therefore be willing to settle for far less than the amount he would expect to recover at the conclusion of protracted litigation. A defendant may believe that it is entirely without fault but might prefer to settle the case quickly as a means of minimizing costs and headaches. The purpose of this evidentiary exclusion is to promote settlement efforts, and the policy assumption underlying this rule is that settlement discussions will be promoted if both parties are comfortable letting their guard down without fear that their efforts will come back to haunt them in the event of a nonsettlement.

This protection does not mean, though, that everything that happens in a negotiation stays in the negotiation. Rule 408 does not require exclusion of evidence that is otherwise discoverable. For example, say you have a videotape of the plaintiff waterskiing the day after his allegedly crippling injury occurred, and you discuss it in settlement talks. The fact that you discussed it in settlement talks may be inadmissible, but you will still be able to introduce the videotape itself. Further, under Rule 408, if the evidence is being offered for a purpose other than to demonstrate liability or validity or to impeach a witness, the evidence can be admitted. This includes, for example, introducing evidence to show bias or prejudice of a witness or to prove a material matter other than liability.

Disputants have even more potential mechanisms for protecting the confidentiality of conversations that take place within the context of a mediation, as opposed to those that are merely part of a negotiation. Federal Rule of Evidence 408 still applies to mediation conversations because a mediation is considered an attempt to settle (or in the words of the FRE, to "compromise" a claim). But a range of other confidentiality-protecting options may be available to mediation participants, depending on the context. Below, we consider three: protective orders, contracts, and privilege. The last of these is the most significant and the most complex, so we will spend most of our time there. But we will start with a survey of protective orders and contracts.

§7.3 PROTECTIVE ORDERS: USING THE COURT TO KEEP IT SECRET

Parties can also use **protective orders** to prevent specified information (like trade secrets or negotiated settlements) from discovery. Federal Rule of Civil Procedure 26(c) provides that parties can make a motion showing that a protective order is necessary to "protect a party or person from annoyance, embarrassment, oppression, or undue burden or expense." Since third parties to a mediation who have not signed the confidentiality agreement are not bound by it, some parties seek a protective order rather than (or in addition to) a confidentiality agreement. Although protective orders are attractive because they carry the weight of a court's potential sanction, they must be approved by the court before they come into effect. Therefore, as a matter of practicality (it takes time to get an order) and strategy (a court is more likely to uphold contractual confidentiality than to grant a protective order), protective orders are not the only mechanism disputants rely on.

§7.4 CONTRACTS: I PROMISE NOT TO TALK

Mediators typically include **confidentiality clauses** in the mediation contracts parties are required to sign at the outset of mediation. These contracts, or agreements to mediate, often provide that the parties agree not to discuss what happens in the mediation (and in some cases, even that mediation took place). The clauses also commonly include an agreement that neither party will testify and that neither will seek testimony from anyone else about the proceedings. The confidentiality agreement can also include provisions that prevent the use of documents or other statements in future litigation (and depending on the terms, may even provide protections broader than Rule 408). Confidentiality agreements typically provide (1) that the mediator will not discuss the mediation with anyone without the parties' permission or as required by law, and (2) that the parties will not subpoena the mediator to testify in a future case. Some confidentiality agreements even provide that the parties will pay for all costs should the mediator be subpoenaed.

It is easy to see why mediators might ask parties to sign these agreements, but the question is whether courts uphold the agreements. After all, you and a drug dealer may sign an agreement not to squeal on each other. Neither of you, however, is going to prevail in a contract action against the other if one of you reneges on some aspect of that agreement. Do courts uphold confidentiality clauses in mediation agreements? For the most part, yes. The logic for upholding these agreements is illustrated by the opinion in *Simrin v. Simrin*, 233 Cal. App. 2d 90 (1965), in which a court upheld a confidentiality agreement signed during a marriage counseling session by Mr. and Mrs. Simrin. This agreement prevented either of them from compelling their rabbi, who acted as their marriage counselor, to testify. The court reasoned that, like mediation, marriage counseling would no longer be helpful if the parties knew that their conversations could be revealed at a later date. With some exceptions, most courts since *Simrin* have followed this general prohibition stemming from contractually based mediation confidentiality.

Courts have a variety of different remedial options if they find that a party breached a confidentiality agreement. Courts have dismissed the case, ordered new trials, and ordered costs in breaches of confidentiality agreements. In one particularly well-known case, *Toon v. Wackenhut Corrections Corp.*, 250 F.3d 950 (5th Cir. 2001), three plaintiffs entered a settlement agreement with a defendant. The settlement agreement included a strict confidentiality clause prohibiting any disclosure of the terms of the agreement. When the defendant failed to make the required payment, the plaintiffs' attorney filed a motion in court seeking to have the agreement enforced. However, the plaintiffs' attorney did not file the motion under seal and, as a result, the terms of the agreement became public. At the request of the defendant, the court sanctioned plaintiffs' counsel by reducing his contingency fee, ordering him to pay a $15,000 sanction to the court, and preventing him from representing any other plaintiff in related claims without the court's permission. Clearly, courts take breaches of confidentiality agreements very seriously.

As with any other contract, a court can also refuse to enforce a confidentiality agreement if it violates public policy. It would violate public policy, for example, if an agreement seeks to prevent parties from sharing information that a party could independently discover outside of the mediation. This also mirrors the provision in Rule 408.

§7.5 PRIVILEGE: THIS RELATIONSHIP IS SPECIAL

As we mentioned earlier, parties may hold a **privilege** in the context of certain special relationships in which candid communication is critical. Drawing an analogy to the doctor-patient and lawyer-client relationship, many courts and legislatures have protected the conversations that occur in mediation under the same theory—that the process cannot be effective unless parties have confidence that the information candidly shared with the mediator will remain confidential.

One of the mechanisms by which a mediation privilege has been created is through common law extension. As the U.S. Supreme Court explained in *Jaffee v. Redmond*, 518 U.S. 1 (1996), under Federal Rule of Evidence 501, a federal judge can create a privilege if it is based on an interpretation of "common law principles . . . in the light of reason and experience." Some courts in states with similar rules of evidence have created a common law privilege for mediation, adopting the same reasoning. Other state courts, however, have held that the creation of a mediation privilege is the province of the legislature, not of a court.

Statutory provisions, therefore, represent the other mechanism by which a privilege is sometimes created. The precise content of these mediation confidentiality statutes varies enormously from one state to another. Most state statutes prohibit participants from compelling a mediator to testify in post-mediation hearings, although most states also carve out a set of exceptions to this broad protection. State statutes often protect communications, such as documents prepared by the participants and the mediator for the purposes of the mediation. Some states base their privilege on Federal Rule of Evidence 408 and require that any records created during mediation be kept confidential if they are relevant to any judicial proceeding. (In these states, if the communications are not relevant to a particular dispute, the documents are not protected by the privilege.) Some states provide no specific exceptions for public policy arguments, while other states permit testimony related to malpractice during the mediation or to criminal acts. Others specifically provide that participants can compel mediator testimony if public policy calls for it. Therefore, it is important to know your specific jurisdiction's rules and whether the privilege is through common law or statute.

Responding to this patchwork of state confidentiality statutes, in an effort to promote uniformity among states, the American Bar Association and the National Conference of Commissioners on Uniform State Laws proposed the Uniform Mediation Act (UMA) in 2001. About a dozen states have adopted the UMA. Nevertheless, most of our analyses below rely on the UMA because it illustrates one relatively straightforward mechanism for creating a mediation privilege. If you understand how the UMA works, you will understand the mechanism (though not necessarily the details) of virtually all state-created privileges. We therefore discuss some of the key aspects of the UMA below.

§7.5.1 Who Holds a Mediation Privilege?

The first issue surrounding the question of a mediation privilege is who exactly holds the privilege, because this determines the level of protection for those involved in a mediation. If the privilege belongs to the parties, can they compel the mediator to testify? If the privilege belongs to the mediator, can the mediator prevent the parties from communicating? Under the UMA, the mediation privilege belongs to both the parties and the mediator. Even nonparty participants (such as experts, relatives, etc.) are granted a form of mediation privilege. UMA §4(b) reads:

> In a proceeding, the following privileges apply:
>
> 1. A mediation party may refuse to disclose, and may prevent any other person from disclosing, a mediation communication.
> 2. A mediator may refuse to disclose a mediation communication, and may prevent any other person from disclosing a mediation communication of the mediator.
> 3. A nonparty participant may refuse to disclose, and may prevent any other person from disclosing, a mediation communication of the nonparty participant.

Essentially, each participant in mediation holds a privilege that protects his or her own mediation communications from disclosure. In addition, mediation parties have a broader privilege, permitting them to prevent disclosure of all mediation communications. The UMA defines a "mediation communication" as a "statement, whether oral or in a record or verbal or nonverbal, that occurs during a mediation or is made for purposes of considering, conducting, participating in, initiating, continuing, or reconvening a mediation or retaining a mediator." Under this definition, the privilege can be rather expansive for the parties and the mediator. For example, even in heart-wrenching cases concerning child abuse in the Catholic Church, the mediator could not be compelled to testify about the settlement terms. In

Leary v. Geoghan, 2002 Mass. App. LEXIS 1706, *1, 2002 WL 32140255, a dispute arose about the enforceability or finality of an agreement allegedly reached in mediation. The plaintiffs argued that the agreement was final, while the defendants (the Catholic Church) argued that the agreement was conditioned on a review for financial viability. The plaintiffs sought to compel testimony from the mediator on the narrow question of whether the agreement contained this conditional clause, but the court upheld the mediator's assertion that under the relevant Massachusetts mediation confidentiality statute, the mediator could not be compelled to testify, even if all of the parties agreed to waive their privileges.

The functioning of a mediation privilege (or what is covered under the privilege) is probably easiest to understand with an illustration. Consider the case of *Folb v. Motion Picture Industry Pension & Health Plans*, 16 F. Supp. 2d 1164 (D. Cal. 1998). Scott Folb, who worked at MPIPHP, reported certain practices of his employers to government regulators, alleging that the practices were illegal. MPIPHP subsequently fired Folb. Folb sued his former employer, alleging that his termination was an illegal response to Folb's whistleblowing. In its defense, MPIPHP asserted that Folb was fired because he allegedly sexually harassed another employee, Vivian Vasquez. Meanwhile, Vasquez filed a lawsuit against MPIPHP alleging sexual harassment. Vasquez and MPIPHP attempted to settle the claim in mediation. No settlement resulted during the mediation, but not long after the mediation, Vasquez and MPIPHP settled the claim for undisclosed terms. Folb sought evidence about MPIPHP's contentions in the context of the Vasquez lawsuit, because Folb asserted that MPIPHP was taking inconsistent positions in the two related pieces of litigation (saying that Folb *had* sexually harassed Vasquez in the Folb lawsuit and *denying* that he had sexually harassed her in the Vasquez lawsuit). The case raised the question of whether Folb could have access to information about what happened in the Vasquez mediation.

How would the UMA resolve the questions this case raises? Under the UMA, both Vasquez and MPIPHP would hold a privilege about any "mediation communication" that took place in their mediation. Undoubtedly, the information Folb sought would fall within the scope of the broad term "mediation communication." So, under the terms of the UMA, Folb would have access to this information only if both of the parties holding a privilege agreed to waive the privilege. In this case, whatever Vasquez's disposition toward the privilege might be, it is highly unlikely that MPIPHP would agree to waive its privilege. Under the UMA, therefore, Folb would have to proceed through his litigation without the benefit of testimony about MPIPHP's stance in the Vasquez settlement efforts.

The *Folb* case arose in federal court before the UMA's adoption, but the court found privilege in common law. As an initial matter, the federal court determined that federal common law governed the question of the existence of a privilege because the case was before the court on federal question jurisdiction. (If this Civil Procedure reference gives you unpleasant flashbacks, just recall that in some cases, a federal court would apply state law to determine this question, and in others, it would refer to federal common law.) The court then analyzed the policy arguments for and against privilege, relying heavily on the *Jaffee* case described above. The court concluded "that encouraging mediation by adopting a federal mediation privilege . . . will provide a public good transcending the normally predominant principle of utilizing all rational means for ascertaining the truth." Folb, therefore, had no access to the mediation conversations that led to the settlement of Vasquez's sexual harassment claim.

§7.5.2 What If I Don't Want the Privilege (or Want to Waive It)?

The existence of a privilege does not mean that the covered information can never be disclosed. A privilege simply means that the information cannot be disclosed without the consent of the party who holds the privilege. This implies, correctly, that there is a mechanism for signaling consent for the discovery or the testimony to proceed. In short, a privilege holder can waive his or her privilege.

Imagine, for example, that in the *Folb* case described above, MPIPHP admitted that Folb had sexually harassed Vasquez. In that event, both MPIPHP and Vasquez *might* decide to waive their privileges, permitting Folb to have access to information about the mediation. (MPIPHP might waive to rebut Folb's assertion that the harassment claim was a pretext for the firing. Vasquez might waive simply to make Folb's life more difficult.) UMA §5 states that "a privilege under Section 4 may be waived . . . if it is expressly waived by all parties to the mediation." So, if both MPIPHP and Vasquez waived privilege, one or both could testify or submit mediation documents into evidence.

Mediators and nonparties also hold privileges that, if not waived, restrict the scope of information about which testimony can occur. For example, even if both of the parties wanted to testify about what happened in mediation, they would not be permitted to testify about "a mediation communication of the mediator," absent a waiver from the mediator. If MPIPHP wanted the mediator to testify about what happened in the mediation between MPIPHP and Vasquez, Vasquez, MPIPHP, *and* the mediator would all have to waive their respective privileges—an extremely unlikely situation. The same kind of three-way waiver requirement also applies to any nonparty participants—the parties and the nonparty participant all must waive their privilege for the nonparty participant to testify. Note how the UMA grants a separate privilege to the mediator. (Remember that in other privileged relationships, the client can waive the lawyer-client privilege and the patient can waive the doctor-patient privilege because it is a client-held or patient-held privilege. Only in the mediation privilege do parties on all sides of this relationship hold a privilege.) This additional provision gives independent power to the mediator (or another privilege holder) to prevent him or her from being subpoenaed.

§7.5.3 Are There Any Exceptions to Privileges?

No privilege is absolute, and the mediation privilege has at least as many exceptions as exist in other privileged relationships. Each state creating a mediation privilege has an opportunity to articulate the circumstances in which the privilege will not apply, and every state of which we are aware has at least some exceptions to mediation privilege. The UMA's set of exceptions are found in §6. In broad terms, UMA §6(a) spells out certain categories of information about which no privilege attaches. For example, the UMA provides no privilege regarding the planned commission of a crime or an intention to inflict bodily injury. Similarly, the UMA does not protect information about which disclosure is otherwise required, like public records laws or mandatory reporting of child abuse.

Most states' exceptions to mediation privilege mirror these exceptions from the UMA. *Angelella v. Pittston Township*, No. 3:06-CV-00120, 2007 U.S. Dist. LEXIS 66968 (M.D. Pa. 2007), is an example of when the mediation privilege does not exist because of public records laws. The lawyer for Pittston Township went on the evening news and discussed the existence of mediation between the two parties. The plaintiff argued as part of her retaliation claim that the township retaliated against her with "undue, unwarranted negative publicity [through the media]." *Id.* at *12. The U.S. District Court held the public's interest in receiving information from public officials that was already on the public record outweighs the privacy interest of the plaintiff. *See id.* at *13. Similarly, in *Perreault v. Free Lance-Star*, 666 S.E.2d 352, 355 (Va. 2008), the Free Lance-Star, a newspaper, wanted the details of a series of wrongful death settlements to be available as a matter of public record. The Virginia Supreme Court found that the trial court had correctly denied the request to keep the settlement private.

Some states deviate from the UMA's approach to mediation confidentiality. For example, the UMA does not protect information about malpractice by attorneys or mediators during the course of a mediation, but not all states have privilege exceptions for cases of alleged malpractice. In *Alfieri v. Solomon*, 365 P.3d 99 (Or. 2015), a client sued his former lawyer for malpractice, alleging that the lawyer provided negligent advice about the client's prospects in litigation and about the merits of a potential settlement—and that this negligent advice occurred before, during, and after the case was in mediation. The Oregon Supreme Court, interpreting an Oregon state statute that deviates from the UMA in this regard, precluded the client from offering evidence specific to the mediation session (for example, the contents of the mediator's proposals), but held that he *could* introduce evidence of the attorney's communications with the client outside of the mediation itself. In California, however, even an allegation of misconduct in the mediation may not trump the requirement of confidentiality. In *Cassel v. Superior Court*, 244 P.3d 1080, 1085 (Cal. 2011), the California Supreme Court held that the California state statute guaranteeing mediation confidentiality "must govern, even though they may compromise petitioner's ability to prove his claim of legal malpractice."

The UMA also sets up a category of circumstances in which a mediation privilege might not exist, depending on the context, thus establishing a balancing test for the court. This kind of balancing test was first used by the court in *Olam v. Congress Mortgage Co.*, 68 F. Supp. 2d 1110 (N.D. Cal. 1999). After balancing the need for the evidence in a case asserting duress, the court in *Olam* admitted the mediator's testimony, and then found no duress in the agreement. This approach to balancing is now reflected in §6(b) of the UMA. Under that provision, in a court proceeding involving a crime or enforcement of the settlement agreement, if a court determines that the evidence is not available through another source and that the need for the evidence substantially outweighs the interest in protecting confidentiality, a mediation party will not be able to assert a privilege against the discovery of the information.

Although mediation promises some level of confidentiality to its participants, it would be inaccurate to say that everything in mediation remains confidential. As we have described above, confidentiality provisions frequently contain many exceptions. Furthermore, like any rule, mediation confidentiality provisions depend in part on voluntary compliance—and not every party keeps quiet, even after promising to do so. Sanctions for breaching confidentiality vary widely (from warnings to sanctions to the possible dismissal of a case), and courts have broad discretion in imposing sanctions in such circumstances.

Examples

The Clearwater Creek Catastrophe

One morning, Paula discovered that chemicals had washed up onto her property on the shores of the legendarily pristine Clearwater Creek. She concluded that one or both of the companies located upstream must be responsible for the pollution, and she filed a lawsuit against both of them. Both Mountain Manufacturing and Valley Vehicles had a history of compliance with environmental regulations, and both launched vigorous defense efforts against Paula's claims.

Early in the lawsuit, Paula, Mountain Manufacturing, and Valley Vehicles agreed to try mediation. They hired Michelle to conduct the mediation. The parties met but no settlement resulted. Eventually, the three parties fired Michelle and the mediation ceased.

The local newspaper ran a story the day after the end of the mediation. The columnist who wrote the story included considerable detail about what allegedly took place during the failed mediation. The story described both Mountain Manufacturing and Valley Vehicles in very negative (and perhaps even libelous) terms. Nowhere in the story did the reporter indicate the source of his information about what happened in the mediation.

After further pretrial litigation, Paula, Mountain Manufacturing, and Valley Vehicles agreed to try mediation a second time. They hired Miranda to conduct the mediation. During the mediation, at the invitation of the parties and Miranda, Paula's neighbor Nancy Norton came in and provided "testimony" about what she saw the morning the pollution first appeared. During the rest of the mediation with Miranda, the attorney for Mountain Manufacturing struck a conciliatory tone, and Paula and Mountain Manufacturing quickly settled. The attorney for Valley Vehicles, however, refused to consider any payment to Paula, and eventually, the mediation ended. Paula continued with her lawsuit against Valley Vehicles.

Assume that the jurisdiction within which all of the above actions took place has adopted a state version of the Uniform Mediation Act.

Paula Versus Valley Vehicles

1a. In the context of Paula's ongoing lawsuit against Valley Vehicles, Valley Vehicles believes that some of the information that came out in each of the mediation sessions would be helpful to its defense. Could Valley Vehicles compel Mountain Manufacturing to testify about what occurred during the mediation sessions?

1b. If, in the context of the litigation between Paula and Valley Vehicles, Mountain Manufacturing volunteered to help out Valley Vehicles by agreeing to testify about what transpired in the mediation sessions, would Mountain Manufacturing be permitted to testify?

1c. Could Valley Vehicles compel either of the mediators to testify about what occurred during the mediation sessions?

1d. Could Valley Vehicles compel Nancy Norton to testify about what occurred during the mediation session when she was present?

1e. Assume that Paula and Mountain Manufacturing included a broad confidentiality clause in the terms of their mediated settlement, which purported to cover not only the discussions leading up to the settlement, but also the terms of the settlement. Could Valley Vehicles compel production of the terms of the settlement between Paula and Mountain Manufacturing?

1f. Encouraged by the number of readers who responded positively to the local newspaper's story about the first mediation, one of its reporters wants to attend any subsequent mediation efforts between Valley Vehicles and Paula. If the parties do not mutually consent to the reporter's presence, is there any way for the reporter to force her way into the sessions?

1g. Assume that both parties in the remaining lawsuit (Valley Vehicles and Paula) have decided to try mediation again. Both are now also expressing interest in permitting the reporter to attend the mediation sessions. What, if any, clauses should the parties include in the new agreement to mediate regarding the reporter's presence and the potential of the reporter testifying about what they observe in the mediation?

Everyone Versus Michelle

2a. Paula, Mountain Manufacturing, and Valley Vehicles all agree that the first mediation effort was a complete waste of time. They believe the mediation failed because of Mediator Michelle's malpractice, and they all sue her. In the context of that lawsuit, could Paula, Mountain Manufacturing, and Valley Vehicles compel Michelle to testify about what happened during the mediation?

2b. Alternatively, in the context of their suit against Michelle, could Paula, Mountain Manufacturing, and Valley Vehicles prevent Michelle from testifying about what happened during the mediation?

2c. Assume that Michelle seeks to settle the dispute with Paula, Mountain Manufacturing, and Valley Vehicles. Identify potential terms for the settlement, consistent with the parties' likely interests.

Manufacturers Versus the Media

3a. Mountain Manufacturing and Valley Vehicles jointly file a lawsuit against the local newspaper and the reporter who wrote the story, alleging that their story about the mediation was libelous. Could Mountain Manufacturing and Valley Vehicles compel the reporter to testify about who leaked information about what transpired in the first mediation session?

3b. In the context of their lawsuit against the newspaper and the reporter, could Mountain Manufacturing and Valley Vehicles testify about what occurred in the first mediation?

3c. The local newspaper and the reporter defend their story, claiming it is true and therefore not libelous. They seek to compel Paula to testify about what happened in the first mediation session. You represent Paula. What advice would you give her about responding to the subpoena?

Valley Vehicles Versus Its Lawyer

4a. After seeing that Mountain Manufacturing easily settled with Paula, Valley Vehicles became convinced that the only reason it did not arrive at a settlement as well was the fault of its attorney. Valley Vehicles files a legal malpractice claim against its attorney, citing the attorney's unnecessarily aggressive and standoffish attitude during the second mediation. Valley Vehicles alleges that, but for the attorney's conduct, Paula would have offered Valley Vehicles the same attractive settlement terms that she offered to Mountain Manufacturing. Could Valley Vehicles compel Paula to testify about the mediation in which the alleged malpractice took place?

4b. Could Valley Vehicles compel Miranda to testify about her observations of the behavior of Valley Vehicles' attorney during the second mediation?

The State Versus Mountain Manufacturing

5a. The state agency charged with enforcing environmental laws brings an action against Mountain Manufacturing. As part of its defense, Mountain Manufacturing wants to present evidence that during the mediation sessions, Valley Vehicles accepted fault for the pollution. Can Mountain Manufacturing testify about statements Valley Vehicles made?

5b. Could the state agency compel either of the mediators to testify about either of the companies' statements during mediation?

5c. Could the state agency charged with enforcing environmental laws compel production of the terms of the settlement agreement between Mountain Manufacturing and Paula?

Explanations

Paula Versus Valley Vehicles

1a. No. The UMA provides certain actors connected with mediations with a set of privileges for "mediation communications." When such privileges attach, they have the effect of making the material in question "not subject to discovery or admissible in evidence" unless the privilege is waived or a specific exception applies. See UMA §4(a). In this case, because Mountain Manufacturing is a mediation party, it clearly holds a privilege regarding the mediation communications in question. Mountain Manufacturing's privilege provides that it "may refuse to disclose, and may prevent any other person from disclosing, a mediation communication." §4(b)(1). Assuming Valley Vehicles is trying to compel Mountain Manufacturing to testify about something that would qualify as a "mediation communication," Mountain Manufacturing will be able successfully to resist providing that information.

1b. Maybe. The UMA does not prohibit all testimony about what occurs within a mediation session. Instead, it provides specific actors with privileges, which they can then exercise or waive. In this case, Mountain Manufacturing holds a privilege as a mediation party. §4(b)(1). Clearly, if it sought to resist testifying about what happened at the mediation, it could do so. (This is the question immediately above.) Here, however, the facts state that Mountain Manufacturing would prefer to testify. We can assume, therefore, that Mountain Manufacturing would be willing to waive its privilege. Similarly, we can assume that Valley Vehicles, also a mediation party and also a holder of the same privilege, would be willing to waive it. But that answers only two-thirds of the question. One mediation party remains—Paula. Under UMA §5(a), a privilege is waived "if it is expressly waived by all parties to the mediation." Therefore, only if Paula is also willing to waive her privilege will Mountain Manufacturing be free to testify about what transpired during the mediation sessions.

1c. No. Under UMA §4(b)(2), a mediator "may refuse to disclose a mediation communication, and may prevent any other person from disclosing a mediation communication of the mediator." Each of the mediators, therefore, holds a privilege that she could exercise. Even if all of the parties waived their privileges under UMA §5(a), it is unlikely that either of the mediators would be willing to waive her privileges. The mediators would probably see little to gain from waiving their privileges and testifying. (Expert witnesses have the potential to make a good living for their work and testimony, but in general, being a witness is an unattractive prospect.) The mediators would probably see plenty to lose from testifying about what transpired in the mediation. Inevitably, the mediator's testimony would be seen as more favorable to one party than to another, and the mediator's understandable interest in preserving a reputation for impartiality would risk being tarnished. As a practical matter, therefore, it is extraordinarily unlikely that Valley Vehicles could compel either of the mediators to testify.

1d. Probably not. The UMA provides a special privilege for "nonparty participants," and Norton appears to qualify as one. (She is "a person [other than a party or mediator] that participate[d] in a mediation." UMA §2(4).) Under UMA §4(b)(3), a nonparty participant holds a privilege permitting the nonparty participant to prevent the disclosure of the nonparty participant's mediation communications. Most likely, therefore, if Valley Vehicles sought to compel Norton to testify about Norton's role in the mediation, Norton would invoke her privilege, and Valley Vehicles would fail.

Even if Norton were favorably disposed toward the idea of testifying about the mediation, each of the mediation parties also holds a relevant (and much broader) privilege. Under UMA §5, every mediation party would also have to waive its privilege before Norton would be free to testify. If Valley Vehicles wanted Norton's testimony to include anything about what the mediator said, the mediator would also hold a privilege under §4(b)(2). Valley Vehicles is extraordinarily unlikely to secure a waiver from both of the other parties, from the mediator, and from Norton; therefore, it is not likely to have the benefit of Norton's testimony about the mediation. Remember, though, that Norton can still testify to the same substance of the testimony she gave in the mediation, as it is independently discoverable.

1e. Probably not. The terms of the settlement agreement itself are not privileged under the UMA. Even if the settlement agreement contained one or more "mediation communications," those terms are explicitly excluded from coverage under UMA §6(a)(1). But the contractual confidentiality provision may not be easy for Valley Vehicles to thwart.

Building on the concepts described in Chapter 3, Valley Vehicles would have two avenues for attacking the confidentiality clause. First, Valley Vehicles could argue that access to the settlement is necessary to prevent prejudice to a third party (like the concrete contractor in *Rittenhouse*, discussed in Chapter 3). Here, however, the settlement does not appear to have been filed with the court, so a court would have no direct mechanism for unsealing that which was never filed or sealed. Second, Valley Vehicles could argue that the settlement hides important environmental information that is needed to protect public health. In some jurisdictions, confidentiality clauses in settlements of claims affecting public health will be stricken as contrary to public policy, but this is a jurisdiction-by-jurisdiction analysis. If Valley Vehicles is in one such jurisdiction, and if Valley Vehicles can argue successfully that the "goop" under dispute constitutes a threat to public health, it will be in luck. Otherwise, Valley Vehicles is unlikely to have access to the settlement terms between Mountain Manufacturing and Paula.

1f. No. Mediation sessions between private disputants are private. If Valley Vehicles or Paula were a state agency, for example, state sunshine laws would almost certainly apply, and access would be more likely. But that is not the case here. This is a private corporation in a dispute with a private individual, contracting for a private third party to provide mediation services. Even if the court ordered the mediation (see Chapter 8 for more on these processes), the basic confidential nature of these proceedings would remain unchanged. Indeed, even if the subsequent alternative dispute resolution effort by Valley Vehicles and Paula were more judicial in nature—for example, a summary jury trial—the logic of *Cincinnati Gas & Electric* (from Chapter 11) would still permit the parties to exclude the reporter from the process.

1g. If Valley Vehicles and Paula decide they want the reporter to be present, they each presumably see some potential benefit to the prospect that the reporter will eventually say something about what they observe in the mediation. If the parties do not want to entertain the risk that the reporter would testify or write something subsequently, they could simply refuse the reporter's request to attend. Assuming neither of the disputants is a public entity, such that open meetings laws might be implicated, the reporter would have no right to force their way into the mediation uninvited.

If the parties want to assure that the reporter has the ability subsequently to testify about a mediation communication, they will need to address the fact that the UMA grants a privilege to each of the disputants. A mutual waiver of that privilege, ex ante, in the mediation agreement should suffice. UMA §3(a)(2) specifies that the privilege only attaches in circumstances in which "the mediation parties and the mediator agree to mediate in a record that demonstrates an expectation that mediation communications will be privileged against disclosure." The mediator would normally still have a privilege permitting them to block the reporter from testifying about the mediator's own mediation communications. But assuming that the parties' express intention that the mediation not be confidential appears in the agreement to mediate—which the mediator would also need to agree to—then the reporter should be competent to testify about the mediation proceedings.

Everyone Versus Michelle

2a. Yes. A mediator holds a privilege that would normally permit the mediator to block testimony about any of her mediation communications. See UMA §4(b)(2). However, the UMA specifically provides an exception to that privilege in the event that the testimony is "sought or offered to prove or disprove a claim or complaint of professional misconduct or malpractice filed against a mediator." UMA §6(a)(5). In the absence of such a privilege, the mediation parties will be able to compel testimony from Michelle. A number of states' mediation privilege laws provide a much narrower set of privilege exceptions than the UMA in the context of alleged malpractice during the mediation. We repeat our advice that you check the particulars of your jurisdiction, with an eye toward whether its exceptions are as broad as those found in the UMA.

2b. No. All parties hold a privilege about what happened in the mediation, and Michelle has a mediator's privilege about her communications. UMA §4(b)(1) and §4(b)(2). However, if Michelle offers her testimony to disprove a claim of malpractice, the exception in §6(a)(5) applies, and the communication is not privileged. Even without this protection, the parties' claim against Michelle may also have the effect of waiving their privilege altogether under UMA §5(b). Under §5(b), the parties cannot assert a privilege that prevents Michelle from defending herself. Thus, under either section, the communication is not privileged, and the parties cannot prevent Michelle from testifying.

Even in contexts in which the UMA does not govern confidentiality, courts will almost always permit mediators to testify about mediation communications in order to defend themselves against allegations of misconduct. For example, in *Allen v. Leal*, 27 F. Supp. 2d 945 (S.D. Tex. 1998), the mother of a child shot by a police officer was attempting to avoid the settlement agreement, which she claimed the mediator coerced. Faced with the question of whether the mediator could testify about what occurred in the mediation, the court held that the plaintiff "'opened the door' by attacking the professionalism and integrity of the mediator and the mediation process, [and hence] the Court was compelled, in the interests of justice, to breach the veil of confidentiality."

2c. The plaintiffs and the mediator likely have some shared (or at least not opposed) interests regarding the potential for a confidentiality clause. The mediator would presumably want to avoid publicity about the alleged malpractice, and the parties would presumably prefer that the mediator not divulge information from the mediation. The settlement would almost certainly include a mutual exchange of waivers, such that the parties would feel secure that this represents full and final resolution of all disputes related to the mediation. The parties may have an opportunity to capitalize on differences in time horizons or discounts rates by settling sooner (or postponing payments, depending on their particular circumstances).

There remains the conspicuous, distributive question about any potential exchange of money regarding the settlement. If the parties were sufficiently disappointed in the mediator's performance, they might not pay the mediator's fee, raising the prospect of a counterclaim by the mediator against the parties. The facts here do not provide enough information to assess accurately the risks and opportunities such litigation might present, nor do we know enough to say much about the scope of any waivers that might be included in a potential settlement.

Manufacturers Versus the Media

3a. Maybe. Nothing in this question implicated UMA privileges. Notice that the reporter is not a party, a mediator, or a nonparty participant in the mediation. Those are the only holders of privileges under the UMA. This makes sense in this case, because the conversation in question—the one between the reporter and the informant—did not actually take place in a mediation session.

The reporter will have to rely on a reporter's privilege to resist testifying about the source of his information. A full discussion of reporters' privileges is far beyond the scope of this chapter, or even this book. The quick summary is that some states offer reporters an absolute privilege against disclosure. Most, however, provide only a qualified privilege. Under this qualified privilege, a party seeking to compel disclosure must typically demonstrate that the reporter's information (1) is highly material and relevant to the claim; (2) is at the "heart of the claim," meaning that it is necessary or critical to maintaining the claim; and (3) cannot be obtained from alternate sources. In cases involving libel claims against reporters, most courts have found that the matter is "at the heart of the claim," and therefore do not recognize a reporter's privilege. Whether the companies can compel testimony from the reporter about the leak, therefore, depends on the jurisdiction's construction of reporters' privileges.

3b. Probably not. If Mountain Manufacturing and Valley Vehicles want to testify, they would clearly be willing to waive the privilege they would otherwise hold, as mediation parties, under UMA §4(b)(1). However, under the terms of UMA §4(a), mediation communications are privileged unless waived, and under the terms of UMA §5, "all parties" to the mediation must waive for a waiver to be effective. Therefore, Mountain Manufacturing and Valley Vehicles will only be able to testify if they secure a waiver from Paula. Given the reality of the other litigation pending between these parties, such a waiver seems unlikely. In short, Paula would have little incentive to be helpful (by waiving the privilege in this case) to someone occupying an adverse position in another piece of litigation.

3c. Paula's immediate choice is about whether she *wishes* to testify.

If Paula would prefer not to testify (for example because of the time, the cost, or the risk of reputational damage), her best strategy would be to seek to quash the subpoena. Under §4(b)(1), a mediation party may refuse to testify about mediation communications. Paula has never waived this privilege, so she should be successful in this regard.

If Paula were inclined to cooperate in the civil libel suit, under normal circumstances, each of the other parties (and potentially the mediator as well, depending on the nature of the evidence being sought) would hold privileges in addition to Paula. Each of them would have to waive those privileges expressly before Paula would be permitted to testify. You would, therefore, presumably advise your client (and likely the lawyers for the newspaper and the reporter) of the need to secure waivers from these other parties before Paula will make herself available to testify.

One potential wrinkle in this is that the newspaper and the reporter could argue that Mountain Manufacturing and Valley Vehicles waived their privileges by bringing this libel action. The argument would be that under UMA §5(b), "a person that discloses or makes a representation about a mediation communication which prejudices another person in a proceeding is precluded from asserting a privilege under Section 4, but only to the extent necessary for the person prejudiced to respond to the representation or disclosure." Here, the companies declared the newspaper account to be false. Whether that constitutes a representation about a mediation communication is arguable. If it is, however, the newspaper and reporter could clearly claim that they have been prejudiced by their claim of falsity, and they would assert the need to compel testimony about what was actually said in order to respond to that representation.

Valley Vehicles Versus Its Lawyer

4a. Yes. For many purposes, as we have illustrated above, both Paula and Mountain Manufacturing would hold privileges that would prevent testimony about the kinds of mediation communications that are likely to be at the heart of Valley Vehicles' claims. But this is an exception to those general circumstances. Under UMA §6(a)(6), no privilege exists if the information is being sought "to prove or disprove a claim or complaint of professional misconduct or malpractice filed against a mediation party, nonparty participant, or representative of a party based on conduct occurring during a mediation." Valley Vehicles' claim against its attorney focuses on the attorney's conduct during the mediation. Therefore, under the UMA, this information is not privileged, and Valley Vehicles will be able to compel Paula's testimony. Recall, however, that some states hold a narrower view of exceptions in the context of alleged malpractice.

4b. No. As we described in the answer immediately above, UMA §6(a)(6) does not make this information the subject of a privilege. However, UMA §6(a)(6) is further modified by UMA §6(c), which provides that "a mediator may not be compelled to provide evidence of a mediation communication referred to in [§6(a)(6)]." As a result, Valley Vehicles could succeed in compelling testimony from other parties—whether they were co-parties or opposing parties—but could not compel testimony from the mediator who was present.

The State Versus Mountain Manufacturing

5a. Probably not, but it depends. The communication in the mediation would generally be protected unless it falls under one of the exceptions in §6 of the UMA. Two exceptions might be relevant to this case. First, there is no privilege for communication that is used to conceal "ongoing criminal activity." UMA §6(a)(4). Mountain Manufacturing might be able to argue that Valley Vehicles' statements are evidence of ongoing criminal activity that violate environmental laws. Second, under §6(b)(1), there is no privilege if a court or administrative agency finds, after a hearing *in camera*, that (1) the evidence is not otherwise available, (2) there is a need for the evidence, and (3) that this is a court proceeding involving a felony or misdemeanor. If the action brought against Mountain Manufacturing is a criminal action (and not just a regulatory civil action), then there is a good argument that Mountain Manufacturing is entitled to have all evidence in its defense available to it. Mountain Manufacturing would need to run through the process outlined in the UMA, but after a hearing, the judge could determine that Valley Vehicles' statements are relevant and not subject to privilege.

5b. Maybe. It most likely depends on whether the state agency's action against Mountain Manufacturing is part of a felony prosecution. If the environmental claim in this case is serious enough to constitute a felony, UMA §6(b)(1) will apply. Under its terms,

> there is no privilege under Section 4 if a court, administrative agency, or arbitrator finds, after a hearing in camera, that the party seeking discovery or the proponent of the evidence has shown that the evidence is not otherwise available, that there is a need for the evidence that substantially outweighs the interest in protecting confidentiality, and that the mediation communication is sought or offered in . . . a court proceeding involving a felony.

The state agency would, therefore, be able to compel testimony about the relevant mediation communications. (Note that it can even compel mediators' testimony, because the mediator shield under UMA §6(c) does not apply to §6(b)(1) cases.) If, however, the agency's action is merely a minor one (for example, a misdemeanor), §6(b)(1) may not apply and the standard privilege will protect a mediator from having to testify.

If the manufacturer's behavior could be characterized as an ongoing crime or an effort to conceal an ongoing crime, the exception under UMA §6(a)(4) would apply. But in this case, the facts do not necessarily support such an assertion.

5c. Probably yes. Neither the UMA nor federal common law protects the terms of the settlement agreement. The contractual agreement between Mountain Manufacturing and Paula is the only thing protecting the confidentiality of the terms. To the extent that the environmental agency would be successful in arguing to a court that the settlement terms relate to the protection of public health in connection with its own enforcement action, it might be able to have the confidentiality clause stricken as contrary to public policy. For more on secret settlements, see Chapter 3.

CHAPTER 8

An Introduction to Arbitration

§8.1 INTRODUCTION

Most students arrive at law school with some idea of what a trial looks like. Their vision of a trial is often the product of television and movies, rather than actual experience, so their initial impressions are frequently mistaken. Still, having that basic model of litigation in mind can be helpful as students begin to navigate the details of procedure and law.

By contrast, very few students arrive at law school having any personal experience with arbitration, and virtually nothing interesting on TV even acknowledges arbitration, much less provides an accurate picture of it. As a result, students studying arbitration often find it difficult to find meaning in the various legal doctrines involved, in part because they have neither a background in nor a mental image of arbitration.

So, with some hesitation, we suggest the following initial mental image as you begin to study arbitration: litigation.

Litigation is an adversarial proceeding in which competing parties make arguments and present evidence before a third party. In litigation, that third party is a randomly assigned judge who will render one or more decisions during the course of the proceeding. The proceeding takes place in a courthouse and includes a high degree of formalism, including things like the judge wearing robes while seated on an elevated bench, with each party assigned to a designated spot in the courtroom. In litigation, a specific set of predictable procedures governs the parties' interactions. Those procedures include rules of pleadings, discovery, and evidence. Furthermore, the judge is bound to apply existing laws to the facts of the particular dispute before the court. At the conclusion, although the results of litigation in a trial court are binding, disappointed parties almost always have at least one opportunity to appeal the outcome.

Arbitration shares some, but not all, of these features. Arbitration, like litigation, is also an adversarial proceeding in which parties present their perspective to a third party, who renders a final decision. Arbitration often has less formality. Arbitration typically occurs in a nice conference room in a law firm office with the arbitrator dressed no differently than the other participants. Procedural and evidentiary rules are typically more relaxed, and in many contexts, the arbitrator may not be obligated to follow the law. Unless otherwise constrained, the arbitrator could, instead, apply their understanding of common business practices, a best guess about the parties' intentions, or a sense of industrial or commercial justice as the basis for a decision. Disputants in an arbitration almost always have a hand in selecting the person who will serve as arbitrator, and there are very few bases upon which one can appeal or contest an arbitrator's final decision.

A final difference—and perhaps the most important one—between arbitration and litigation is that arbitration is fundamentally a creature of contract. Parties participate in binding arbitration because at some point they agreed to do so. While most parties adopt the less formal procedural rules the major arbitration services providers offer, they can, of course, design the procedures themselves. If the parties' contract spells out a set of procedures identical to litigation, those will govern the arbitration. If they want the arbitrator to wear a robe, that's probably fine as well. As Judge Posner colorfully put the matter in *Baravati v. Josephthal, Lyon & Ross, Inc.*, 28 F.3d 704, 709 (7th Cir. 1994), "[S]hort of authorizing trial by battle or ordeal or, more doubtfully, by a panel of three monkeys, parties can stipulate to whatever procedures they want to govern the arbitration of their disputes; parties are as free to specify idiosyncratic terms of arbitration as they are to specify any other terms in their contract."

Because of this flexibility, any effort to describe arbitration generically must include the caveat that arbitration process depends on "what the parties agreed to." This description is no exception. We have just described one version of arbitration, albeit a typical one. Still, this is a starting point from which you can begin to appreciate the important legal and policy issues that arise in arbitration.

The most fundamental distinction between arbitration and most other forms of dispute resolution outside of court is that arbitrators decide the matters submitted to them. Arbitration—in all its various forms—is an adjudicative process. And, in almost all forms of arbitration, arbitrators' decisions are binding on the disputants.

§8.1.1 Arbitration Is Not Litigation

Now that we've set up a mental image of arbitration as similar to litigation, it might be helpful to compare arbitration to litigation. In most of your law school classes, the chronological "life" of a dispute appears to begin with some unfortunate incident occurring between two or more parties. (You have surely noticed by now that if two people coexist happily, we are unlikely to study their interactions in law school.) Sometime after the incident, the dispute finds its way to court. After some form of adjudication (for example, a dispositive motion or a verdict at trial), the court enters a judgment. The court's judgment then takes effect. The simplified "timeline" of a litigated case, therefore, looks something like this:

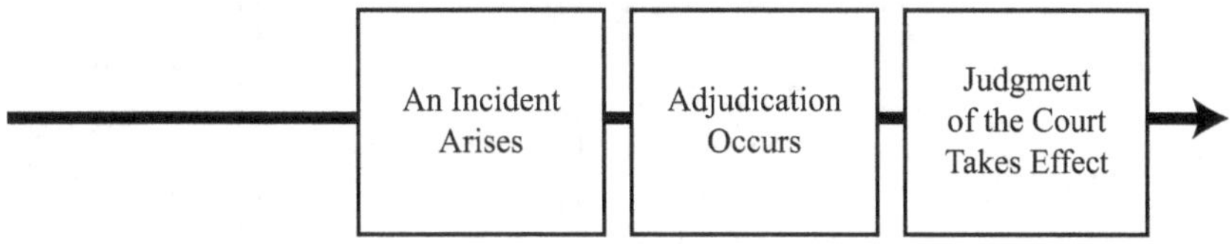

This simplified timeline omits, of course, the possibility that the parties had some relationship prior to the incident. In any contract claim or divorce, for example, one would expect to see a box before the incident—one in which the parties at least arguably entered a relationship with each other.

This timeline also ignores the increasingly prominent role of ADR in modern litigation. ADR appears in the timeline of modern litigation in a number of possible places, depending on the type of ADR in question. For example, it would be perfectly normal (though perhaps surprising to students after their first year of law school) for one party to pick up the phone and call the other person following an incident to see if they can work it out. Perhaps the parties will hire lawyers to negotiate on their behalf. Or perhaps they will engage the services of a mediator to explore the possibility of settlement before the dispute ripens into a lawsuit.

Negotiation and mediation may also occur after a lawsuit has commenced. For example, as we discuss in Chapter 6, some jurisdictions require litigants to pursue some form of ADR before they proceed to trial. Parties might, therefore, try mediation just before or just after discovery to see if they might prefer a possible settlement to further litigation. In some systems, opportunities for ADR extend even beyond the end of trial. For example, appellate mediation programs, which seek to promote a post-verdict settlement before a matter appears before appellate courts, are increasingly common. At every step along the timeline pictured above, opportunities for negotiation and mediation arise.

§8.1.2 Arbitration Is a Contractual Substitute for Litigation

Arbitration, the most formal of the ADR methods you are likely to study, operates in most instances as a true substitute for litigation through the courts. Those in arbitration are not, for the most part, simultaneously pursuing litigation. As a binding[1] method of alternative dispute resolution, arbitration takes place *in lieu* of trial.

One way in which an arbitration's timeline differs from that of litigation is that binding arbitration only occurs if the parties agreed to arbitrate. (We discuss in later chapters the range of behaviors that are treated as constituting "agreement to arbitrate" for purposes of enforcing arbitration clauses.) Notice the basic chronology of arbitration, illustrated below.

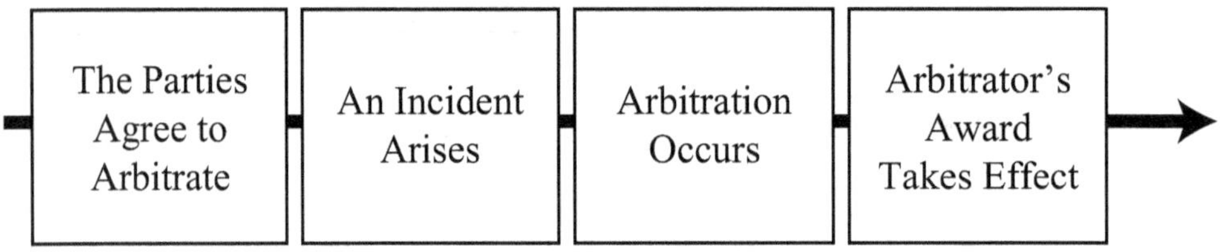

We should also note that in some cases, parties with no prior contractual relationship may find themselves in a dispute and may agree to arbitrate their existing dispute. In that event, the order of the first two of these boxes would be reversed. But the basic idea remains the same: Arbitration necessarily involves an agreement to submit the dispute to arbitration.

As you learned in your first-year Contracts course, parties enter contractual relationships all the time. (A consumer buys a product. An employee takes a job. Two businesses set up a joint venture. A patient checks into a hospital. A union and a company enter a collectively bargained agreement. And so on.) In the process of entering that relationship, parties sometimes wisely anticipate that something could go wrong down the road. Though predicting future problems may not be the kind of thing one would normally expect at the blissful moment of entering into an exciting contract of some sort, few lawyers survive law school without noticing that a fair percentage of deals wind up going sour. Lawyers tend to be good at envisioning bad scenarios, and the best lawyers craft contracts that address those scenarios effectively.

1. As we discuss in Chapter 11, a nonbinding version of arbitration exists. For purposes of simplicity, when we refer to arbitration in this chapter, we speak of the version in which the arbitrator's decision is binding on the participants.

One common approach to dealing with the possibility of a future dispute is to insert a clause describing how the parties will resolve future disputes. This clause might include, for example, choice of law and choice of forum provisions. Increasingly, this clause also calls for the parties to enter arbitration (rather than litigation) to resolve those future disputes.

To return to the major point of this section: Arbitration, in most of its forms, is entirely a creature of contract. If the parties agreed to arbitrate a dispute, they will be held to that agreement, and either party will be able to block the other from pursuing an action in court. The corollary is that if the parties did not agree to resolve their dispute through arbitration, they cannot be compelled to resolve their dispute through arbitration. As a preview of some of the materials we cover in Chapter 9, however, you should know that many courts have been expansive in their assessment of what constitutes "agreeing" to arbitrate. In many circumstances, you are deemed to have agreed to arbitrate by accepting employment, by purchasing a product, or by paying for a service. It would be inaccurate to assume, therefore, that all of arbitration can be avoided if one simply prefers to litigate. (For example, if you bought this book through certain online vendors, you may have already agreed to submit any disputes related to the purchase of this book to arbitration, whether you were aware of it or not. And we're sorry about that.)

§8.1.3 Arbitration Is Not Mediation

Do *not* confuse arbitration with mediation. The principal difference between the two lies in the authority of the third party. Put most succinctly, arbitrators render decisions and mediators don't. A mediator might offer suggestions; make predictions about what a court would do; facilitate conversation between the disputants; and engage in a wide variety of activities aimed at helping the disputants to find a mutually acceptable outcome. But a mediator does not render a binding decision. A mediation ends one of two ways: Either the parties reach a settlement with each other, or they don't. An arbitration ends one way: The arbitrator makes a final decision. This is a modest overstatement, of course, because just as litigants can agree to settle on the courthouse steps or while the jury is deliberating, parties to arbitration can agree to settle even during the course of the arbitration. The important difference is that mediation is explicitly designed to promote settlement, whereas litigation and binding arbitration are designed to produce a judgment.

Although arbitration is a confidential process, it does not enjoy the same kind of confidentiality protection as mediation. (See Chapter 7 for more on confidentiality in mediation.) Arbitration leads to resolutions almost entirely outside of the public view. In arbitration, transcripts are not necessarily required, the arbitrator can issue a decision without any opinion explaining the reasoning underlying the decision, and the hearing itself is rarely open to public access. Further, because a dispute that finds itself in arbitration tends to stay in arbitration before the same arbitrator, there is rarely a reason for outside interest in the arbitration proceedings. The combination of these factors means that arbitration is usually characterized by relative secrecy. Of course, if there is a motion either to confirm or vacate a decision, certain aspects of the arbitration will become part of a public court filing.

While privacy is important to many who choose to mediate, the primary reason mediation confidentiality receives statutory protection is because we want to provide an incentive for participants to engage fully. Engaging fully in mediation might involve acknowledging the other side's perspective, suggesting compromise options, disclosing your own priorities, etc. In arbitration, by contrast, confidentiality is not needed to provide this incentive, because arbitration is an adversarial proceeding, akin to litigation. In adversarial proceedings, we imagine that both parties present the best evidence and make the best arguments they can. There is no reason for them to hold back on these arguments, even in the absence of formal confidentiality protections, because they want to win the case. Thus, courts and legislatures have not given arbitration parties the same array of confidentiality protections as mediation.

Still, issues of confidentiality in arbitration do sometimes arise. The leading case on arbitration confidentiality is *United States v. Panhandle Eastern Corp.*, 118 F.R.D. 346 (D. Del. 1988). The United States, on behalf of the Maritime Administration, brought a civil action against Panhandle and its affiliates to protect its security interest as a guarantor of ship financing bonds. As part of discovery, the United States requested documents concerning an earlier arbitration conducted between Panhandle and Sonatrach (the Algerian National Oil and Gas Company). Panhandle made a motion for a protective order to prevent disclosure of the Sonatrach documents, including the parties' arbitration briefs. It argued that disclosure of the arbitration documents to third parties would severely prejudice its ongoing business relationship with Sonatrach and the Algerian government. The court found this argument unpersuasive, holding that Panhandle had failed to demonstrate good cause for the protective order. As a result, the arbitration documents were discoverable and admissible. Arbitration parties who would prefer additional confidentiality are only *sometimes* able to achieve it by including confidentiality clauses in their contracts.

§8.1.4 Comparing Litigation, Arbitration, and Mediation

	Final Decision Maker	How it Starts	Role of the Third Party	Role of the Courts	Outcome
Litigation	Judge (and sometimes jury)	Plaintiff files a complaint with the court	Final decision maker	Comprehensive > Oversee all pretrial, trial, and enforcement	Binding judgment, enforceable in court
Binding Arbitration	Arbitrator	Party files a claim pursuant to arbitration agreement procedures	Final decision maker	Minimal > Sometimes needed to compel parties to arbitration, to stay litigation. > Available to enforce arbitral award. > Rarely available for review or appeal.	Arbitral award, enforceable in court
Mediation	Parties	Parties consent to meet in mediation Or Parties are compelled to try mediation by rule or by court	Facilitator of negotiations	Minimal > Sometimes needed to compel mediation participation. > Available to enforce terms of agreement reached in mediation – whether through contract or consent order.	Either: Settlement. An enforceable contract or a consent judgment. No agreement. Parties go forward with another process.

§8.2 A BRIEF HISTORY OF THE LAW OF ARBITRATION

The idea of submitting a dispute to a third party and having that party render a decision is by no means a recent development. In one very common form, the third party is someone who has a degree of control over the disputants. Historically, the third party might be a ruler, a leader, or a monarch, for example. (Any parent with two or more children has seen this instinct to call in a higher authority—probably more times than the parent would prefer.) Perhaps the most famous maternity dispute in history involved two women, each claiming to be the mother of the child in question, who submitted the dispute to Solomon.[2] As the story is commonly told, we might imagine that the women chose Solomon because he was "wise." In fact, he was the king (although many also thought him to be wise and used this story as proof of his cleverness).

The notion of submitting a dispute to someone in a position of general authority has considerable appeal. If the person rendering the decision is also capable of assuring compliance with that decision, the service is even more valuable. This trend continues to this day. Many disputants take their disputes to judges (through the vehicle of litigation), because the state has a system of mechanisms for assuring that judges' decisions are binding.

Evidence of arbitration in the United States dates to colonial times, but arbitration was used only modestly in most contexts until the twentieth century. Some labor disputes were resolved through binding arbitration more than one hundred years ago. There were also some well-known international arbitration cases between countries. For example, the United States and Great Britain arbitrated the Alabama Claims in 1871, stemming from the U.S. allegation that Great Britain violated its neutrality during the U.S. Civil War by aiding the Confederacy.[3]

Businesses that were engaged in regular commerce with one another also frequently sought the speed, efficiency, and expertise arbitration offered. But standing in the way of broad application of arbitration to resolve disputes was judicial reluctance to enforce arbitral agreements. Arguing that arbitration agreements inappropriately "ousted" the courts of their proper jurisdiction, many U.S. courts refused to give effect to arbitration agreements or the awards of arbitrators. That is, the courts saw arbitration as an illegitimate intrusion into their "turf." Without any assurance that an agreement to arbitrate a dispute would be enforced, parties saw little reason to include one in a contract. Similarly, unless parties were assured that an arbitrator's decision would be respected, they had little reason to submit a case to arbitration. As a result, for some time, arbitration enjoyed only moderate usage.

In 1925, responding to the business community's displeasure over courts' reluctance to give effect to arbitration agreements, Congress passed the Federal Arbitration Act (the FAA). The FAA essentially commands courts to treat arbitration clauses in contracts the same way that they treat all other

2. You might recall that Solomon decided that the baby should be split in two. In response, one of the two claimants backed down, agreeing that the other woman should have the baby. Solomon then deemed the woman who refused to permit the baby to be divided to be the true mother. The story is the origin of the commonly used phrase "to split the baby."

3. See Frank Warren Hackett, *Reminiscences of the Geneva Tribunal of Arbitration 1872: The Alabama Claims* (Houghton Mifflin, 1911).

clauses in contracts. On the front end, the FAA ensures the enforceability of an agreement to arbitrate. On the back end, the FAA ensures that the courts will enforce the arbitration award and offers limited review of such awards. Following the FAA's enactment, arbitration came to be common in resolving contract disputes among repeat-player businesses (those that frequently do business with each other). Arbitration also enjoyed a prominent role in resolving labor disputes, and many of the most significant arbitration decisions of the U.S. Supreme Court in the mid-twentieth century arose in the context of labor arbitrations.

Beginning in the 1970s and 1980s, arbitration started to expand to other categories of disputes. It was no longer just sophisticated businesses and those with ongoing commercial relationships that were entering arbitration agreements. Instead, arbitration clauses began to appear in employment contracts and in consumer sales as businesses took advantage of the efficiencies, cost savings, and control offered by arbitration. The expansion of arbitration into these realms has added a layer of complexity to arbitration, and the courts continue to sort out the boundaries of this expansion. Unlike the attitude from one hundred years ago, however, modern courts embrace arbitration agreements in a wide variety of settings, supporting what these courts perceive as "a federal policy favoring arbitration." We will discuss this evolution further in Chapter 9.

§8.3 MAKING THEM PLAY: HOW COURTS COMPEL PARTICIPATION IN ARBITRATION

The usefulness of arbitration agreements hinges significantly on the ability of each party to hold the other to the terms of the arbitration agreement. After all, what good is an agreement to arbitrate if you are unable to compel the other side to arbitrate? What good is winning a case before an arbitrator if the arbitrator's judgment cannot be enforced? These questions overstate the issue somewhat. There are ways in which an agreement or an award could have some utility, even if they were unenforceable. But the bulk of the attraction of arbitration clauses is that parties can bind themselves (or more accurately, that they can bind the other side) into arbitration in an enforceable way.

To give arbitration this certainty and finality requires a particular relationship with the courts, because courts are the ones with the established power of the state to compel or prohibit certain behavior. The rest of this chapter examines the contours of the relationship between arbitration and the courts.

In its most simplistic form, arbitration is entirely private. Two parties enter a contract together (a wholly private act), and they include an arbitration clause in that contract. Then they get into some kind of dispute. (This is still private, assuming neither one called the police or involved the state in some way.) They mutually recognize that they had previously anticipated this possibility in their contract, so they agree (privately) to hire a private arbitrator. They engage in the arbitration (still no state involvement), and the arbitrator rules in favor of one party over the other. The loser does whatever the arbitrator orders, and the matter is resolved completely privately. In fact, most arbitrations are conducted without the state being involved in any way.

Potential complications arise when the private arbitration process intersects with the public litigation process during a dispute. For example, what happens when, during litigation, one party argues that the parties entered a pre-dispute agreement to arbitrate the dispute in question?

The Federal Arbitration Act provides the statutory framework for the relationship between courts and arbitration. However, as you will see in Chapter 10, various state laws also shape this relationship, and in some cases, federal and state laws differ. But, as to the subject of this chapter—enforcement—both federal and state laws adopt virtually identical mechanisms for governing the relationship between arbitration and the courts.

§8.3.1 Motions to Stay the Litigation

What happens if a plaintiff files a complaint in federal court, and the defendant believes that the matter is properly the subject of an agreement to arbitrate? Under the authority of §3 of the Federal Arbitration Act, the defendant would file a *motion to stay the litigation* in court.

In a simple case, the defendant seeking to have the claim heard in arbitration would file a motion to stay with the court, show the court the written arbitration agreement, and demonstrate that the subject of the lawsuit is covered by the arbitration agreement. Upon satisfaction of these conditions, the court would grant the stay, and no further litigation nor an appeal from the grant of the motion to stay would be permitted until the arbitration had run its course. Assuming the arbitration clause was sufficiently broad to cover everything that the litigation would have addressed, nothing will be left for the court to do upon the conclusion of the arbitration. In short, an order staying litigation under FAA §3 can effectively end the dispute's life in court.

You can probably think of many ways in which this sequence might be more complicated in practice. In later chapters, we take up such questions as, "What if it's not clear that the contract containing the arbitration clause is enforceable?" or "What if it's not clear whether the arbitration agreement covers the subject of the plaintiff's complaint?" (Chapter 9); and, "What if state and federal laws conflict about the answer to any of these questions?" (Chapter 10). For now, you should simply understand that if a party believes that a claim should be heard in arbitration rather than in litigation, the party can file a motion to stay the litigation, pending the outcome of the arbitration.

§8.3.2 Motions to Compel Arbitration

What if one party believes that arbitration is required, but the other party refuses to participate in arbitration? Again, the party seeking to enforce an arbitration agreement can go to court, this time by seeking an order to compel arbitration of the matter. The federal statutory basis for such an order appears in §4 of the Federal Arbitration Act, under which parties can compel arbitration if they are "aggrieved by the alleged failure, neglect, or refusal of another to arbitrate under a written agreement for arbitration."

As with motions to stay the litigation, before granting a motion to compel arbitration, a court must be satisfied that a contract containing a relevant arbitration clause exists. This raises all kinds of possible legal wrinkles that we will cover in the next chapters. The big picture is that a party can use the coercive powers of the court enforce the agreement to arbitrate.

In some cases, a party might file both a §4 motion to compel arbitration and a §3 motion to stay litigation. For example, a defendant against whom a plaintiff has filed a lawsuit, but who believes that arbitration is called for, might go to the court and say, "Send this ne'er-do-well plaintiff to arbitration because he agreed to arbitrate. Relatedly, and for the same reasons, please stop this litigation." In practical terms, this could be overkill, because success with the first would necessarily bring about the desired effect from the second. Still, you should be aware that many of the important cases we discuss in these chapters concerning the relationship between arbitration and the courts arose in contexts in which one party sought both to stay the litigation and to compel arbitration.

§8.3.3 Defaults in Arbitration

What if a party files a claim in arbitration, and the defendant refuses to show up? As you may recall from Civil Procedure, if someone sues you in court and you fail to show up, you are at great risk of having the court declare you to be in default. In fact, the procedural rules in virtually every jurisdiction provide for the entry of default and, quickly thereafter, the entry of default judgment against an absent defendant. That default judgment, like any judgment of a court, can be enforced against you. The plaintiff can get the assistance of local law enforcement to seize your property to satisfy a judgment against you if you refuse to pay it.

The picture is not all that different in arbitration, though the mechanisms vary depending on the jurisdiction and the terms of the arbitration agreement itself. Under a variety of laws—many states' arbitration laws, the Uniform Arbitration Act, the new Revised Uniform Arbitration Act, and the Federal Arbitration Act—an arbitrator may enter a default judgment against an absent party, provided the party had adequate notice of the hearing. Arbitrations that are administered under some organizations' rules handle absent parties differently. For example, under the rules of the American Arbitration Association or the International Chamber of Commerce,[4] an arbitrator cannot enter a judgment by default. The arbitrator must still hear the claim of the party who is present and render a decision. Of course, as you might imagine, if you don't even show up, it's going to be hard for you to win.

Therefore, as a practical matter, the capacity to compel the participation of an absent party is not always central to the functioning of arbitration.

§8.3.4 The Preclusive Effects of Arbitral Awards

Motions to stay or to compel represent two methods to assure that a dispute is processed in the forum of the disputants' choosing. But what if the dispute goes to one place, gets resolved, and then one of the disputants tries to bring the case again in another forum? In most instances in litigation, disputants have only one bite at the apple because of the effects of the preclusion doctrines.

Preclusion is an umbrella term that encompasses two separate affirmative defenses. The first is the doctrine of *res judicata*, or claim preclusion. If *res judicata* applies, a plaintiff is precluded from bringing his or her entire claim on the theory that the plaintiff already litigated (or had a chance to litigate) this claim in a previous action. *Res judicata* acts like a sledgehammer, eradicating entire claims. By contrast, the second form of preclusion, collateral estoppel (also known as issue preclusion), only prevents the relitigation of certain issues that were already litigated in a previous action. If collateral estoppel applies, the rest of the claim may proceed through litigation, but some issues within that litigation will already be decided.

In the context of your Civil Procedure course, these doctrines probably appeared in the discussion of two sequential court actions. The first case went to court and was resolved in some way. Then a party filed a second action in court, and the other party sought to preclude the relitigation of some or all of what happened in the first lawsuit. But what if one or the

4. As will be discussed more fully below, many arbitration agreements identify an organization that will provide to them an arbitrator to resolve their dispute and default rules for them to follow if a dispute arises. The American Arbitration Association and the International Chamber of Commerce are two such provider organizations.

other (or both) of the two cases instead appeared before an arbitrator? How do the preclusion doctrines affect arbitration?

If a party seeks to preclude an issue or a claim in court, citing a prior arbitration, the court must decide whether the preclusion doctrines apply to arbitral awards. Courts are split on this. More than two decades ago, the Supreme Court, in *McDonald v. City of West Branch*, 466 U.S. 284 (1984), held that an arbitration is not a "judicial proceeding," and therefore denied the application of the Full Faith and Credit Clause to its enforcement. For the same reasons, it held that the federal court in question should not give the arbitral award preclusive effect under the usual common law preclusion doctrines, either. In many cases, federal courts have some discretion about whether to give preclusive effect to arbitral awards. Some state courts, however, routinely give full preclusive effects to arbitral awards, treating the awards as if they were court judgments. For example, the Connecticut Supreme Court, in *Corey v. Avco-Lycoming Div.*, 307 A.2d 155 (Conn. 1972), holding that a prior arbitration barred a subsequent lawsuit, wrote that it saw "[n]o satisfactory reason . . . why an award, which the parties have expressly stipulated should be final as to the subject submitted, should not be as conclusive as a court-rendered judgment."

As an additional note, international arbitrations are often given greater preclusive deference than their domestic counterparts, because the Convention on the Recognition and Enforcement of Foreign Arbitral Awards does not line up precisely with the Federal Arbitration Act. We discuss the enforcement of international arbitral awards later in this chapter.

The best rough summary of the law of preclusion, as applied to arbitral awards, is this: Most courts are particularly inclined to grant preclusive effect to arbitral awards when the arbitration procedures in the first case included the kinds of procedures one would expect to find in litigation.

The preclusion doctrines typically also run smoothly in the other direction. That is, what if the first case was in court and resulted in a final judgment on the merits, and the second one appeared before an arbitrator? Could the party who was victorious in the first (litigated) case avoid readjudication of the same claim or issue in the second case (in arbitration)? In short, yes. This principle is outlined in John Morrell & Co. v. Loc. Union 304A of United Food & Com. Workers, AFL-CIO, 913 F.2d 544, 561–62 (8th Cir. 1990). The details of the enforcement of preclusion-based defenses are beyond the scope of this book, but the big picture is that a party who fails in court will not find in arbitration a refuge in which to try again.

However, the above analysis is often irrelevant in practice because many victorious arbitration parties seek (successfully) to have the arbitrator's award entered as a judgment of the court. Once it is given the status of a court's judgment, there is no question that it will be given preclusive effect. Courts play virtually no role in reviewing or supervising the entry of the award, as we discuss later in the chapter, yet this simple act gives the arbitrator's decision clear preclusive effect in subsequent actions.

§8.4 GETTING YOUR WAY: HOW COURTS HANDLE REVIEWS OF ARBITRATORS' DECISIONS

Arbitration is an adjudicative, adversarial process. In most cases, it produces winners and losers. What can a losing party do about the undesired outcome, beyond complaining bitterly? Can the losing party somehow have the arbitrator's award vacated?

The short answer is probably not. One of the attractions of arbitration, at least to many parties, is its finality. In the words of the court in *Moncharsh v. Heily & Blase*, 832 P.2d 899, 903 (Cal. 1992), "The arbitrator's decision should be the end, not the beginning, of the dispute." Arbitration, therefore, presents very few opportunities to succeed with an appeal.

§8.4.1 Challenging Arbitral Awards Under the FAA

The four principal grounds for challenging a domestic arbitral award are outlined in §10 of the FAA. An unhappy arbitration party must satisfy one of the four grounds to successfully avoid the outcome of the arbitration. But the task is more difficult than it might seem. Each of the FAA's grounds for vacatur is crafted narrowly, and courts have construed these narrowly crafted grounds even more narrowly. When you review the four FAA grounds for vacatur, notice that the party seeking to avoid the award does not merely argue that the arbitrator made an incorrect decision. In fact, a court is unlikely to be willing even to hear such a complaint. This section is about procedural flaws—something that went wrong with the process that led to the outcome—not about the substantive outcome itself. Of course, if the party is seeking to avoid the award, it's certainly because the party is unhappy with the award. But vacatur is available under FAA §10 only when one of a limited number of procedural flaws led to the losing party's unhappiness. We describe each of the four grounds for vacatur below.

1. **"The arbitrator was duped!"** FAA §10(a)(1) provides that a court may make an order vacating an arbitral award "where the award was procured by corruption, fraud, or undue means." This provision addresses the prospect that the arbitrator might have been influenced by something other than the appropriate considerations one would expect of a decision maker. In the case of §10(a)(1), the question is

whether the arbitrator's decision was based on corruption or fraudulent evidence.

A typical case involving §10(a)(1) involves an allegation that one of the witnesses committed perjury during the arbitration hearing. If the perjured testimony was central to the case and the arbitrator relied on it to decide, the losing party might convince a court to vacate the award on the basis of §10(a)(1). This was the outcome in *Bonar v. Dean Witter Reynolds, Inc.*, 835 F.2d 1378 (11th Cir. 1988). Typically, to prove that an award was procured by undue means, the party seeking vacatur must show that the fraud [or corruption] was (1) not discoverable upon the exercise of due diligence prior to the arbitration, (2) materially related to an issue in the arbitration, and (3) established by clear and convincing evidence" MCI Constructors, LLC v. City Of Greensboro, 610 F.3d 849, 858 (4th Cir. 2010). In *Bonar*, the plaintiffs presented an "expert" witness to testify in an arbitration hearing involving a dispute over securities. The expert claimed to have degrees in finance and accounting, as well as experience in the banking industry. The arbitrators heard the expert's testimony and, consistent with that testimony, imposed punitive damages against one of the named defendants. When that defendant learned that the "expert" had fabricated his credentials, the defendant sought to have a federal court vacate the arbitrator's award under FAA §10(a). The court held that §10(a)(1) requires that the challenger establish fraud by clear and convincing evidence, that the fraud in question must not have been discoverable before or during the arbitration, and that the fraud was material to the decision. In *Bonar*, the court found that the defendant satisfied all three elements. Because the arbitration rules in *Bonar* did not permit prehearing exchanges of witness lists, there was no real opportunity for the defendant to discover the fraud. And the arbitrators would not have permitted "expert" testimony from the witness if they had known that the witness held no relevant credentials. As a result, a court vacated the arbitrators' imposition of punitive damages against the defendant and ordered a rehearing before a new panel of arbitrators.

2. **"The arbitrator was on the take!"** FAA §10(a)(2) provides that a court may refuse to enforce an arbitrator's award if there was "evident partiality or corruption in the arbitrators." As with §10(a)(1), the complaining party does not need to demonstrate any error in the arbitrator's decision. It suffices to demonstrate that the arbitrator deviated so significantly from the presumption of impartiality that attaches to arbitration that it makes no sense to enforce the arbitrator's award. For example, if an arbitrator fails to disclose that his son

is an executive in one of the organizations appearing in the arbitration, a court would very likely deem this to be evident partiality for purposes of FAA §10(a)(2). Citing §10(a)(2), the Supreme Court has held that if an arbitrator has a history of dealings that might create an impression of bias, the arbitrator must disclose those dealings. In *Commonwealth Coatings Corp. v. Continental Casualty. Co.*, 393 U.S. 145 (1968), a plurality of the Court wrote:

> It is true that arbitrators cannot sever all their ties with the business world, since they are not expected to get all their income from their work deciding cases, but we should, if anything, be even more scrupulous to safeguard the impartiality of arbitrators than judges, since the former have completely free rein to decide the law as well as the facts and are not subject to appellate review. We can perceive no way in which the effectiveness of the arbitration process will be hampered by the simple requirement that arbitrators disclose to the parties any dealings that might create an impression of possible bias.

In some cases, therefore, a court may refuse to enforce an arbitral award under §10(a)(2) even if there is no showing of actual bias, corruption, or partiality in the arbitrator.

3. **"The arbitrator conducted a sham hearing!"** FAA §10(a)(3) provides that a court may refuse to enforce an arbitral award "[w]here the arbitrators were guilty of misconduct in refusing to postpone the hearing, upon sufficient cause shown, or in refusing to hear evidence pertinent and material to the controversy; or of any other misbehavior by which the rights of any party have been prejudiced." For example, in the case of *Tempo Shain Corp. v. Bertek, Inc.*, 120 F.3d 16 (2d Cir. 1997), arbitrators refused to postpone a hearing to permit the testimony of one of the executives of Bertek, the defendant corporation. The executive, who the defendants argued was at the center of the events giving rise to the arbitration claim and who would have offered testimony favorable to Bertek, was temporarily unable to testify because his wife had been diagnosed with cancer and he needed to attend to her. Based on evidence that did not include the executive's testimony, the arbitrators found against Bertek. But the Second Circuit held that the arbitrators were guilty of misconduct under FAA §10(a)(3). Calling the proceeding "fundamentally unfair," the appellate court vacated the arbitrators' ruling against Bertek.
4. **"The arbitrator did something, but not what the contract told the arbitrator to do!"** The final provision of the FAA §10 grounds for vacatur provides that a court may refuse to enforce "[w]here the arbitrators exceed their powers, or so imperfectly executed them that a mutual, final, and definite award upon the subject matter submitted was not made." Some parties have tried to stretch this ground into a broad opportunity for review of the substance of the award.

(The logic goes, "We didn't contractually authorize the arbitrator to make an error of law, so this erroneous ruling exceeds the arbitrator's authority.") But this logic has not swayed courts. Instead, the logic of the opinion in *United Paperworkers Int'l Union v. Misco, Inc.*, 484 U.S. 29 (1987), prevails: "As long as the arbitrator is even arguably construing or applying the contract and acting within the scope of his authority, that a court is convinced he committed serious error does not suffice to overturn his decision."

FAA §10(a)(4) is reserved for the relatively rare instance in which the arbitrator's decision is flawed in a way that makes enforcement problematic. For example, an award will not be enforced if it is unintelligible. ("We can't figure out what the heck this decision means.") An award is also subject to vacatur if the scope of the arbitrator's award does not match the scope of the arbitrator's contractual mandate.

In some cases, an arbitrator does less than what the contract called for. For example, in *Escobar v. Shearson Lehman Hutton, Inc.*, 762 F. Supp. 461 (D.P.R. 1991), Andres Escobar and Pedro Escobar each held accounts with a brokerage firm, and each filed claims against the firm. The claims were consolidated for the arbitral hearing, the arbitrator took evidence about both accounts, and the dealer defended against both claims. The arbitrator ruled in favor of the claimants, but the arbitrator's award only referred to one of the two disputed accounts. On motion for vacatur, the court held that this constituted an "imperfectly executed" award and refused to enforce it.

Similarly, an award is subject to vacatur if it clearly exceeds the boundaries of the question put before the arbitrator. ("We disagreed about the value of the defective widgets, so we submitted it to arbitration. But the arbitrator issued an award naming the value at $1.2 million, ordered me to do community service, and ordered the other party to hand over my dachshund. The arbitrator had no authority to order me to do community service, and we never agreed to arbitrate anything about the ownership of any dog.") In *Stolt-Nielsen v. AnimalFeeds*, 559 U.S. 662 (2010), the Supreme Court held that the arbitrator exceeded his power by permitting a class arbitration when the contract was silent as to whether class-wide arbitrations were permissible. We discuss this case further in Chapter 9. The short summary is that the Court held that the arbitrators' decision stemmed from the arbitrators' view of proper public policy. The majority of the Court said that this exceeded the authority given to them under the terms of the arbitration agreement—creating a basis for vacatur under §10(a)(4).

As with the other FAA §10 grounds, however, you should assume that vacatur is unlikely except in the most extraordinary circumstances.

§8.4.2 Challenging Arbitral Awards on Nonstatutory Grounds

In addition to statutory grounds for vacatur, certain common law bases *may* exist for overturning an arbitrator's decision. (Most examples of these nonstatutory bases for vacatur appear in state common law decision. In Chapter 10 we will return to the question of the applicability of state laws relevant to arbitration, given the potential for federal preemption.) These nonstatutory grounds examine the substance of an arbitrator's award more than the FAA does, because the FAA cares largely only about unearthing and overturning flaws in the *process* leading to the arbitrator's award. The headline on these nonstatutory bases is that they are available only in narrow circumstances.

One example of a nonstatutory basis for challenging an arbitrator's award is a challenge arguing that the arbitrator's award should not be upheld on the grounds that the award violates *public policy*. The Supreme Court narrowly construes the "public policy" basis for overturning an arbitrator's decisions. For example, in *Eastern Associated Coal v. United Mine Workers Dist. 17*, 531 U.S. 57 (2000), the Court reviewed an arbitrator's award stemming from a dispute that arose in a collective bargaining context. The contract signed by the UMW on behalf of all employees stipulated that an employee could be fired only for "just cause." James Smith, a unionized driver with EAC, tested positive for marijuana use. When the company tried to dismiss Smith, the union filed a claim with an arbitrator. The arbitrator determined that this failed test did not constitute "just cause" for termination, and the arbitrator ordered Smith reinstated. Some time later, Smith tested positive for drugs again. The company again fired Smith, and again the union appealed on Smith's behalf. The second arbitrator considered Smith's testimony about the second relapse, again judged the firing not to be "just cause," and ordered Smith both to undergo treatment and to submit a signed resignation letter for use in the event that Smith was ever caught again in the future. The employer sought to have the arbitrator's award vacated on the grounds that it violates public policy. The Court upheld the arbitrator's award, saying that the question is *not* whether the Court agrees with the arbitrator's decision. Instead, the Court instructs us to assume that the contract says and means whatever the arbitrator rules it says and means. The question then becomes if the contract says and means *that*, is that contract unenforceable on the grounds that it violates public policy? In this case, the Court found that there were competing interests at play. On the one hand, society has a keen interest in assuring that the people who operate heavy, mobile machinery are not under the influence of drugs. On the other hand, society has a strong interest in providing rehabilitation to those who struggle with addiction. Both of these policies have statutory bases and both are legitimate. Because the arbitrator's interpretation of the contract's terms is given deference, the court treated the contract as though it had those explicit terms and left the arbitrator's decision intact.

Some parties to arbitration contracts have sought to create *contractual* bases for reviewing an arbitrator's award beyond those spelled out in the FAA. What if the contracting parties mutually agree to greater post-arbitration opportunities for judicial scrutiny? Can parties agree to expand these bases for judicial review? Until 2008, courts were split on this question. In *Hall Street Assocs. v. Mattel, Inc.*, 552 U.S. 1396 (2008), the Supreme Court declared that the answer is no. Although the Court was closely divided, the majority held that the grounds listed in FAA §10 and §11 are, essentially, the "exclusive" grounds under the FAA. The Court left the door open for other statutory and common law bases for review outside of the FAA (perhaps, for example, a "public policy" objection). But it closed the door on agreements to expand judicial review of arbitral awards.

Many jurisdictions historically overturned arbitral decisions when they demonstrated "manifest disregard of the law." The "manifest disregard" standard has two basic components, each of which must be met before a party challenging an arbitral award will be successful. First, the arbitrator must have made an error that is so profound as to be apparent (or "manifest") on the face of the award. This category does not, therefore, cover mistakes in procedure or errors in evidentiary rulings, for example. Instead, the law in the area must be so clear, and the arbitrator's decision must be so clearly contrary to that law, that the arbitrator's decision can be called "manifestly" contrary to that law. Second, the arbitrator must have clearly "disregarded" the relevant law. It is not enough to demonstrate that the arbitrator was utterly ignorant of the law. It is not enough to demonstrate that the arbitrator made a mistake in applying the law. Instead, the party seeking to have the arbitral award vacated must demonstrate that the arbitrator knew the relevant law and chose to disregard it in rendering a decision. The *Hall Street* decision has called into question the ongoing viability of the common law "manifest disregard" standard for reviewing arbitral awards since that is not an explicit ground for vacatur under the FAA. Since the *Hall Street* decision, federal courts have split on the question of whether the "manifest disregard" standard survives as a basis for overturning an arbitrator's decision. Because of this circuit split and because the standard has been so important in the development of this area of the law, it is important for you to understand its parameters.

§8.5 MAKING THEM PAY: HOW COURTS ENFORCE ARBITRAL AWARDS

The simplest progression of events related to arbitration looks like this: Two parties agree to arbitrate, a dispute arises, the parties bring their dispute before an arbitrator, the arbitrator rules in favor of one party, and the parties abide by the arbitrator's decision.

The mechanisms by which a party can be compelled to give effect to an arbitral award vary somewhat depending on the nature of the arbitration. The most significant distinction is between domestic arbitrations and those involving international awards. We address each briefly below.

§8.5.1 Disputes at Home: Entering Arbitral Awards as Judgments

Courts have certain coercive powers. If a court orders a litigant to do (or refrain from doing) something, the litigant must either appeal the order or abide by it. If the litigant simply refuses to follow the order, she may be found in contempt of court, and she may face the prospect of fines or imprisonment. Similarly, if a court enters judgment against a litigant, that judgment is given effect unless it is overturned on appeal or a jurisdictional defect is successfully raised in a collateral attack.

An arbitrator's award, by contrast, is not itself an order or a judgment of the court. The Federal Arbitration Act and its state equivalents, therefore, provide a formal mechanism by which an arbitrator's award is treated as a judgment of the court. Parties' contractual agreements to arbitrate virtually always include language specifying that the decision of an arbitrator will be final and may be entered as judgment (commonly called *confirming the arbitral award*) in one or more courts. Under §9 of the FAA, "any party to the arbitration may apply to the court so specified [in the agreement to arbitrate] for an order confirming the award, and thereupon the court must grant such an order unless the award is vacated, modified, or corrected." In the event the parties did not specify a particular court, the FAA provides that application may be made to the court located where the arbitrator issued the award. Commonly, parties drafting arbitration clauses will include far more expansive language about the entry of judgment on the arbitrator's award. For example, the American Arbitration Association suggests a clause providing that "judgment on the award rendered by the arbitrator(s) may be entered in any court having jurisdiction thereof." In essence, under FAA §9, if the winning party can obtain court confirmation of the arbitrator's award, it is enforceable in the same way that any other judgment from that court would be enforceable.

You should notice that the court to which an application to confirm an arbitral award is made has very little discretion. It must confirm the award (and therefore enter it as a judgment of the court) unless the award is "vacated, modified, or corrected." For now, you should know that a losing party in arbitration is extremely unlikely to get out from under the arbitrator's award.

§8.5.2 Disputes Without Borders: International Arbitral Awards

Companies from different countries routinely do business together, and as a result, companies from different countries routinely get in disputes with one another. What happens when international parties disagree? In some ways, their choices are similar to domestic disputes. They can negotiate, mediate, arbitrate, or go to court. Of course, if you are going to court, you'd prefer a "home field" advantage with your laws, your language, and your customs. But so would the other side. One explanation for the appeal of arbitration in the international business context is that arbitration offers international businesses an opportunity to negotiate over the forum and the governing law relevant to any future disagreements. Rather than either side necessarily securing a home field advantage, the contracting parties can agree to submit the dispute to a predetermined international arbitration provider whose location and rules are acceptable to both sides.

Enforceability of foreign arbitration awards, versus foreign court awards, is probably even more important to the selection of arbitration as the alternative dispute resolution method of choice in international commerce. Unlike domestic court orders, orders from foreign courts are not automatically enforceable in a different country. Unless both of the relevant countries have a treaty regarding the enforcement of civil judgments across borders, enforcement is questionable at best, and only some such treaties exist. In arbitration, by contrast, virtually all countries are signatories to the New York Convention (the common name for the 1958 Convention on Recognition and Enforcement of Foreign Arbitral Awards), which makes the enforcement of arbitral awards extraordinarily easy—even in cross-border circumstances. So once parties decide to adjudicate their disputes (versus settle on their own), they frequently conclude that it makes much more sense to arbitrate than litigate.

Consider a Canadian company that has a dispute with a Brazilian company with which it has a joint venture in Mexico. If the parties have no contractual dispute resolution provisions, a dispute would quite possibly result in the sort of transnational choice-of-law mess that law professors would enjoy (but businesspeople would hate). Now assume instead that the terms of their joint venture include an agreement to arbitrate disputes arising under the contract. Assume it sets forth the arbitration procedures and even specifies a venue (for example, London, Singapore, or New York). An arbitrator's decision in this case will be easily enforced not only in the venue in which the arbitration took place, but also (and more important) in the country where the losing company's assets are located. (In general, arbitration awards are easy to enforce, but one should confirm this in the country where the judgment will be enforced.) In short, arbitral awards are more portable internationally than court orders, making arbitration much more attractive as the international adjudication process of choice.

Examples

Larry, Moe, and Curly entered a joint venture to produce blockbuster motion pictures, with a view toward distributing them throughout the United States and possibly globally. In the contract establishing their joint venture, they agreed to arbitrate "any and all disputes related to the formation, performance, or breach of this agreement." At a recent meeting of the three partners, an arguably comical melee broke out when each came to believe that the other two had done none of the things required under the terms of the joint venture. None of the partners sustained lasting injuries in the fisticuffs, but each was livid about the others' apparent breach of the joint venture agreement.

1. **A race to somewhere.** Each of the three venture partners consulted with separate legal counsel, contemplating possible legal actions against the other two. The first to act was Larry, who raced to the local courthouse and filed a complaint against Moe and Curly, alleging breach of contract and breach of fiduciary duty. The next day, Moe filed a claim against Larry and Curly with an arbitrator, pursuant to the procedures set forth in the joint venture agreement, alleging breach of contract. Curly, confused, sat back and waited to figure out where he should bring his claim against his other two partners. What options does each party have for pursuing his claims in the forum of his choice?

2. **Where is that wise guy?** Moe filed an arbitration claim against Larry and Curly, pursuant to the arbitration procedures set forth in the joint venture agreement, alleging breach of contract. Curly appeared in the arbitration, responded to Moe's allegations, and filed a set of counterclaims against Moe. Larry, however, was nowhere to be found. The arbitration rules specified in their contract do not permit the arbitrator to enter a default judgment. Both Moe and Curly were eager to have Larry be part of the action because he has comparatively deep pockets and because they believe his breach was particularly egregious. What options do Moe and Curly have?

3. **Where is that wise guy's money?** With respect to the claims between Moe and Curly, the arbitrator ruled in Curly's favor. The arbitrator found that Curly met his obligations under the contract and Moe breached his. The arbitrator held that Moe owed Curly $100,000. Immediately upon receiving the award, Curly had the award confirmed in the nearest court. Weeks later, however, Moe has still not paid Curly. What could Curly do to try to collect from Moe, and what are his prospects of success?

4. **Slapping Larry again.** Moe filed a claim against Larry in arbitration, alleging breach of contract. Larry defended himself vigorously in the arbitration hearing, but the arbitrator found for Moe in the amount of $50,000. Moe went to court and had the award confirmed. Larry grumblingly paid the money to Moe. A month later, Moe filed a lawsuit in federal court against Larry, seeking to recover additional money for the same injuries stemming from the same set of facts that gave rise to Moe's arbitration claim against Larry. What options does Larry have?

5. **Slapping Moe again.** Curly filed a claim against Moe in arbitration, alleging breach of contract. Moe defended himself vigorously in the arbitration hearing, but the arbitrator found for Curly in the amount of $50,000. Moe grumblingly paid the money to Curly. A month later, Curly filed a lawsuit in federal court against Moe, seeking damages stemming from the same set of facts that gave rise to Curly's arbitration claim against Moe. What options does Moe have?

6. **You call that an expert?** Larry, Moe, and Curly appeared in arbitration, and each party asserted a claim against each of the other two. The dispute hinged on whether any of the parties' conduct constituted a breach of their moviemaking joint venture agreement. During the course of the arbitration hearing, Larry called Willy Woopwoop as an "expert" witness. Moe and Curly objected to Woopwoop's credentials as an expert. Woopwoop testified that he had a degree in cinematography, an MBA, and ten years of experience in the movie business. On this basis, the arbitrator permitted Woopwoop's testimony as an expert. Woopwoop told the arbitrator that Larry was the only one of the three who made defensible business decisions. The arbitrator subsequently ruled for Larry on all claims. Moe and Curly, still angry about the damning expert testimony, hired an investigator to look into Woopwoop's background. A week later, the investigator produced evidence that Woopwoop never received even a college degree and that his only experience in the movie industry was as a frequent patron of a local cinema. Would Moe and Curly succeed in having a court vacate the arbitrator's award?

7. **One hairy hearing.** Larry and Curly appeared before an arbitrator to resolve each of their claims that the other had attempted to embezzle money from the joint venture. About an hour into the rather heated hearing, Curly confronted Larry by saying, "That isn't even your real hair, is it? Remember that you're under oath." Larry angrily shouted, "Of course it's my real hair, you imbecile!" An animated exchange of slaps ensued, and eventually the arbitrator declared that she had heard enough testimony. Not long afterward, the arbitrator issued an award in favor of Larry. Not long after that, Curly came into possession of a

videotape of Larry putting on a wig, along with sworn testimony from one of Larry's former employees, insisting that Larry has not had hair in years. If Curly seeks to have the arbitrator's award vacated on the basis of fraud, will he succeed?

8. **Curly's perpetual parade of pals.** During an arbitration involving Larry and Curly, Larry presented two witnesses and rested his case. Curly began presenting his evidence by calling one of his friends to serve as a character witness. At the conclusion of that friend's testimony, the arbitrator asked if Curly had anyone else to call. "Soitenly!" replied Curly, who then called another friend as a character witness. At the conclusion of that friend's testimony, the arbitrator again asked if Curly was finished yet. But Curly kept calling witnesses, one after the other, and each of them testified about Curly's unfailing veracity. Eventually, the arbitrator grew tired of the parade of witnesses, and refused to permit any further testimony from either party. If the arbitrator rules against Curly, what chance would Curly have of convincing a court to vacate the award?

9. **Shemp, man of reason.** In anticipation of an arbitration involving Larry, Moe, and Curly, a dispute arose about who would serve as arbitrator. The parties reviewed a list of candidates and eventually settled on a man named Shemp. Shemp conducted the hearings in accordance with the procedures articulated in the parties' agreement, and he issued an award in favor of Larry against the other two. Later, Moe and Curly discovered that Shemp and Larry are business partners. Would Moe and Curly be likely to persuade a court to vacate the arbitral award issued against them?

10. **Arbitral snoozing.** Larry and Moe submitted their dispute to an arbitrator, according to the procedures specified in their contract. The arbitrator rendered an award in favor of Larry. Moe sought to have the award vacated, claiming that the arbitrator slept during most of the portion of the hearing when Moe was presenting his evidence. Is Moe likely to be successful in his efforts to resist the arbitrator's award?

11. **The opinion of a knucklehead.** Moe brought a claim against Larry in arbitration, alleging that Larry violated a noncompete clause in their contract. Moe introduced as evidence a signed employment contract between Larry and a competing film studio, timesheets signed by Larry, testimony from the competing studio's payroll officer, and a videotape of Larry handing out the competing studio's business cards at a film festival. Larry presented, as his defense, a copy of his bank account, showing that his earnings from the other film studio were not quite as significant as Moe had alleged. Larry also pled, during the arbitration hearing, "I'm sorry, Moe. Please forgive me!" The arbitrator issued an

award in favor of Larry, writing that she "found Larry's evidence more persuasive," and spending several pages in her opinion detailing the bases for her decision. What chances would Moe have of convincing a court to vacate the arbitrator's award?

12. **The opinion of a chowderhead.** Curly brought an arbitration action against Larry, alleging that Larry unlawfully discriminated against Curly on the basis of Curly's "follicularly challenged coiffure." Curly presented as evidence a document showing that bald members of the joint venture received less favorable benefits than those with "more lustrous locks." Larry argued vigorously that the law does not recognize any protected class on the basis of hair, noting that no discrimination claim could possibly survive if the plaintiff is not in some way protected. In her opinion, the arbitrator wrote, "Discrimination isn't about just certain classes of people. I don't care what the law says. Anybody can feel bad if they're left out. And that's wrong." The arbitrator concluded by ruling in favor of Curly and awarded him $1 million in compensatory and punitive damages. What is the likelihood that Larry would succeed in having the award vacated?

13. **What's the big idea?** In the same dispute between Curly and Larry described in the example immediately above, would it make any difference if the arbitrator had merely found in favor of Curly, but had issued no written opinion at all?

Explanations

1. **A race to somewhere.** Moe filed his claim against the other two in arbitration. On the face of things, this appears to be consistent with the partners' agreement. Moe presumably preferred to have his claim heard by an arbitrator. The only possible threat to this would be if Larry's court case were to proceed, because the result of the court case risks precluding Moe's claim in arbitration. As a result, the best course of action for Moe would be to file a motion to stay the litigation in court under FAA §3 and a motion to compel arbitration under §4. The court would then need to satisfy itself that "the making of the agreement for arbitration or the failure to comply therewith is not in issue." Here, nothing suggests impropriety in the formation of the arbitration agreement. The agreement clearly covers the alleged claim, and Moe did everything required under the arbitration agreement. Therefore, the court would grant Moe's motion to stay the litigation, as required by *Smith v. Spizzirri*, No. 22–1218 slip op. (May 16, 2024). If something remains of Larry's claim following the arbitration, Larry may return to court to have the court resolve the unresolved issues. But most likely, Moe will succeed in having the entire set of disputes related to the alleged breaches heard in arbitration.

The procedural option available to Larry to try to maintain the action in court would be to file a motion to stay the arbitration. Motions to stay arbitration will be granted in circumstances in which the court is satisfied that no arbitration agreement legitimately applies to a dispute, and an arbitrator's decision risks creating inappropriate preclusive effects or conflict with existing litigation. Here, however, for the reasons described above, Larry appears to have a weak claim that this case belongs in court rather than in arbitration. His motion to stay the arbitration, therefore, has little chance of being granted.

Curly has not yet filed a claim in either forum. If the action were maintained in court, the joinder doctrines you encountered in Civil Procedure would certainly permit Curly to add his claims against the other two. (Here, the joinder would likely take the form of a counterclaim and a cross-claim.) But as described above, the litigation is almost certain to be stayed, pending the outcome of the arbitration. The arbitration procedures to which the three parties agreed likely included procedures for adding claims—probably something akin to the civil procedure rules on this point. Curly will most likely figure out that arbitration is where the action will take place and therefore will join his claims in that forum.

2. **Where is that wise guy?** Moe and Curly have two basic options. First, under FAA §4, Moe and Curly are "aggrieved by the alleged failure, neglect, or refusal of another to arbitrate under a written agreement for arbitration." They could, therefore, file a motion to compel Larry to arbitrate. Assuming the court sees this agreement to arbitrate as valid, binding, and applicable to this dispute, the court would grant the motion. If Larry subsequently failed to arbitrate, he not only would be in violation of his contractual duty, but also (and more seriously) would be in violation of a court order. The court's contempt power to sanction parties who refuse to adhere to a court order make this an effective mechanism for compelling Larry's participation.

   The second option for Moe and Curly would be to proceed with the arbitration even in the absence of Larry. The arbitration agreement does not permit the arbitrator to enter a judgment by default. Thus, the arbitrator would be permitted to hear the merits of the case and render a decision. If Larry is not there to present his case, the arbitrator is likely to render a decision that Larry will not like. Assuming Moe and Curly follow all of the procedures properly, the arbitrator's award would be binding against Larry.

3. **Where is that wise guy's money?** Because Curly had the arbitrator's award confirmed with the court (either under FAA §9 or a state equivalent), the award is treated the same as any judgment of the court. Each jurisdiction has its own specific procedures for the enforcement of

judgments. In most cases, Curly would be able to enlist the services of a local law enforcement officer (such as a sheriff) to enforce the court judgment. Enforcement might take the form of seizing Moe's property and selling it to satisfy the judgment. And again, because the court confirmed the award, Curly could even enforce the award as a judgment in other states under the Full Faith and Credit Clause. Unless Moe is so poor as to be effectively judgment-proof, Curly's prospects for recovery are excellent.

4. **Slapping Larry again.** Larry should assert the affirmative defense of *res judicata* in the subsequent court action. The complaint in court rests upon the same set of facts as those asserted in the prior arbitration. *Res judicata* acts to preclude claims that were (or could have been) brought in the prior action, provided the prior action resulted in a valid, final judgment on the merits. Here, the arbitrator's award appears to satisfy all of those requirements. And because Moe confirmed the arbitrator's award in court, there are none of the difficulties that sometimes arise about the preclusive effects of an arbitral award. Here, the award is treated as a judgment of the court. Larry will not have to face the prospect of a second dose of liability for the same wrongdoing.

5. **Slapping Moe again.** This is exactly the same scenario as the question immediately above, except that this time the prevailing party did not have the arbitrator's award confirmed in court. The Supreme Court, in *McDonald v. City of West Branch*, 466 U.S. 284 (1984), suggested that arbitration alone (without judicial confirmation) did not constitute a "judicial proceeding," and therefore carried no preclusive effect in subsequent litigation. By contrast, some state courts accord preclusive effect to unconfirmed arbitration awards.

   In a case like this, where the losing party immediately paid the adverse arbitral award, the winning party would have no real reason to have the award confirmed. Moe already paid up, so what would Curly stand to gain by taking the award to court? To refuse Moe's assertion of *res judicata* on this matter would, in effect, punish Moe for living up to his promise to abide by the arbitrator's decision. Had he been a bad sport and refused to pay the award, Curly would have needed to go to court to have the award confirmed and enforced. And if that happened, *res judicata* would plainly be available to Moe. It is unlikely that a court would, in this circumstance, refuse the application of *res judicata*, but it is less certain than the example immediately above.

6. **You call that an expert?** Probably yes. The standards for successfully challenging an arbitrator's decision are limited, but in this case the court would probably find that the arbitrator's decision was based on fraudulent testimony from Woopwoop and thus subject to vacatur under

FAA §10(a)(1). In *Bonar v. Dean Witter Reynolds, Inc.*, 835 F.2d 1378 (11th Cir. 1988), as described earlier, a purported expert witness deceived the arbitrator about his credentials, and a court subsequently vacated the arbitral award for fraud. The same would likely occur in this case, for the same reasons. The testimony of Woopwoop was material, and it was presented to the arbitrator only because of fraud. Assuming Moe and Curly had no reasonable opportunity to unearth and challenge the fraud before or during the course of the arbitration, FAA §10(a)(1) would permit vacatur.

7. **One hairy hearing.** No. It is true that FAA §10(a)(1) permits parties to avoid arbitral awards that were procured on the basis of fraud. Even if we assume, however, that Larry's testimony about his hair was knowingly false, it is difficult to imagine that an arbitrator would have based her decision on this testimony. Unless the testimony was material, it cannot be the basis of vacatur under §10(a)(1). Curly's best argument would be that if the arbitrator had known Larry's propensity for falsifying some things (like the true state of his hair), the arbitrator would have found it easier to believe that Larry would falsify other things (like the allegedly embezzled money). But the distance between Larry's locks and embezzlement is too wide to make vacatur likely.

8. **Curly's perpetual parade of pals.** Curly would have little chance of convincing a court to vacate the arbitrator's award if the only alleged defect in the hearing was the arbitrator's decision to cut off testimony from Curly's redundant parade of character witnesses. FAA §10(a)(3) provides that courts may refuse to enforce arbitral awards when they were the product of a flawed process, for example, if the arbitrator "refus[ed] to hear evidence pertinent and material to the controversy." (Recall the *Tempo Shain Corp. v. Bertek, Inc.* case, in which the executive caring for his sick wife never got to testify and the award was vacated). However, in this case, Curly was not prejudiced by the arbitrator's decision. There is no evidence that the arbitrator ignored all of the testimony that had come up to that point. Clearly, the arbitrator must have some discretion in controlling against a filibuster version of arbitration hearings. Even if there is a gray area in the question of how much an arbitrator must permit in general, the arbitrator's decision this case is presents no meaningful risk of prejudice. A motion to vacate would be denied.

9. **Shemp, man of reason.** Probably yes. FAA §10(a)(2) permits vacatur "where there was evident partiality" in the arbitrator. Even though there is no particular accusation that Shemp's conduct was inappropriate, his relationship with one of the arbitration parties creates such a substantial impression of impropriety and bias that a court might refuse

to enforce his award. In the case of *Julius Erving v. Virginia Squires Basketball Club*, 349 F. Supp. 716 (E.D.N.Y. 1972), the Virginia Squires sought an injunction preventing Erving (a.k.a. "Dr. J") from playing with any other basketball team. Part of Erving's contract included an arbitration clause, which specified that the arbitrator would be the commissioner of the American Basketball Association (the league in which the Virginia Squires competed). In an order compelling arbitration, the court took notice of the fact that the newly appointed commissioner was a named partner in the law firm representing the Virginia Squires. As a result, the court ordered arbitration, but ordered that a different, "neutral" arbitrator be appointed. Even though the case involving Shemp is in a different posture than the Julius Erving case, the fact that the partiality of the arbitrator was not evident until after the proceedings had concluded would probably lead a court to the conclusion that the arbitral award cannot stand.

10. **Arbitral snoozing.** Moe's best shot at having the arbitrator's award vacated would be under FAA §10(a)(3), which permits a court to vacate an award where the arbitrator engaged in "misbehavior by which the rights of any party have been prejudiced." As incredible as these circumstances may sound, according to the party who was seeking to have an arbitral award vacated in *National Post Office Mailhandlers v. USPS*, 751 F.2d 834 (6th Cir. 1985), the arbitrator "dozed" during their presentation of evidence. Following a motion to vacate, the court held an evidentiary hearing and asked each party about its recollection of the arbitrator's apparent inattention. As you might imagine, each side recalled the arbitrator's conduct differently. The court eventually determined that whatever lack of arbitral attention occurred was not significant enough to constitute misbehavior under FAA §10(a)(3), holding that "the standard for judicial review of arbitration procedures is merely whether a party to arbitration has been denied a fundamentally fair hearing."

    Moe's chances of having the arbitrator's award vacated, therefore, depend on whether Moe can actually demonstrate that (1) the arbitrator napped during the presentation of Moe's evidence, and (2) the arbitrator napped during such an important part of Moe's presentation of evidence that Moe's rights have been prejudiced. Given the uncertainties involved, however, Moe's better course of action would have been to waken the slumbering arbitrator and request a continuance or a caffeine break.

11. **The opinion of a knucklehead.** Moe's chances of having the award vacated are slim. Nothing in the facts suggests any defect in the arbitration proceeding itself, so nothing in the FAA is likely to support Moe's efforts. Furthermore, nothing in the arbitrator's award comes near to constituting a violation of public policy. Moe's best chance for vacatur, therefore, would come from asserting that the arbitrator's decision

constitutes "manifest disregard of the law." Many jurisdictions, however, have interpreted the *Hall Street* opinion as preempting that objection. Even in those jurisdictions that recognize manifest disregard, often as a "gloss" on § 10(a)(4), which permits vacatur when an arbitrator exceeds their powers, courts generally refuse to second-guess the legal conclusions, much less the fact finding, of arbitrators. Nothing suggests that the arbitrator disregarded a clearly applicable law here. Even if an arbitrator reaches a decision that is against the clear weight of the evidence, a court is extraordinarily unlikely to disturb the award.

12. **The opinion of a chowderhead.** If Larry is in a jurisdiction that still recognizes the "manifest disregard" basis for objecting to an arbitrator's decision, he has as good a chance of having this award vacated as any "manifest disregard" claim is likely to have. For a manifest disregard assertion to succeed, the party contesting the arbitral award must show that "(1) the arbitrator knew of a governing legal principle yet refused to apply it or ignored it altogether, and (2) the law ignored by the arbitrator was well defined, explicit, and clearly applicable to the case." This is a high standard and, as we have discussed, is exceedingly rare. For instance, in *Montes v. Shearson Lehman Bros.*, 128 F.3d 1456 (11th Cir. 1997), a former employee charged Shearson Lehman with violating federal overtime laws. During the arbitration hearing, the attorney for the defendant urged the arbitrators to "ignore the law," and the arbitrators subsequently ruled in favor of the defendants. The Eleventh Circuit acknowledged that manifest disregard is an extremely narrow circumstance, but nonetheless vacated the award and sent the case back for a new arbitration. In Curly's action against Larry, given Larry's defense based solely on the sound legal principle that bald people do not belong to a protected class, and given the arbitrator's apparent understanding of this law, a court would be likely to view the arbitrator's award as being the product of manifest disregard of the law. In a jurisdiction in which the FAA is the exclusive ground for appeal, Larry would have a difficult time. Assuming "manifest disregard" is available, however, Larry would be likely to succeed with his request that the award be vacated.

13. **What's the big idea?** Maybe. If the jurisdiction in question recognizes only FAA grounds for challenging an arbitrator's award, Larry would be forced to argue that the arbitrator "imperfectly executed" her powers under §10(a)(4). But such an argument would be unlikely to prevail, since the facts do not specify that the parties' arbitration agreement required a written opinion.

    Even in jurisdictions in which the "manifest disregard" standard remains valid, courts are split over how to deal with the situation in which the arbitrator failed to write a reasoned opinion. Recall that arbitrators are under no obligation to explain their decisions unless the parties' contract calls for a reasoned decision. Does silence make it virtually impossible to assess the arbitrator's thought process, and therefore make it virtually impossible to say what the arbitrator knew or disregarded? Or does silence invite the court to assume knowledge in a way that makes it more likely to overturn arbitral awards?

Both lines of logic find support. A federal judge, concurring in *Federated Dep't Stores v. JVB Indus.*, 894 F.2d 862, 871 (6th Cir. 1990) (Martin, J., concurring), described the exercise of trying to determine whether an arbitrator manifestly disregarded the law, when the arbitrator issued no written opinion, as a "judicial snipe hunt." For example, in *DiRussa v. Dean Witter Reynolds*, 121 F.3d 818 (2d Cir. 1997), a former securities dealer, DiRussa, brought a claim against his former employer alleging age discrimination in violation of the Age Discrimination in Employment Act (ADEA). Consistent with the terms of DiRussa's employment contract, the case went to arbitration, where DiRussa sought compensatory damages, punitive damages, and attorneys' fees. The arbitrator found in favor of DiRussa and awarded him compensatory damages but denied all other relief. Noting that the ADEA mandates that attorneys' fees be granted to successful claimants, DiRussa filed a motion to vacate or modify the award to include attorneys' fees on the basis that the arbitrator's refusal to award attorneys' fees constituted manifest disregard of the law. The court agreed that the ADEA does mandate attorneys' fees. But the court nonetheless upheld the arbitrator's award (without attorneys' fees) because there was no evidence that the arbitrators knew that the ADEA had this requirement. Absent this knowledge, the arbitrators could not be held to have disregarded the law.

By contrast, in *Halligan v. Piper Jaffray, Inc.*, 148 F.3d 197 (2d Cir. 1998), Halligan, a salesman, was fired from his job shortly before his retirement. Halligan alleged age discrimination, and during the arbitration hearing, his former employer admitted that Halligan was "basically qualified." Halligan produced evidence showing that he was among the top-producing salespeople at the company, and he presented witnesses who testified about Halligan having been "pushed out" of the job. The arbitrator ruled in favor of the company and issued no written opinion. In considering a motion to vacate, the court wrote, "[W]hen a reviewing court is inclined to hold that an arbitration panel manifestly disregarded the law, the failure of the arbitrators to explain the award can be taken into account. Having done so, we are left with the firm belief that the arbitrator here manifestly disregarded the law or the evidence or both."

It appears that the weight of cases leans in favor of the *DiRussa* logic—that an arbitrator's award that is silent about the arbitrator's logic cannot serve as the basis of a manifest disregard objection. Recalling that many jurisdictions no longer recognize any form of "manifest disregard" objection, the prospect of vacatur here is limited unless some statutory basis exists.

CHAPTER 9

Must This Dispute Go to Arbitration?

§9.1 INTRODUCTION

Not everyone wishes to resolve their disputes through arbitration. Even those who entered into a contract with an arbitration clause may, once a dispute has arisen, decide that they prefer to litigate their dispute in court. Why might some disputants prefer court? Maybe they want the publicity associated with public adjudication. Maybe they love the idea of a jury deciding the factual questions or they hope to establish binding precedent. Maybe they like the formality a trial can offer. Maybe their lawyers are simply more familiar with litigation. There are many legitimate reasons why some parties might prefer to litigate their disputes rather than to arbitrate them. Whatever the reason, in virtually all circumstances, a party seeking to avoid arbitration does so because it perceives a strategic advantage to appearing in court rather than arbitration.

This chapter examines the range of different avenues available to a disputant who seeks to *avoid* arbitration. It might seem counterintuitive that in a section of an ADR book devoted entirely to arbitration, we will spend the bulk of our time and space dealing with ways to avoid arbitration. The reality is that much of modern law and litigation about arbitration relate precisely to the question of whether parties will be compelled to submit their disputes to arbitration.

§9.2 WHAT PART OF THE ARBITRATION AGREEMENT IS BEING CHALLENGED? THE DOCTRINE OF SEPARABILITY

Binding arbitration is a creature of contract. From that basic observation, it stands to reason that one of the simplest ways to prevent another party from enforcing an arbitration agreement is to attack the agreement the way you would any other contract. So, for example, an arbitration agreement between two companies is unlikely to be enforceable if the contract was printed in six-point font in ancient Sanskrit and the only signature on the contract is a block-letter crayon effort by the five-year-old daughter of one company's receptionist. We pledge not to force you to relive your entire Contracts class in this chapter, but we will give you a survey of some of the most common contract-based defenses parties raise in seeking to avoid arbitration.

Contract-based strategies for avoiding arbitration essentially boil down to one of two lines of attack. One is to assert that there was no contractual agreement to arbitrate. The other is to assert that although the parties entered into a contract, some part of it is unenforceable. In the following sections, we explain the range of contract-based challenges to arbitration in terms of one of these two categories.

We begin, however, by asking about the target of the contractual challenge. In short, is the party challenging the enforceability of the entire contract, or just the arbitration agreement?

Many contracts contain arbitration agreements, and most follow a similar structure. First, there is the basic contract (for example, to rent a car, to enter an employment relationship, to receive health care, or to launch a joint venture). The contract spells out the duties and rights of each party in some level of detail. Then, somewhere in that "container" contract, there is an arbitration clause that spells out the conditions under which future disputes will be resolved through arbitration. Within some arbitration clauses, there may be an additional clause called a "delegation" clause, which specifies whether an arbitrator or a court will be called upon to resolve any disputes about the arbitration clause.

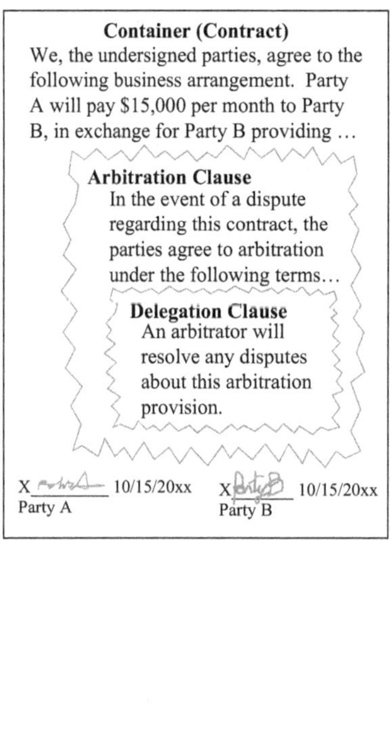

A party seeking to avoid arbitration might challenge any of these three agreements — the container agreement, the arbitration provision embedded in the container agreement, or the delegation provision embedded in the arbitration provision. The same contractual bases for challenges are available for any of these three targets. But the question of who decides the challenge depends greatly on the target of the challenge, as we describe in the next section.

§9.3 WHO DECIDES CONTRACTUAL CHALLENGES?

Before we examine each of the methods a party might use to avoid arbitration, we will talk about *who* decides each of these challenges (a court or an arbitrator). A party who seeks to avoid arbitration would almost certainly prefer to have a court hear challenges to arbitration. ("After all, if I'm trying to avoid arbitration, it's because I don't want an arbitrator deciding things.") And a party who believes she entered a binding arbitration agreement wants to have that agreement take effect without going through the machinery of court. ("After all, what's the point of agreeing to arbitrate any disputes that may arise if it all just winds up before a judge anyway?") As you will see, the test for resolving the question of who decides depends on the precise portion of the contract a party is challenging and on the nature of the challenge being raised.

§9.3.1 Challenges to the Container Agreement

Typically, when a party has one or more of the contract-based arguments against the enforceability of a contract, such as fraud, duress, unconscionability, or public policy, its objections apply to the entire contract, not just to the arbitration clause. A party is likely to claim that the *entire container agreement* was fraudulently induced, rather than merely the arbitration provision falling within the container agreement. Or a party will claim that the entire agreement is unenforceable because it is unconscionable. Or, like the plaintiff in *Buckeye Check Cashing, Inc. v. Cardegna*, 546 U.S. 440 (2006), a party will assert that the entire contract is unenforceable because one provision within the contract (for example, a usurious interest rate) renders the contract itself illegal. Attacks on enforceability typically target the container agreement, not just the arbitration clause.

Who decides those challenges to the container agreement? The accurate, but not always immediately helpful, answer is "whoever the parties agreed to have hear these challenges." The parties could have, for example, specifically contemplated the prospect of such challenges. If their arbitration clause specified that they agreed to have a court hear all such challenges, those challenges would fall outside of the arbitration agreement and a court would hear them. The far more common condition, however, is one in which the parties' contract is silent on the question of who decides challenges to the container agreement, or one in which the parties generically say that "any and all disputes related to the contract" will go to arbitration. What happens then?

The Supreme Court addressed this question with its articulation of the concept of separability in *Prima Paint Corp. v. Flood & Conklin Mfg. Co.*, 388 U.S. 395 (1967). Flood & Conklin Manufacturing (F&C) entered into a business contract with Prima Paint, which contained an agreement to arbitrate "any controversy or claim arising out of the agreement." Not long after the parties entered the contract, a dispute arose. F&C accused Prima Paint of failing to live up to its obligations and sought to commence an action in arbitration. Prima Paint responded by commencing an action in federal court, alleging that because F&C had fraudulently induced Prima Paint into signing the contract in the first place, Prima Paint should not be bound by the agreement to arbitrate. The merits of the case, of course, would ultimately hinge on this relatively basic contract dispute. The preliminary question, however, was *who* (the court or an arbitrator) would be assessing the merits of the challenge to the contract.

The Supreme Court answered this preliminary question by sending the dispute to an arbitrator to assess both the breach alleged by F&C and the fraud alleged by Prima Paint. The Supreme Court explained:

> [E]xcept where the parties otherwise intend, arbitration clauses . . . are "separable" from the contracts in which they are embedded, and that where no claim is made that fraud was directed to the arbitration clause itself, a broad arbitration clause will be held to encompass arbitration of the claim that the contract itself was induced by fraud.[1]

Section 4 of the FAA requires a court to compel arbitration once it is satisfied that "the making of the arbitration agreement" is not in issue. In the case of *Prima Paint*, the Court concluded that the making of the arbitration agreement was not in issue, even if the enforceability of the entire contract *was* in issue.

1. *Prima Paint*, 388 U.S. at 402.

§9.3.2 Challenges to the Arbitration Clause Specifically

Two parties with an existing dispute could (and sometimes do) enter a stand-alone agreement that commits them to arbitrate the dispute. For example, imagine that your classmate's laptop spontaneously combusts, causing damage to some of your property. You and your classmate surely do not have an existing contract that would cover such a contingency. One option for you would be to file a lawsuit against your classmate (and/or possibly many other parties). Alternatively, your classmate could approach you and suggest that the two of you enter an agreement to have your claim resolved by an arbitrator. If the two of you enter an agreement to arbitrate, it is a contract and will be as binding as any other agreement. Now, what if you have second thoughts and want to challenge the enforceability of the agreement you entered with your classmate (for example, by saying that there was no consideration supporting the agreement to arbitrate, that it was procured by fraud, or that it was unconscionable). Who would hear your objections? Unless the parties agreed to have an arbitrator resolve such challenges, the answer is: *a court*. The idea is that the basis of the challenge is directed specifically at the agreement to arbitrate, and if the agreement to arbitrate was itself so flawed as to be unenforceable, the allegation should not be referred to an arbitrator to decide.

In the context of arbitration agreements appearing inside container agreements, the same basic principle applies: A challenge to the validity of an arbitration clause is a question for a court. For example, if a party says that it was coerced into accepting the arbitration component of the contract, that objection will appear before a court. In short, if the challenge is to the arbitration clause itself, rather than to the container agreement, and if there is no provision delegating the resolution of such challenges to an arbitrator, then a court, rather than an arbitrator, will decide the merits of the objection.

§9.3.3 Challenges to the Delegation Clause Specifically

One extra wrinkle is that modern contracts often include arbitration clauses that contain at least two provisions: (a) one providing for arbitration of any claims arising under the broader contract, and (b) one providing for an arbitrator to resolve any challenges to the enforceability of the contract, including its arbitration provisions.

What if someone wants to challenge the enforceability of such an arbitration clause—for example, because it was allegedly unconscionable? In *Rent-A-Center v. Jackson*, 561 U.S. 63 (2010), the Supreme Court held that an arbitrator would hear that challenge. Applying the separability doctrine, the Court reasoned that the challenge was to the entire arbitration clause ((a) + (b)), not merely a challenge to the delegation clause (b). If the challenge were only about (b), a court would resolve it. But essentially, the Court treated the unconscionability challenge as if it were a challenge to a container agreement, even though the "container" in this case is simply a lengthy arbitration provision. We return to a more detailed discussion of this point below in §9.6.

The Supreme Court had to address a similar issue in which some lower courts were taking on decision making in disputes where one party contended that the argument for arbitration of a particular dispute was "wholly groundless." These lower courts looked past the arbitration agreements' clauses delegating arbitrability decisions to the arbitrator. The Supreme Court, in *Henry Schein Inc. v. Archer and White Sales Inc.*, 139 S. Ct. 524 (2019), made short work of this judicially-created doctrine, rejecting the "wholly groundless" exception as inconsistent with the FAA and problematic because it "confuses the question of who decides arbitrability with the separate question of who prevails on arbitrability." Unsurprisingly, the Court found that lower courts must respect parties' decision to delegate arbitrability to the arbitrator.

In the next five sections, we walk through the basic forms of objections a party seeking to avoid arbitration might raise. These categories are neither sequential nor hierarchical, but they do capture the range of possible bases upon which a party might challenge the referral of a case to arbitration.

§9.4 OBJECTION #1: "WHAT CONTRACT? I NEVER AGREED TO ARBITRATE ANYTHING."

Court's Role	**Nature of the Objection to Arbitration**	Arbitrator's Role
Decide whether a contract exists. If a contract with an arbitration clause exists, send the case to arbitration.	"What contract? I never entered a contract."	None.

With the exception of certain court-annexed, nonbinding forms of arbitration (which we discuss briefly in Chapter 11), arbitration occurs only when the parties contract to send a dispute to arbitration. Perhaps the most obvious objection a party can raise to arbitration, therefore, would be that they did not reach such an agreement.

Entering into a contract is typically not a terribly complicated matter. It takes only a few things—like offer, acceptance, and consideration—all of which are surely familiar from your first-year Contracts class. But just as you discovered in your Contracts class, disagreements sometimes arise about each of those seemingly straightforward concepts. Was there an offer? Was there an acceptance or substantial performance? Was there consideration? In the sections below, we provide a brief survey of the landscape of contract-based objections likely to arise in the context of arbitration.

§9.4.1 Mutual Assent

Among the most basic principles in contract law is that a contract is not enforceable unless there was an **offer** and **acceptance**. An offer means showing a willingness to enter a particular bargain so that the other party has the ability to accept. An acceptance means showing an agreement to the terms of the offer in the way invited or required by the offer. Of course, as you learned in your first-year Contracts class, contracting is not always as simple as that, but the basic proposition still stands: Unless there was an offer and acceptance, a contract is not enforceable.

Agreements to arbitrate are no different: They require an offer and acceptance. Imagine that you are walking to school when a runaway delivery truck drives up onto the sidewalk, runs into you, and causes you some minor injuries. You file a tort claim against the driver of the truck in a local court. Could the driver convince that court to stay the litigation and order you to arbitrate your claim despite your preference to have your claim heard in court? No. You never agreed to arbitrate this claim against the truck driver, he never offered to arbitrate the claim, and you certainly never assented to the terms of an arbitration agreement. Without those elements, no contract exists, and there is no basis for the court to send your claim to arbitration.

Some kinds of contracts must be in writing in order to be enforceable. (Recall the Statute of Frauds.) The Federal Arbitration Act includes a provision that limits its applicability to *written* arbitration agreements. "Acceptance," however, is governed by state contract law. In *Caley v. Gulfstream Aerospace Corp.*, 428 F.3d 1359, 1368 (11th Cir. 2005), for example, the court held that "while the FAA requires that the arbitration agreement be in writing, it does not require that it be signed by the parties." Arbitration clauses in unilateral contracts (ones in which acceptance is demonstrated by performance, not by a signature) meet the FAA's requirement that the arbitration agreement be "written." See also, Galloway v. Santander Consumer USA, Inc., 819 F.3d 79 (4th Cir. 2016).

Of course, an agreement to arbitrate does not have to precede the incidents giving rise to the claim in question. The truck driver, having run you over, could jump out of his truck, help you to your feet, apologize profusely, and then ask you if you would be willing to sign an agreement to arbitrate any and all claims arising out of the incident. If you assent to the arbitration agreement, but then file a claim in court, the court might very well direct you to arbitration. As a basic matter, if you did not form a contract in which you agreed to arbitrate your claim, the other party cannot compel you to arbitrate the claim.

§9.4.2 Consideration

Contracts also require consideration, which requires examining parties' bargained-for exchanges. These bargained-for exchanges are only enforceable if the promisor (the person making the promise) benefits somehow or the promisee (the person to whom the promise is made) incurs a detriment of some sort. For example, your first-year casebook probably mentioned *Hamer v. Sidway*, 27 N.E. 256 (N.Y. 1891), the case involving an uncle who promised his nephew a large sum of money on the condition that the nephew forbear drinking, gambling, and swearing. The court deemed the detriment the nephew incurred (forsaking swearing, for example, something he would have otherwise had a right to do) as adequate consideration to support the contract.

In the arbitration context, a common and straightforward illustration of adequate consideration would be two companies planning the terms of a joint venture. They agree to include an arbitration clause in their contract, agreeing requiring them to submit "any and all disputes" related to the joint venture to binding arbitration. In that case, each receives the benefit of having secured arbitration, and each incurs the detriment of having forgone the possibility of adjudicating subsequent contract claims in court. Another common scenario is when you purchase something, a laptop, for example, and the warranty of the laptop includes an arbitration provision. You received a benefit—a brand-new computer—as part of an exchange that included handing over your money and agreeing to the manufacturer's arbitration clause. These types of agreements are often called adhesion contracts.

Consideration becomes more complicated in the arbitration context when there was some prior relationship between parties, and *then* contractual terms were modified to include an arbitration agreement. For example, it is now common for employees to agree to a thick set of terms in their employee handbooks. The terms included in the handbook are (for the most part) going to be binding on the employee, assuming they are not outrageous. And there is no consideration problem because these were the terms the employee signed on to when the employee accepted the employment.

Now, imagine that an employer sent out an e-mail notice to all employees saying, "Good morning, employees. The company intends to amend the Employee Handbook to include an arbitration clause. If you continue to work for us after next week, we will deem that acceptance of our new policy." Would the arbitration clause be binding? You might first analyze whether there was an offer (clearly yes) and acceptance (yes, courts consider your performance constructive acceptance if you keep working after notice like this). Consideration is also present because in exchange for the detriment of the arbitration clause (to the extent you view that as a detriment), you receive the benefit of a paying job. That is plenty.

If the above scenario troubles you, that's probably good. You are likely imagining all kinds of potential abuses. What if the employer sneaks some terrible provisions into that new arbitration clause? What if the handbook is now crazily lopsided in its treatment of employees? What if the employees really don't have time to read or review the new clause? What if the employer keeps changing the terms around? Isn't there some limit to all of this? Yes. We discuss those near the end of this section when we talk about unconscionability.

§9.4.3 Capacity, Authority, and Legality

Consideration and mutual assent are necessary for creating an enforceable contract, but other factors can affect the enforceability of an agreement. For example, a person must have sufficient capacity before they will be held to their agreements. An elementary school student's signature on an otherwise unobjectionable contract would create an enforceability problem.

Similarly, if someone signing an agreement on behalf of someone else does not have authority to bind that other person, the contract may not be enforceable. The case of *First Options v. Kaplan*, 514 U.S. 938 (1995), highlights this point. Kaplan, signing an agreement on behalf of his company with First Options, did not consent to arbitration on his individual behalf and therefore was not bound by the arbitration clause, even though the company on whose behalf he signed was bound to arbitrate. There are circumstances, however, in which individuals may be bound by organizational commitments to arbitration. For example, until earlier this century, unionized employees (who operate under a collectively bargained contract) were not generally bound to arbitrate their individual, statutory claims against their employers. However, in *14 Penn Plaza v. Pyett*, 556 U.S. 247, 258 (2009), the Supreme Court held that "[n]othing in the law suggests a distinction between the status of arbitration agreements signed by an individual employee and those signed by a union representative." One should note, however, that if the union refuses to take the employee's grievance to arbitration, the employee will be permitted to proceed alone. Finally, if an agent who is authorized to act on your behalf, agrees to arbitrate, the agreement will be treated as if it were your own. For example, in *Kindred Nursing Ctr. Ltd. P'ship v. Clark*, 581 U.S. 246 (2017), an elderly man gave his wife, Beverley Wellner, a general power of attorney. She later signed various agreements on his behalf as he chécked into a nursing home operated by Kindred Nursing Centers. The nursing home's agreement included an arbitration clause that stated, "any and all claims or controversies arising out of or in any way relating to . . . the Resident's stay at the Facility" would be resolved through "binding arbitration" rather than a "lawsuit." Unfortunately, Mr. Wellner passed away while under the care of Kindred, and Mrs. Wellner filed a wrongful death lawsuit in court. Kindred moved to compel arbitration according to the contract. Kentucky courts held that, as a matter of Kentucky law, "a power of attorney could not entitle a representative to enter into an arbitration agreement without specifically saying so." The Supreme Court reversed, holding that (for reasons that may become clearer after Chapter 10) even though much may be at stake with respect to arbitration clauses, states cannot require a greater level of authority for agents with respect to arbitration agreements than they do with other contractual terms.

State contract law declares contracts containing certain kinds of agreements "illegal" and, therefore, unenforceable. For example, contracts with usurious interest rates, contracts for the sale of human body parts, or contracts to commit crimes would not withstand challenge. However, as a preview, the preemption doctrines we describe in Chapter 10. Limit states' ability to target arbitration clauses for special scrutiny if the parties' agreement involves interstate commerce.

§9.5 OBJECTION #2: "YES, I SIGNED A CONTRACT WITH AN ARBITRATION CLAUSE, BUT THE CONTRACT ISN'T ENFORCEABLE"

Court 's Role	**Nature of the Objection to Arbitration**	Arbitrator's Role
None (send to arbitrator), unless the parties specify otherwise in the contract.	"This whole contract is unenforceable, including the arbitration clause."	Decide the enforceability of the contract. (Recall *Prima Paint* and the separability doctrine.)

The section above focused on those circumstances in which the person seeking to avoid arbitration is arguing that no agreement to arbitrate existed. But that's not the only way a party can avoid arbitration. More often, the parties will have agreed to arbitrate, but the party seeking to avoid arbitration will argue that their agreement to arbitrate should not be enforced because the container agreement is unenforceable or because the arbitration clause itself is unenforceable.

Your Contracts class surely provided you with a number of different ideas about circumstances in which a court might not treat an agreement as enforceable. Some of the most significant avenues you likely studied (for example, indefiniteness and the statute of frauds) do not commonly arise in the context of arbitration. Other contract defenses, however (like fraud, public policy, duress, and, especially, unconscionability), are more typical avenues for opposing the enforcement of arbitration. Below, we survey some of the most significant bases for challenging the enforceability of an agreement to arbitrate.

As a practical matter, most of the contractual defenses we discuss below are usually asserted as challenges to the container agreement rather than to the arbitration clause in particular. Alleged fraud is likely to be fraud about the entire contractual relationship. Alleged duress applies to the entire agreement, not just the clause about arbitration. And so forth. Under the logic of *Prima Paint*'s separability, therefore, an arbitrator, not a court, will hear virtually all of these challenges.

§9.5.1 Fraud

A contract is not enforceable if it was fraudulently induced. A party can avoid a contract on the basis of fraud if the fact was material *and* the listener was reasonable and justified in relying on the misrepresented fact. Each component of that statement is subject to pages and pages of definition, clarification, application, exception, and refinement. But the basic idea stands: Contracts—including arbitration clauses—are not enforceable if they were the product of fraud.

Most of the time, when fraud is committed in the formation of a contract, the alleged material misrepresentation has to do with some aspect of the contract *other* than the arbitration clause that happens to be included in the overall contract. For example, the other side lies to you about the nature of the product being sold. ("This can opener also serves as a cellular phone in Europe.") They misrepresent their assets. ("We own the patent on this device.") They fail to correct inaccurate assertions they made earlier about their prior performance. ("The financial report we gave you last week covered everything from the past three years.") And so on.

Of course, it is possible that a lie will relate specifically to the arbitration clause itself. For example, a representative of a circus company could say, "I know that our proposal specifies that the arbitrations will take place under the rules of the ClownCo Arbitration Association. And I know their website is down right now. But don't worry, their procedures precisely mirror those of the American Arbitration Association," when, in fact, the procedures are nothing like those of the American Arbitration Association. If you can demonstrate that the false claims relate directly to the arbitration clause, are material or knowingly false, that you reasonably relied on them to your detriment, and that there is no provision delegating enforceability challenges to the arbitrator, a court will not enforce an arbitration clause against you.

§9.5.2 "Public Policy" Objections

As a general matter, contracts contrary to public policy will not be enforced. For example, even if you and a drug dealer on the street corner execute an otherwise flawless contract for the purchase and sale of cocaine, the court will not entertain a civil lawsuit if one of you reneges on the agreement. Of course, the line between what is and is not consistent with public policy is not necessarily easily defined.

You might be thinking, "Wait, I thought there was a well-established policy *favoring* arbitration. What could possibly be the problem?" It is certainly true that courts have, in recent decades, developed an expansive jurisprudence stemming from the basic proposition that courts should favor enforcing agreements to arbitrate. But this does not mean that courts will enforce any agreement to arbitrate under any circumstances. The agreement must still withstand a challenge that its enforcement would violate public policy.

For many years, courts applied the "public policy" doctrine to strike down arbitration clauses that purported to cover claims involving statutorily created rights. As you know, many legal claims derive from common law rather than statutory rights. But within the past several decades, statutorily created rights have become increasingly common, particularly at the federal level. For example, most antidiscrimination lawsuits are based not in the common law, but rather in a set of statutes. We refer to these and other rights as statutorily created rights. Agreements to arbitrate were not enforced in the context of many of these statutory rights for a long time. For example, in *Wilko v. Swan*, 346 U.S. 427 (1953), the U.S. Supreme Court pointed out that arbitrators are not required to have legal training, that arbitrators operate "without judicial instruction on the law," and that arbitrators are not required to provide reasoned awards nor preserve a record of their proceedings. The combination of these factors, the Court concluded, rendered unenforceable arbitration agreements relating to claims under the Securities Act, despite the public policy generally favoring arbitration. The logic, at the time, was that arbitration would simply frustrate the public policy underlying statutes like the Securities Act, particularly when those acts create causes of action that aim to provide relief for consumers or others with relatively less sophistication or power.

During the 1980s, however, the Supreme Court took a different approach and eventually overruled *Wilko*, making statutory rights broadly amenable to arbitration. The Court rejected what it called "generalized attacks on arbitration" in which the assertion is that arbitration is inherently unfair or biased. See *Gilmer v. Interstate/Johnson Lane Corp.*, 500 U.S. 20, 30 (1991). Instead, the Court has said that arbitration is not necessarily inconsistent with the vindication of statutory rights, even in circumstances in which arbitration procedures differ from court procedures. In response, Congress could choose to draft a statute precluding arbitration of that particular right. In most cases, however, statutes are silent about arbitration, and a contract sending those claims to arbitration does not run afoul of public policy.

An arbitration clause would violate public policy if it prevented parties from bringing actions to vindicate their statutory rights. As a practical matter, however, this is difficult to establish. In *American Express v. Italian Colors*, 570 U.S. 228 (2013), for example, a group of merchants sought to sue American Express, as a class, for antitrust violations. However, each merchant's contract included an arbitration agreement with a class-action waiver. The merchants argued that the class waiver in the arbitration clause should not be enforced because it would make it cost prohibitive for any of them to win an antitrust claim. The costs associated with the expert analysis required in an antitrust case far exceeded the recovery any individual claimant could reasonably expect. The Court drew a distinction between the effective right to *bring* an action and the effective right to *prevail* in an action. Nothing in the arbitration agreement precluded an individual from *bringing* an action in antitrust (for example by requiring prohibitively high arbitration filing fees), and as a result, it upheld the class waiver and the arbitration clause.

The door is still open to the possibility that *some* arbitration agreement, in some form, in some context, will be so inconsistent with the statutory purposes underlying a particular claimant's cause of action that it will be stricken on the basis of public policy. An arbitration agreement that prohibited all access to discovery materials, restricted the scope of awards, and fundamentally stripped away a claimant's ability to prevail in a statutory claim would probably not be enforced. But, at this point, it is an uphill battle for the party seeking to avoid arbitration on the basis that the contract providing for arbitration is contrary to public policy.

Of course, Congress may expressly prohibit arbitration of a statutory claim. Many statutes creating causes of action were passed when *Wilko* was still good law (and therefore, there was no clear reason for Congress to have specified that arbitration would be an inappropriate forum for vindicating the statutory rights in question). In the years since *Wilko* was overturned, however, Congress failed to amend most of these statutes creating rights of action. As a result, without an express congressional prohibition against arbitrating a statutorily based claim, the presumption is that arbitration is merely a different, but still entirely valid, forum for vindicating these rights. See *Rodriguez de Quijas v. Shearson/American Express*, 490 U.S. 477 (1989). Proposals often surface in Congress to prohibit the arbitration of certain statutory rights, but, to date, very few of these proposals have passed. One exception is the 2007 Defense Authorization Act, which now protects service members from mandatory arbitration with their creditors.

An additional proposal-turned law is the Ending Forced Arbitration of Sexual Assault and Sexual Harassment Act (EFAA). Passed in March 2022, EFAA amended the FAA by precluding employers from requiring employees to agree, pre-dispute, to arbitrate sexual assault and harassment claims. Thus, employee sexual assault or sexual harassment claims may go directly to court. The Act also allows claimants to avoid pre-dispute agreement class action waivers for sexual assault or sexual harassment claims. Because EFAA amends the FAA itself, the exemption applies to all arbitration agreements covered by the FAA, not just employment disputes.

§9.5.3 Duress

As we discussed in Chapter 3 on the Law of Negotiation, an agreement that results from an exchange beginning with the phrase "your money or your life" and ending with the target of the phrase opting to relinquish his money is not an enforceable contract. Briefly, when one party wrongfully coerces the other into a circumstance in which there is no reasonable alternative but to accept, economic duress exists and the contract will not be enforceable. Traditionally, a party alleging economic duress must show (1) that he or she has been the victim of a wrongful or unlawful act or threat, and (2) that the act or threat deprived the victim of free or unfettered will. In addition to economic duress, some courts have also recognized emotional duress (for example, demanding a prenuptial agreement on the eve of the wedding). As with most contract law, this formulation varies from state to state. Still, high-pressure situations in which one party enjoys disproportionately greater influence may suggest the presence of duress.

§9.5.4 Unconscionability

A court will refuse to enforce a contract if it is convinced that the contract is unconscionable. As we outlined in Chapter 3, Judge Skelly Wright, in the case of *Williams v. Walker-Thomas Furniture*, 350 F.2d 445 (D.C. Cir. 1965), articulated the concept of unconscionability this way: "Unconscionability has generally been recognized to include an absence of meaningful choice on the part of one of the parties together with contract terms which are unreasonably favorable to the other party." Essentially, unconscionability includes two components: procedural unconscionability and substantive unconscionability. In most jurisdictions, a contract will be deemed unconscionable only if both of these factors are present, at least to some degree. The analysis of these factors presents something of a sliding scale. In a contract involving grotesque substantive unconscionability, for example, the party challenging the contract needs to show comparatively less procedural unconscionability.

Procedural unconscionability asks about the process for reaching the agreement. How lopsided was the bargaining? To what extent did each party have a meaningful choice? Any context involving contracts of adhesion, for example, are marked by an absence of meaningful choice. Similarly, if a party has greater bargaining power and wields that power in a way that creates surprise or oppression, the agreement may be deemed procedurally unconscionable. In one of the early law review articles on this topic, issues of procedural unconscionability were described as "bargaining naughtiness."[2]

Substantive unconscionability asks about the terms of the contract in question. How lopsided are the terms of the deal? As you might imagine, there is no formulaic, bright-line test for determining whether a deal is substantively unconscionable. No single term is likely to be dispositive on its own. Rather, a court will examine the totality of the contract to determine whether it exceeds acceptable boundaries.

The question of unconscionability is a significant one in the realm of arbitration. Arbitration clauses now appear in a vast array of adhesion contracts—ranging from employment agreements to consumer sales to health care. The party drafting an arbitration clause has an incentive to make it very favorably skewed toward its interests, *just barely* on the acceptable side of the line between enforceable and unconscionable. Whether a court will actually deem an arbitration agreement unconscionable depends not only on the particulars of the agreement and its formation, but also on the contract laws of the jurisdiction in which the arbitration agreement is under dispute.

You can be certain that attorneys for companies drafting arbitration clauses have been spending considerable time testing the limits. Common targets include placing limits on arbitrators' powers to award certain kinds of remedies. For example, many arbitration clauses prohibit arbitrators from ordering injunctive relief or awarding punitive damages. Still others target the joinder doctrines, placing limits on the ability of parties to join together—for example, in a class action. Lower courts had been divided on whether a contract requiring arbitration but barring class-wide proceedings would be unconscionable. However, the Supreme Court settled the debate in *Concepcion*, overturning on preemption grounds lower court rulings that

2. Arthur A. Leff, *Unconscionability and the Code—The Emperor's New Clause*, 115 U. Pa. L. Rev. 485, 487 (1967).

sought to apply state prohibitions against such waivers. See *AT&T Mobility LLC v. Concepcion*, 563 U.S. 333 (2011).

A great example of an unconscionable arbitration agreement (at least "great" in the sense of providing a clear illustration) arose in the case of *Hooters of America, Inc. v. Phillips*, 173 F.3d 933 (4th Cir. 1999). In that case, a bartender who worked at a Hooters restaurant brought suit against her employer, alleging sexual harassment in violation of Title VII. Hooters filed a motion to compel arbitration, citing the arbitration clause within an ADR policy the company had presented to employees two years earlier. The arbitration clause was a caricature of a biased procedure. It imposed pleadings and discovery burdens only on the employee. At the same time, Hooters reserved special privileges only for itself, such as dispositive motions, revocation, and fixing the composition of the pool of potential arbitrators. In the end, the court concluded that the Hooters rules were "so one-sided that their only possible purpose is to undermine the neutrality of the proceeding." It called the overall policy "a sham system unworthy even of the name of arbitration" and refused to enforce the arbitration clause.

There are also several examples of courts overturning arbitration agreements that restrict the professional backgrounds of arbitrators. For example, in *Broemmer v. Abortion Services of Phoenix*, 840 P.2d 1013 (Ariz. 1992), the court refused to enforce an arbitration agreement that limited the arbitral panel to licensed obstetricians and gynecologists. Similarly, in *Graham v. Scissor-Tail, Inc.*, 623 P.2d 165 (Cal. 1981), a court refused to enforce a requirement that an arbitrator be a member of a particular musicians' union because one of the disputants was a member of the same union. On the other hand, a contract designating a potentially interested party acting as arbitrator does not necessarily constitute an unconscionable agreement. For example, the Second Circuit upheld an arbitration conducted by NFL commissioner Roger Goodell regarding the "deflategate" case. NFL Mgmt. Council II, 820 F.3d 527 (2d Cir. 2016).

Of course, most arbitration clauses do not overreach so dramatically. As a result, the analysis involved in deciding whether a given set of arbitration terms is unconscionable demands far more balancing, judgment, and case-by-case analysis. What if the Hooters clause had merely contained one or two of these lopsided provisions, rather than an entire set of them? Or what if Hooters had provided more opportunity for its employees to read, consider, and even opt out of the arbitration agreement? A party seeking to avoid arbitration on the basis of unconscionability must demonstrate that the arbitration provisions were imposed in an unfair, adhesive manner (procedural unconscionability) and that they contain unreasonably burdensome terms (substantive unconscionability).

But the burden to prove unconscionability rests on the party attempting to avoid arbitration. The Supreme Court considered an assertion that an arbitration clause was unconscionable in the case of *Green Tree Financial Corp. Alabama v. Randolph*, 531 U.S. 79 (2000). In that case, Larketta Randolph bought a mobile home and financed the purchase through Green Tree Financial Corp. The loan document Randolph signed included a clause requiring the parties to resolve "all disputes, claims, or controversies" related to the loan through arbitration. The clause said nothing about how the costs and fees associated with arbitration would be allocated. Randolph later sued Green Tree, alleging violations of various federal laws aimed at protecting borrowers. Green Tree filed a motion to compel arbitration. (See Chapter 8 for more on these mechanics.) Randolph argued that the arbitration clause was unconscionable because the expenses associated with arbitration were so high that she might be effectively unable to pursue her claims against Green Tree. On appeal, the Court acknowledged the possibility that *some* arbitration clauses might create such a significant burden on prospective plaintiffs as to be unconscionable. In this case, however, a divided Court found that Randolph had not adequately demonstrated a sufficient risk that she would be encumbered with an actually unmanageable expense. It wrote, "[W]here, as here, a party seeks to invalidate an arbitration agreement on the ground that arbitration would be prohibitively expensive, that party bears the burden of showing the likelihood of incurring such costs. Randolph did not meet that burden."

As a side note, we should mention that the analysis for unconscionability (and other contract-based challenges that we discuss) depends primarily on state law. In Chapter 10, we will turn to the question of the FAA's impact on all of this. The short preview is that state law still governs the unconscionability analysis—provided the state unconscionability doctrines do not single out arbitration agreements for different treatment than other contracts. If a limit on damages is unenforceable as a matter of *general* state contract law, for example, a damage cap in the context of arbitration will also be unenforceable.

§9.6 OBJECTION #3: "THE ARBITRATION CLAUSE ITSELF IS UNENFORCEABLE"

Court 's Role	**Nature of the Objection to Arbitration**	Arbitrator's Role
Unless there is a clause delegating enforceability challenges to an arbitrator, decide whether the arbitration clause is enforceable. (Recall *Prima Paint* and the separability doctrine.) If the clause is enforceable, send the case to arbitration.	"Regardless of the enforceability of the contract as a whole, this arbitration clause itself is not enforceable."	If there is a clause delegating enforceability challenges to an arbitrator, and the challenge is not specific to the delegation clause, decide whether the arbitration clause is enforceable. (Recall *Rent-A-Center*.)

In the section immediately above, we discussed the standards a court (or an arbitrator) would apply in assessing a challenge to the enforceability of an agreement containing an arbitration clause. In this section, we consider the possibility that a party might specifically challenge the enforceability of an arbitration or delegation provision. Two questions arise in this context: What substantive standards will apply? and Who will decide such challenges?

In theory, parties can use any available contract theory when attacking the enforceability of an arbitration provision. As a practical matter, some of the objections described in the section immediately above do not readily apply. For example, it is unlikely that a party will be able to say that an arbitration clause was secured under duress (but the rest of the contract was fine) or that an arbitration clause should fail for want of consideration (but the rest of the contract was fine) or that there was no capacity to enter the arbitration part of the agreement (but the rest of the contract is fine). The major avenues of attack, however, remain available: A party might claim fraud with respect to the terms of an arbitration provision even though the rest of the contract was unaffected. Or a party might claim that the terms of an arbitration agreement are unconscionable or contrary to public policy, even though the other terms in the contract are unobjectionable.

Which part of the contract is being challenged?
And what clauses does that contract contain?

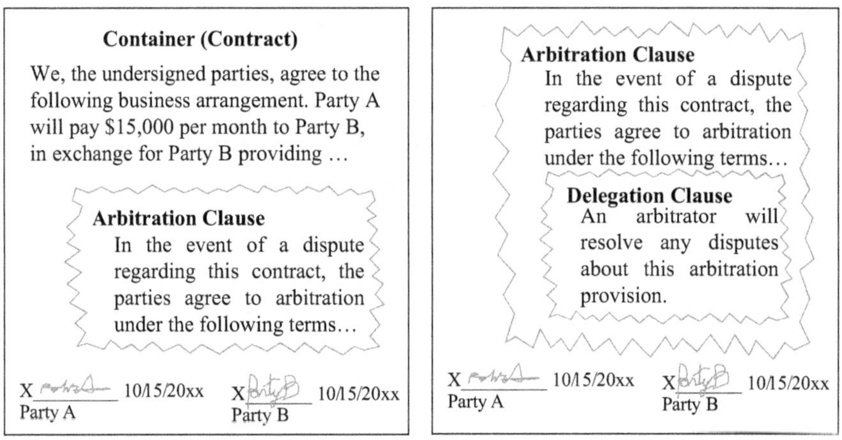

The answer to "who decides" directly parallels the analysis for arbitration clauses generally. Going back to first principles, a dispute is sent to arbitration only if the parties agreed to have such disputes go to arbitration. See *First Options*. But the separability doctrine forces us to look carefully at which part of an agreement is being challenged. See *Prima Paint*. As we know, if a party is challenging the enforceability of a contract that does not contains an arbitration clause, it will go to court. If a party challenges the enforceability of a contract with an arbitration clause, it will go to an arbitrator. If a party challenges the enforceability of the arbitration clause specifically, it will go to a court *unless* the contract also contains a delegation clause specifying that an arbitrator should hear challenges to the arbitration clause. See *Rent-A-Center*. In essence, the arbitration clause is treated as its own separate contract, and absent an arbitration provision (in the form of a delegation clause), contractual challenges must be heard by the court.

In theory, one could extend this logic ad infinitum: What happens if a party challenges the delegation clause specifically, rather than the arbitration clause or the container agreement? The dissent in *Rent-A-Center* likened the extension of the Supreme Court's current logic to Russian nesting dolls, creating potentially infinite layers of severability. As a practical matter, the more focused the target within a contract, the more limited the bases upon which one could raise a contractual objection. But in theory, the same logic would apply: the party's challenge to a delegation clause would be heard by a court, unless the parties had delegated *those* kinds of challenges to an arbitrator.

§9.7 OBJECTION #4: "THIS PARTICULAR DISPUTE DOES NOT FALL WITHIN THE SCOPE OF THE ARBITRATION CLAUSE"

Court 's Role	**Nature of the Objection to Arbitration**	Arbitrator's Role
	"This dispute does not fall within the scope of our arbitration clause."	
Decide whether the dispute is substantively arbitrable. (Recall strong presumption in favor of arbitration, *Steelworkers* and *Mitsubishi*.) If the dispute is arguably within the scope of the agreement, send the case to arbitration.		None, unless the parties "clearly and unmistakably" specified that they wanted an arbitrator to decide this. (*First Options*.) If the parties intend for an arbitrator to decide substantive arbitrability questions, the same presumption in favor of arbitration exists.

Here, we consider circumstances in which the disputants contest neither the existence of a contract containing an arbitration clause nor the enforceability of the agreement to arbitrate. Instead, they contend *as a matter of contractual interpretation* that the contract does not compel them to arbitrate their specific dispute or claim, in this particular circumstance. The set of objections within this umbrella of contractual interpretations are commonly referred to as questions of *arbitrability*. This term, though, lacks a precise and uniformly shared definition. Arbitrability can mean anything from whether the contract compels arbitration to whether the contract is enforceable. For purposes of clarity, we intend to limit our usage of the term "arbitrability" in this section to whether the contract compels parties into arbitration, but you should be aware that the term operates almost as a chimera in this area of the law.

Arbitrability presents two distinct avenues for parties seeking to avoid arbitration. The first, commonly called **substantive arbitrability**, examines the scope of the parties' agreement to arbitrate. A challenge based on substantive arbitrability asserts that even if there is a valid agreement to arbitrate, the parties never intended for that arbitration agreement to cover the particular dispute in question. The second, commonly called **procedural arbitrability**, examines the processes and conditions spelled out in the parties' agreement to arbitrate. A challenge based on procedural arbitrability asserts that the dispute should not be sent to arbitration because the party seeking to send the case to arbitration failed to satisfy some procedural prerequisite from the arbitration agreement Procedural arbitrability is the subject of §8.8 below.

One of the many ways in which parties can customize or tailor their agreement to arbitrate is with the *scope* of the arbitration agreement. Arbitration need not be a binary matter. ("Either we arbitrate everything, or we arbitrate nothing.") Instead, parties can specify precisely the kinds of disputes they want to send to arbitration. When a dispute arises, the substantive arbitrability question simply asks whether the dispute falls within the scope of the parties' arbitration agreement.

For example, imagine that two companies entering a joint venture include a provision in their contract in which they agree to arbitrate "any disputes regarding the formation of this contract or the representations made prior to the launch date of this joint venture." If a dispute arose in which one company claimed that the other misstated its assets during the negotiations, the arbitration clause would cover it. (It would be "substantively arbitrable.") If, on the other hand, a dispute arose in which one company claimed that the other side subsequently failed to make the final installment payment under the terms of the contract, the dispute would fall outside of the scope of the arbitration agreement because the incident arose after the launch date of the joint venture. Neither company could force the other into arbitration on that claim because it does not fall within the scope of their agreement and would, therefore, not be substantively arbitrable.

§9.7.1 Standards for Deciding If a Dispute Is Substantively Arbitrable

Sometimes the scope of an arbitration agreement will be so plain that no detailed analysis will be necessary to determine substantive arbitrability. For example, some arbitration clauses are narrowly and precisely crafted, spelling out in great detail which kinds of disputes are to be resolved through arbitration. ("We agree to arbitrate any and all disputes regarding whether the widgets in question conform to the contractual specifications set forth in Appendix B.") Other arbitration clauses are so broad that they encompass absolutely any dispute that could possibly arise. ("We agree to arbitrate any and all disputes related to or arising out of the formation, performance, nonperformance, breach, termination, or interpretation of this contract.") Substantive arbitrability is not a significant issue in either of these circumstances, because the substantive scope of the agreement is clear.

But what if the contract's scope is ambiguous? It is not easy to draft provisions in a way that prevents multiple interpretations. If an arbitration agreement has a scope that is *arguably* broad enough to encompass the particular dispute in question, what happens?

The U.S. Supreme Court first tackled this question in an opinion from the famous *Steelworkers* trilogy, a series of Supreme Court cases in 1960 addressing arbitration questions. In *United Steelworkers v. Warrior & Gulf Navigation Co.*, 363 U.S. 574 (1960), the union claimed that the somewhat ambiguous terms of a contract required the arbitration of a particular grievance involving work that had been contracted to non-union employees, and the company argued that the grievance fell outside the scope of the arbitration clause. In its ruling, favoring the union's position, the Supreme Court announced that all "doubts should be resolved in favor of coverage." This is a *strong* presumption of arbitrability. As long as the dispute arguably falls within the scope of the arbitration agreement, the dispute is sent to arbitration.

For some time, a question remained whether this presumption of arbitrability applied only in the relatively narrow context of collective bargaining. In 1985, however, the Supreme Court returned to the question of substantive arbitrability—this time outside the context of a labor-management contract. It reaffirmed the broad presumption of arbitrability in *Mitsubishi Motors Corp. v. Soler Chrysler-Plymouth, Inc.*, 473 U.S. 614 (1985), a commercial dispute between an automobile manufacturer and an automobile dealer. The Supreme Court said, with respect to substantive arbitrability, "[T]he parties' intentions control, but those intentions are generously construed as to issues of arbitrability." In other words, the presumption that an arbitration clause is broad enough to encompass a dispute is strong, and it applies even beyond the collective bargaining context.

Why make this assumption? Why not the opposite assumption? Part of the reason lies in the Supreme Court's consistent finding since the early 1980s that there is a strong federal policy favoring arbitration. The other part is that this is a circumstance in which the parties have clearly agreed to arbitrate *some* things. As the Court reasoned, the parties knew they would be called upon to arbitrate in some contexts, and it would have been easy enough for the parties to specify if there were certain kinds of instances in which they would prefer *not* to arbitrate.

§9.7.2 Who Decides Whether a Dispute Is Substantively Arbitrable?

The scope of an arbitration clause is to be broadly construed, so that the presumption is in favor of declaring a dispute to be substantively arbitrable. But who makes this determination—a court or an arbitrator?

The question of "who decides" substantive arbitrability was the subject of a significant Supreme Court case, *First Options of Chicago, Inc. v. Kaplan* (discussed earlier in §9.4.3). First Options submitted a claim to arbitration, citing a contractual arbitration provision. Kaplan asserted in the arbitration that the claim in question was not subject to arbitration, but the arbitrators ruled that First Options properly brought the claim to arbitration, and then ruled against Kaplan on the merits of First Options' claim. Kaplan sought a court order vacating the arbitral award against him, again arguing that a court (rather than the arbitrators) should have heard Kaplan's objections to arbitrability. The Supreme Court eventually sided with Kaplan, ruling that a court should review the arbitrability of the claim.

The first component of the Supreme Court's opinion in *First Options* set out the basic principle that if the parties have agreed who decides arbitrability, the parties' decision will control. In so holding, the Court returned to the principle that arbitration is a matter of contract between the parties. "[T]he question 'who has the primary power to decide arbitrability' turns upon what the parties agreed about *that* matter." If the parties agreed to have a court determine arbitrability, the court should resolve the question. And if the parties agreed to have an arbitrator resolve arbitrability, an arbitrator's decision should control on this question.

The second component of the Court's *First Options* analysis is that if there is contractual silence about who should decide arbitrability, or if the agreement is ambiguous as to the question of arbitrability, then the court is the presumptive decision maker. The Court held that *a court* is the presumptive decision maker in a dispute over substantive arbitrability, unless the parties "clearly and unmistakably" agreed that an arbitrator should resolve it.

This creates an interesting dichotomy: The court has a presumption in favor of arbitration for resolving the *merits* of a substantive arbitrability fight, but a presumption in favor of having a judge decide *who* decides whether the case is arbitrable. The Court in *First Options* called this discrepancy "understandable." It suggested that parties who knowingly enter into an agreement to arbitrate can reasonably be expected to anticipate that they would need to be clear if they want a particular type of dispute to stay out of arbitration. By contrast, with respect to the question of who decides substantive arbitrability, the Court admitted that the question is "rather arcane." The Court reasoned that having arbitrators as the presumptive decision makers about arbitrability questions "might too often force unwilling parties to arbitrate a matter they reasonably would have thought a judge, not an arbitrator, would decide."

The short answer, therefore, to who decides substantive arbitrability is whoever the parties say. But if there is any doubt about the parties' intended decison maker or whether an arbitration agreement applies to a particular dispute, the court should decide. For instance, in *AT&T Technologies, Inc. v. Communications Workers of America*, 475 U.S. 643 (1986), a union challenged AT&T's decision to lay off a set of employees, claiming the layoffs violated the collective bargaining agreement. The union demanded arbitration, which was available for many kinds of disputes under the collective bargaining agreement. But AT&T asserted that the layoffs in question were because of a "lack of work," a condition it claimed fell outside the scope of the collective bargaining agreement's arbitration clause. The Supreme Court held that, in the absence of specific language providing that an arbitrator decide the question, a district court must review the agreement to determine whether the parties intended to submit such disputes to arbitration. (Recall from *Steelworkers* and *Mitsubishi*, however, that the court's presumption in the analysis will be in favor of sending disputes to arbitration.)

§9.8 OBJECTION #5: "THEY DIDN'T DO WHAT THE ARBITRATION AGREEMENT REQUIRES THEM TO DO"

Court 's Role	**Nature of the Objection to Arbitration**	Arbitrator's Role
None (send to an arbitrator).	"They haven't done what they need to do to send this to arbitration." →	Decide the procedural arbitrability question, including conditions precedent. (Recall *Howsam.*)

The terms of an arbitration agreement are, in some ways, like a set of privately constructed litigation procedures. Mercifully, most contracting parties do not have to craft their arbitration rules from scratch. Typically, the parties choose a fully written set of arbitration rules from one of a number of sources. For example, some arbitration organizations promulgate rules for arbitration (in part because they hope disputants will hire their organization to administer arbitrations). Some professional associations have sample arbitration procedures. For example, homebuilders have a set of proposed arbitration rules, as do architects, as do developers. The idea is that contracting parties might, with relatively little investment of time, easily find a set of arbitration procedures they will find appropriate to govern future disputes.

Now, what happens if one or both of the parties fail to follow the procedures that appear in their arbitration agreement? And who decides whether the parties have, in fact, followed the agreed-upon procedures?

For minor procedural rules governing the conduct of the arbitration, the question sits in the lap of an arbitrator. If, for example, the arbitration procedures indicate that parties must give each other 72 hours' notice of any witnesses they intend to call, and one of the parties (arguably) gives the other side only 60 hours' notice, the resulting dispute then falls within the province of the arbitrator to determine. Such intra-arbitration disputes are virtually never subject to judicial review. (For more on the limited possibility of judicial review of arbitrators' decisions, see Chapter 8.)

The important questions within this category arise when the dispute in question concerns a so-called gateway matter. We should warn you that the term "gateway dispute," like the term "arbitrability," is used in such a wide range of settings that it risks being unhelpful. Nevertheless, the Supreme Court continues to refer to certain matters as "gateway," and it is, therefore, important to discuss the various things that might fall under this umbrella. Some gateway disputes concern the question of whether a binding contract exists at all. Other gateway disputes hinge on whether the parties have done the things they need to have done to bring the arbitration clause into effect under the terms of their arbitration agreement. It is this latter category of concerns that we are calling issues of "procedural arbitrability" in this section.

§9.8.1 Standards for Deciding If Conditions Precedent to Arbitration Have Been Satisfied

Like many of the other areas of arbitration law we have been discussing, regular contract law governs the question of how to decide if a party has followed the arbitration procedures or has met the prerequisites to arbitration.

Unlike many other subtopics we have discussed, however, no arbitration-specific presumptions tip the balance one way or the other. A party alleging that the other party has not met some contractual condition precedent to arbitration has the burden of showing that failure. Similarly, a party alleging that some arbitration procedure was not followed, like providing notice of claims, has the burden of demonstrating that failure.

§9.8.2 Who Decides Whether a Dispute Is Procedurally Arbitrable?

As with the question of the enforceability of an arbitration contract, many of the procedural arbitrability disputes center on the question of *who* decides whether the parties have properly satisfied the contractual conditions that would send them to arbitration. And the answer for *procedural* arbitrability is different than for *substantive* arbitrability. In short, arbitrators, not courts, resolve disputes over procedural arbitrability.

In *Howsam v. Dean Witter Reynolds, Inc.*, 537 U.S. 79 (2002), the Supreme Court addressed the question of allocating decision-making authority regarding procedural arbitrability issues. In that case, Howsam, on the advice of her Dean Witter advisor, bought an interest in a set of limited partnerships. The partnerships did not fare as well as Howsam hoped, and she believed that Dean Witter had misrepresented certain aspects of the purchase. The terms of Howsam's investment contract with Dean Witter included an arbitration provision, which specified that the arbitration rules of the National Association of Securities Dealers (NASD) would apply. Howsam sought to bring her claim against Dean Witter to arbitration. Dean Witter responded by pointing to a clause in the NASD rules that held that no dispute would be eligible for arbitration "where six (6) years have elapsed from the occurrence or event giving rise to the dispute." The question before the Supreme Court was not whether that amount of time had passed, but rather *who decides* whether Howsam's claim was timely. The Supreme Court held that this was a matter "where parties would likely expect that an arbitrator would decide the gateway matter. Thus, 'procedural' questions which grow out of the dispute and bear on its final disposition are presumptively *not* for the judge, but for an arbitrator, to decide."

§9.9 THE SPECIAL CASE OF CLASS-WIDE CLAIMS

The basic theme of the previous sections has been that the parties' intentions should control both whether a matter goes to arbitration and also who should decide that particular question. The baseline presumption in those analyses depends, in part, on whether the challenge relates to procedural arbitrability or substantive arbitrability. The line between substantive arbitrability and procedural arbitrability is not always perfectly clear, however, and in some circumstances, much is at stake in that line drawing. That is particularly true with respect to class-wide claims, but the Court's unwillingness to allow arbitrators leeway in interpreting silent or ambiguous class waivers may be sui generis, i.e. unique to class processes, as explained below.

If a contract specifically provides for class arbitrations and all parties agree to that provision, a case can clearly proceed on that basis. If a contract precludes class-wide arbitration, then an arbitrator who purported to conduct a class arbitration nonetheless would surely be exceeding her or his powers. But what if an arbitration clause in a contract is silent about whether class-wide arbitration is available? Should that be treated as a procedural matter for the arbitrator to resolve or a substantive matter for the court?

In *Stolt-Nielsen v. AnimalFeeds*, 559 U.S. 662, 685–87 (2010), a majority of the Supreme Court held that

> [a]n implicit agreement to authorize class-action arbitration . . . is not a term that the arbitrator may infer solely from the fact of the parties' agreement to arbitrate. This is so because class arbitration changes the nature of arbitration to such a degree that it cannot be presumed the parties consented to it by simply agreeing to submit their [bilateral] disputes to an arbitrator. . . . We think that the differences between bilateral and class-action arbitrations are too great for arbitrators to presume, consistent with their powers under the FAA, that the parties' mere silence on the issue of class-action arbitration constitutes consent to resolve their disputes in class proceedings.

The rule created in *Stolt-Nielsen* continues the theme of recent court interpretation: Parties are only compelled to class arbitration if the parties contracted for class arbitrations. However, this *relatively* straightforward rule is complicated in application. What if the arbitration clause is ambiguous regarding class arbitration? What if the parties submitted to class arbitration anyway? Courts, as always, will attempt to honor the contract between the parties and uphold the outcome that parties seemed to intend—sometimes by explicit action and sometimes by inference.

In *Oxford Health Plans, LLC v. Sutter*, 569 U.S. 564 (2013), Sutter and a group of doctors sued Oxford Health Plans, alleging insufficient and delayed payments for serving patients covered by the insurance company.

Oxford moved to compel arbitration of the class action under their arbitration clause, which read, "No civil action concerning any dispute arising under this Agreement shall be instituted before any court." The doctors sought to proceed as a class, and Oxford argued that their agreement did not permit class-wide arbitration. The arbitrator found that the parties' contract evidenced an intention "to vest in the arbitration process everything that is prohibited from the court process." The arbitrator, therefore, held that the contract permitted class-wide arbitration. Oxford appealed and argued vigorously that the arbitrator's interpretation of the contract was badly mistaken—so badly mistaken that the court should overturn the decision under FAA §10, on the grounds that the arbitrator had exceeded his authority. But the Supreme Court held that the arbitrator's interpretation had at least "arguably construed" the contract, and the parties had bargained for having an arbitrator do just that. The Court concluded that "the arbitrator's construction holds, however good, bad, or ugly. In sum, Oxford chose arbitration, and it must now live with that choice." The case, therefore, proceeded on a class-wide basis, but in arbitration.

However, as you might imagine, lawyers now often provide great specificity about class arbitration in the clauses they draft. In *Epic Systems Corp. v. Lewis*, 584 U.S. 497 (2018), an employee named Steven Morris attempted to avoid an arbitration agreement with his employer. The employee's contract provided that disputes must be arbitrated *and* that any arbitration must be brought individually, rather than as a class action. Morris sought to bring a class action nonetheless, arguing that the clause's effective prohibition against collective claims violated federal labor law. The Supreme Court disagreed, finding no conflict and holding that the FAA's "savings clause" requires the terms to be enforced, as written. (For more on the "savings clause," see Chapter 10.) As a result, many critics of this form of arbitration now observe that an employer can effectively remove all risk of class actions by (1) requiring arbitration, and (2) requiring all arbitrations to be adjudicated individually.

In fact, employers and others who include arbitration clauses in adhesion contracts can avoid class arbitrations *even if* the contracts they have drafted are ambiguous about the question. In *Lamps Plus v. Varela*, 587 U.S. 176 (2019), a data breach led to the disclosure of more than one thousand employees' tax information. The employees sought class-wide adjudication of their claim against the company, and the employment agreement was ambiguous. The Supreme Court held that because "the shift from individual to class arbitration is a 'fundamental' change," provision for class-wide arbitration would have to be unambiguous, even though the usual common law canons would suggest that ambiguous contract terms should be interpreted against the drafter (here, the company and therefore permitting class arbitration).

Creative lawyers, in response to the Court's limitations on class processes, have now developed the concept of mass arbitration, whereby individuals with arbitration agreement file thousands of claims against companies, who previously agreed to pay arbitration filing fees. Courts have been unsympathetic to company complaints about the mass arbitration process. Concerned about this financial exposure, companies began settling these claims. But they also turned to the arbitration providers, like AAA, to request new rules that would address the mass arbitration issue. Many of these new rules require the "batching" of cases. A typical batching process rule might state that, if claimants file more than 50 similar arbitration claims, the parties must select a specific number of claims for individual arbitration, and direct the remaining claims into a global mediation process. It is unclear how these new rules will impact existing arbitration agreements or if companies will start to include class arbitration in their future clauses.

§9.10 PULLING IT ALL TOGETHER AND A PREVIEW OF THE PREEMPTION DOCTRINE

As we said at the start of this chapter, arbitration is a creature of contract, and you remember from your first year of law school that contract law is a state law issue. There is, however, a Federal Arbitration Act, and that fact complicates matters considerably. According to the preemption doctrine, if a valid federal law is in conflict with a state law, the federal law will trump. To what extent do the terms of the FAA conflict with (and therefore preempt) state contract laws? What can (or can't) a state do if it wants to regulate arbitration agreements? In Chapter 10, we will examine the question of the interaction between state law and federal law in resolving questions about enforcing arbitration agreements.

With some hesitation about oversimplifying what is an evolving and complex area of the law, we offer the following summary of the past two chapters on the following page.

9. Must This Dispute Go to Arbitration?

Court's Role	**Nature of the Objection to Arbitration**	Arbitrator's Role
Decide whether a contract exists. If a contract with an arbitration clause exists, send the case to arbitration.	"What contract? I never entered a contract."	None.
None (send to arbitrator), unless the parties specify otherwise in the contract.	"This whole contract is unenforceable, including the arbitration clause."	Decide the enforceability of the contract. (Recall *Prima Paint* and the separability doctrine.)
Unless there is a clause delegating enforceability challenges to an arbitrator, decide whether the arbitration clause is enforceable. (Recall *Prima Paint* and the separability doctrine.) If the clause is enforceable, send the case to arbitration.	"Regardless of the enforceability of the contract as a whole, this arbitration clause itself is not enforceable."	If there is a clause delegating enforceability challenges to an arbitrator, and the challenge is not specific to the delegation clause, decide whether the arbitration clause is enforceable. (Recall *Rent-A-Center*.)
Decide whether the dispute is substantively arbitrable. (Recall strong presumption in favor of arbitration, *Steelworkers* and *Mitsubishi*.) If the dispute is arguably within the scope of the agreement, send the case to arbitration.	"This dispute does not fall within the scope of our arbitration clause."	None, unless the parties "clearly and unmistakably" specified that they wanted an arbitrator to decide this. (*First Options*.) If the parties intend for an arbitrator to decide substantive arbitrability questions, the same presumption in favor of arbitration exists.
None (send to an arbitrator).	"They haven't done what they need to do to send this to arbitration."	Decide the procedural arbitrability question, including conditions precedent. (Recall *Howsam*.)

Examples

Working for the Grape

Grapalicious Grapes is a small vineyard and wine-making operation. The Grapalicious Employee Handbook, which is incorporated by reference into every employee's contract, includes a alternative dispute resolution provision. That provision reads, in part:

> Employer and Employee agree to endeavor to resolve any and all differences, grievances, and disputes through the most efficient, least formal mechanism possible. To that end, Employer and Employee agree that any complaint or grievance will be presented to the other side, in writing, within four months of the circumstances giving rise to the complaint or grievance. Further, neither the Employer nor the Employee will initiate any formal action against the other without having first engaged in a good-faith effort to resolve the matter consensually.
>
> In the event Employer and Employee are unable to resolve their differences through informal negotiations, Employer and Employee agree to submit to binding arbitration the following disputes:
>
> a. Any and all disputes concerning wages and benefits, and
> b. Any and all disputes concerning the termination of this employment relationship.
>
> Except as provided herein, the arbitration will be conducted according to the Employment Arbitration Rules of the American Association of Grapegrowers.

1. **Sour grapes.** Ernest was a Grapalicious employee for more than a year. Three months ago, he was fired from his job. Having now examined his final paycheck more carefully, Ernest believes that Grapalicious incorrectly calculated his overtime pay for the weeks before he was fired. Ernest called Grapalicious and tried to work things out, but he got nowhere. If Ernest were to bring a claim against Grapalicious, would Grapalicious be able to force him to bring it before an arbitrator, rather than in court?

2. **Sour grapes, version two.** Assume the same set of facts as in question 1, except that Ernest brought his claim concerning the overtime calculations directly to an arbitrator immediately upon discovering the error in his paycheck. Would Grapalicious have any grounds for opposing the submission of the case to arbitration? Who decides this?

3. **Sour grapes, the digital version.** When Ernest began work, he logged into a program, aptly named "e-forms." He followed a multi-step process for signing documents where the user signs in with a username (his employee id number) and a password. Then the user scrolls through

the whole agreement and checks a box which results in his username appearing as the signature. When Ernest attempts to avoid arbitration by filing his complaint in court, Grapalicious moves to compel arbitration, attaching the document with his user id signature on it to prove that he "signed" it. Ernest claims he did not, asserting that it must have been his supervisor or a fellow employee who inputted his signature, because he never saw the arbitration agreement. Should this dispute go to court or to an arbitrator to decide whether Ernest is bound to arbitrate his claim?

4. **Overripe grapes.** Emilia was a Grapalicious employee for almost a decade. For the entire period of her employment, she worked a somewhat irregular schedule. She and her supervisor would simply set a schedule at the start of each month, customizing it to her needs and to the needs of the company. Some weeks, she would work as many as 50 hours, and some weeks, she would work as few as ten. On average, by the end of the year, it always worked out that she was working about two-thirds time with Grapalicious. About a year ago, Emilia got a new supervisor. About ten months ago, her supervisor stopped giving her large assignments. In the past eight months, she has never worked more than 15 hours a week. Emilia is convinced that her new boss has made these adverse employment decisions for discriminatory reasons, and she files a lawsuit against Grapalicious. If Emilia attempted to resolve this issue with her employer and failed before filing a complaint, would Grapalicious succeed in an effort to compel Emilia to bring her claim before an arbitrator instead? Who decides this?

5. **Grape gripe.** Emmanuel is a salesman for Grapalicious. For years, he has been assigned to the Rocky Mountain region. When he is not on the road, Emmanuel works from the basement of his home (which is located in the region). Grapalicious paid for all of the costs of maintaining the home office—something it has done for no other members of its sales force. Three months ago, Emmanuel's boss told him that he would soon be responsible for the Southeast region and advised him to put his house on the market right away. Emmanuel filed a letter of complaint with his boss, citing, among other things, the extraordinary burden it would place on his family. Grapalicious refused to change the assignment, and now it is also refusing to pay to set up a similar home office in Emmanuel's new home in the Southeast. After trying unsuccessfully to resolve this matter consensually with Grapalicious, Emmanuel filed his claim—about the transfer and about the refusal to pay for a new home office—with an arbitrator. If Grapalicious filed a motion in court seeking to stay the arbitration, what arguments would it make, and would Grapalicious be successful?

6. **Discriminating palate?** Eleanor was an executive at Grapalicious for several years. Almost immediately after a new CEO came on board, Eleanor was fired. She is convinced that her discharge was the product of unlawful discrimination. Three months later, she filed a lawsuit against Grapalicious in federal court. Grapalicious attempted to contact Eleanor to discuss the matter, which she refused to do. Would Grapalicious succeed if it sought to compel Eleanor to pursue her claim in arbitration? In addition to her employment discrimination claim, what if Eleanor added a claim that the new CEO sexually assaulted her?

Doing Business with the Grape

7. **Missing bottles.** Grapalicious has a contract with BottleCo to supply bottles for wine and other products made at the Grapalicious vineyard. The contract includes an arbitration clause that provides for arbitration only in cases of "intentional breach of contract." One shipment of bottles never arrived at Grapalicious, causing Grapalicious to fail to meet the deadline for entering and selling wine at the biggest "new release" wine show of the season. Grapalicious files a claim in arbitration against BottleCo, citing the arbitration clause in the contract between Grapalicious and BottleCo. BottleCo responds by filing a motion to stay the arbitration, pointing to the limited reach of the arbitration clause. As part of its motion, BottleCo maintains that the missing shipment was an innocent mistake rather than an intentional breach. Who rules on the motion, and how will the court or arbitrator rule on the motion to stay arbitration?

8. **Complaining on the clock.** Grapalicious gets another shipment of bottles from BottleCo. This time, several of the bottles are cracked and others are misshapen. Grapalicious promptly calls BottleCo to complain. BottleCo responds by saying, "Let's meet in person to work all of this out." Because of scheduling difficulties, the parties are not able to meet until a few months later. At the meeting, BottleCo tells Grapalicious that it cannot discuss the problem because Grapalicious failed to bring the defective bottles to the meeting. Their meeting adjourns. Grapalicious later sends photos of the broken bottles to BottleCo. After some further delay, about a year after the disputed shipment in question took place, BottleCo responds by saying, "We're going to need you to put all of this in writing." Grapalicious, finally fed up with dealing with BottleCo, files an arbitration claim against BottleCo. BottleCo then files a motion in court to stay the arbitration, citing the contractual provision requiring the complaining party to bring any arbitration action under the contract within one year of the event that gave rise to the claim. How will the court (or arbitrator if applicable) rule on the motion to stay arbitration?

9. **The grape's rules.** Grapalicious has a supply contract with SuperScrewper to manufacture screw tops to seal all of Grapalicious's wine bottles. According to the contract with SuperScrewper, "any and all disputes regarding the quality of the bottle screw tops described in this contract shall be resolved through arbitration." A dispute arises from the most recent SuperScrewper shipment. Grapalicious files a lawsuit in court against SuperScrewper, alleging that (1) the entire shipment of screw tops was late, (2) too few screw tops were sent, and (3) some of the screw tops were bent and unusable. Will SuperScrewper be able to compel Grapalicious to bring these claims in arbitration instead of court?

10. **The grape's rules, part two.** Assume the same set of facts as in question 9. The arbitration agreement between Grapalicious and SuperScrewper also specifies that "any such arbitration shall be conducted according to the Commercial Arbitration Rules of the American Association of Grapegrowers." What impact would this clause have if, according to those rules, questions of substantive arbitrability are to be resolved by the arbitrator?

Arbitrating Burgers

11. **The Burger Pit's falling arches.** The Burger Pit is a local drive-thru fast food restaurant. You pull up in your car and place an order at the window of the restaurant. While you are waiting for your Belly Buster Bacon Burger, the enormous silver-colored arches that normally sit on the roof of the Burger Pit come crashing down onto your car. You receive your burger and a ride to the hospital. After you recover from your injuries, you file a lawsuit against Burger Pit in the local county court. Burger Pit appears in court and files a motion to stay the litigation and compel arbitration. What would a court do with the motion?

12. **The Burger Pit's drive-thru waiver.** Fully recovered, you pull up in your car at Burger Pit to place an order at the window of the restaurant. While you are waiting for a Burger Pit employee to take your order, you notice a small sign that says, "By placing an order with us you are agreeing to arbitrate any and all disputes arising out of or relating to your purchase. For details of the arbitration agreement, visit our website." You order, pay for, and receive a Belly Buster Bacon Burger. Shortly after you eat it, you become terribly ill with food poisoning. After you recover, you file suit against Burger Pit in the local county court. Burger Pit appears in court and files a motion to stay the litigation and compel arbitration, which you oppose. What arguments would each side likely make, and how would the court likely rule on the motion?

13. **The Burger Pit doesn't deliver.** During your planning for the company picnic, you enter a catering contract with Burger Pit. Burger Pit's

catering contract contains a clause that says, "By signing this agreement, you are agreeing to arbitrate any and all disputes arising out of or relating to this catering agreement." You and Burger Pit negotiate over the price and the specifications for the catering job, and eventually you both sign the agreement. You send Burger Pit payment in advance, as is required under the contract, and you wait. The day of the company picnic arrives, but Burger Pit never does. Despite your frantic calls to the Burger Pit hotline, no food is ever delivered. You file a lawsuit in the nearest court alleging breach of contract. Burger Pit files a motion to stay the litigation, citing the arbitration clause in the catering contract. What would the court do with Burger Pit's motion?

14. **Le Burger's arbitration menu.** Le Burger is an upscale hamburger restaurant, complete with crisp table linens and snooty servers. At the bottom of each page of the Le Burger menu is a notice that reads, "By placing an order with us, you are agreeing to arbitrate any and all disputes arising out of or relating to your purchase. For a complete copy of the arbitration agreement, see the back side of our menu." On the back of the Le Burger menu appear the details of an arbitration agreement. After waiting for weeks to secure a reservation at Le Burger, you finally get a table late one evening. You order a range of food from the menu, and the snooty server has you initial a short form indicating that you read, understood, and accepted the Le Burger arbitration policy. Shortly after your meal is over, you become terribly sick with food poisoning. You bring suit against Le Burger in court, and Le Burger seeks to stay the litigation, citing the arbitration policy on its menu. What would a court likely do with Le Burger's motion?

15. **Le Burger's pricy arbitration menu.** Le Burger has the same menu as the one described in question 14, except that the arbitration agreement included on the back of its menu specifies a set of arbitration procedures under which a claimant must pay an unrecoverable filing fee of $2,000 to commence an action. Does this clause change the enforceability of the arbitration agreement?

16. **Le Burger: home of chauvinist pigs.** You and a group of your female friends go to Le Burger after work one day. The Le Burger maître d' seats you, and you notice that the menu includes an arbitration clause that purports to cover "any and all claims arising out of or related to your visit to Le Burger." You and the waiter joke about the clause, and you agree to its terms in writing when you place your order. The waiter brings you and your friends your entrees. When it comes time for dessert, your waiter tells you and your party, "Women don't need dessert. That's particularly true for your group. You are done with your meal." You are so offended that you storm out. You and your friends want to

sue Le Burger for unlawful discrimination. Would you be able to file the claim in court, or would you be forced to bring it in arbitration?

17. **Le Burger: home of Stone Age policies.** Tonya Tartare works as a char-broiling engineer in the Le Burger kitchen. When she accepted the job with Le Burger, she signed an employment contract, one part of which included an arbitration clause covering "any and all claims related to this employment or the termination thereof." After six months of working at Le Burger, Tartare discovers that all of her male colleagues make considerably more money than she does. Tartare confronts her manager, who tells her that it is "Le Burger policy to offer women one-third less than guys, because the silly dames always seem to accept lower pay without question." Tartare files a lawsuit against Le Burger, and Le Burger files a motion to stay the litigation, citing the arbitration clause in Tartare's employment contract. How would the court rule on Le Burger's motion?

18. **Le Burger: home of no class.** Assume the same facts as question 17, except that the arbitration clause also specifically prohibits representative or class-action suits. Tartare wants to bring an action on behalf of all female Le Burger employees. Would she be able to do so?

19. **Le Burger: home of the home court advantage.** Reuben Rubin, a busboy, was one of the longest-serving employees at Le Burger, having been there for almost a decade. One day, at the beginning of his shift, his supervisor handed him a document entitled, "New Arbitration Policy." The document spelled out the terms of a new arbitration provision applicable to all Le Burger employees. According to the policy, "any and all disputes related to or arising out of" Rubin's employment were subject to arbitration. The agreement also specified that all arbitrations would take place in a forum to be selected by Le Burger and that the arbitrator of any such disputes would be required to have "at least 15 years of experience in restaurant ownership or management." Rubin's supervisor told him that he had until the end of his shift to accept or decline, and indicated that he could continue his employment only if he accepted. Rubin hastily accepted, signed the policy, handed it back to her, and began his shift. About a month later, Rubin saw restaurant staff egregiously violating a number of health and safety regulations, and he raised the issue with his supervisor, who said she would take care of things. The next day, Le Burger fired Rubin. Rubin brought a lawsuit against Le Burger alleging breach of contract and violation of state whistleblower protection laws. Le Burger files a motion to stay the litigation, and Rubin contests the enforceability of the arbitration agreement. Who would hear Rubin's objections, and what is the likely outcome?

20. **Burger Pit: home of liars.** You enter into a franchise agreement with Burger Pit to operate a fast food restaurant in your hometown. During negotiations over the franchise agreement, you specifically ask the Burger Pit representative about the availability of its mouthwatering "secret sauce." The Burger Pit representative tells you, "As part of your agreement, you will have access to an unlimited amount of our secret sauce. After all, that sauce is the heart and soul of Burger Pit's business." Burger Pit requires six months' payment up front. Immediately after signing the agreement, you learn that the Food and Drug Administration had just listed Burger Pit's secret sauce as a banned, toxic substance. You are convinced that Burger Pit knew about the FDA ban at the time of your negotiations. You file a lawsuit alleging fraud and breach of contract against Burger Pit. Burger Pit appears in court and files a motion to stay the litigation, citing an arbitration clause in the franchise agreement that says that "any and all disputes arising out of or related to the formation, performance, breach, or nonperformance of this contract" shall be arbitrated. What would a court do with Burger Pit's motion?

21. **Le Burger: home of creative signatures.** One day, during the busiest season of the year, the manager of Le Burger was in desperate need of additional help in the kitchen. She hastily agreed to hire the first applicant who came to the restaurant, a man named Stephen Stylo, and put him to work immediately that evening. After only a few weeks, Le Burger fired Stylo. Shortly after that, Stylo files a lawsuit in federal court against Le Burger alleging that his termination was unlawful and discriminatory. Le Burger appears in court and moves to stay the litigation. To its motion, Le Burger attaches a copy of its employment contract, with a broad arbitration clause highlighted and with a signature appearing just above Stylo's name. Stylo argues that he has never seen this contract before, swears that he never signed any employment contract with Le Burger, and says that the signature appearing on the contract looks nothing like his own. What would the court do with Le Burger's motion to stay the litigation?

Explanations

Working for the Grape

1. **Sour grapes.** Yes. Based on the facts before us, the Grapalicious employment contract—including the arbitration clause contained in the contract—appears to have no defects. For example, nothing in the contract suggests that the employee handbook was imposed inappropriately on the employees, and nothing suggests that the handbook's provisions unconscionably favor Grapalicious over the employees. We might want to know more about the Employment Arbitration Rules of the American

Association of Grapegrowers to assess their fairness, but on these facts, nothing suggests that the contract itself is anything but binding.

As to the question of substantive arbitrability, the arbitration clause within this contract specifies a relatively narrow scope of disputes that are subject to arbitration. Rather than saying "any and all disputes about anything," it names two categories of disputes that must be arbitrated. Such terms are to be read expansively, however, under the logic of the federal policy favoring arbitration, as articulated in the Supreme Court's *Steelworkers* trilogy. Here, the dispute concerns both wages and the termination of Ernest's employment. The dispute is, therefore, substantively arbitrable, and Grapalicious will be able to compel Ernest to arbitrate this dispute.

2. **Sour grapes, version two.** Yes. Although it may appear counterintuitive, Grapalicious might be able to resist having this heard in arbitration by arguing that Ernest failed to satisfy the conditions precedent to arbitration specified in the employee handbook. According to the handbook, Ernest was supposed to present his complaint to Grapalicious in writing, and he was supposed to exhaust good-faith bargaining efforts. Nothing in the facts suggests that he did so. Therefore, Ernest may be blocked from imposing the arbitration provision against Grapalicious, if Grapalicious wishes to avoid having an arbitrator resolve the dispute.

   Notice, however, that all of these objections that Grapalicious might raise fall into the category of "procedural arbitrability" questions—so-called gateway issues that the parties would reasonably expect the arbitrators to decide. As a result, an arbitrator (rather than a court) would resolve disputes about Ernest's compliance with these provisions. A court would hear the substance of this dispute if an arbitrator determined that Ernest's failure to adhere to the procedural requirements of the contract bars him from compelling arbitration.

3. **Sour grapes, the digital version.** Under most state laws, an electronic signature is legally valid only when the individual who the signature purports to represent is the one who engages in the action of signing. Here, Ernest's user ID, which is the electronic signature, appeared at the end of an entire employment agreement, which contained an arbitration clause. Ernest's claim that he did not sign it and his claim that his supervisor or another worker could have used his user ID to create an account and sign the agreement, creates a question of fact as to the existence of the arbitration agreement. Because this is an issue of whether the arbitration agreement exists, the court, not an arbitrator, must decide it.

4. **Overripe grapes.** Grapalicious would probably be unable to compel Emilia to bring her claim before an arbitrator. This question hinges on the substantive arbitrability of Emilia's claim. The contract specifies the two

types of claims subject to arbitration. Unless the dispute falls within the categories the parties consented to present to an arbitrator, Grapalicious would have no grounds to compel arbitration. Emilia's claim does not, on its face, appear to be a dispute over wages and benefits, though one could argue that the customized work schedule was a benefit of some sort. Nor does the dispute technically concern the termination of her employment (as evidenced by the fact that she remains employed at Grapalicious). As a result, therefore, unless the arbitration clause is read extraordinarily expansively, Grapalicious is unlikely to succeed in compelling arbitration.

Now, who makes this determination—a court or an arbitrator? In most cases, a court would resolve this question of substantive arbitrability. Some states appear to resolve this question differently, sending the matter to arbitration. But as a general matter, under the logic of *First Options*, the question of substantive arbitrability would be sent to an arbitrator only if the parties' agreement evidenced a "clear and unmistakable" intention to do so. Here, no such indication exists, so a court would resolve the question.

Notice that how the parties frame the litigation can make a big difference. Is this a simple matter of work assignments—a matter not identified as subject to arbitration? If so, a court would refuse to compel arbitration. Or is this a case of a wage and hour dispute, and because both were significantly decreased, a case of constructive termination? If so, the matter appears to fall within the scope of the arbitration clause, particularly given the broad presumption in favor of substantive arbitrability.

5. **Grape gripe.** Grapalicious's best argument would be that Emmanuel's claims are not substantively arbitrable. Grapalicious would argue that nothing in these facts relates to the termination of Emmanuel's employment, and that the transfer itself does not involve wages and benefits. Quite plainly, Emmanuel was not fired, so that aspect of the arbitration clause's scope does not affect the analysis.

The question is whether any of this involves a dispute over "wages and benefits." The transfer itself does not appear to fall within the arbitration clause's scope. But the company's refusal to reimburse expenses for setting up a new home office might constitute a dispute over benefits. Given the strong federal policy favoring arbitration and the corresponding presumption of arbitrability, it is certainly conceivable that one might consider this to be at least partially a dispute over benefits—and therefore, at least partially substantively arbitrable.

If the dispute over benefits (the home office expenses) is deemed substantively arbitrable, Grapalicious would fail in its motion to stay the arbitration—at least as to that issue. To the extent the parties contracted to arbitrate disputes like this one, a court would hold off on deciding the merits of the remaining legal claims until the arbitration had run its course. (Recall the preclusion doctrine reasons requiring this sequence. If the court were to go first, it might make a ruling that precluded an arbitrator from deciding that which the parties agreed to have an arbitrator decide.)

The fight in question in this chapter is not about whether a claimant wins. It is about the forum in which an aggrieved party must bring a claim. In this case, conceivably, Emmanuel might have to bring his claims in two separate fora.

6. **Discriminating palate?** Yes. Eleanor might object to being compelled to arbitrate a claim involving a statutory right (in this case, antidiscrimination laws). However, a public policy objection will not succeed absent some statutory language making it clear that the type of discrimination claim in question is not subject to arbitration agreements. (See Chapter 8 for more on public policy objections.) The agreement, therefore, is enforceable. Grapalicious appears to have complied with the conditions precedent to arbitration by endeavoring to resolve the dispute consensually, so the arbitrator is likely find the matter procedurally arbitrable.

   If Eleanor added a claim of sexual assault to her discrimination claim, the End Forced Arbitration of Sexual Harassment and Sexual Assault Act would come into play. Under the new Act, employees cannot be compelled to arbitrate sexual assault or sexual harassment claims. Courts have not resolved whether an employee who has claims in addition to their sexual assault or sexual harassment claim, must arbitrate those claims even though they cannot be compelled to arbitrate their sexual assault or harassment claims. Thus, it is possible that the sexual assault claim would continue in court, while the sex discrimination claim would proceed in arbitration. Lower courts are just beginning to address the question and are generally coalescing around two points of view – some courts are finding that if a complaint contains even one sexual assault or harassment allegation, then it cannot enforce an arbitration agreement as to *any* of the claims within the complaint while others consider whether claims brought at the same time as a sexual assault claim arise from "a common nucleus of operative facts." If so, those arising from the common nucleus of facts would proceed in court.

Doing Business with the Grape

7. **Missing bottles.** The enforceability of the contract between BottleCo and Grapalicious is not in question, so this raises a substantive arbitrability question at the outset. Responsibility for determining whether Grapalicious's claim falls within the scope of the arbitration clause rests initially with the court.

In deciding the motion to stay litigation (which hinges on a determination of substantive arbitrability), the court will be guided by the *Steelworkers* presumption of arbitrability. The clause specifically limits its arbitration to incidents of "intentional breaches of contract," and it might be difficult for Grapalicious to demonstrate that BottleCo's breach was intentional. Nevertheless, given the broad presumption of arbitrability, the court may decide that the matter is at least arguably within the scope of the clause.

The Supreme Court addressed a somewhat similar question in *PacifiCare Health v. Book*, 538 U.S. 401 (2002). In that case, the arbitration clause in question prohibited the arbitrator from awarding any "punitive" damages. The plaintiffs brought a claim alleging a RICO violation, and sought the treble damages that statute makes available to successful claimants. When the defendants sought to compel arbitration, the plaintiffs objected on the grounds that they might be unable to receive the relief they deserved in arbitration. The litigants argued over whether treble damages were an example of "punitive" damages (which the arbitrator was not empowered to award) or "remedial" or "compensatory" damages (which would fall within the arbitrator's authority). The Supreme Court found the argument premature and compelled arbitration, largely on the grounds that arbitrators should resolve questions concerning ambiguous contractual terms.

In the dispute involving Grapalicious's claim, it is therefore likely that a court would deny BottleCo's motion to stay the arbitration.

8. **Complaining on the clock.** This raises a procedural arbitrability issue. Neither party contends that the contract is unenforceable, and neither party contends that the dispute fails to fall within the scope of the disputes they agreed to arbitrate. Instead, BottleCo is asserting that Grapalicious failed to adhere to the procedural requirements of the arbitration agreement and therefore should be barred from proceeding in arbitration against BottleCo.

   This procedural arbitrability issue falls within the scope of "gateway matters" that the parties would, as the Supreme Court in *Howsam* wrote, "likely expect that an arbitrator would decide." The arbitrator might decide that Grapalicious gave BottleCo constructive notice or that BottleCo engaged in misbehavior that prevents it from asserting this defense to arbitration. In that case, the arbitrator would then proceed to determine the merits of the claim. Alternatively, the arbitrator might decide that the contract's procedural requirements were clear and that Grapalicious failed to meet them. If that happens, the dispute would be dismissed from arbitration, and Grapalicious would have to pursue its claim in court. (And a court may very well interpret the time clause as creating a waiver of any right to pursue an action in court, even if the otherwise relevant statute of limitations would not yet bar the action.) In either event, BottleCo's procedural arbitrability defense would be sent to an arbitrator to decide, and as such, BottleCo's motion to stay the arbitration would be denied.

9. **The grape's rules.** Any effort by SuperScrewper to compel arbitration will hinge on the substantive arbitrability question of whether Grapalicious's claims fall within the category of "disputes regarding the quality of the bottle screw tops." Remember, the language of the contract itself is the first element to examine. Such matters are properly for a court to resolve, so the trial court would make this determination. Operating under the presumption of arbitrability articulated in the *Steelworkers* trilogy, the court would almost certainly find that the third of Grapalicious's allegations (that some tops were bent and unusable) falls within the scope of the arbitration clause. The questions of the timing and quantity of the shipment are less obviously disputes "regarding the quality of the screw tops." Even with the "generous" construction dictated by the Supreme Court in *Mitsubishi*, a court would likely find only the last of these disputes arbitrable. It would, therefore, grant an order compelling arbitration of the third (but not the first two) of Grapalicious's claims and would likely allow the other two claims to proceed in litigation. The court could then stay the proceedings while the arbitration goes forward.

10. **The grape's rules, part two.** The usual presumption is that questions of substantive arbitrability are the province of courts rather than arbitrators. In the *First Options* case, the Supreme Court held that a court "should not assume that the parties agreed to arbitrate arbitrability unless there is 'clear and unmistakable' evidence that they did so." The contract clearly incorporates the arbitration rules of the American Association of Grapegrowers. (Incidentally, many of today's major arbitration providers' standard rules contain this provision.) The question is whether this incorporation by reference constitutes the parties' "clear and unmistakable" intention to arbitrate arbitrability. The majority of federal courts that have looked at this question have held that incorporation by reference is sufficient to meet the demands of *First Options*, particularly where, as in the case here, the contract drafters are both sophisticated parties. However, some federal courts have held, in similar circumstances, that the incorporation by reference is not enough, suggesting that the parties were unlikely to have truly considered the matter when just referencing boilerplate arbitration provisions. If the incorporated arbitration rules declare a delegation clause, delegating all arbitrability questions to the arbitrator, the court will send the matter to an arbitrator to determine whether the claims fall within the scope of the arbitration agreement.

Arbitrating Burgers

11. **The Burger Pit's falling arches.** Burger Pit's motion would be denied, and your case would stay in court. Nothing in the facts suggests that you and Burger Pit ever entered a contractual relationship of any sort beyond the purchase of your burger. No agreement to arbitrate exists. (You could have agreed to arbitrate this dispute with them after the incident, but nothing in these facts suggests that you did.) Burger Pit may now want to arbitrate, but it never offered you arbitration, and you certainly never accepted it. Without an agreement to arbitrate, there is no basis for the court to compel arbitration.

12. **The Burger Pit's drive-thru waiver.** The court would be unlikely to enforce the arbitration agreement in this case, though this one is less certain than the previous example.

    The arguments against arbitration in this case are strong. First, the sign was small, hard to notice, and you were probably trapped in line already by the time you saw it. Second, you were very likely not made aware of the actual terms of the arbitration agreement. If you didn't know the actual terms of the arbitration agreement (assuming you didn't go to the website and read the rules while waiting in line), there was no "meeting of the minds" about this bargain. If you didn't know the terms of the offer, you didn't accept them. And finally, there is some question about whether the notice of arbitration would constitute a "written agreement" under the FAA's terms. Here, the link between your ordering and your accepting an arbitration clause that was written somewhere is quite tenuous.

    Burger Pit's best argument is that it provided clear notice of the arbitration agreement's inclusion in any transaction. Burger Pit would point out that you saw the sign and ordered food nonetheless, implying that you accepted the terms. Surely, no matter how hungry you were, this is not a circumstance that constitutes duress.

13. **The Burger Pit doesn't deliver.** The court would almost certainly stay the litigation. These facts describe an enforceable contract. Nothing in the description suggests a defect in the offer, the acceptance, or the consideration. There was enough of a balance in the bargaining power (as evidenced by the fact that you got Burger Pit to change some of the terms in the contract) to dispel any scent of procedural unconscionability. Nothing in the facts suggests that the arbitration clause was remarkable or problematic in any way. You agreed to arbitrate disputes about this catering contract, and this is a dispute about the catering contract. You are going to have to bring your claim in arbitration.

14. **Le Burger's arbitration menu.** The court would be likely to grant Le Burger's motion to stay the litigation. A court would not proceed with

litigation if it is satisfied that an agreement to arbitrate was made. In this case, no contractual defects appear in the facts. You had notice of the arbitration clause, and nothing in these facts suggests that the clause itself was somehow flawed. Your claim against Le Burger would likely be heard by an arbitrator, pursuant to the arbitration procedures printed on the back of the Le Burger menu.

15. **Le Burger's pricy arbitration menu.** Probably yes. You have a much better chance of avoiding arbitration in this circumstance than in the previous example. You could argue, for example, that the fee structure renders the arbitration agreement unconscionable. Normally, to demonstrate unconscionability, you would need to show both procedural and substantive unconscionability. In this case, nothing appears to be fatally wrong with the process by which this contract was formed. But there is at least some chance that the burden created by the arbitrator fees (particularly compared to the product prices) will be significant enough that a court would refuse to enforce the arbitration agreement.

    In the case of *Brower v. Gateway 2000, Inc.*, 676 N.Y.S.2d 569 (N.Y. App. Div. 1998), a computer manufacturer included a form contract in the boxes in which it shipped computers to consumers. According to the arbitration clause appearing on that form, consumers had to pay at least $4,000 to the arbitration provider up front, and at least half of that fee was nonrecoverable. The New York appeals court considered an unconscionability argument (in light of the fact that these sums exceeded the cost of virtually all of the products the manufacturer sold) and sent the case back for the parties to substitute a less expensive alternative.

    To prevail in this line of argument, however, the burden would be on you to demonstrate that the fees create an *actual*, prohibitive burden, rather than merely the risk of a burden. This was the conclusion of the Supreme Court in *Green Tree Financial Corp. Alabama v. Randolph*, 531 U.S. 79 (2000). In that case, the arbitration clause was silent about the allocation of arbitration fees, and the Court refused to strike the arbitration clause down on the basis of a mere "risk." Here, therefore, you would have to demonstrate that the fee in fact creates the kind of burden that would effectively bar you from an opportunity to bring a claim. The arbitration fee of $2,000, which when compared to your dinner bill makes it highly unlikely that you would ever pursue a claim, may just be sufficient to demonstrate that burden.

16. **Le Burger: home of chauvinist pigs.** Your discrimination claim would probably be heard before an arbitrator. As with each of the examples immediately above, nothing appears to be wrong with the process by which the arbitration agreement was formed. Nothing in these facts suggests that there is anything wrong with the substantive provisions of the arbitration agreement itself. And nothing in the language

articulating the scope of the arbitration agreement could be read to exclude any categories of disputes.

Antidiscrimination claims are almost always statutory, and there are some circumstances in which certain kinds of arbitration agreements will be inconsistent with these kinds of statutory rights. But to prevail with such an objection, you would need to demonstrate that some aspect of the particular arbitration agreement in question frustrates the public policy underlying the statute. (*Gilmer.*) Nothing in the facts suggests that Le Burger's arbitration provision is inconsistent with antidiscrimination laws. As a result, your claim would be likely headed to arbitration.

17. **Le Burger: home of Stone Age policies.** Given these facts, the court would grant the motion to stay the litigation. Even if the discrimination in this case is terrible and clearly unlawful, the question of who will decide the merits of the claim is governed by the parties' agreement. In this case, nothing suggests any defect in the formation of Tartare's employment agreement or the arbitration clause contained therein. Tartare has a great claim, and she is going to have to present it to an arbitrator.

18. **Le Burger: home of no class.** No. The clause unambiguously points away from class-wide arbitration, precluding an argument under *Oxford Health Plans*. Unless Tartare succeeds in convincing a court that the class-action waiver is unenforceable, therefore, she would be barred from initiating a representative action—in court or in arbitration. *AT&T v. Concepcion* will make it very difficult for Tartare to succeed. The Court in *Concepcion* prevented a party from proceeding with a class arbitration in circumstances similar to Tartare's. Indeed, Tartare's claim of unconscionability may be weaker than the Concepcion's because her claims have the prospect of greater financial recovery than would be present in a typical low-level consumer claim. Tartare is likely, therefore, to have to proceed in a non-representative action against Le Burger. Of course, an arbitration agreement does not preclude Tartare from filing a discrimination claim with the EEOC. See *EEOC v. Waffle House*, 534 U.S. 279 (2002).

19. **Le Burger: home of the home court advantage.** Rubin's challenge would almost certainly be based on unconscionability, and while there are no bright-line rules or precise definitions for unconscionability, this arbitration clause appears to overreach enough to be unenforceable.

    On the issue of procedural unconscionability, Rubin would point to the process by which his consent was secured. It is not per se procedurally unconscionable to require an employee to agree to an arbitration provision as a condition of employment. Here, though, the fact that Le Burger drafted it, presented it in an adhesive manner, gave him only a brief opportunity to review it, and provided no opportunity to revoke his acceptance weighs considerably against Le Burger. On the matter of the substance of the agreement, Rubin can make at least two arguments, each of which has merit. First, he will point to the unilateral choice of forum granted to Le Burger and will argue that it presents an unbearable risk of creating excessive costs. Recall that the mere risk of costs is not necessarily dispositive of an arbitration provision's enforceability. (This was the crux of the Supreme Court's opinion in *Randolph*, described above.) But in this case, Le Burger retains the option to designate a forum in a way that makes it particularly difficult for Rubin to specify the expenses he would incur.

Second, Rubin would point to the restriction on the identity of the arbitrators and argue that by restricting the arbitrators to experienced restaurant owners, Le Burger has created a sham procedure with structural biases against claimants. On balance, the combination of these factors makes it likely that the arbitration agreement is unconscionable.

Now, who is the appropriate decision maker? In this case, the alleged unconscionability is specific to the arbitration agreement itself—not to the container agreement more broadly. Under the *Prima Paint* reasoning, attacks specific to the arbitration agreement are the province of the courts. It is a court, therefore, that would judge the merits of Rubin's challenge.

20. **Burger Pit: home of liars.** Your claim against Burger Pit would almost certainly be headed to arbitration. The Burger Pit representative's statements about the availability appear to be fraudulent, on the basis of these facts. (It was a knowing misrepresentation of a material fact, and your reasonable reliance on that assertion caused you harm.) But the question presented here is not whether your claim has merit. The question is about the forum in which your claim will be heard.

    The separability doctrine, articulated in the Supreme Court's decision in *Prima Paint*, guides the analysis in this case. According to the facts, the contract clearly contained a broad agreement to arbitrate. Nothing in the facts suggests a defect in the formation of the arbitration clause in particular. Instead, the alleged defect (the fraud) tainted not just the arbitration clause, but also the entire container agreement. Under the logic of the *Prima Paint* decision, therefore, the court must give effect to the parties' intent to have disputes (including challenges to the container agreement in which the arbitration clause sits) resolved by an arbitrator.

21. **Le Burger: home of creative signatures.** In this case, Stylo is not merely attacking the enforceability of a contract with an arbitration provision. Instead, he is attacking even the *existence* of a contract with an arbitration provision. A court would not compel arbitration until it is satisfied that the parties entered an agreement with an arbitration provision. If the

challenge is about the *existence* of a contract, rather than just its enforceability, the challenge must be resolved by a court.

In this way, fraud in the inducement is treated differently from forgery of a signature on a nonexistent contract. Judge Easterbrook, in *Sphere Drake Insurance Ltd. v. All American Insurance Co.*, 256 F.3d 587 (7th Cir. 2001), explained the distinction this way:

> A claim of fraud in the inducement—which boils down to "we wouldn't have signed this contract had we known the full truth about our trading partner"—supposes that the unhappy party did agree, but now wishes it hadn't. If a claim of "we wish we hadn't agreed" could be litigated, even when the arbitration clause is so broad, this would move a good portion of contract disputes back to court and defeat this part of the agreement at the outset, for it is easy to cry fraud. . . . But whether there was any agreement is a distinct question. . . . A person whose signature was forged has never agreed to anything.

This does not mean that Stylo will necessarily have the substance of his discrimination claim heard by a court. If Stylo prevails in his assertion that the signature in question is a forgery, the court will proceed to hear the substance of Stylo's claim against Le Burger. However, if the court finds the signature to be valid, it will grant Le Burger's motion to stay the litigation, and Stylo will be forced to arbitrate his discrimination claim.

CHAPTER 10

Federal Preemption and the Law(s) of Arbitration

§10.1 INTRODUCTION

The law of arbitration is, in many ways, more complex than the laws related to other alternative dispute resolution processes (other than litigation). In part, the complexity stems from the comparatively greater formality one finds in arbitration than in other ADR processes. Another factor in the complexity of arbitration law is the juxtaposition of both state and federal laws. In this final arbitration chapter, we examine the relationship between these state and federal laws and their effects on arbitration.

At least two fundamental principles inform this area of the law. Each, independently, is relatively straightforward. The first principle is that not everyone loves arbitration. You probably realized this while reading earlier chapters in this book. Just as individual preferences vary, so do those of the states in terms of favoring arbitration.. States' legislative processes are influenced by a variety of factors. For example, a state with a history of strong consumer protection laws is likely to have a different set of laws than a state with a history of laws supporting unfettered commerce.

The second of the important principles in this area is that federal law strongly promotes the enforcement of arbitration agreements. At the heart of the federal-state relationship pertaining to arbitration is Section 2 of the Federal Arbitration Act (see Appendix 2, p. 307). FAA §2 provides that an arbitration provision "shall be valid, irrevocable, and enforceable, save upon such grounds as exist at law or in equity for the revocation of any contract"—the so-called "Savings Clause."

So we have two simple principles—not everyone loves arbitration, and federal law promotes arbitration. The combination of these two principles, however, creates a complex patchwork of laws governing arbitration. What happens when these two principles collide? What if a state law is less favorable to arbitration than is suggested by the FAA? Does it matter if the dispute appears in state court as opposed to federal court? To what extent should the answer to these questions be influenced by the terms of the parties' arbitration agreement? These difficult, but critically important, questions form the basis of this chapter.

§10.2 SOME BACKGROUND ON THE PREEMPTION DOCTRINE

Because we have a federal system of government, we frequently encounter circumstances in which federal and state laws diverge. Before examining the peculiar intersection of state and federal arbitration laws, we offer the following brief overview of the general laws of preemption.

Put most basically, the preemption doctrine provides that federal laws generally trump state laws. Drawn from the Supremacy Clause of the Constitution, the preemption doctrine is the vehicle for assuring that federal law is the "supreme law of the land." In *Jones v. Rath Packing Co.*, 430 U.S. 519 (1977), for example, the U.S. Supreme Court considered competing federal and state standards regarding bacon packaging. According to both federal and state laws, bacon labels must accurately state the weight of the packaged food. However, the federal law provided for "reasonable variations caused by loss or gain of moisture during the course of good distribution practices," while the state law had no provision allowing for variation. A bacon producer that was fined for violating the state standard asserted that its bacon packages met the looser federal law and that the federal law preempted the stricter state standard. The Supreme Court agreed, finding that the federal law must preempt the state standard.

In some cases, Congress clearly intends for a particular law to preempt specific state laws to the contrary. For example, when Congress passed the federal Controlling the Assault of Non-Solicited Pornography And Marketing (CAN-SPAM) Act, it specifically stated that the act supersedes any state statute, regulation, or rule that expressly regulates the use of electronic mail to send commercial messages. Circumstances like these do not present complicated questions.

Preemption can also occur when the federal law is silent about preempting state laws, but when the federal laws dominate the area. Some federal schemes of laws are so complete that they leave no room in the field for state law. In *Campbell v. Hussey*, 368 U.S. 297 (1961), for example, the Supreme Court held that a state law pertaining to the labeling of tobacco was preempted through so-called field preemption by federal regulation of the tobacco industry because Congress intended to create "uniform standards" for tobacco labeling. Preemption, therefore, sometimes occurs even when a state law does not directly contradict any federal law, and Congress has not expressly denied states the power to create laws in the area.

In still other cases, a state law is preempted through so-called conflict preemption if it creates obstacles (or actually makes it impossible) to comply with federal law. For example, in *McDermott v. Wisconsin*, 228 U.S. 115 (1915), the Court held that the state could not enact legislation regarding the labeling of syrup that interfered with federal regulation of the same activity. Still, these articulations of the boundaries of the preemption doctrine leave considerable room for ambiguity.

You probably encountered the Supremacy Clause for the first time during your Civil Procedure course, in the context of the *Erie* doctrine. The *Erie* doctrine addresses questions about which law (state or federal) should govern the various questions that arise in litigation. In brief, federal courts have a set of rules of civil procedure. And federal courts sometimes hear cases involving federal subject matter such as patent cases, antitrust cases, or federal discrimination cases. In those cases, a federal court applies federal laws and federal procedures in overseeing the adjudication. But federal courts also hear "diversity of citizenship" cases—ones in which the underlying basis of the claim is state law (a tort claim, a property dispute, or a contract claim, for example). What laws should a federal court apply in those cases? As a general matter, federal courts sitting in diversity apply federal procedures and state substantive law. (This is, of course, dangerously overbroad for purposes of answering a Civil Procedure exam, but it will do for our purposes here.) Finally, state courts often hear claims that are based at least in part on federal law. State courts wind up using state procedures while enforcing the federal substantive law. This collection of broad principles is often referred to as the *Erie* doctrine, though in reality the relevant legal issues are broader than the *Erie* case alone. At the heart of it all is the Supremacy Clause and its effects on the enforceability of state laws.

§10.3 FEDERAL ARBITRATION LAW AS SUBSTANTIVE LAW

The Federal Arbitration Act forms the basis of the federal law of arbitration. Almost all of the FAA's provisions refer to the duties and obligations of "United States courts" or of "any United States district court." FAA §2, however, does not make specific reference to federal courts. Instead, it merely provides that arbitration agreements "shall be valid, irrevocable, and enforceable, save upon such grounds as exist at law or in equity for the revocation of any contract."

A fundamental question, therefore, is whether Congress intended FAA §2 to be binding on state courts as well as federal courts. Should FAA §2 be enforced as substantive federal law? The text and the legislative history of the FAA do not point to an obvious answer to these questions and this silence has led to vociferous debate. Nevertheless, the Supreme Court answered these questions in the affirmative in *Southland Corp. v. Keating*, 465 U.S. 1 (1984). As a result, the FAA is treated as substantive federal law, preempting state laws to the contrary. In *Southland*, a group of franchisees who operated 7-Eleven stores brought suit against Southland, the owner of the 7-Eleven franchises in California. Citing the franchise agreement's arbitration clause, Southland filed motions to compel arbitration. The California Supreme Court refused to compel arbitration, because the California Franchise Investment Law required that franchisees' claims be brought to court, rather than to arbitration. Southland appealed, and the U.S. Supreme Court reversed. The Court cited the federal policy favoring arbitration, and held that FAA §2 rests on the constitutional authority of the Commerce Clause. It wrote that the FAA "creates a body of federal substantive law . . . applicable in state and federal courts."

Despite this far-reaching language, the *Southland* opinion was not, at the time of the opinion, viewed as a declaration that the FAA preempts the entire field of arbitration. This left room for some state laws in the area of arbitration, and the question became which state laws avoid preemption. In the intervening years, however, the opportunities for states to legislate have narrowed considerably.

§10.4 FIVE CATEGORIES OF STATE LAWS RELATED TO ARBITRATION

State legislatures frequently consider proposals to amend state laws in ways that would affect some aspect of the way arbitration operates. In addition to the usual policy tradeoffs at the heart of legislative decisions, anything related to arbitration must also raise possible preemption questions.

For purposes of simplicity, we suggest five categories of state laws, each of which has the potential to affect arbitration in some way. Some of these laws would plainly not be preempted by federal law (for example, because they support arbitration's efficient functioning in a way that is consistent with the FAA). Some of these laws would plainly be preempted by federal law (for example, because they present an irreconcilable conflict with an explicit FAA provision). Others sit in the murkier in-between area with respect to preemption. As you might expect, the boundaries between these categories may, in some cases, be blurry. And to be clear, this spectrum of categorization is our own, rather than a framework memorialized in a particular judicial opinion. However, we think that it captures the current legal landscape.

Categories of State Laws Related to Arbitration

1. State laws affecting all contracts
2. State laws enforcing arbitration clauses
3. State laws enforcing arbitration clauses, but only with some modifications or restrictions
4. State laws disfavoring arbitration clauses and some other subset of contracts
5. State laws disfavoring only arbitration clauses

§10.4.1 State Laws Affecting All Contracts

A considerable portion of the law of contracts is a matter of state law. State law governs what constitutes adequate consideration. State law sets the parameters of the doctrines of fraud and duress. State law establishes tests for determining whether a contract is unconscionable. Each of these state laws is potentially relevant to arbitration because arbitration is a creature of contract. An arbitration clause is enforceable, therefore, only if it satisfies the laws governing contract formation and performance. At a basic level, nothing in the FAA disrupts states' predominance in this area. FAA §2 provides that an arbitration clause is enforceable "save upon such grounds as exist at law or in equity for the revocation of any contract." State laws related to general contract defenses applicable to any contract are safe from preemption. Even if they are applied in a way that causes an arbitration clause to be unenforceable, they do not run afoul of the FAA.

§10.4.2 State Laws Enforcing Arbitration Clauses

As we described in Chapter 8, the FAA provides a statutory basis for giving effect to arbitration agreements. Under the FAA, a party to an arbitration agreement can file a motion to compel arbitration or to stay litigation. Similarly, the FAA provides the basis for entering an arbitrator's award as a judgment of the court, making it enforceable through the familiar machinery of the judiciary.

But what about state courts? The FAA's provisions routinely refer to "courts of the United States." What happens to parties whose case presents no basis for appearing in federal court? The answer is that state law routinely provides for enforcement of arbitration in ways similar to (and in some cases, identical to) the federal provisions. Many states, for example, have adopted either the Uniform Arbitration Act (UAA) or the Revised Uniform Arbitration Act (RUAA). Both the RUAA and the UAA have provisions that permit parties to compel or stay arbitration, to enter an arbitral award, or to challenge the award on some narrow basis. The RUAA and UAA apply when the FAA does not apply, i.e. in cases where interstate commerce is not present.

State arbitration laws illustrate that the FAA does not entirely preempt state law, particularly when the state law promotes arbitration. As an initial matter, preemption occurs only when the state law and the federal law are in conflict. Where the state law accomplishes the same thing as the federal law, a preemption analysis is unnecessary.

§10.4.3 State Laws Enforcing Arbitration Clauses, but Only with Some Modifications or Restrictions

Some state laws target arbitration specifically, but cannot properly be characterized as singling out arbitration for wholesale hostile treatment like the laws described below. Instead, these state laws provide for the enforcement of arbitration contracts—with some caveats or conditions. In general, the more onerous the conditions, the more likely a court is to view the state law as unlawfully in conflict with the federal law governing arbitration.

For example, the California Judicial Council promulgated a set of state ethics standards regarding arbitrators' disclosures. The standards required more disclosure than would be required under FAA §10 (the provision that spells out the bases upon which a court can vacate an arbitral award). In a high-profile dispute between Hollywood figures Michael Ovitz and Catherine Schulman, an arbitrator issued an award in favor of Ovitz. Schulman then sought to have the award vacated after discovering that the arbitrator had not disclosed that he was engaged in arbitrating another dispute involving Ovitz's law firm. Schulman argued that disclosure of this relationship was required under the California arbitrator ethics rules, and Ovitz argued that the FAA preempted the application of those rules. A California court of appeals sided with Schulman, finding that the state ethics rules do not

> reflect hostility to arbitration or an attempt to limit the ability to enter arbitration agreements. The California scheme seeks to enhance both the appearance and reality of fairness in arbitration proceedings, thereby instilling public confidence. With increased public confidence, arbitration is more attractive as a means of resolving private disputes. Hence, far from posing an obstacle to implementing the purpose of the FAA, [the disclosure requirement] actually serves that purpose.

Ovitz v. Schulman, 133 Cal. App. 4th 830, 35 Cal. Rptr. 3d 117 (App. 2 Dist. 2005).

As you might expect, however, this area of the law is evolving and filled with gray areas. Those seeking to enforce state laws affecting arbitration frame the laws as if they are mere "modifications" or "enhancements," arguing that they are consistent with the letter and the spirit of the FAA. Those seeking to avoid state laws affecting arbitration frame the laws as "hostile" to the FAA and to arbitration generally. The more tinkering a state attempts to do with the enforceability of arbitration contracts or arbitral awards, the more likely it is to be preempted under the FAA.

§10.4.4 State Laws Disfavoring Arbitration Clauses and Some Other Subset of Contracts

Some state laws do not single out arbitration specifically but nonetheless have the effect of treating arbitration clauses (and some other kinds of contracts) differently from contracts generally. Although not as clearly contrary to the FAA as those state laws that specifically target arbitration, these state laws are nonetheless likely to be preempted by the FAA.

For example, the case of *OPE International v. Chet Morrison Contractors*, 258 F.3d 443 (5th Cir. 2001), revolved around a Louisiana statute regulating construction contracts and subcontracts. Under the terms of the Louisiana statute, a construction contract is "null and void and unenforceable as against public policy" if it "requires a suit or arbitration proceeding to be brought in a forum or jurisdiction outside of this state." A dispute arose between a Texas corporation and a Louisiana subcontractor. According to their contract, any disputes were to be resolved by arbitration in Texas. In contesting a motion to compel arbitration, the subcontractor argued that the arbitration contract was invalid because its choice of forum provision violated the Louisiana statute. Notice here that the Louisiana statute does not single out arbitration as the only type of contract to be unenforceable. Instead, it invalidates all contracts—including arbitration contracts—that would require a forum outside of the state. Citing *Southland*, the court held that the FAA preempted the Louisiana statute because it conditioned the enforceability of the arbitration provision on selection of a Louisiana forum, a requirement that does not apply to contracts generally. Under the *OPE International* court's logic, because the state statute had the *effect* of invalidating an arbitration clause, the FAA would not permit the state statute to operate.

Similarly, the Delaware Supreme Court upheld arbitration in the case of *Graham v. State Farm*, 565 A.2d 908 (Del. 1989), despite the presence of a state law right to a jury that was arguably implicated by the agreement. In *Graham*, an insurance company sought to enforce an arbitration agreement in the plaintiff's insurance policy. The plaintiff argued that the insurance policy was a contract of adhesion, that the arbitration clause was not even part of the agreement at the time the plaintiff signed up for the insurance, and that enforcement of the arbitration clause would constitute a waiver of the plaintiff's state law—protected right to a jury. Citing the strong policy in favor of arbitration, the Delaware Supreme Court held that the arbitration clause should be enforced against the plaintiff.

The Supreme Court summarized this area of the law in *Kindred Nursing Ctr. Ltd. P'ship v. Clark*, 581 U.S. 246 (2017), as establishing "a sort of 'equal-treatment' rule for arbitration contracts." *Epic Systems Corp. v. Lewis*, 584 U.S. 497(2018). (*Kindred* was the case, discussed in Chapter 9, where the state could not require a higher level of scrutiny for powers of attorney in arbitration agreements versus other types of agreements.) Gray area still exists, as the "equal-treatment" is not self-defining. But the clear trend is to view as preempted any state laws that invalidate a set of contracts if that set includes arbitration contracts.

§10.4.5 State Laws Disfavoring Only Arbitration Clauses

State laws that target and disfavor arbitration (for example by expanding the contractual bases for challenging arbitration agreements, without doing the same for all agreements) are preempted The Supreme Court arrived at this conclusion in the case of *Doctor's Assocs., Inc. v. Casarotto*, 517 U.S. 681 (1996). In *Casarotto*, a Montana state law provided that arbitration clauses would be enforceable only if the first page of the contract in question contained a notice of an arbitration clause printed in underlined, capital letters. A dispute arose involving a contract containing an arbitration agreement, but the first page included no notice of arbitration, much less one in underlined, capital letters. The Supreme Court held that the Montana state law could not be applied consistent with the FAA. Noting that the state law singles out arbitration for separate treatment, the Supreme Court deemed the state law to be preempted, and it enforced the arbitration agreement.

Some states are sufficiently skeptical of arbitration in certain contexts that they have passed laws designed to prevent the enforcement of arbitration clauses in those contexts. Typically, a state's concerns focus on commercial and employment settings—ones characterized by a large disparity in the power or sophistication of the parties.

For example, California's Franchise Investment Law—the one at issue in the *Southland* case—aimed to protect franchisees from abusive contractual terms imposed by franchisors. Among the terms deemed invalid under the California law were arbitration clauses. As you know from the *Southland* case, the Supreme Court struck down these laws that single out arbitration and render them unenforceable. FAA §2 permits state law to invalidate arbitration contracts, but only "upon such grounds as exist at law or in equity for the revocation of any contract."

Nor does it matter whether the state law in question is statutory or common law. For example, the West Virginia legislature passed a statute prohibiting the enforcement of predispute waivers "of the right to commence an action" against nursing homes. Citing this provision, the West Virginia Supreme Court refused to enforce a predispute arbitration clause in a case involving wrongful death and personal injury. The U.S. Supreme Court reversed, in *Marmet Healthcare v. Brown*, 565 U.S. 530 (2012), stating that the FAA preempted West Virginia's policy because it specifically targeted arbitration instead of applying generally to all contracts.

§10.5 WHAT IF THE PARTIES SPECIFICALLY CHOOSE TO HAVE STATE LAW GOVERN THE QUESTION?

A further potential complication in the law of arbitration preemption arises when the parties' contract specifies that a particular state's law should govern the resolution of the dispute. Choice of law clauses (for example, "this contract shall be governed by the law of Oklahoma") are common in modern contracts, and you probably encountered them in your Civil Procedure course. The idea behind a choice of law provision is to add clarity and predictability to the contract. Absent a choice of law provision, there is some risk that the parties will wind up fighting not only about what happened, but also about what body of law should govern the question of what should happen. And so these clauses are common, particularly in commercial contracts.

The arbitration wrinkle is quite easily illustrated this way: Assume the parties' contract specifies that the laws of State X will govern all disputes related to the contract. Now assume that certain laws in State X would disallow an arbitration clause that would otherwise be permitted under federal law. Which law controls?

Recall the two competing, important policies at play in this circumstance. On the one hand, the whole idea of arbitration is to permit parties, through the contracting process, to agree mutually to shape their own alternative dispute resolution procedure. This logic would suggest that the state's law should be applied, because doing so permits the parties to "have their own way." On the other hand, the whole idea of the FAA is to prevent states from overriding parties' agreements to arbitrate. This logic would suggest that the state's law should be preempted, because doing so results in the case being resolved through arbitration.

The question turns on the choice of law provision. Choice of law provisions come in three basic flavors, two of which produce clear answers to the preemption question. In the third case, unfortunately, we are stuck with "it depends"—or its even less satisfying cousin, "it's hard to say."

§10.5.1 If the Parties Specify State Law Only as to Substance

Imagine that in addition to an agreement to arbitrate, the contract contains a choice of law provision that says simply, "If either party alleges that the other committed fraud in connection with this contract, we want our conduct to be judged against the standards set forth in State X's articulation of the law of fraud." In that case, if a dispute arose in which one party alleged that the other committed fraud, it is clear that the contract specifies State X law for determining whether the conduct in question constitutes fraud.

What if State X also had a set of arbitration laws that would cause some aspect of the parties' arbitration agreement to be nullified? It would not matter. This is a simple case of parties intending to arbitrate a dispute and state law trying to prevent them from doing so. Because the parties have not expressed an intention to be bound by state arbitration law, there is no conflict between the pro-arbitration federal law and the parties' autonomy. Federal law would preempt any such state law as easily as it did in the *Southland* case.

§10.5.2 If the Parties Specify State Law as to Arbitration

The typical federal preemption circumstance in arbitration involves a state law that treats arbitration agreements with more hostility than it treats other contracts. The logic of FAA preemption is to protect parties' ability to enter into binding arbitration agreements and to avoid state hostility to the implementation of those agreements. But what if the parties want their arbitration agreement to be more restricted than the FAA would otherwise specify? Building on the principle that the parties control the terms of their arbitration agreements, it is possible for parties to incorporate state law terms into their agreements—even if the FAA would otherwise preempt those state law provisions.

Although parties could accomplish a wide range of things in drafting arbitration clauses by spelling them out in precise terms, they commonly seek drafting efficiencies by incorporating other materials by reference. For example, many arbitration clauses may point to the rules then in existence of some arbitration provider organization. Choice of law clauses operate in much the same way: Parties do not need to spell out all possible, relevant laws. They can instead simply agree that the laws of State X shall apply. This raises the question, however, about what "counts" as a state law. In *DirecTV v. Imburgia*, 577 U.S. 47 (2015), the Supreme Court faced such a question. The arbitration clause contained a provision under which the *entire* arbitration agreement would be stricken if the "law of your state" prohibits waivers of class arbitrations. California had, at the time the parties entered their contract, a provision prohibiting waivers of class arbitrations. But the Supreme Court subsequently ruled, in *Concepcion*, (discussed in Chapter 9, §9.5.4 that any such statutes would be struck on preemption grounds. In the *DirecTV* case, the Court then held that the "law of your state" would not include the now-preempted California law. As a result, the arbitration provision was maintained.

§10.5.3 If the Parties' Choice of Law Provision Is Ambiguous About the Scope of Its Coverage

Imagine that the parties' choice of law provision is less precise (the typical case) and says simply, "All disputes regarding this contract shall be resolved pursuant to the laws of State X." What happens if a dispute arises and one party challenges the enforceability of some aspect of the arbitration clause in the contract, pointing to State X laws? Should State X laws be applied (even though they are not entirely hospitable to arbitration)? Or should federal law preempt State X law (even though doing so ignores the parties' choice of law provision)?

This circumstance demands a trade-off between the two competing policies underlying this area of the law. Courts are most likely to try to guess whether the parties' choice of law provision is more like the first or the second of the scenarios described immediately above. That is, a court will ask itself, "Did the parties intend to name State X law to govern just the substantive legal questions related to this dispute, or did they intend to incorporate State X arbitration law as well?"

In some circumstances, the state law in question will be such that the most reasonable assumption about the parties' intention is that the parties intended to incorporate the state arbitration laws' provisions into their arbitration agreement. For example, in *Volt Info. Sciences, Inc. v. Bd. of Trustees of Leland Stanford Junior Univ.*, 489 U.S. 468 (1989), the parties outlined broadly that California law would govern any disputes. A multiparty dispute arose, one piece of which involved parties who had not signed the arbitration agreement. As a result, some pieces of the dispute would be heard in arbitration, and some pieces would be heard before a court. The question became which pieces of the dispute would go first (with some of the parties obviously concerned about the prospect of preclusion, depending on the outcome of whichever went first). California state law authorized the court to stay the arbitration between some parties pending the result of the litigation involving the other parties. Under the FAA, however, the court would not be entitled to stay the litigation. The Supreme Court upheld the trial court's decision to stay the arbitration, explaining that the parties' choice of law provision "incorporated California rules of arbitration into their arbitration agreement." In essence, the Court said this was more like the second category above—that the parties intended for California's arbitration stay provisions to be part of the parties' selected arbitration rules. The Court saw no FAA preemption problem here because "parties are generally free to structure their arbitration agreements as they see fit. Just as they may limit by contract the issues which they will arbitrate, so too may they specify by contract the rules under which that arbitration will be conducted."

In circumstances where the state law inhibits arbitration, however, courts will view broad choice of law provisions as not intending to include state law *limitations* on arbitrators. For example, in *Mastrobuono v. Shearson Lehman Hutton, Inc.*, 514 U.S. 52 (1995), the parties designated New York law in their choice of law provision. A dispute arose and proceeded to arbitration, and the arbitrator awarded punitive damages against the defendant. The defendant sought to have the award vacated on the grounds that New York state law does not permit arbitrators to award punitive damages. The Supreme Court upheld the arbitrator's award, explaining that the parties' choice of law provision intended to include only "New York's substantive rights and obligations, and not the State's allocation of power between alternative tribunals." In other words, the Supreme Court believed that these parties intended for New York law to govern only substantive disputes (for example, what legal standards should be applied to determine whether a fraud occurred), not arbitration-related disputes (for example, what powers an arbitrator has).

In some regards, when parties specify a particular arbitration provider in their contracts, the rules of that provider act much like a choice of law provision. In *Preston v. Ferrer*, 552 U.S. 346 (2008), for example, the parties' contract included a comprehensive arbitration clause ("any dispute . . . relating to [the contract] shall be submitted to arbitration in accordance with the rules of the American Arbitration Association") along with a general choice of law provision specifying California law. A dispute arose in which Preston sought to recover management fees from Ferrer (television's "Judge Alex"), and Preston initiated arbitration proceedings against Ferrer. Ferrer alleged that because Preston was an unlicensed talent agent, the contract was void. California law specifies that such claims should be heard initially by the California Labor Commissioner. California state courts enjoined Preston from proceeding in arbitration against Ferrer, at least until he had appeared before the state administrative agency. The U.S. Supreme Court, however, held that the FAA preempts the California law on this matter because the parties referred "any dispute" to arbitration, without carving out exceptions like those that the California state law would have created.

Volt, *Preston*, and *Mastrobuono* stand generally for a principle that the FAA does not preempt state procedural rules that are pro-arbitration but preempts substantive laws that are inconsistent with the FAA's pro-arbitration policy.

§10.6 CONFLICTS BETWEEN FEDERAL LAW AND THE FAA

While this is not strictly a preemption question, competing *federal* laws are still in the category of laws that might disrupt the functioning of the FAA. A state law in conflict with the FAA will be preempted. But what if the FAA is in conflict with some aspect of another federal law? In *Epic Systems v. Lewis*, 138 S. Ct. 1612 (2018), the Supreme Court considered—and ultimately rejected in a 5-4 opinion—a challenge to an arbitration clause on the grounds that it conflicted with a subsequently-passed federal law. The challengers had noted that the National Labor Relations Act (passed in 1935) protects workers' right to engage in "concerted activities." This, they argued, was inconsistent with a ruling that the FAA compels enforcement of an arbitration clause prohibiting class or collective arbitrations. The narrowly-divided Court ruled instead that the two statutes could each be given effect, finding that the NLRA's language about collective action was in reference to union organizing activity, not about consolidated civil litigation. In the absence, then, of statutory language mandating particular dispute resolution procedures, courts will enforce arbitration agreements even when they contain a class waiver.

Examples

1. **The Sweat Factory's youthful look.** The Sweat Factory is a fast-growing set of fitness center franchises, targeted at a young, urban clientele.

   Ben, a baby-faced 16-year-old health fanatic, applied for a position as a fitness coach at the first Sweat Factory to open its doors in his home state. Nowhere on the employment application did the Sweat Factory ask about Ben's age, and he never mentioned it. In the course of filling out his application for employment, Ben did initial a box labeled "acknowledgment of receipt and acceptance of arbitration provisions." The arbitration provision contained in the contract mandates arbitration of "any and all disputes related to the applicant's employment or termination thereof."

   Two weeks into his employment, Ben's boss fired him for "unprofessional and unacceptable personal hygiene." Ben sued the Sweat Factory for wrongful termination. The Sweat Factory filed a motion to compel arbitration, citing the employment agreement. Ben responded by revealing his age and claiming that the arbitration clause appearing in the contract is not binding on him as a matter of state law. The state in which Ben lives and worked provides that the age of majority for contract formation is 18. The Sweat Factory contends that the arbitration clause is binding on Ben because the FAA preempts the application of this state law in this case.

Will a court or an arbitrator hear the merits of Ben's claims against the Sweat Factory?

2. **That isn't just sweat I smell.** In a fit of post-holiday guilt, Jen decides to sign up for a membership at the Sweat Factory. After an unusually quick tour of the facilities, the manager of the Sweat Factory presents her with their standard membership form. He invites her to take it home and read it, but she insists on signing up immediately. Included in the membership agreement is an arbitration clause that reads, "The Member agrees to resolve any and all claims against the Sweat Factory through binding arbitration." Jen separately initialed the arbitration clause, signed the agreement, and paid the membership fees.

   One week later, as she was working out, Jen noticed a curious musty odor and later contracted a severe cough. Her health deteriorated enough that she sought medical attention, and her doctors speculated that she had been exposed to harmful mold. After a full recovery, she returned to the Sweat Factory and noticed that almost all of the walls and many of the machines had a thin (but disgusting) layer of mold on them. Jen also noticed that the Sweat Factory's posted health license had expired six months before her membership began.

   Jen filed a lawsuit against the Sweat Factory, alleging improper maintenance and violations of the state health code. The Sweat Factory filed a motion to compel arbitration, citing Jen's membership agreement. Jen responded by arguing that the arbitration clause is unenforceable as a matter of state law because the Sweat Factory was unlicensed when she signed her membership agreement. Under the relevant state law, a consumer contract is per se unenforceable if it is issued by an unlicensed business. The Sweat Factory argues that the FAA preempts the application of state law in this case.

   Who will hear the substance of Jen's claim against the Sweat Factory—an arbitrator or a court?

3. **Buy a bottle, get arbitration for free.** Veronica was passing by a Sweat Factory center one hot day when she noticed a stack of giant plastic "Sweat Factory Thirstquencher" water bottles in the window. She went inside and asked to purchase one of the enormous water bottles. Upon learning that Veronica was not a member of the Sweat Factory, the Sweat Factory cashier asked Veronica to sign a "Sweat Factory NonMember Consumer Agreement" before selling her the bottle. The agreement consisted of nothing more than an arbitration clause providing that "any and all" disputes related to any consumer purchases at the Sweat Factory would be resolved through arbitration. Veronica signed the agreement, purchased the $10 water bottle, filled it with cold water, and went on her way.

Later that day, Veronica became terribly sick, and she believes that her illness was caused by toxic chemicals leaching from the Sweat Factory water bottle. She filed a lawsuit against the Sweat Factory, and the Sweat Factory moved to compel arbitration, citing the consumer agreement.

In preparing to oppose the motion to compel arbitration, Veronica's attorney discovered a state law that provides, in part, "As a matter of state law, no clause requiring the arbitration of a dispute will be enforceable if it is contained in a contract for purchase or sale of a consumer good costing less than $1,000."

What effect is this state law likely to have on the enforceability of the arbitration agreement?

4. **Arbitration clauses in the small (electronic) print.** Archie, a perennial couch potato, saw a Sweat Factory advertisement on television late one night. Inspired, he immediately went online to sign up for a Sweat Factory membership. The membership agreement on the Sweat Factory website included an all-encompassing arbitration clause. Archie skimmed the agreement quickly and clicked "I accept." One month later, Archie was shocked to receive his first bill from the Sweat Factory. The bill included a $500 start-up fee and a monthly fee of $150. Archie claims that the website included no mention of a start-up fee, and that it listed the monthly fee as $15, rather than $150.

   Archie filed a lawsuit in state court against the Sweat Factory seeking treble damages under the state's consumer protection statute. The Sweat Factory moved to compel arbitration, citing the clause in the contract Archie "accepted" online. Archie opposes the motion to compel arbitration on the grounds that the state's consumer protection laws specifically require that any arbitration clause be separately signed (if it is in hard copy) or be separately accepted (for example, by clicking a separate "I accept" button in a pop-up window, if the contract was entered online). Here, Archie argues, he neither signed nor separately accepted the arbitration clause. Will the state consumer protection law help Archie to avoid having his claim heard in arbitration?

5. **Fraud and the franchisee.** Betty, an aspiring entrepreneur with a passion for fitness, decided to open a Sweat Factory franchise. The franchise agreement between Betty and General Urban Training Corporation (GutCo), the owner and franchisor of the Sweat Factory fitness centers, included a broad arbitration clause.

   Betty's operation of her first Sweat Factory franchise did not have nearly the success she expected. She stopped paying the franchise fees set forth in her agreement with GutCo. GutCo then filed a claim against her in arbitration, consistent with the terms of the franchise agreement.

Betty intends to file a counterclaim against GutCo, alleging fraud in the financial projections GutCo provided to her as a prospective franchisee. She would prefer, however, for the entire dispute to be litigated, rather than arbitrated. Betty files a motion to stay the arbitration, citing a state law that expressly prohibits franchise agreements from containing binding arbitration clauses. Will Betty's motion to stay the arbitration succeed, in light of the state law on point?

6. **How to waive a jury.** Ricardo signed a membership agreement with the Sweat Factory. Buried deep in the membership agreement was an arbitration clause requiring "any and all disputes" related to Ricardo's membership to be resolved through binding arbitration.

   After Ricardo failed to pay his monthly fee, the Sweat Factory imposed a fine of $1,000 on Ricardo, along with a notice that the fine would increase exponentially if it went unpaid. Ricardo claims that the fine is a violation of the membership agreement, and he is pretty sure it violates state usury laws as well. He files a complaint in state court against the Sweat Factory, and the Sweat Factory moves to compel arbitration.

   In opposing the motion to compel arbitration, Ricardo cites a State Supreme Court decision in which the court struck down a jury waiver provision in a consumer contract. In that case, the State Supreme Court wrote:

   > Our state's constitution tolerates the enforcement of a contractual waiver of the right to a jury only when such waiver is entered voluntarily, knowingly, and intelligently. Further, such waiver must clearly, unequivocally, and unambiguously express a waiver of this right.

   What, if any, effect is the State Supreme Court's decision on jury waivers likely to have on the motion to compel arbitration in Ricardo's case?

Explanations

1. **The Sweat Factory's youthful look.** The question here hinges entirely on whether the FAA preempts the state contract law defining the age of majority for contract formation. The arbitration clause in the contract clearly covers this dispute, and no other potential contract defects appear in the facts to make us question whether the claim should head to arbitration. If state law declares Ben, a minor, to be incapable of entering this contract, he will be able to have his claim heard in court. If, however, the FAA were to preempt the application of the state majority law, Ben will be bound by the terms of the contract and an arbitrator would hear the merits of his claim.

   Here, the state law in question does nothing to target or single out arbitration. Instead, this state law declares the age of majority for any contract formation. The law applies to all contracts in all contexts—including arbitration agreements. As such, it is entirely consistent with the FAA because its application strikes down arbitration contracts only on a ground that "exist[s] at law or in equity for the revocation of any contract." (Recall that this language is drawn directly from FAA §2.) Because preemption kicks in only when a conflict arises between federal law and state law, the FAA does nothing to disrupt the application of this state law and Ben's claim will be heard in court.

2. **That isn't just sweat I smell.** If, as Jen asserts, the relevant state law is applicable to all consumer contracts involving unlicensed businesses, the FAA will not preempt the state law. Under the FAA's terms, an arbitration contract must be enforced "save upon such grounds as exist at law or in equity for the revocation of any contract." The state law rendering these contracts unenforceable arguably renders *any* contract unenforceable—not just arbitration contracts. As a result, Jen should prevail in her efforts to have the merits decided by a court rather than an arbitrator. The Sweat Factory would prevail (at least in the sense of having an arbitrator hear the initial question about arbitrability) if this were an instance of Jen arguing that she had been fraudulently induced to sign the entire contract. Her real objection, however, is that the entire contract is unenforceable for state law reasons that apply to all contracts, not singling arbitration contracts out in any way. That objection would properly lie with a court.
3. **Buy a bottle, get arbitration for free.** The state law is unlikely to have any effect, because the FAA preempts it. The state law singles out arbitration for nonenforcement and therefore does not treat arbitration clauses on par with other contractual provisions. This is precisely the kind of state law the Supreme Court has determined to offend the FAA. The state law treats arbitration provisions less favorably than it treats all contract provisions. As a result, it conflicts with FAA §2 and its application will be preempted in this case.
4. **Arbitration clauses in the small (electronic) print.** The state law will not prevent the enforcement of the arbitration clause in Archie's case. The state law here is inconsistent with the Supreme Court's interpretation of the FAA because it forces arbitration clauses to adhere to higher standards than all other contract provisions. As such, it will be preempted.
5. **Fraud and the franchisee.** Betty will be bound by the arbitration clause appearing in her franchise agreement with GutCo. It is easy to understand why the state may have an interest in protecting franchisees, given their relative lack of sophistication in most circumstances. And it may be easy to understand why a state would view arbitration clauses drafted by

franchisors skeptically. As a policy matter, the state law may make sense. The problem for Betty is that *Southland* clearly held such antiarbitration laws to be inconsistent with (and preempted by) the FAA.

6. **How to waive a jury.** Courts are most likely to view this kind of jury waiver limitation as targeting (or at least affecting) arbitration clauses differentially—in violation of the savings clause of the FAA. Some state supreme courts have come out the other way, viewing jury waivers as facially neutral statutes raising no preemption claims. But the clear trend is toward viewing the FAA as preempting such statutes' application in the context of arbitration clauses.

CHAPTER 11

Dispute Resolution Within the Court System

§11.1 INTRODUCTION

Even though your law school probably teaches so-called "alternative" dispute resolution separately from litigation, litigation other forms of dispute resolution are in many ways inextricably linked in modern practice. It is inaccurate to assume that ADR only happens outside of a courthouse and litigation only happens inside a courthouse. The judiciary is involved in both formal and informal ADR processes. Sometimes, judges engage in mediation, or at least in mediation-like behaviors, in an effort to resolve disputes. Other times, judges or other court personnel suggest that litigants consider using the services of one or another ADR provider to search for possible settlements. And, of course, what the parties expect to happen inside the courtroom influences their private negotiations and settlement efforts.

In this chapter, we focus on the most intertwined version of this relationship between the judiciary and various forms of non-litigation dispute resolution: court-ordered ADR. First, we examine the sources of courts' authority to compel parties to engage in ADR. Second, we consider the boundaries of courts' authority, looking at what courts can and cannot order. Third, we focus on the requirements of participation and what good-faith participation entails. Finally, we look at what happens when parties disobey a court's order to participate in ADR.

§11.2 WHY A COURT HAS THE AUTHORITY TO ORDER ADR

At some point, virtually every parent has asserted the authority to impose some unwanted restriction, deadline, or responsibility on a child, by citing the authority, "Because I said so, and because I am the parent." Judicial authority, at least theoretically, is more limited than this vision of parental authority. If the court is compelling litigants to participate in ADR, some rule, statute, or common law principle must give the court the authority to do so.

In re Atlantic Pipe Co., 304 F.3d 135 (1st Cir. 2002), provides a useful survey of the possible basis of judicial authority to order ADR. In that case, the First Circuit Court of Appeals listed four potential sources of authority for a federal court to order mediation: (1) Federal Rule of Civil Procedure 16; (2) applicable federal statutes; (3) a court's local rules; and (4) the court's inherent powers. Below, we examine each of these four sources. We also note that a fifth source, state rules, provide the foundation for the vast array of ADR processes made available in state judicial systems.

§11.2.1 Rule 16 of the Federal Rules of Civil Procedure

Rule 16 has provided for pretrial judicial conferences ever since the adoption of the Federal Rules of Civil Procedure in 1938. In its original form, Rule 16 conferences were relatively straightforward, requiring judges and litigants to set expectations about the nature, schedule, and boundaries of the forthcoming litigation. For example, Rule 16 conferences routinely limit certain discovery requests and create a timetable for dispositive motions. In 1983, however, Rule 16(a) was amended to include the explicit suggestion that these Rule 16 conferences also be used for the purpose of "facilitating settlement." Citing Rule 16(a), judges have engaged in a variety of activities to promote the settlement of claims during Rule 16 conferences.

Rule 16(c)(2)(I) also explicitly anticipates the creation of local rules concerning ADR, stating that "the court may consider and take appropriate action on . . . settling the case and using special procedures to assist in resolving the dispute when authorized by statute or local rule." Courts have interpreted "appropriate action" to include not only encouraging but also requiring that litigants engage in ADR. Once these local rules (which we discuss below) exist, Rule 16 authorizes the court to order the parties to use ADR procedures.

§11.2.2 Federal Statutes and Local Rules

A second potential source of a court's authority to compel participation in ADR comes from federal statutes such as the Civil Justice Reform Act of 1990 and the subsequent Alternative Dispute Resolution Act of 1998 (ADR Act), 28 U.S.C. §652. The Civil Justice Reform Act created pilot programs in which federal courts required ADR programs, and the ADR Act extended the pilot programs to all federal jurisdictions. In fact, the ADR Act requires that each federal district establish some type of non-litigation dispute resolution system for the cases within its jurisdiction and that the district court "require that litigants in all civil cases consider the use of an alternative dispute resolution process at an appropriate stage in the litigation."

Based on this requirement, each federal district has established an ADR system. In some cases, the system includes a brief protocol for a single ADR process. For example, in the court-annexed mediation program for the Eastern District of Pennsylvania, the local rules include guidelines about the selection and training of mediators, the assignment of cases, and the mediation process. The judge can order mediation or the parties can request mediation themselves. In other jurisdictions, such as the Ninth Circuit, the model rules for district courts include descriptions of a wide range of ADR processes, case management rules, preprocess requirements, and far more detail about the options available to litigants. Furthermore, some jurisdictions' local rules explicitly authorize judges to order the parties to engage in some type of ADR process. Finally, some local rules even spell out the requirements of that participation as well as sanctions for violating a court order to participate in ADR.

§11.2.3 The Court's Inherent Powers

The inherent power of the court holds the most sweeping source of judicial authority to order the parties to pursue settlement opportunities. Inherent powers rest on the implied statutory or constitutional provisions entrusting the judicial function to the courts. As a result, these powers are not the product of a specific, delineated grant of authority the way the previous sources of authority are. As such, it is important to understand the parameters of, and limits to, the exercise of such authority.

For example, in *In re Atlantic Pipe Co.*, described above, the parties were involved in a complex web of claims and counterclaims originating from the failure of a massive public works construction project. Hoping to simplify matters, the district judge ordered the parties to participate in mediation and to share the costs of mediation equally. One of the parties objected and claimed the district court did not have the authority to order participation on these terms, even though the mediation itself would not produce any binding agreement on the parties without their consent. The court of appeals concluded that the district court had the power to enact local rules either pursuant to a statutory provision or under the ADR Act of 1998. Further, the court stated that even in the absence of these forms of authority, the district court could order mediation through its inherent judicial powers. The court of appeals qualified this grant of discretionary power by asserting that when the district court uses this inherent power to mandate mediation, the mediation must include certain safeguards. The opinion in *In re Atlantic Pipe Co.* suggested that a court's inherent powers are constrained by at least four limiting principles.

> First, inherent powers must be used in a way reasonably suited to the enhancement of the court's processes, including the orderly and expeditious disposition of pending cases. Second, inherent powers cannot be exercised in a manner that contradicts an applicable statute or rule. Third, the use of inherent powers must comport with procedural fairness. And, finally, inherent powers must be exercised with restraint and discretion.

The court of appeals held that the mediation in this case must have a time limit and that the mediator's fees must be capped at a reasonable amount. This case illustrates that a court has substantial discretion in mandating mediation so long as it orders a reasonable process.

§11.2.4 State ADR Systems

Court-ordered ADR is not a uniquely federal phenomenon. Many states have adopted one or more ADR systems in association with their courts, while other states have mandated forms of nonbinding ADR for entire categories of cases. In California, for example, the civil procedure code requires mediation for all civil cases valued at less than $50,000. In contrast, Texas grants judges the discretion to order mediation in virtually any civil case. In Minnesota, all parties in civil cases are required to discuss ADR options, and the court has the authority to require an ADR process at its discretion. Clearly, some states have developed much more thorough ADR systems than federal courts, while others have relatively less robust ADR systems in place. Most important, you should keep in mind that court-ordered ADR is not a uniquely federal phenomenon.

§11.3 WHAT A COURT CANNOT COMPEL THE PARTIES TO DO

As outlined in the section above, courts frequently have the authority to order litigants to participate in certain nonbinding forms of ADR. To help give shape to the scope of that authority, we begin by exploring that which a court cannot do.

§11.3.1 A Court Can't Make Me Settle!

It may sound obvious, but we start with the basic proposition that a court cannot (under any of the sources of authority listed above) compel litigants to settle. A court cannot, therefore, order litigants to mediation and threaten to hold them in contempt if they fail to settle their case. Similarly, in the context of a judicial settlement conference, a judge can try to persuade parties to settle, but cannot force them to do so under threat of penalty. For example, in *Kothe v. Smith*, 771 F.2d 667 (2d Cir. 1985), the trial court judge, in a pretrial conference, suggested that the $2 million claim should be settled for between $20,000 and $30,000. The plaintiff indicated to the judge that she would accept an offer in that range, but the judge never communicated this willingness to the defendant. The defendant did not settle the claim in the pretrial conference, and later made a $5,000 offer, which the plaintiff refused. After one day of the trial, the defendant offered to settle the case for $20,000, and the plaintiff accepted. The trial court judge then imposed sanctions on the defendant, citing the defendant's unwillingness to settle earlier during the pretrial conference. On appeal, the Second Circuit described the settlement process as complex and ruled that sanctions for a failure to settle were inappropriate, especially since the trial court judge never expressed the plaintiff's indication that it would be willing to settle in that range. The court stated that Rule 16 "was not designed as a means for clubbing the parties—or one of them—into an involuntary compromise." Courts can order the parties to the bargaining table and require the parties have the authority to settle, but the courts cannot require a settlement.

§11.3.2 A Court Can't Make Me Make an Offer!

The court also cannot require the parties to make an offer. In *Avril v. Civilmar*, 605 So. 2d 988 (Fla. Dist. Ct. App. 1992), the plaintiff demanded $2 million for claims stemming from an automobile accident. In mediation, the defendant offered to settle for $1,000. The defendant explained that the reason for the relatively low offer was that the plaintiff had suffered only soft-tissue injuries, and the defendant and his insurer had not yet had a chance to conduct an investigation in the two months since the accident. Upon motion from the plaintiff's attorney, the Florida trial court imposed sanctions on the defendant for failing to act in good faith during the mediation. The appellate court overturned that ruling, stating that the "plaintiff's only basis for sanctions is merely that defendants were unwilling to make an offer of settlement satisfactory to him . . . there is no requirement that a party even make an offer at mediation, let alone offer what the opposition wants to settle." Thus, a court can order parties to mediation, but it cannot punish parties who fail to make an offer or fail to make an offer that is attractive to the other party.

§11.3.3 A Court Can't Force the Terms of an Offer (but Can Sometimes Punish Me If I Turn Down a Good Offer)!

Although it is true that a court cannot order parties to make offers or to accept particular terms of an agreement, many judges and many policies strongly "encourage" parties to settle. In some cases, that encouragement may be so strong that parties wind up feeling real pressure to resolve their claims. An example of permissible encouragement appears in offer-of-judgment provisions such as the one found in Federal Rule of Civil Procedure 68. Under Rule 68, the plaintiff has to pay the defendant's costs and fees incurred after the date of the offer of judgment if

1. a defendant makes an offer of settlement in writing,
2. the plaintiff rejects that offer,
3. the dispute goes forward in litigation, and
4. the plaintiff's eventual recovery is less than the defendant's prior offer of settlement.

The parties must meet both express and implied requirements in order to trigger Rule 68 protection. First, the offer must be made in writing. Second, the offer must have been presented to the plaintiff in a timely manner, as determined by each jurisdiction (under the federal rule, roughly two weeks before the trial is set to begin). Third, the terms of the offer must be clear. Finally, if the plaintiff accepts the offer, it must do so unconditionally and in writing. Note that if the parties go to trial, the court considers the offer automatically withdrawn, and it is inadmissible as evidence. Prior to trial, however, the defendant can make additional offers, and each offer is subject to the same conditions.

Many states also have offer-of-judgment statutes in their rules of civil procedure, and they tend to operate like Rule 68. When a party rejects a settlement offer, and it turns out to be more attractive than that party's award at trial, offer-of-judgment statutes require the rejecting party to pay costs and fees from the time of the offer. For example, assume that the defendant offers to settle the dispute with the plaintiff for $50,000 on October 15. The plaintiff refuses and takes the dispute through litigation. On December 15, at the conclusion of trial, the plaintiff is only awarded $20,000. The plaintiff is now responsible for paying the defendant's costs incurred from October 15 to December 15, excluding attorneys' fees. For more on how these kinds of incentives may affect parties' settlement decision making, see Chapter 2.

The theory behind an offer-of-judgment rule is twofold. First, the rule is supposed to discourage plaintiffs from rejecting reasonable offers. On the theory that some cases persist needlessly in court because plaintiffs have fantasies about jackpot juries, offer-of-judgment statutes can provide extra incentive for a plaintiff *not* to roll the dice. If plaintiffs are punished for continuing through litigation when they should have accepted the offer, they will be more likely to accept the offer. Second, this rule is also designed to encourage defendants to make a reasonable offer and to make it sooner rather than later. (A defendant's incentive is to offer early, in order to maximize the costs and fees potentially recovered if the plaintiff inappropriately turns down the offer.)

Offer-of-judgment statutes, therefore, represent examples of "encouraging" settlement (which is permitted) without imposing particular terms of settlement (which is not permitted).

§11.4 WHAT A COURT CAN COMPEL THE PARTIES TO DO

§11.4.1 A Court Can Compel a Particular (Nonbinding) Form of ADR

Up until now, we have largely been speaking of court authority to order litigants to go through some form of ADR. In certain jurisdictions, this is all that courts do. The court presents litigants with a menu of different ADR options and says, in effect, "Choose something, and don't come back until you've given it a try." In other jurisdictions, courts can order litigants to participate in a particular form of ADR—either one mandated for all litigants or one specially selected by the judge for the particular case in question.

In all cases, the courts' authority to compel participation in ADR mechanisms is limited to **nonbinding** forms of ADR. A court order compelling parties to engage in binding ADR would deprive the litigants of the opportunity to present their claims in court. In some cases, this would violate the litigants' right to a jury trial (a right that is available in only certain circumstances of civil litigation, contrary to popular belief). In all events, such an order would violate the litigants' due process rights. As a result, courts may only compel nonbinding forms of ADR.

§11.4.1.1 Mediation

One of the most recognizable forms of court-ordered ADR is mediation. As we discuss in Chapter 6, mediation can take many different forms, and the court-ordered versions are no different. Litigants sent to court-ordered mediation must still navigate strategic and practical issues about mediator selection and type of mediation. Further, the court systems ordering mediation must carefully consider the mechanisms for providing adequate judicial supervision of the mediation system. Many of the issues raised elsewhere in this book about confidentiality and quality control in mediation become even more salient when a court is overseeing the process. Some jurisdictions have created rosters of mediators and established certain qualifications (training, education, experience, etc.) trying to ensure that parties have a quality mediation experience. Courts are also concerned with the type of participation that parties have in a court-ordered process, and we will examine this issue of good-faith participation later in this section.

§11.4.1.2 Nonbinding Arbitration

A second major form of ADR that litigants are frequently ordered to attend is **nonbinding arbitration**. As you will learn, an arbitration (even a nonbinding one) looks much like a trial. It involves a decision maker, similar to a judge, who hears the arguments of each side and renders a decision. Nonbinding arbitrations rarely have the formality of court and are designed to move quickly and efficiently. For example, because parties often believe that arbitrators have sufficient expertise to assess evidence appropriately, without formal exclusionary rules, arbitrations may proceed quickly, with more relaxed (and speedier) evidentiary rules.

Why would litigants want to go through arbitration if the arbitrator's decision is not binding? First, there is some chance that the arbitration process will satisfy a range of different interests the litigants may have in bringing their claims. It may provide them with an opportunity to tell their stories, to confront their counterparts, and to hear the opinion of an impartial third party. That alone could make the process worthwhile to some litigants.

Second, the arbitrator's opinion often provides useful information to both parties about how their cases are perceived, which might encourage the parties to settle.

Third, nonbinding arbitration impacts litigants because the order to participate in it frequently includes a cost-shifting mechanism similar to offer-of-judgment rules like Rule 68. For example, in *Richardson v. Sport Shinko*, 880 P.2d 169 (Haw. 1994), a nonbinding arbitrator issued a $60,000 nonbinding award in favor of the plaintiffs to compensate for an injury suffered at the defendant's hotel. Dissatisfied with that amount, the plaintiffs demanded a trial de novo, but at trial, the jury found entirely in favor of the hotel. Immediately after the trial, the defendant filed a motion for sanctions under a Hawaii statute that provides for recovery in the event the party demanding a trial de novo fails to improve upon the arbitrator's award by a certain percentage. The Hawaii Supreme Court upheld the sanctions against the plaintiffs, and as a result, instead of *receiving* $60,000, the plaintiffs wound up *owing* the defendants more than $5,000.

§11.4.1.3 Early Neutral Evaluation

Early neutral evaluation (ENE) is another form of nonbinding arbitration that courts can order. The ADR Act of 1998 specifically mentions the possibility of courts adopting rules regarding ENE, and many have done so. ENE is typically even more casual than nonbinding arbitration, although it operates similarly in some regards. For example, ENE parties prepare memos, outline the dispute and their respective legal positions, and give short explanations of their desired outcomes to an evaluator. The evaluator (typically selected for their significant prior experience with similar cases) can ask questions before rendering a written case evaluation. Like in evaluative mediation (see Chapter 6), the evaluation usually predicts a specific amount the evaluator believes a party will recover at trial or a range for reasonable recovery under the circumstances. ENE highlights both the legal merits of each party's position and the likely outcome of litigation. Parties often use the evaluation as the basis for a settlement or use this information to pursue some other agreement. Because ENE is nonbinding, however, either party can choose to disregard the evaluation and proceed to trial.

§11.4.1.4 Summary Jury Trials

A **summary jury trial** (SJT) differs from a regular trial in two important ways. First, as the name suggests, it is shorter. Typically, each side is permitted a limited amount of time to present its best case, and then a jury deliberates and renders a decision. Second, in a summary jury trial, the jury's verdict is nonbinding. In many cases, the jury knows that its decision will not be binding, although this is not always so. Furthermore, i the parties are typically given an opportunity to discuss the case with the jurors to understand better why they reached a particular decision.

Like nonbinding arbitration and ENE, the principal intention of a summary jury trial is to promote settlement. However, unlike nonbinding arbitration, summary jury trials virtually never include a cost-shifting mechanism. Instead, they typically seek to promote settlement by requiring the key decision makers from each side to attend the summary jury trial. The theory is that parties may be more inclined to settle once they have seen the other side's best arguments made to a jury and have heard the jury's interpretation of those arguments.

§11.4.2 A Court Can (but Doesn't Always) Compel Good-Faith Participation

In many jurisdictions, courts are explicitly authorized to compel parties to participate in nonbinding ADR in **good faith**. At least two dozen states currently have a good-faith statutory requirement, and a similar number of federal district courts have adopted local rules with a good-faith requirement.

When two disputants appear in a binding dispute resolution process, like litigation or arbitration, they will usually take the matter seriously. After all, if they do not, the decision maker is more likely to find against them, given the adversarial nature of those proceedings. Further, the decision maker in each of those binding processes typically can penalize bad behavior that goes beyond simple inattention or lack of seriousness.

When two parties voluntarily agree to engage in an ADR process, there is reason to believe that they will take the process seriously. After all, they chose to be there. Each party can walk away whenever they want to. There is no incentive in bad behavior except that, unfortunately, even in voluntary ADR processes, there is some risk that one or both of the parties will use the process for a purpose other than settlement. A party might use an ADR process as a "fishing expedition," to try to assess the other side's case before trial. Or worse, a party might use an ADR process as a means to delay trial, to harass the other side, or to drive up expenses.

When courts order parties into nonbinding ADR processes, however, there is even more reason to worry about potential abuse and bad behavior. We are not suggesting that ADR only works if both parties behave well and like each other. Few disputants like each other by the time a dispute reaches litigation, and many parties, driven by unhappiness and by strategic or competitive considerations, act in less than helpful ways throughout the ADR process. If the success of ADR hinged on each party behaving perfectly, ADR would never be very useful. But there is a boundary beyond which parties' behavior is certain to spoil the effectiveness of any ADR process. What would it mean if a court could order parties to participate in ADR and then permit them to engage in behavior that thwarted any chance the ordered ADR process had of producing a settlement?

Thus, the context of court-ordered ADR, more than voluntary ADR, presents a clash of policy interests. On the one side, you have the interest in preserving the integrity of the court's order and in promoting settlement through nonbinding ADR mechanisms. On the other side, you have the interest in preserving the parties' autonomy and control over the fate of their own dispute. Good-faith requirements aim to strike a balance by preserving the parties' autonomy to manage the dispute, as long as they do so in a way that respects the integrity of the court and the opposing party.

§11.4.2.1 What Constitutes Good-Faith Participation?

There are plenty of reasons why parties might not settle a lawsuit. They might believe that the case is important to take to trial in order to establish some principle or legal precedent. They might paint themselves into a corner publicly in a way that makes settlement too costly. Parties might hate each other so much that they cannot bring themselves to agree to anything. Their attorneys may have given them bad advice. They may lack sufficient information, resources, time, or authority to reach a deal. They might not be sufficiently creative to see their way through the problem.

As we noted above, courts cannot compel parties to settle. What courts can do, through the mechanism of a good-faith requirement, is remove at least some of the potential barriers to settlement. For example, a case is less likely to settle if one of the parties is absent, unprepared, or lacks the authority to reach an agreement. Courts have, therefore, focused on the elements of attendance, preparation, and authority in shaping the legal boundaries of what constitutes good-faith participation.

Attendance is the easiest item to measure in terms of good faith, and courts have consistently found that failing to show up to an ordered mediation constitutes bad faith. For example, in *Graham v. Baker*, 447 N.W.2d 397 (Iowa 1989), a seller commenced forfeiture proceedings against a buyer who had defaulted on installment payments for purchased land. Pursuant to a statute requiring parties to such disputes to "participate" in mediation, the parties' attorneys (each of whom had the power of attorney) met in a mediation session. However, once at the mediation, the seller's attorney, Flagg, insisted that the entire matter was "nonnegotiable." A court reviewing Flagg's behavior wrote:

> Flagg's behavior, which ranged between acrimony and truculency, precluded any beneficial result to the parties from the mediation process. It has cost his clients considerable time and expense. Nevertheless, his inappropriate behavior is not determinative. We find that Flagg's presence at the mediation meeting satisfied the minimal participation required by the statute.

Clearly, a court would not deem every absence to constitute a sanctionable lack of good-faith participation. But having a good excuse after the fact is far less likely to be forgiven than having a good excuse beforehand and seeking the court's approval for your absence. For example, in *Hernando County School Bd. v. Nazar*, 920 So. 2d 794 (Fla. Dist. Ct. App. 2006), a party and his attorney both failed to appear at a court-ordered mediation. When the party who did appear filed a motion for sanctions, the absent party explained that he was out of town assisting relatives victimized by a hurricane, and his attorney informed the court that he had experienced medical problems requiring a doctor's appointment. The court nevertheless imposed sanctions for failure to attend, indicating that the parties should have cleared their absences in advance of the mediation, rather than after the fact. Another court took the same basic approach in *Raad v. Wal-Mart Stores, Inc.*, 1998 WL 272879, 1998 U.S. Dist. LEXIS 11881, a case in which some of the parties unexpectedly telephoned into a mediation session, rather than appearing in person. The court held that mere telephonic presence was not in compliance with the requirement to attend mediation but left open the possibility that if telephonic presence had been discussed prior to the mediation, it might have been allowed. This logic was endorsed by the court in *In re Marriage of Pebbles*, 2004 Iowa App. LEXIS 1304, *2, in which one party did not attend the mediation in person. Instead, he sent his attorney to the mediation and was available via telephone. Over the objection of the party who did attend in person, the court held that under the particular terms of the mediation order in this case, the attorney's presence satisfied the requirement to "attend."

A second component of good-faith participation hinges on the **preparation** each party has engaged in prior to the ADR process. For example, disputants (or even worse, attorneys for the disputants) who show up to a mediation without really understanding the nature of the case or the relevant interests have little chance of engaging in the process in a meaningful way. Preparation, however, is not always easy to measure. Therefore, courts mostly review complaints based on inadequate preparation and look at externally verifiable forms of preparation. For example, if a mediator (or a court) has requested a premediation memorandum, experts' reports, or other preparation in advance, failure to comply will constitute bad-faith participation.

A third component of good-faith participation in the context of ADR relates to assuring that those who attend the mediation have sufficient **settlement authority** to make resolution possible. A mediation in which the CEOs of each company are present is far more likely to settle than one in which one side sends only the summer intern from the accounting department. In *G. Heileman Brewing Co. v. Joseph Oat Co.*, 871 F.2d 648 (7th Cir. 1989), the court specifically ordered corporate representatives with settlement authority to appear at a pretrial settlement conference. Upholding this order, the Seventh Circuit declared the power to compel participation to be within the court's inherent authority, as discussed earlier in this chapter. This holding has been extended to other court-ordered ADR processes as well. Although the court cannot force the parties to settle, this requirement seeks to assure that the ADR process at least has a possibility of producing a settlement.

Measuring good (or bad) faith is more difficult when the conduct in question is more subjective. Is it bad faith to have a nasty attitude? Is it bad faith to seem disengaged? Is it bad faith not to listen carefully? And so on. Trying to punish behavior like this poses at least two significant challenges. First, it raises considerable questions of proof. Demonstrating that a party was not at the mediation is one thing; demonstrating that the party was not paying careful attention is quite another. Second, complicating all of this is the question of confidentiality. In almost all jurisdictions, mediators are barred (because of confidentiality considerations) from testifying about parties' behavior during mediation. (See Chapter 7 for more on mediation confidentiality.)

Foxgate Homeowners' Ass'n v. Bramalea, 25 P.3d 1117 (Cal. 2001), provides a useful example of the tension between enforcing good-faith requirements and maintaining confidentiality. The plaintiff homeowners' association brought a claim for a construction defect against the developer Bramalea. After working with the parties for several months, the mediator scheduled a five-day mediation session to which both sides were ordered to bring experts and claims representatives. The parties were also supposed to serve experts' reports on each other before the mediation. On the first morning, the plaintiff showed up with its attorney and nine experts. In contrast, the defendant's attorney showed up 30 minutes late and with no experts. When the defendant would not promise to show up with experts at any time, the subsequent mediation sessions were canceled. The mediator filed a report with the court supporting plaintiff's motion for sanctions, detailing the attorney's "obstructive bad-faith tactics," and then resigned from the case. The California Supreme Court held that, under the relevant California confidentiality statute, a mediator is not allowed to report even sanctionable bad-faith behavior. Here, the court had no problem with the concept of sanctioning what was clearly a series of nonappearances and failure to comply with even the most basic premediation discovery orders. Yet the issue of who reported the bad faith was problematic, and the court held that the rules concerning confidentiality trumped the interest of good-faith participation.

The *Foxgate* balancing, however, has not been adopted in all states. Indeed, some states' statutes specifically authorize (or even require) a court-affiliated mediator to report a party's failure to participate in good faith. For example, the U.S. Bankruptcy Court for the Southern District of New York in *In re A.T. Reynolds & Sons, Inc.*, 452 B.R. 374 (S.D.N.Y. 2011), specifically ordered that the "mediator shall report any willful failure to attend or to participate in good faith in the mediation process of conference." When the mediator in that case reported that one party had refused to engage in risk analysis and instead stuck only to a predetermined negotiation posture, the bankruptcy court held that party in violation of the order to participate in good faith. On appeal, the sanction was overturned. The court made it clear that it was within the bankruptcy court's authority to order good-faith participation, but it held that failure to engage in risk analysis and failure to make a more attractive offer did not constitute a violation of that good-faith requirement.

Even if one were able to overcome the challenges associated with proving bad behavior in mediations while adhering to the confidentiality limits, there is also a risk that punishing such behavior will create unmanageable and unwise restrictions on party autonomy. Some parties will choose to adopt a problem-solving stance in bargaining. Some will be aggressive. Some will be passive. Some will engage in hard bargaining. Parties are (and must be) permitted to choose their approach to negotiating with their counterparts. Hard bargaining, or even obnoxious behavior, might not be pleasant, and is probably not very effective in most circumstances (see Chapter 1 on negotiation), but that does not mean that the behavior is (or should be) subject to sanction.

Even an explicit good-faith requirement does not mean that a party has to give up on its positions or cave in to the other party. It is certainly not bad faith for someone to bargain hard to get a favorable settlement. For example, in *Hunt v. Woods*, 1996 WL 8037, 1996 U.S. App. LEXIS 1420 (6th Cir. 1996), the plaintiff, Hunt, was injured in a car accident, and sued Woods, the driver of the other car, for damages. Hunt and Woods were sent to pretrial mediation to try to work out a settlement. Woods's attorney attended the mediation with authorization to settle for some amount less than the limit of Woods's $25,000 policy. Hunt, however, entered mediation with a firm anchor of not less than $25,000. The mediator told Woods that it would be a waste of time to make an offer below that anchor point. Agreeing, Woods did not respond to Hunt's $25,000 proposal. The case went to trial, where Woods stipulated to liability and Hunt was awarded $37,000. Hunt then tried to get pretrial interest, arguing that because Woods knew he did not have a defense against his liability, and because he did not make a settlement offer, he was not mediating in good faith. On appeal, the court rejected the idea that Woods was bargaining in bad faith. The court noted that he entered mediation prepared to make an offer, but was convinced by the mediator that anything below $25,000 would be rejected out of hand. Woods adopted a strategy that, ultimately, appears to have been unwise, but it was not evidence of bad faith.

Hard bargaining with a nominal offer of settlement can also be perfectly defensible. In *Gray v. Eggert*, 635 N.W.2d 667 (Wis. Ct. App. 2001), a school bus driven by Gray and a county transit bus driven by Eggert collided. Gray sued for damages, but Eggert denied all liability, arguing that the school bus had run into him while he was stopped, and any injuries she sustained were due to her own negligence. The trial court ordered the two parties to mediation, where Eggert stuck to his assertion that he was not liable. Gray offered to settle for $5,000, and Eggert responded by offering $100. The trial court then imposed sanctions on Eggert for failing to make a good-faith effort to settle. The appeals court, however, overturned this decision, holding that although the trial court could order mediation, it could not require that the parties settle, nor could the trial court judge (who was not present at the mediation) use the nominal settlement offer as evidence that Eggert was acting in bad faith.

§11.4.2.2 What Happens to Those Who Cross the Line?

If a judge finds that a party has acted in bad faith, the judge has considerable discretion in crafting an appropriate sanction. Typically, the judge chooses a sanction designed to make the aggrieved party whole. For example, in *Raad v. Wal-Mart Stores, Inc.*, discussed previously, Wal-Mart failed to follow the judge's order to mediate when it did not send a representative with settlement authority to the mediation. The trial court judge issued penalties that included the plaintiff's attorneys' fees, the expense of bringing the motion for sanctions, the money the defendant saved by not sending someone to the mediation, and the costs to other litigants from the court taking time to resolve this motion and not resolve other cases. The trial judge in this case was mainly concerned with returning all of the adversely affected parties to their financial situations prior to the failed mediation.

On occasion, the penalties can be far more severe for failure to participate in good faith. In *Nick v. Morgan's Foods*, 99 F. Supp. 2d 1056 (E.D. Mo. 2000), for example, the court sanctioned the defendant for failing to mediate in good faith because the defendant refused to provide the mediator with a mediation memorandum and to send someone with authority to settle to the mediation. The court ordered Morgan's Foods to pay all of the opposing party's attorney's fees, to pay the mediation fees, to pay the plaintiff for his time wasted at the mediation, and to pay $1,500 to the Clerk of the United States District Court (Clerk) as a sanction. The court further ordered the attorney for Morgan's Foods to pay $1,250 to the Clerk as sanctions for filing a frivolous motion associated with these sanctions.

At the far end of the spectrum of sanctions, some incidents of bad faith result in dismissal or default. For example, in *Triad Mack Sales & Serv. v. Clement Bros. Co.*, 438 S.E.2d 485 (N.C. Ct. App. 1994), the court ordered each party to send someone with settlement authority to a mediation session. When the defendant failed to do so, the defendant's attorney merely offered an unsworn statement that the president of the defendant corporation was ill and that "all other officers, directors, and employees were out of state." The court issued an order striking the defendant's answer and placing the defendant company in default. The appellate court, reviewing an appeal of the order, acknowledged that the trial court judge could have crafted a lesser sanction, but upheld the default as falling within the discretion of the trial court judge.

§11.5 ENFORCING MEDIATED SETTLEMENT AGREEMENTS

An agreement reached through mediation may typically be enforced in one of two ways: First, it can be enforced as a contract between the parties.

In most cases, a mediated settlement agreement is enforceable on exactly the same terms and using the same enforcement mechanisms as any other contract. Some jurisdictions have additional requirements of contracts constituting mediated agreements. For example, in California, a mediated settlement is only enforceable if the parties state in a writing signed by each party or on the record that the mediated settlement is "enforceable or binding or words to that effect." Cal. Evid. Code §1123(b) (2019). Generally, enforcement and challenges of agreements reached in mediation and memorialized in the form of a contract are treated as any other contract.

The second method of enforcing a mediated agreement arises in circumstances in which the agreement is filed with and approved by the court. This can happen when the parties file the settlement with the presiding court and incorporate the terms of the settlement agreement into the order of dismissal, or when the parties provide explicitly in the dismissal order that the trial judge retains jurisdiction over any issue arising out of enforcement or interpretation of the mediated settlement. (Both of these methods are discussed in *Kokkonen v. Guardian Life Insurance Co. of America*, 511 U.S. 375 (1994).) All federal courts and most state courts allow either of the above options for retained jurisdiction, post-dismissal.

A party seeking to avoid the enforcement of the terms of a mediated agreement would almost always seek to employ traditional contract defenses, like duress, unconscionability, misrepresentation, mutual mistake, or changed circumstances. (Chapter 3 has more on these bases for attacking a settlement agreement.) Other defenses specific to the mediation process, like mediator misbehavior, discussed in Chapter 6, may prevent enforcement as well. For example, in *Vitakis-Valchine v. Valchine*, 793 So. 2d 1094 (Fla. Dist. Ct. App. 4th Dist. 2001), a husband and wife entered into a divorce settlement after mediation and incorporated the settlement into a judgment of divorce. The wife later moved to set aside the agreement because of mediator misconduct, including alleged coercion and improper influence. The court determined that some of the wife's claims, if proven to be true on remand, could demonstrate mediator misconduct such that the mediated agreement would be unenforceable.

Examples

Snow White has been the talented and trusted bookkeeper for the Seven Dwarfs for many years. However, keeping track of the Dwarfs' spending habits while managing the accounting of their diamond mining business is not easy. Snow White believed that every year she would receive a salary increase at least equal to the cost of living, for her dedicated efforts, and she received such a raise every year until two years ago. For the past two years, however, she has been receiving the same wage, which sits far below market value for the work she does. After she heroically handled an accounting disaster when Dopey failed to report a purchase for an entirely new mine (he forgot where the old one was located and decided to buy another), she decided to sue for back wages. The Dwarfs claim that her past raises were purely discretionary and she is not entitled to any past wages.

1. **Hi-ho, hi-ho, it's off to mediation we go.** During an initial judicial conference with the judge assigned to the case of *Snow White v. Seven Dwarfs*, the judge issues the following order: "The parties shall, within 30 days of this order, select a mediator from the approved court roster. Within 30 days of the selection of the mediator, the parties shall meet at least once to try to work out a settlement." Before even engaging in the mediator-selection process, the Dwarfs indicate to Snow White that they have no intention of going to mediation. If the Dwarfs believe the court lacks the authority to order mediation, could they simply ignore the order? If they ignore the order, what options would Snow White have?
2. **The wicked mediator.** The judge orders Snow White and the Dwarfs to mediation, and the judge's order specifies that the mediator in the case will be Wicked Witch. Wicked Witch is not listed on the court's approved-mediator roster, does not appear to have conducted any mediations prior to this one, and has not taken any mediation courses. However, Wicked Witch is a close, personal friend of the judge. What options does Snow White have if she would prefer not to participate in mediation with Wicked Witch?
3. **Hi-ho, it's off to summary jury trial we go?** In lieu of sending the parties to mediation, the judge orders Snow White and the Dwarfs to conduct a summary jury trial. As part of the order, the judge specifies that the principal clients must attend in person. Snow White and her attorney are worried about the summary jury trial, because their best witness, Sleeping Beauty, is a secret. At a minimum, Snow White and her attorney would prefer not to have Sleeping Beauty testify about the diamond industry until the trial. What options does Snow White have?
4. **Don't be a dope in mediation.** Snow White and the Dwarfs are ordered into mediation, and the relevant local rules specify that the parties must participate in good faith. Snow White arrives at the mediation ready to discuss the merits of the case. She expects the Dwarfs to send Doc, the Dwarf who possesses full settlement authority in this matter. Instead, the only Dwarf to show up is Dopey. Dopey arrives at the mediation 20 minutes late, eating a cupcake from a party he just attended. When confronted about his failure to submit a premediation memo and documents, he simply attempts to appease Snow White with a bite of his cupcake. Outraged that the Dwarfs do not appear to be taking the mediation seriously, Snow White storms out. She files a motion for sanctions, accusing the Dwarfs of participating in bad faith in the mediation. How is the court likely to rule on Snow White's motion?

5. **While you were sleeping.** After making no progress in the first mediation session with Dopey, the Dwarfs decide to send Sleepy to the next session. Once Sleepy arrives, the mediator convinces both participants to sit down together and begins to ask each side to discuss their underlying interests. Snow White goes into depth about her feelings, shedding some tears about not being appreciated at the Dwarf house. After Snow White is done wiping her eyes, she looks up and finds that Sleepy has been asleep the whole time! Snow White is outraged that she just poured her heart out to a Dwarf who did not hear a word—he might as well have stayed home! She files another motion for sanctions with the court, again asserting that the Dwarfs have not engaged in the mediation in good faith. How is the court likely to rule on Snow White's motion?

6. **Grumpy behavior in a mediation.** In their third mediation session, the Dwarfs realize that they need to take this situation seriously. Their lucrative diamond mining industry will not be able to survive the negative press that would follow if this case were litigated. Seeking to protect their business, they send Grumpy to the next round of negotiations. Grumpy is easily the shrewdest negotiator among the Dwarfs, having personally negotiated many big-money deals for the Dwarfs' business. However, Grumpy is primarily known for his angry and uncompromising personality. He has a long track record of strained relationships with Snow White and with many of the Dwarfs. Because he feels that Snow White was an ungrateful and demanding employee, Grumpy approaches the negotiations with an even bigger chip on his shoulder than normal. He starts out with an unreasonably low settlement offer, and then refuses to engage in any meaningful discussion about a compromise. As the session continues, it becomes clear that he does not take Snow White's claim seriously and has no desire to offer her a larger settlement. Annoyed and offended by Grumpy's lack of respect for her claim, Snow White files a motion for sanctions with the judge who ordered the mediation. How is the court likely to rule on Snow White's motion?

7. **Too shy to show up.** In a closed-door meeting, the Dwarfs evaluate their negotiation strategy and conclude they have made some big mistakes in choosing their representatives. They decide that they will have more success if they send someone with a calm and welcoming personality to foster a productive mediation session, and choose to send Bashful to day four's session. However, on the morning of the mediation, Bashful becomes, unsurprisingly, bashful at the thought of having to speak candidly in front of Snow White and her attorney. On the verge of an anxiety attack, Bashful decides that the only effective way he can represent the Dwarfs' interests at the mediation is to appear by telephone. He calls in to the session and begins talking in calm and friendly tones. Snow White, however, is outraged that the Dwarfs did not send a representative in person. She

storms out and files a motion for sanctions with the judge who ordered the mediation. How is the court likely to rule on Snow White's motion? Would the outcome have been any different if it had been a nonbinding arbitration to which the Dwarfs failed to show, rather than a mediation?

8. **Not the happily ever after we wanted.** During a court-mandated summary jury trial (SJT), the jury found that the Dwarfs owed Snow White backpay in an amount that far exceeded even Snow White's aggressive demand for relief in her complaint. The Dwarfs and their lawyer believe that the jury must have made either one of two errors: either the jury members believed that they were empowered to award punitive damages, or they simply made a mathematical error. In either event, the Dwarfs and their lawyer are confident that this kind of award would warrant remittitur or a new trial, if this were before the court. What options do the Dwarfs have in response to the SJT?

9. **Too short on cash.** Outside of the context of mediation, the Dwarfs send Snow White a written settlement offer. Under the terms of the offer, Snow White would receive a 40% pay raise, a lump sum of $40,000 to cover back wages, and up to $20,000 to cover Snow White's attorney fees, in exchange for a comprehensive mutual waiver of any and all claims. Fed up with the Dwarfs and uncertain whether she has any interest in returning to work for them, Snow White refuses the settlement offer. The case goes to trial, and a jury sides with Snow White, but awards only a total of $15,000 in damages, with no attorney fees. Following the entry of judgment, the Dwarfs file a motion to recover the litigation costs and their own attorneys' fees they incurred since the date of their offer to Snow White. How is the court likely to rule on the Dwarfs' motion?

Explanations

1. **Hi-ho, hi-ho, it's off to mediation we go.** The Dwarfs are at risk of being found in contempt of court if they refuse to follow the court's order. Even if the Dwarfs are correct in their assertion that the court lacks the authority to order the parties into mediation, it is a terrible idea simply to ignore a court's order. In terms of procedure, if the Dwarfs never objected to being sent to mediation in the first place, they could try filing a motion with the judge seeking to be excused from the mediation. If they raised an objection at the time of the order, the Dwarfs could file a motion to reconsider the court's order. And if all else fails, they might be able to seek interlocutory appellate review of the trial court judge's order.

   However, the Dwarfs are unlikely to succeed in challenging the court's order that the case go through mediation. Recall that in *In re Atlantic Pipe Co.*, the court named inherent powers as one of four possible sources for a court's authority to order parties into mediation. Nothing in the facts of this case suggests that the order is improper or beyond the scope of the court's inherent powers. Nothing suggests that the order conflicts with local rules or statutes, that the ordered mediation is somehow unfair, or that the court's order was otherwise improper. Even if the Dwarfs appeal the court's order compelling mediation, the order will almost certainly stand.

The question here also asks about Snow White's options. Assuming Snow White does not want to find herself at risk of being held in contempt along with the Dwarfs, she will need to take independent steps to carry out at least as much of the court's order as she can. For example, she should send letters to the Dwarfs, urging their participation in the mediator selection process. She should indicate her willingness to participate in mediation. And so on. Snow White cannot yet file a motion with the court seeking to enforce the court's order that the Dwarfs participate in mediation. Technically, because the 30 days specified in the judge's order have not yet passed, the Dwarfs are not yet in violation of the court's order. Presumably, they may yet change their minds and engage in mediation—a prospect made even more likely if Snow White takes steps to give effect to the judge's order.

2. **The wicked mediator.** Under the logic of *In re Atlantic Pipe Co.*, a court's authority to compel parties into mediation is bound by certain constraints. For example, it suggests that a court's use of its inherent powers "must comport with procedural fairness." In this case, we know nothing about the actual mediation process Wicked Witch would conduct, so we cannot say for certain that Snow White would succeed in characterizing the process as unfair. Snow White would probably argue that parties' autonomy and self-determination in mediation must include at least some say in the selection of the mediator—particularly here, where the parties have not independently chosen to go to mediation.

   Snow White might further argue that the judge's reliance on the court's inherent powers was not done with "restraint and discretion." If Wicked Witch were merely unqualified, Snow White might not be able to overcome the deference that would normally be afforded to the trial court's discretionary order. If Wicked Witch were merely a friend of the judge, the appearance of impropriety might not be sufficient to overcome an order specifying a particular mediator. But the combination of these two factors weighing against propriety makes it very likely that a court reviewing the trial judge's order would side with Snow White and order mediation with a different mediator.

   We do not have enough information about the facts here to know whether the judge would face the prospect of independent sanctions for improper behavior. Clearly, government officials cannot self-deal—they cannot expend public resources or use their public offices in ways to enrich themselves. In many circumstances, this ban extends to relatives and even friends. Without knowing more of the details of the relationship between Wicked Witch and the trial judge, it is unclear whether Snow White could bring a complaint against the trial judge for this order. In all events, though, if Snow White objects to the appointment of Wicked Witch, she should raise the matter with the trial court to preserve the objection.

3. **Hi-ho, it's off to summary jury trial we go?** As an initial matter, Snow White could seek to have the order compelling participation in the summary jury trial (SJT) reversed. She could file a motion with the court asking it to reconsider its order, or she could file an appeal seeking the same. The prospect of success with either of these efforts is likely to hinge on the degree to which the court has the authority to order parties to summary jury trial. Some jurisdictions plainly view summary jury trials as within the scope of ADR mechanisms to which courts have the inherent power to order parties. (For example, in *Cincinnati Gas & Electric v. General Electric*, 854 F.2d 900 (6th Cir. 1988) (discussed in Chapter 3), the Sixth Circuit upheld orders to attend a summary jury trial.) In *Strandell v. Jackson County*, 838 F.2d 884 (7th Cir. 1987), the Seventh Circuit found that neither the court's inherent powers nor the relevant rules permitted a judge to order this particular form of ADR. Note, however, that the *Strandell* decision predates the 1992 amendments to FRCP 16, which authorizes "settling the case and using special procedures to assist in resolving the dispute when authorized by statute or local rule." Most likely, therefore, depending on her jurisdiction, Snow White has little likelihood of escaping the judge's order altogether.

   If Snow White is not released from the order compelling an SJT, Snow White and her attorney would need to carefully weigh the possibility of conducting the SJT *without* calling Sleeping Beauty to the stand. Nothing in an order compelling SJT could compel a disputant to take a particular approach to prosecuting or defending its case. It would infringe far too much on party autonomy, and there is no precedent suggesting that a party would be limited in a full trial to that which he or she presented in an initial, summary jury trial. If Snow White otherwise puts on her case in earnest, she runs little risk of being held to have participated in violation of the court's order.

   Depending on the terms of the SJT process, however, Snow White may have a strong incentive to perform as well as possible in the process—including by calling her secret star witness. If the SJT included a cost-shifting mechanism akin to that found in Rule 68's offer-of-judgment statute, Snow White would find herself functionally compelled to do her best, even if no legal rule requires it. However, as described above, such a cost-shifting mechanism virtually never accompanies an

SJT process. To impose such a feature on the parties would truly illustrate the tension between a party's autonomy with respect to the course of its lawsuit and the court's inherent powers to manage cases.

Further, Snow White probably exaggerates the potential benefit of keeping Sleeping Beauty's testimony (and even her identity) out of the summary jury trial process. Television often suggests that trials are filled with surprise witnesses that turn a case in dramatic fashion. The reality of modern litigation, with procedures ranging from liberal discovery to pretrial practice, makes trial by ambush exceedingly rare.

4. **Don't be a dope in mediation.** The court is likely to find that the Dwarfs' participation failed to meet the "good faith" standard required under the terms of the court order. Good faith is not a self-defining concept, of course, but we can draw guidance from the various jurisdictions that have considered the boundaries of good faith in other contexts. For example, courts appear to have reached relative consensus on the idea that good faith includes, at a minimum, having a representative at the mediation who has appropriate settlement authority. To the extent that Dopey lacked settlement authority, the participation may be found to be in bad faith. Further, if mediators require an initial submission (for example, a mediation memo), and a party fails to provide it, courts have held that the party has breached its duty to participate in good faith. These externally measurable criteria (attendance, authority, submissions) all point to an absence of good faith, and probably make this a relatively easy question for a court.

   By contrast, behaviors within the mediation session (for example, Dopey's bizarre introduction of a partially eaten cupcake into the conversation) are much more difficult for a court to consider in assessing the extent to which parties have engaged in good faith. Confidentiality and the subjectivity involved in assessing mediation behaviors make these internal-to-mediation activities less prone to judicial review under good-faith standards. Here, however, the case is relatively easy because Dopey's lack of settlement authority is sufficient to support Snow White's complaint.

   The court has discretion to mete out punishment for failure to participate in good faith Typically, a court would fine the Dwarfs for the costs of that day's mediation, including the costs of the mediator, the mediator's travel costs, the costs Snow White incurred by taking the time away from her bookkeeping, and Snow White's attorneys' costs for the day. For example, in *G. Heileman Brewing Co. v. Joseph Oat Corp.*, 871 F.2d 648 (7th Cir. 1989), multiple parties to a commercial contract were engaged in a bitter dispute. A federal magistrate ordered each party to send a corporate representative with the authority to settle to a pretrial conference for the purpose of discussing the positions of the parties and discussing possible settlements. One company sent an attorney authorized to speak for the company, but with no authority to settle. The court imposed sanctions on that company for not sending a representative with full authority to settle. On appeal, the court upheld the sanctions imposed for violating the court order, and imposed sanctions of nearly $6,000 for the other companies' costs and attorneys' fees.

5. **While you were sleeping.** If Snow White is able to demonstrate to the court that, in fact, Sleepy was sleeping throughout the mediation, she may prevail. Although a court would not normally inquire deeply into the nature of a disputant's participation in the course of a mediation, Snow White may successfully argue that a participant who is asleep is the functional equivalent of a participant who is absent. And then, using the line of cases holding that presence is a minimal component of good-faith participation, Snow White would make the case for sanctions.

   In his defense, Sleepy would probably (1) dispute the allegation that he was asleep the whole time, and (2) point out the difficult line-drawing exercise this case presents even if he did doze off at some point. As to the first, Snow White may face a difficult proof issue stemming from the confidentiality that typically attaches to mediation sessions. (For more on the confidentiality that attaches to mediation sessions, see Chapter 7.) As to the second, Sleepy would probably suggest a slippery slope to the court. Is it bad faith to be tired? To be distracted? To fail to pay careful attention? Again, if the proof were easy to access, a court would probably rule in favor of Snow White's motion for sanctions, but the proof could be elusive.

   If the court does find bad faith, it is likely to order the Dwarfs to pay all costs associated with the mediation for that day, including attorneys' fees, making Snow White technically whole again (even though she is likely to be emotionally drained at this point). Because this is the Dwarfs' second attempt at mediation and their second good-faith violation, a judge may find it necessary to give them a harsher punishment. Local court rules can permit a court to impose fairly harsh penalties on parties that fail to mediate in good faith. Penalties may range, depending on the jurisdiction, from a simple fine all the way to dismissal, and in most cases, the trial court judge has discretion to make the decision.

6. **Grumpy behavior in a mediation.** Grumpy's behavior might not meet the conventional, popular definition of good-faith participation, but it is very unlikely that a court would fine him for any of the behaviors described here. Grumpy was present, had settlement authority, had prepared his case, and he had even made a settlement offer (albeit a very low one). As the court in *Gray v. Eggert*, described above, concluded, a low settlement offer alone is not evidence of bad-faith participation. Courts typically examine the full range of circumstances surrounding

an allegation of bad faith before making a determination. For example, in *Francis v. Women's Obstetrics & Gynecology Group*, 144 F.R.D. 646 (W.D.N.Y. 1992), the defendant was physically present at the mediation but failed to submit the required preparation materials in a timely fashion. Once the mediation commenced, the defendant informed the plaintiff that the defendant had not yet secured authorization from its insurance carrier for coverage, rendering the exercise largely moot. In granting the plaintiff's motion for sanctions, the court decried the defendant's "cavalier attitude" toward the process. Here, however, Grumpy was "merely" a hard bargainer. His strategy might not be successful. It might not even comport with the vast majority of existing "best practices" among negotiators. A court would not, however, find that his participation here breached the requirement to participate in good faith.

7. **Too shy to show up.** The court would be well within its discretion to sanction the Dwarfs for failing to participate in good faith. Bashful's reluctance to appear in person may be understandable. Indeed, there are surely circumstances in which the best, most efficient arrangement would be to have some or all of the participants in mediation appear by phone. But a disputant should not assume that he or she can unilaterally opt for this nonconventional mode of participation at the last minute. In this case, Bashful made no mention of the possibility that he would appear by phone. Instead, he simply called in rather than appearing in person. Just as in *Raad v. Wal-Mart Stores, Inc.*, described above, Bashful did not secure permission ahead of time for this mode of appearance. In this case, it is not clear that Snow White's reaction (storming out immediately) was entirely justified. However, without prior or contemporaneous consent to the appearance by phone, the court could deem Bashful's absence a failure to participate in good faith. As with previous examples, the court will have broad discretion in crafting an appropriate punishment for failure to adhere to the court's order. The most likely sanction would be fee shifting aimed at making Snow White whole for the failed mediation session.

   If the proceeding had been a mandatory, nonbinding arbitration hearing, rather than mediation, the Dwarfs might be in even more trouble. Under some arbitration rules, if one party fails to appear, the absent party is considered in default. Even if no rules providing for default exist, if only one party is present to offer evidence to the arbitrator, the arbitrator will almost certainly find in favor of the party who is present. In a binding arbitration, that would be the end of the story. But what about a nonbinding arbitration? In theory, as the name suggests, the arbitrator's finding is nonbinding and the losing party can demand a trial de novo. But at least some courts have concluded that a party who fails to appear at a mandatory, nonbinding arbitration has waived any right to demand a trial de novo, essentially rendering the nonbinding arbitrator's decision final. See, for example, *New England Merchants National Bank v. Hughes*, 556 F. Supp. 712 (E.D. Pa. 1983) (refusing to grant trial de novo following defendant's failure to appear in a nonbinding arbitration).

8. **Not the happily ever after we wanted.** The Dwarfs may have good reason to be unhappy with the results of the SJT, but they have no conspicuous legal options for contesting its outcome. The purpose of a summary jury trial is to facilitate settlements by providing each party with a snapshot of what *might* happen at trial. In this case, the Dwarfs may believe that some aspect of the SJT process was flawed in a way that rendered it not predictive of trial. Perhaps Snow White would agree, or perhaps she and her lawyers will determine that they undervalued their case—a result that might make settlement *less* likely. But summary jury trials are nonbinding, and there is no evidence that Snow White (or the jurors) engaged in any misconduct. So, the Dwarfs have no legal recourse here. Their best course of action would be to learn from the SJT jurors, with an eye toward avoiding this kind of outcome if the case proceeds to trial.

9. **Too short on cash.** It may depend on whether the action is taking place in federal court or state court. In federal court, the Dwarfs' motion would fall under Federal Rule of Civil Procedure 68. The facts do not specify otherwise, so we should assume that the Dwarfs' written offer was sufficiently unambiguous and unconditional to fall within the scope of the rules. Under Rule 68, because "the judgment finally obtained by the offeree [Snow White] is not more favorable than the offer, the offeree must pay the costs incurred after the making of the offer." The Dwarfs' *costs*, therefore, will be recoverable. However, Rule 68 limits the opportunity for recovery to costs (which include small-ticket items like filing fees, stenographers' fees, etc.). The largest portion of the Dwarfs' expenses most likely came in the form of attorneys' fees. Many states have offer-of-judgment rules identical to that in FRCP 68, but some states have statutes that provide for the recovery of attorneys' fees as well. Absent such a rule, however, the Dwarfs would recover only some of the money they seek from Snow White.

APPENDIX 1

The Uniform Mediation Act

The Uniform Mediation Act (UMA) was drafted by the National Conference of Commissioners on Uniform State Laws (NCCUSL). The NCCUSL approved the final draft in 2002 and then amended it in 2003 to add provisions from the United Nations Commission on International Trade Law. Through its Section on Dispute Resolution, the American Bar Association collaborated in the drafting. The ABA along with the American Arbitration Association, Judicial Arbitration and Mediation Service (JAMS), the CPR Institute for Dispute Resolution and the National Arbitration Forum have endorsed the UMA. As of the printing of this edition, more than a dozen states and the District of Columbia have adopted a version of the UMA. For an update on enactments, see https://www.uniformlaws.org/committees/community-home?communitykey=45565a5f-0c57-4bba-bbab-fc7de9a59110#LegBillTrackingAnchor.

SECTION 1. TITLE.

This [Act] may be cited as the Uniform Mediation Act.

SECTION 2. DEFINITIONS.

In this [Act]:

(1) "Mediation" means a process in which a mediator facilitates communication and negotiation between parties to assist them in reaching a voluntary agreement regarding their dispute.

(2) "Mediation communication" means a statement, whether oral or in a record or verbal or nonverbal, that occurs during a mediation or is made for purposes of considering, conducting, participating in, initiating, continuing, or reconvening a mediation or retaining a mediator.

(3) "Mediator" means an individual who conducts a mediation.

(4) "Nonparty participant" means a person, other than a party or mediator, that participates in a mediation.

(5) "Mediation party" means a person that participates in a mediation and whose agreement is necessary to resolve the dispute.

(6) "Person" means an individual, corporation, business trust, estate, trust, partnership, limited liability company, association, joint venture, government; governmental subdivision, agency, or instrumentality; public corporation; or any other legal or commercial entity.

(7) "Proceeding" means:

(A) a judicial, administrative, arbitral, or other adjudicative process, including related pre-hearing and post-hearing motions, conferences, and discovery; or

(B) a legislative hearing or similar process.

(8) "Record" means information that is inscribed on a tangible medium or that is stored in an electronic or other medium and is retrievable in perceivable form.

(9) "Sign" means:

(A) to execute or adopt a tangible symbol with the present intent to authenticate a record; or

(B) to attach or logically associate an electronic symbol, sound, or process to or with a record with the present intent to authenticate a record.

SECTION 3. SCOPE.

(a) Except as otherwise provided in subsection (b) or (c), this [Act] applies to a mediation in which:

(1) the mediation parties are required to mediate by statute or court or administrative agency rule or referred to mediation by a court, administrative agency, or arbitrator;

(2) the mediation parties and the mediator agree to mediate in a record that demonstrates an expectation that mediation communications will be privileged against disclosure; or

(3) the mediation parties use as a mediator an individual who holds himself or herself out as a mediator, or the mediation is provided by a person that holds itself out as providing mediation.

(b) The [Act] does not apply to a mediation:

(1) relating to the establishment, negotiation, administration, or termination of a collective bargaining relationship;

(2) relating to a dispute that is pending under or is part of the processes established by a collective bargaining agreement, except that the [Act] applies to a mediation arising out of a dispute that has been filed with an administrative agency or court;

(3) conducted by a judge who might make a ruling on the case; or

(4) conducted under the auspices of:

(A) a primary or secondary school if all the parties are students or

(B) a correctional institution for youths if all the parties are residents of that institution.

(c) If the parties agree in advance in a signed record, or a record of proceeding reflects agreement by the parties, that all or part of a mediation is not privileged, the privileges under Sections 4 through 6 do not apply to the mediation or part agreed upon. However, Sections 4 through 6 apply to a mediation communication made by a person that has not received actual notice of the agreement before the communication is made.

SECTION 4. PRIVILEGE AGAINST DISCLOSURE; ADMISSIBILITY; DISCOVERY.

(a) Except as otherwise provided in Section 6, a mediation communication is privileged as provided in subsection (b) and is not subject to discovery or admissible in evidence in a proceeding unless waived or precluded as provided by Section 5.

(b) In a proceeding, the following privileges apply:

(1) A mediation party may refuse to disclose, and may prevent any other person from disclosing, a mediation communication.

(2) A mediator may refuse to disclose a mediation communication, and may prevent any other person from disclosing a mediation communication of the mediator.

(3) A nonparty participant may refuse to disclose, and may prevent any other person from disclosing, a mediation communication of the nonparty participant.

(c) Evidence or information that is otherwise admissible or subject to discovery does not become inadmissible or protected from discovery solely by reason of its disclosure or use in a mediation.

SECTION 5. WAIVER AND PRECLUSION OF PRIVILEGE.

(a) A privilege under Section 4 may be waived in a record or orally during a proceeding if it is expressly waived by all parties to the mediation and:

(1) in the case of the privilege of a mediator, it is expressly waived by the mediator; and

(2) in the case of the privilege of a nonparty participant, it is expressly waived by the nonparty participant.

(b) A person that discloses or makes a representation about a mediation communication which prejudices another person in a proceeding is precluded from asserting a privilege under Section 4, but only to the extent necessary for the person prejudiced to respond to the representation or disclosure.

(c) A person that intentionally uses a mediation to plan, attempt to commit or commit a crime, or to conceal an ongoing crime or ongoing criminal activity is precluded from asserting a privilege under Section 4.

SECTION 6. EXCEPTIONS TO PRIVILEGE.

(a) There is no privilege under Section 4 for a mediation communication that is:

(1) in an agreement evidenced by a record signed by all parties to the agreement;

(2) available to the public under [insert statutory reference to open records act] or made during a session of a mediation which is open, or is required by law to be open, to the public;

(3) a threat or statement of a plan to inflict bodily injury or commit a crime of violence;

(4) intentionally used to plan a crime, attempt to commit or commit a crime, or to conceal an ongoing crime or ongoing criminal activity;

(5) sought or offered to prove or disprove a claim or complaint of professional misconduct or malpractice filed against a mediator;

(6) except as otherwise provided in subsection (c), sought or offered to prove or disprove a claim or complaint of professional misconduct or malpractice filed against a mediation party, nonparty participant, or representative of a party based on conduct occurring during a mediation; or

(7) sought or offered to prove or disprove abuse, neglect, abandonment, or exploitation in a proceeding in which a child or adult protective services agency is a party, unless the

[Alternative A: [State to insert, for example, child or adult protection] case is referred by a court to mediation and a public agency participates.]

[Alternative B: Public agency participates in the [State to insert, for example, child or adult protection] mediation.].

(b) There is no privilege under Section 4 if a court, administrative agency, or arbitrator finds, after a hearing in camera, that the party seeking discovery or the proponent of the evidence has shown that the evidence is not otherwise available, that there is a need for the evidence that substantially outweighs the interest in protecting confidentiality, and that the mediation communication is sought or offered in:

(1) a court proceeding involving a felony [or misdemeanor]; or

(2) except as otherwise provided in subsection (c), a proceeding to prove a claim to rescind or reform or a defense to avoid liability on a contract arising out of the mediation.

(c) A mediator may not be compelled to provide evidence of a mediation communication referred to in subsection (a)(6) or (b)(2).

(d) If a mediation communication is not privileged under subsection (a) or (b), only the portion of the communication necessary for the application of the exception from nondisclosure may be admitted. Admission of evidence under subsection (a) or (b) does not render the evidence, or any other mediation communication, discoverable or admissible for any other purpose.

SECTION 7. PROHIBITED MEDIATOR REPORTS.

(a) Except as required in subsection (b), a mediator may not make a report, assessment, evaluation, recommendation, finding, or other communication regarding a mediation to a court, administrative agency, or other authority that may make a ruling on the dispute that is the subject of the mediation.

(b) A mediator may disclose:

(1) whether the mediation occurred or has terminated, whether a settlement was reached, and attendance;

(2) a mediation communication as permitted under Section 6; or

(3) a mediation communication evidencing abuse, neglect, abandonment, or exploitation of an individual to a public agency responsible for protecting individuals against such mistreatment.

(c) A communication made in violation of subsection (a) may not be considered by a court, administrative agency, or arbitrator.

SECTION 8. CONFIDENTIALITY.

Unless subject to the [insert statutory references to open meetings act and open records act], mediation communications are confidential to the extent agreed by the parties or provided by other law or rule of this State.

SECTION 9. MEDIATOR'S DISCLOSURE OF CONFLICTS OF INTEREST; BACKGROUND.

(a) Before accepting a mediation, an individual who is requested to serve as a mediator shall:

(1) make an inquiry that is reasonable under the circumstances to determine whether there are any known facts that a reasonable individual would consider likely to affect the impartiality of the mediator, including a financial or personal interest in the outcome of the mediation and an existing or past relationship with a mediation party or foreseeable participant in the mediation; and

(2) disclose any such known fact to the mediation parties as soon as is practical before accepting a mediation.

(b) If a mediator learns any fact described in subsection (a)(1) after accepting a mediation, the mediator shall disclose it as soon as is practicable.

(c) At the request of a mediation party, an individual who is requested to serve as a mediator shall disclose the mediator's qualifications to mediate a dispute.

(d) A person that violates subsection [(a) or (b)] [(a), (b), or (g)] is precluded by the violation from asserting a privilege under Section 4.

(e) Subsections (a), (b), [and] (c), [and] [(g)] do not apply to an individual acting as a judge.

(f) This [Act] does not require that a mediator have a special qualification by background or profession.

[(g) A mediator must be impartial, unless after disclosure of the facts required in subsections (a) and (b) to be disclosed, the parties agree otherwise.]

SECTION 10. PARTICIPATION IN MEDIATION.

An attorney or other individual designated by a party may accompany the party to and participate in a mediation. A waiver of participation given before the mediation may be rescinded.

SECTION 11. INTERNATIONAL COMMERCIAL MEDIATION.

(a) In this section, "Model Law" means the Model Law on International Commercial Conciliation adopted by the United Nations Commission on International Trade Law on 28 June 2002 and recommended by the United Nations General Assembly in a resolution (A/RES/57/18) dated 19 November 2002, and "international commercial mediation" means an international commercial conciliation as defined in Article 1 of the Model Law.

(b) Except as otherwise provided in subsections (c) and (d), if a mediation is an international commercial mediation, the mediation is governed by the Model Law.

(c) Unless the parties agree in accordance with Section 3(c) of this [Act] that all or part of an international commercial mediation is not privileged, Sections 4, 5, and 6 and any applicable definitions in Section 2 of this [Act] also apply to the mediation and nothing in Article 10 of the Model Law derogates from Sections 4, 5, and 6.

(d) If the parties to an international commercial mediation agree under Article 1, subsection (7), of the Model Law that the Model Law does not apply, this [Act] applies.

SECTION 12. RELATION TO ELECTRONIC SIGNATURES IN GLOBAL AND NATIONAL COMMERCE ACT.

This [Act] modifies, limits, or supersedes the federal Electronic Signatures in Global and National Commerce Act, 15 U.S.C. Section 7001 et seq., but this [Act] does not modify, limit, or supersede Section 101(c) of that Act or authorize electronic delivery of any of the notices described in Section 103(b) of that Act.

SECTION 13. UNIFORMITY OF APPLICATION AND CONSTRUCTION.

In applying and construing this [Act], consideration should be given to the need to promote uniformity of the law with respect to its subject matter among States that enact it.

SECTION 14. SEVERABILITY CLAUSE.

If any provision of this [Act] or its application to any person or circumstance is held invalid, the invalidity does not affect other provisions or applications of this [Act] which can be given effect without the invalid provision or application, and to this end the provisions of this [Act] are severable.

SECTION 15. EFFECTIVE DATE.

This [Act] takes effect ______________________________.

SECTION 16. REPEALS.

The following acts and parts of acts are hereby repealed:

(1)

(2)

(3)

SECTION 17. APPLICATION TO EXISTING AGREEMENTS OR REFERRALS.

(a) This [Act] governs a mediation pursuant to a referral or an agreement to mediate made on or after [the effective date of this [Act]].

(b) On or after [a delayed date], this [Act] governs an agreement to mediate whenever made.

APPENDIX 2

The Model Standards of Conduct for Mediators

The Model Standards of Conduct for Mediators was prepared in 1994 by the American Arbitration Association, the American Bar Association's Section of Dispute Resolution, and the Association for Conflict Resolution. A joint committee consisting of representatives from the same successor organizations revised the Model Standards in 2005. Both the original 1994 version and the 2005 revision have been approved by each participating organization.

PREAMBLE

Mediation is used to resolve a broad range of conflicts within a variety of settings. These Standards are designed to serve as fundamental ethical guidelines for persons mediating in all practice contexts. They serve three primary goals: to guide the conduct of mediators; to inform the mediating parties; and to promote public confidence in mediation as a process for resolving disputes.

Mediation is a process in which an impartial third party facilitates communication and negotiation and promotes voluntary decision making by the parties to the dispute.

Mediation serves various purposes, including providing the opportunity for parties to define and clarify issues, understand different perspectives, identify interests, explore and assess possible solutions, and reach mutually satisfactory agreements, when desired.

NOTE ON CONSTRUCTION

These Standards are to be read and construed in their entirety. There is no priority significance attached to the sequence in which the Standards appear.

The use of the term "shall" in a Standard indicates that the mediator must follow the practice described. The use of the term "should" indicates that the practice described in the standard is highly desirable, but not required, and is to be departed from only for very strong reasons and requires careful use of judgment and discretion.

The use of the term "mediator" is understood to be inclusive so that it applies to co-mediator models.

These Standards do not include specific temporal parameters when referencing a mediation, and therefore, do not define the exact beginning or ending of a mediation.

Various aspects of a mediation, including some matters covered by these Standards, may also be affected by applicable law, court rules, regulations, other applicable professional rules, mediation rules to which the parties have agreed and other agreements of the parties. These sources may create conflicts with, and may take precedence over, these Standards. However, a mediator should make every effort to comply with the spirit and intent of these Standards in resolving such conflicts. This effort should include honoring all remaining Standards not in conflict with these other sources.

These Standards, unless and until adopted by a court or other regulatory authority, do not have the force of law. Nonetheless, the fact that these Standards have been adopted by the respective sponsoring entities should alert mediators to the fact that the Standards might be viewed as establishing a standard of care for mediators.

STANDARD I. SELF-DETERMINATION

A. A mediator shall conduct a mediation based on the principle of party self-determination. Self-determination is the act of coming to a voluntary, uncoerced decision in which each party makes free and informed choices as to process and outcome. Parties may exercise self-determination at any stage of a mediation, including mediator selection, process design, participation in or withdrawal from the process, and outcomes.

1. Although party self-determination for process design is a fundamental principle of mediation practice, a mediator may need to balance such party self-determination with a mediator's duty to conduct a quality process in accordance with these Standards.

2. A mediator cannot personally ensure that each party has made free and informed choices to reach particular decisions, but, where appropriate, a mediator should make the parties aware of the importance of consulting other professionals to help them make informed choices.

B. A mediator shall not undermine party self-determination by any party for reasons such as higher settlement rates, egos, increased fees, or outside pressures from court personnel, program administrators, provider organizations, the media or others.

STANDARD II. IMPARTIALITY

A. A mediator shall decline a mediation if the mediator cannot conduct it in an impartial manner. Impartiality means freedom from favoritism, bias or prejudice.

B. A mediator shall conduct a mediation in an impartial manner and avoid conduct that gives the appearance of partiality.

1. A mediator should not act with partiality or prejudice based on any participant's personal characteristics, background, values and beliefs, or performance at a mediation, or any other reason.
2. A mediator should neither give nor accept a gift, favor, loan or other item of value that raises a question as to the mediator's actual or perceived impartiality.
3. A mediator may accept or give de minimis gifts or incidental items or services that are provided to facilitate a mediation or respect cultural norms so long as such practices do not raise questions as to a mediator's actual or perceived impartiality.

C. If at any time a mediator is unable to conduct a mediation in an impartial manner, the mediator shall withdraw.

STANDARD III. CONFLICTS OF INTEREST

A. A mediator shall avoid a conflict of interest or the appearance of a conflict of interest during and after a mediation. A conflict of interest can arise from involvement by a mediator with the subject matter of the dispute or from any relationship between a mediator and any mediation participant, whether past or present, personal or professional, that reasonably raises a question of a mediator's impartiality.

B. A mediator shall make a reasonable inquiry to determine whether there are any facts that a reasonable individual would consider likely to create a potential or actual conflict of interest for a mediator. A mediator's actions necessary to accomplish a reasonable inquiry into potential conflicts of interest may vary based on practice context.

C. A mediator shall disclose, as soon as practicable, all actual and potential conflicts of interest that are reasonably known to the mediator and could reasonably be seen as raising a question about the mediator's impartiality. After disclosure, if all parties agree, the mediator may proceed with the mediation.

D. If a mediator learns any fact after accepting a mediation that raises a question with respect to that mediator's service creating a potential or actual conflict of interest, the mediator shall disclose it as quickly as practicable. After disclosure, if all parties agree, the mediator may proceed with the mediation.

E. If a mediator's conflict of interest might reasonably be viewed as undermining the integrity of the mediation, a mediator shall withdraw from or decline to proceed with the mediation regardless of the expressed desire or agreement of the parties to the contrary.

F. Subsequent to a mediation, a mediator shall not establish another relationship with any of the participants in any matter that would raise questions about the integrity of the mediation. When a mediator develops personal or professional relationships with parties, other individuals or organizations following a mediation in which they were involved, the mediator should consider factors such as time elapsed following the mediation, the nature of the relationships established, and services offered when determining whether the relationships might create a perceived or actual conflict of interest.

STANDARD IV. COMPETENCE

A. A mediator shall mediate only when the mediator has the necessary competence to satisfy the reasonable expectations of the parties.

1. Any person may be selected as a mediator, provided that the parties are satisfied with the mediator's competence and qualifications. Training, experience in mediation, skills, cultural understandings and other qualities are often necessary for mediator competence. A person who offers to serve as a mediator creates the expectation that the person is competent to mediate effectively.

2. A mediator should attend educational programs and related activities to maintain and enhance the mediator's knowledge and skills related to mediation.

3. A mediator should have available for the parties information relevant to the mediator's training, education, experience and approach to conducting a mediation.

B. If a mediator, during the course of a mediation, determines that the mediator cannot conduct the mediation competently, the mediator shall discuss that determination with the parties as soon as is practicable and take appropriate steps to address the situation, including, but not limited to, withdrawing or requesting appropriate assistance.

C. If a mediator's ability to conduct a mediation is impaired by drugs, alcohol, medication or otherwise, the mediator shall not conduct the mediation.

STANDARD V. CONFIDENTIALITY

A. A mediator shall maintain the confidentiality of all information obtained by the mediator in mediation, unless otherwise agreed to by the parties or required by applicable law.

1. If the parties to a mediation agree that the mediator may disclose information obtained during the mediation, the mediator may do so.

2. A mediator should not communicate to any non-participant information about how the parties acted in the mediation. A mediator may report, if required, whether parties appeared at a scheduled mediation and whether or not the parties reached a resolution.

3. If a mediator participates in teaching, research or evaluation of mediation, the mediator should protect the anonymity of the parties and abide by their reasonable expectations regarding confidentiality.

B. A mediator who meets with any persons in private session during a mediation shall not convey directly or indirectly to any other person, any information that was obtained during that private session without the consent of the disclosing person.

C. A mediator shall promote understanding among the parties of the extent to which the parties will maintain confidentiality of information they obtain in a mediation.

D. Depending on the circumstance of a mediation, the parties may have varying expectations regarding confidentiality that a mediator should address. The parties may make their own rules with respect to confidentiality, or the accepted practice of an individual mediator or institution may dictate a particular set of expectations.

STANDARD VI. QUALITY OF THE PROCESS

A. A mediator shall conduct a mediation in accordance with these Standards and in a manner that promotes diligence, timeliness, safety, presence of the appropriate participants, party participation, procedural fairness, party competency and mutual respect among all participants.

1. A mediator should agree to mediate only when the mediator is prepared to commit the attention essential to an effective mediation.

2. A mediator should only accept cases when the mediator can satisfy the reasonable expectation of the parties concerning the timing of a mediation.

3. The presence or absence of persons at a mediation depends on the agreement of the parties and the mediator. The parties and mediator may agree that others may be excluded from particular sessions or from all sessions.

4. A mediator should promote honesty and candor between and among all participants, and a mediator shall not knowingly misrepresent any material fact or circumstance in the course of a mediation.

5. The role of a mediator differs substantially from other professional roles. Mixing the role of a mediator and the role of another profession is problematic and thus, a mediator should distinguish between the roles. A mediator may provide information that the mediator is qualified by training or experience to provide, only if the mediator can do so consistent with these Standards.

6. A mediator shall not conduct a dispute resolution procedure other than mediation but label it mediation in an effort to gain the protection of rules, statutes, or other governing authorities pertaining to mediation.

7. A mediator may recommend, when appropriate, that parties consider resolving their dispute through arbitration, counseling, neutral evaluation or other processes.

8. A mediator shall not undertake an additional dispute resolution role in the same matter without the consent of the parties. Before providing such service, a mediator shall inform the parties of the implications of the change in process and obtain their consent to the change. A mediator who undertakes such a role assumes different duties and responsibilities that may be governed by other standards.

9. If a mediation is being used to further criminal conduct, a mediator should take appropriate steps including, if necessary, postponing, withdrawing from or terminating the mediation.

10. If a party appears to have difficulty comprehending the process, issues, or settlement options, or difficulty participating in a mediation, the mediator should explore the circumstances and

potential accommodations, modifications or adjustments that would make possible the party's capacity to comprehend, participate and exercise self-determination.

B. If a mediator is made aware of domestic abuse or violence among the parties, the mediator shall take appropriate steps including, if necessary, postponing, withdrawing from or terminating the mediation.

C. If a mediator believes that participant conduct, including that of the mediator, jeopardizes conducting a mediation consistent with these Standards, a mediator shall take appropriate steps including, if necessary, postponing, withdrawing from or terminating the mediation.

STANDARD VII. ADVERTISING AND SOLICITATION

A. A mediator shall be truthful and not misleading when advertising, soliciting or otherwise communicating the mediator's qualifications, experience, services and fees.

1. A mediator should not include any promises as to outcome in communications, including business cards, stationery, or computer based communications.
2. A mediator should only claim to meet the mediator qualifications of a governmental entity or private organization if that entity or organization has a recognized procedure for qualifying mediators and it grants such status to the mediator.

B. A mediator shall not solicit in a manner that gives an appearance of partiality for or against a party or otherwise undermines the integrity of the process.

C. A mediator shall not communicate to others, in promotional materials or through other forms of communication, the names of persons served without their permission.

STANDARD VIII. FEES AND OTHER CHARGES

A. A mediator shall provide each party or each party's representative true and complete information about mediation fees, expenses and any other actual or potential charges that may be incurred in connection with a mediation.

1. If a mediator charges fees, the mediator should develop them in light of all relevant factors, including the type and complexity of the matter, the qualifications of the mediator, the time required and the rates customary for such mediation services.

2. A mediator's fee arrangement should be in writing unless the parties request otherwise.

B. A mediator shall not charge fees in a manner that impairs a mediator's impartiality.

1. A mediator should not enter into a fee agreement which is contingent upon the result of the mediation or amount of the settlement.

2. While a mediator may accept unequal fee payments from the parties, a mediator should not use fee arrangements that adversely impact the mediator's ability to conduct a mediation in an impartial manner.

STANDARD IX. ADVANCEMENT OF MEDIATION PRACTICE

A. A mediator should act in a manner that advances the practice of mediation. A mediator promotes this Standard by engaging in some or all of the following:

1. Fostering diversity within the field of mediation.

2. Striving to make mediation accessible to those who elect to use it, including providing services at a reduced rate or on a pro bono basis as appropriate.

3. Participating in research when given the opportunity, including obtaining participant feedback when appropriate.

4. Participating in outreach and education efforts to assist the public in developing an improved understanding of, and appreciation for, mediation.

5. Assisting newer mediators through training, mentoring and networking.

B. A mediator should demonstrate respect for differing points of view within the field, seek to learn from other mediators and work together with other mediators to improve the profession and better serve people in conflict.

APPENDIX 3

The Federal Arbitration Act

The Federal Arbitration Act was originally enacted in 1925 and was codified into its modern form in 1947. The first major amendment of the act occurred with the passage of the Ending Forced Arbitration of Sexual Assault and Sexual Harassment Act of 2021.

9 U.S.C. 1 ET SEQ.

SECTION 1. "MARITIME TRANSACTIONS" AND "COMMERCE" DEFINED; EXCEPTIONS TO OPERATION OF TITLE

"Maritime transaction," as herein defined, means charter parties, bills of lading of water carriers, agreements relating to wharfage, supplies furnished vessels or repairs to vessels, collisions, or any other matters in foreign commerce which, if the subject of controversy, would be embraced within admiralty jurisdiction; "commerce," as herein defined, means commerce among the several States or with foreign nations, or in any Territory of the United States or in the District of Columbia, or between any such Territory and another, or between any such Territory and any State or foreign nation, or between the District of Columbia and any State or Territory or foreign nation, but nothing herein contained shall apply to contracts of employment of seamen, railroad employees, or any other class of workers engaged in foreign or interstate commerce.

SECTION 2. VALIDITY, IRREVOCABILITY, AND ENFORCEMENT OF AGREEMENTS TO ARBITRATE

A written provision in any maritime transaction or a contract evidencing a transaction involving commerce to settle by arbitration a controversy thereafter arising out of such contract or transaction, or the refusal to perform the whole or any part thereof, or an agreement in writing to submit to arbitration an existing controversy arising out of such a contract, transaction, or refusal, shall be valid, irrevocable, and enforceable, save upon such grounds as exist at law or in equity for the revocation of any contract or as otherwise provided in chapter 4 [See Section 401-402 below].

SECTION 3. STAY OF PROCEEDINGS WHERE ISSUE THEREIN REFERABLE TO ARBITRATION

If any suit or proceeding be brought in any of the courts of the United States upon any issue referable to arbitration under an agreement in writing for such arbitration, the court in which such suit is pending, upon being satisfied that the issue involved in such suit or proceeding is referable to arbitration under such an agreement, shall on application of one of the parties stay the trial of the action until such arbitration has been had in accordance with the terms of the agreement, providing the applicant for the stay is not in default in proceeding with such arbitration.

SECTION 4. FAILURE TO ARBITRATE UNDER AGREEMENT; PETITION TO UNITED STATES COURT HAVING JURISDICTION FOR ORDER TO COMPEL ARBITRATION; NOTICE AND SERVICE THEREOF; HEARING AND DETERMINATION

A party aggrieved by the alleged failure, neglect, or refusal of another to arbitrate under a written agreement for arbitration may petition any United States district court which, save for such agreement, would have jurisdiction under title 28, in a civil action or in admiralty of the subject matter of a suit arising out of the controversy between the parties, for an order directing that such arbitration proceed in the manner provided for in such agreement. Five days' notice in writing of such application shall be served upon the party in default. Service thereof shall be made in the manner provided by the Federal Rules of Civil Procedure. The court shall hear the parties, and upon being satisfied that the making of the agreement for arbitration or the failure to comply therewith is not in issue, the court shall make an order directing the parties to proceed to arbitration in accordance with the terms of the agreement. The hearing and proceedings, under such agreement, shall be within the district in which the petition for an order directing such arbitration is filed. If the making of the arbitration agreement or the failure, neglect, or refusal to perform the same be in issue, the court shall proceed summarily to the trial thereof. If no jury trial be demanded by the party alleged to be in default, or if the matter in dispute is within admiralty jurisdiction, the court shall hear and determine such issue. Where such an issue is raised, the party alleged to be in default may, except in cases of admiralty, on or before the return day of the notice of application, demand a jury trial of such issue, and upon such demand the court shall make an order referring the issue or issues to a jury in the manner provided by the Federal Rules of Civil Procedure, or may specially call a jury for that purpose. If the jury find that no agreement in writing for arbitration was made or that there is no default in proceeding thereunder, the proceeding shall be dismissed. If the jury find that an agreement for arbitration was made in writing and that there is a default in proceeding thereunder, the court shall make an order summarily directing the parties to proceed with the arbitration in accordance with the terms thereof.

SECTION 5. APPOINTMENT OF ARBITRATORS OR UMPIRE

If in the agreement provision be made for a method of naming or appointing an arbitrator or arbitrators or an umpire, such method shall be followed; but if no method be provided therein, or if a method be provided and any party thereto shall fail to avail himself of such method, or if for any other reason there shall be a lapse in the naming of an arbitrator or arbitrators or umpire, or in filling a vacancy, then upon the application of either party to the controversy the court shall designate and appoint an arbitrator or arbitrators or umpire, as the case may require, who shall act under the said agreement with the same force and effect as if he or they had been specifically named therein; and unless otherwise provided in the agreement the arbitration shall be by a single arbitrator.

SECTION 6. APPLICATION HEARD AS MOTION

Any application to the court hereunder shall be made and heard in the manner provided by law for the making and hearing of motions, except as otherwise herein expressly provided.

SECTION 7. WITNESSES BEFORE ARBITRATORS; FEES; COMPELLING ATTENDANCE

The arbitrators selected either as prescribed in this title or otherwise, or a majority of them, may summon in writing any person to attend before them or any of them as a witness and in a proper case to bring with him or them any book, record, document, or paper which may be deemed material as evidence in the case. The fees for such attendance shall be the same as the fees of witnesses before masters of the United States courts. Said summons shall issue in the name of the arbitrator or arbitrators, or a majority of them, and shall be signed by the arbitrators, or a majority of them, and shall be directed to the said person and shall be served in the same manner as subpoenas to appear and testify before the court; if any person or persons so summoned to testify shall refuse or neglect to obey said summons, upon petition the United States district court for the district in which such arbitrators, or a majority of them, are sitting may compel the attendance of such person or persons before said arbitrator or arbitrators, or punish said person or persons for contempt in the same manner provided by law for securing the attendance of witnesses or their punishment for neglect or refusal to attend in the courts of the United States.

SECTION 8. PROCEEDINGS BEGUN BY LIBEL IN ADMIRALTY AND SEIZURE OF VESSEL OR PROPERTY

If the basis of jurisdiction be a cause of action otherwise justiciable in admiralty, then, notwithstanding anything herein to the contrary, the party claiming to be aggrieved may begin his proceeding hereunder by libel and seizure of the vessel or other property of the other party according to the usual course of admiralty proceedings, and the court shall then have jurisdiction to direct the parties to proceed with the arbitration and shall retain jurisdiction to enter its decree upon the award.

SECTION 9. AWARD OF ARBITRATORS; CONFIRMATION; JURISDICTION; PROCEDURE

If the parties in their agreement have agreed that a judgment of the court shall be entered upon the award made pursuant to the arbitration, and shall specify the court, then at any time within one year after the award is made any party to the arbitration may apply to the court so specified for an order confirming the award, and thereupon the court must grant such an order unless the award is vacated, modified, or corrected as prescribed in sections 10 and 11 of this title. If no court is specified in the agreement of the parties, then such application may be made to the United States court in and for the district within which such award was made. Notice of the application shall be served upon the adverse party, and thereupon the court shall have jurisdiction of such party as though he had appeared generally in the proceeding. If the adverse party is a resident of the district within which the award was made, such service shall be made upon the adverse party or his attorney as prescribed by law for service of notice of motion in an action in the same court. If the adverse party shall be a nonresident, then the notice of the application shall be served by the marshal of any district within which the adverse party may be found in like manner as other process of the court.

SECTION 10. SAME; VACATION; GROUNDS; REHEARING

(a) In any of the following cases the United States court in and for the district wherein the award was made may make an order vacating the award upon the application of any party to the arbitration

(1) where the award was procured by corruption, fraud, or undue means;

(2) where there was evident partiality or corruption in the arbitrators, or either of them;

(3) where the arbitrators were guilty of misconduct in refusing to postpone the hearing, upon sufficient cause shown, or in refusing to hear evidence pertinent and material to the controversy; or of any other misbehavior by which the rights of any party have been prejudiced;

(4) where the arbitrators exceeded their powers, or so imperfectly executed them that a mutual, final, and definite award upon the subject matter submitted was not made.

(b) If an award is vacated and the time within which the agreement required the award to be made has not expired, the court may, in its discretion, direct a rehearing by the arbitrators.

(c) The United States district court for the district wherein an award was made that was issued pursuant to section 580 of title 5 may make an order vacating the award upon the application of a person, other than a party to the arbitration, who is adversely affected or aggrieved by the award, if the use of arbitration or the award is clearly inconsistent with the factors set forth in section 572 of title 5.

SECTION 11. SAME; MODIFICATION OR CORRECTION; GROUNDS; ORDER

In either of the following cases the United States court in and for the district wherein the award was made may make an order modifying or correcting the award upon the application of any party to the arbitration:

(a) Where there was an evident material miscalculation of figures or an evident material mistake in the description of any person, thing, or property referred to in the award.

(b) Where the arbitrators have awarded upon a matter not submitted to them, unless it is a matter not affecting the merits of the decision upon the matter submitted.

(c) Where the award is imperfect in matter of form not affecting the merits of the controversy.

The order may modify and correct the award, so as to effect the intent thereof and promote justice between the parties.

SECTION 12. NOTICE OF MOTIONS TO VACATE OR MODIFY; SERVICE; STAY OF PROCEEDINGS

Notice of a motion to vacate, modify, or correct an award must be served upon the adverse party or his attorney within three months after the award is filed or delivered. If the adverse party is a resident of the district within which the award was made, such service shall be made upon the adverse party or his attorney as prescribed by law for service of notice of motion in an action in the same court. If the adverse party shall be a nonresident then the notice of the application shall be served by the marshal of any district within which the adverse party may be found in like manner as other process of the court. For the purposes of the motion any judge who might make an order to stay the proceedings in an action brought in the same court may make an order, to be served with the notice of motion, staying the proceedings of the adverse party to enforce the award.

SECTION 13. PAPERS FILED WITH ORDER ON MOTIONS; JUDGMENT; DOCKETING; FORCE AND EFFECT; ENFORCEMENT

The party moving for an order confirming, modifying, or correcting an award shall, at the time such order is filed with the clerk for the entry of judgment thereon, also file the following papers with the clerk:

(a) The agreement; the selection or appointment, if any, of an additional arbitrator or umpire; and each written extension of the time, if any, within which to make the award.

(b) The award.

(c) Each notice, affidavit, or other paper used upon an application to confirm, modify, or correct the award, and a copy of each order of the court upon such an application.

The judgment shall be docketed as if it was rendered in an action.

The judgment so entered shall have the same force and effect, in all respects, as, and be subject to all the provisions of law relating to, a judgment in an action; and it may be enforced as if it had been rendered in an action in the court in which it is entered.

SECTION 14. CONTRACTS NOT AFFECTED

This title shall not apply to contracts made prior to January 1, 1926.

SECTION 15. INAPPLICABILITY OF THE ACT OF STATE DOCTRINE

Enforcement of arbitral agreements, confirmation of arbitral awards, and execution upon judgments based on orders confirming such awards shall not be refused on the basis of the Act of State doctrine.

SECTION 16. APPEALS

(a) An appeal may be taken from

(1) an order

(A) refusing a stay of any action under section 3 of this title,

(B) denying a petition under section 4 of this title to order arbitration to proceed,

(C) denying an application under section 206 of this title to compel arbitration,

(D) confirming or denying confirmation of an award or partial award, or

(E) modifying, correcting, or vacating an award;

(2) an interlocutory order granting, continuing, or modifying an injunction against an arbitration that is subject to this title; or

(3) a final decision with respect to an arbitration that is subject to this title.

(b) Except as otherwise provided in section 1292 (b) of title 28, an appeal may not be taken from an interlocutory order

(1) granting a stay of any action under section 3 of this title;

(2) directing arbitration to proceed under section 4 of this title;

(3) compelling arbitration under section 206 of this title; or

(4) refusing to enjoin an arbitration that is subject to this title.

CHAPTER 4—ARBITRATION OF DISPUTES INVOLVING SEXUAL ASSAULT AND SEXUAL HARASSMENT

SECTION 401. DEFINITIONS

In this chapter:

(1) Predispute arbitration agreement.—The term "predispute arbitration agreement" means any agreement to arbitrate a dispute that had not yet arisen at the time of the making of the agreement.

(2) Predispute joint-action waiver.—The term "predispute joint-action waiver" means an agreement, whether or not part of a predispute arbitration agreement, that would prohibit, or waive the right of, one of the parties to the agreement to participate in a joint, class, or collective

action in a judicial, arbitral, administrative, or other forum, concerning a dispute that has not yet arisen at the time of the making of the agreement.

(3) Sexual assault dispute.—The term "sexual assault dispute" means a dispute involving a nonconsensual sexual act or sexual contact, as such terms are defined in section 2246 of title 18 or similar applicable Tribal or State law, including when the victim lacks capacity to consent.

(4) Sexual harassment dispute.—The term "sexual harassment dispute" means a dispute relating to conduct that is alleged to constitute sexual harassment under applicable Federal, Tribal, or State law.

SECTION 402. NO VALIDITY OR ENFORCEABILITY

(a) In General.—Notwithstanding any other provision of this title, at the election of the person alleging conduct constituting a sexual harassment dispute or sexual assault dispute, or the named representative of a class or in a collective action alleging such conduct, no predispute arbitration agreement or predispute joint-action waiver shall be valid or enforceable with respect to a case which is filed under Federal, Tribal, or State law and relates to the sexual assault dispute or the sexual harassment dispute.

(b) Determination of Applicability.—An issue as to whether this chapter applies with respect to a dispute shall be determined under Federal law. The applicability of this chapter to an agreement to arbitrate and the validity and enforceability of an agreement to which this chapter applies shall be determined by a court, rather than an arbitrator, irrespective of whether the party resisting arbitration challenges the arbitration agreement specifically or in conjunction with other terms of the contract containing such agreement, and irrespective of whether the agreement purports to delegate such determinations to an arbitrator.

Table of Authorities

Cases

14 Penn Plaza v. Pyett, 556 U.S. 247, 258 (2009), 227

Allen v. Leal, 27 F. Supp. 2d 945 (S.D. Tex. 1998), 181
American Express v. Italian Colors, 570 U.S. 228 (2013), 231
Angelella v. Pittston Township, No. 3:06-CV-00120, 2007 U.S. Dist. LEXIS 66968 (M.D. Pa. 2007), 173
AT&T Mobility LLC v. Concepcion, 563 U.S. 333 (2011), 234
AT&T Technologies, Inc. v. Communications Workers of America, 475 U.S. 643 (1986), 241
Avril v. Civilmar, 605 So. 2d 988 (Fla. Dist. Ct. App. 1992), 287

Bank of America v. Hotel Rittenhouse Associates, 800 F.2d 339 (3d Cir. 1986), 71
Baravati v. Josephthal, Lyon & Ross, Inc., 28 F.3d 704, 709 (7th Cir. 1994), 188
Bonar v. Dean Witter Reynolds, Inc., 835 F.2d 1378 (11th Cir. 1988), 201, 214
Broemmer v. Abortion Services of Phoenix, 840 P.2d 1013 (Ariz. 1992), 234
Brower v. Gateway 2000 Inc., 676 N.Y.S.2d 569 (N.Y. App. Div. 1998), 67, 261
Buckeye Check Cashing, Inc. v. Cardegna, 546 U.S. 440 (2006), 221

Caley v. Gulfstream Aerospace Corp., 428 F.3d 1359, 1368 (11th Cir. 2005), 225
Campbell v. Hussey, 368 U.S. 297 (1961), 267
Cassel v. Superior Court, 244 P.3d 1080, 1085 (Cal. 2011), 174
Cincinnati Gas & Elec. Co. v. General Electric Co., 854 F.2d 900 (6th Cir. 1988), 73, 85, 303
Commonwealth Coatings Corp. v. Continental Cas. Co., 393 U.S. 145 (1968), 202
Corey v. Avco-Lycoming Div., 307 A.2d 155, 160 (1972), 199

DirecTV v. Imburgia, 577 U.S. 47 (2015), 274
DiRussa v. Dean Witter Reynolds, 121 F.3d 818 (2d Cir. 1997), 217
Doctor's Assocs., Inc. v. Casarotto, 517 U.S. 681 (1996), 272

Eastern Associated Coal v. United Mine Workers Dist. 17, 531 U.S. 57 (2000), 204
Epic Systems Corp. v. Lewis, 584 U.S. 497 (2018), 245, 272, 277
Escobar v. Shearson Lehman Hutton, Inc., 762 F. Supp. 461 (D.P.R. 1991), 203
Evans v. Jeff D., 475 U.S. 717 (1986), 101

Federated Dep't Stores v. JVB Indus., 894 F.2d 862, 871 (6th Cir. 1990), 217
First Options v. Kaplan, 514 U.S. 938 (1995), 227
Folb v. Motion Picture Industry Pension & Health Plans, 16 F. Supp. 2d 1164 (D. Cal. 1998), 171
Foxgate Homeowners' Ass'n v. Bramalea, 25 P.3d 1117 (Cal. 2001), 295
Francis v. Women's Obstetrics & Gynecology Group, 144 F.R.D. 646 (W.D.N.Y. 1992), 306
Furia v. Helm, 111 Cal. App. 4th 945 (Ct. App. 2003), 148

G. Heileman Brewing Co. v. Joseph Oat Corp., 871 F.2d 648 (7th Cir. 1989), 294, 304
Gilmer v. Interstate/Johnson Lane Corp., 500 U.S. 20, 30 (1991), 231
Graham v. Baker, 447 N.W.2d 397 (Iowa 1989), 293
Graham v. Scissor-Tail, Inc., 623 P.2d 165 (Cal. 1981), 234
Graham v. State Farm, 565 A.2d 908 (Del. 1989), 271
Gray v. Eggert, 635 N.W.2d 667 (Wis. Ct. App. 2001), 296, 305
Gray v. Eskimo Pie Corp., 244 F. Supp. 785 (D. Del. 1965), 49
Green Tree Fin. Corp. Ala. v. Randolph, 531 U.S. 79 (2000), 234, 261

Hall Street Assocs. v. Mattel, Inc., 552 U.S. 1396 (2008), 205
Halligan v. Piper Jaffray, Inc., 148 F.3d 197 (2d Cir. 1998), 217
Hallowich v. Range Resources Corporation, 2012 Pa. Super.234 (Pa. Super. Ct. Dec. 7, 2012), 200
Hamer v. Sidway, 27 N.E. 256 (N.Y. 1891), 226
Hernando County School Bd. v. Nazar, 920 So. 2d 794 (Fla. Dist. Ct. App. 2006), 293
Hoffman v. Red Owl Stores, 26 Wis. 2d 683 (1965), 49
Hooters of America, Inc. v. Phillips, 173 F.3d 933 (4th Cir. 1999), 234
Howsam v. Dean Witter Reynolds, Inc., 537 U.S. 79 (2002), 243
Hunt v.Woods, 1996 WL 8037, 1996 U.S. App. LEXIS 1420 (6th Cir. 1996), 296

In re A.T. Reynolds & Sons, Inc., 452 B.R. 374 (S.D.N.Y. 2011), 295
In re Atlantic Pipe Co., 304 F.3d 135 (1st Cir. 2002), 284–86, 301, 302
In re Brown, 453 P.2d 958 (Ariz. 1969), 113
In re Eichholz, 2007 WL 1223613, 2007 U.S. App. LEXIS 11201, 114
In re Lewis, 463 S.E.2d 862 (Ga. 1995), 114
In re Marriage of Pebbles, 2004 Iowa App. LEXIS 1304, 294
In re Panel File Number 99-5, 607 N.W.2d 429 (Minn. 2000), 116
In re Potter, 952 P.2d 936 (Kan. 1998), 111
In re Ragland, 697 N.E.2d 44 (Ind. 1998), 113

Jaffe v. Redmond, 518 U.S. 1 (1996), 169
Janus Films, Inc. v. Miller, 801 F.2d 578 (2d Cir. 1986), 69
Jones v. Rath Packing Co., 430 U.S. 519 (1977), 266
Julius Erving v.Va. Squires Basketball Club, 349 F. Supp. 716 (E.D.N.Y. 1972), 215

Kindred Nursing Ctr. Ltd. P'ship v. Clark, 581 U.S. 246 (2017), 228, 272
Kentucky Bar Ass'n v. Geisler, 938 S.W.2d 578 (Ky. 1997), 60
Kokkonen v. Guardian Life Ins. Co of Am., 511 U.S. 375 (1994), 298
Kothe v. Smith, 771 F.2d 667 (2d Cir. 1985), 287

Leap Systems, Inc. v. MoneyTrax Inc., 638 F.3d 216 (3d Cir. 2011), 72
Luethke v. Suhr, 650 N.W.2d 220 (Neb. 2002), 115

Marmet Healthcare v. Brown, 565 U.S. 530 (2012), 273
Mastrobuono v. Shearson Lehman Hutton, Inc., 514 U.S. 52 (1995), 276
McDermott v.Wisconsin, 228 U.S. 115 (1915), 267
McDonald v. City of West Branch, 466 U.S. 284 (1984), 199, 213
Mitsubishi Motors Corp. v. Soler Chrysler-Plymouth, Inc., 473 U.S. 614 (1985), 239
Moncharsh v. Heily&Blase', 832 P.2d 899, 903 (Cal. 1992), 200
Montes v. Shearson Lehman Bros., 128 F.3d 1456 (11th Cir. 1997), 216

National Post Office Mailhandlers v. USPS, 751 F.2d 834 (6th Cir. 1985), 215
New England Merchants National Bank v. Hughes, 556 F. Supp. 712 (E.D. Pa. 1983), 307
Nick v. Morgan's Foods, 99 F. Supp.2d 1056 (E.D. Mo. 2000), 297
NLRB v. General Electric Co., 418 F.2d 736 (2d Cir. 1969), 49

Olam v. Congress Mortgage Co., 68 F. Supp.2d 1110 (N.D.Cal. 1999), 174
OPE International v. Chet Morrison Contractors, 258 F.3d 443 (5th Cir. 2001), 271
Ovitz v. Schulman, 133 Cal. App. 4th 830, 35 Cal. Rptr. 3d 117 (App. 2 Dist. 2005), 270
Oxford Health Plans, LLC v. Sutter, 569 U.S. 564 (2013), 244

PacifiCare Health v. Book, 538 U.S. 401 (2002), 258
Perreault v. Free Lance-Star, 666 S.E.2d 352, 355 (Va. 2008), 173
Preston v. Ferrer, 552 U.S. 346 (2008), 276
Prima Paint Corp. v. Flood & Conklin Mfg. Co., 388 U.S. 395 (1967), 222

Raad v.Wal-Mart Stores, Inc., 1998 WL 272879, 1998 U.S. Dist. LEXIS 11881, 294, 297, 306
Rent-A-Center v. Jackson, 561 U.S. 63 (2010), 223
Richardson v. Sport Shinko, 880 P.2d 169 (Haw. 1994), 290
Rodriguez de Quijas v. Shearson/American Express, 490 U.S. 477 (1989), 232

Saini v. Int'l Game Tech., 434 F. Supp. 2d 913, 923 (D. Nev. 2006), 86
Simrin v. Simrin, 233 Cal. App. 2d 90 (1965), 168
Southland Corp. v. Keating, 465 U.S. 1 (1984), 268

Sphere Drake Ins. Ltd. v. All American Ins. Co., 256 F.3d 587 (7th Cir. 2001), 264
Stambovsky v. Ackley, 572 N.Y.S.2d 672 (N.Y. App. Div. 1991), 61
Stare v. Tate, 21 Cal. App. 3d 432 (1971), 63, 82
Stolt-Nielsen v. Animal-Feeds, 559 U.S. 662 (2010), 203, 244
Strandell v. Jackson County, 838 F.2d 884 (7th Cir. 1987), 303

Tempo Shain Corp. v. Bertek, Inc., 120 F.3d 16 (2d Cir. 1997), 202, 214
Toon v. Wackenhut Corrections Corp., 250 F.3d 950 (5th Cir. 2001), 168
Triad Mack Sales & Serv. v. Clement Bros. Co., 438 S.E.2d 485 (N.C. Ct. App. 1994), 297

United Paperworkers Int'l Union v. Misco, Inc., 484 U.S. 29 (1987), 203
United States v. Panhandle Eastern Corp., 118 F.R.D. 346 (D. Del. 1988), 192
United Steelworkers v. Warrior & Gulf Navigation Co., 363 U.S. 574 (1960), 239

Vitakis-Valchine v. Valchine, 793 So. 2d 1094 (Fla. Dist. Ct. App. 4th Dist. 2001), 298
Volt Info. Sciences, Inc. v. Bd. Of Trustees of Leland Stanford Junior Univ., 489 U.S. 468 (1989), 275

Wagshal v. Foster, 28 F.3d 1249 (D.C. Cir. 1994), 146
Wilko v. Swan, 346 U.S. 427 (1953), 230
Williams v. Walker-Thomas Furniture Co., 350 F.2d 445 (D.C. Cir. 1965), 67, 232

Statutes and Rules

ABA Formal Ethics Op. 06-439, p. 3, (2006), 57
Alternative Dispute Resolution Act, 28 U.S.C. §652 (1998), 285
Ark. Code Ann. §16-7-204 (2018), 108

California Evidence Code Section 1123 (2019), 298
Civil Justice Reform Act, 28 U.S.C. §652(1990), 285

Federal Arbitration Act, 9 U.S.C. §10 (2002), 200–203, 205, 214–215, 270
Federal Arbitration Act, 9 U.S.C. §11 (2002), 205
Federal Arbitration Act, 9 U.S.C. §2 (2002), 265, 267–269, 272, 281
Federal Arbitration Act, 9 U.S.C. §3 (2002), 196–197, 211
Federal Arbitration Act, 9 U.S.C. §4 (2002), 197, 212
Federal Arbitration Act, 9 U.S.C. §9 (2002), 206–207, 212
Federal Rule of Civil Procedure 16 (2013), 284
Federal Rule of Civil Procedure 23(e) (2013), 70
Federal Rule of Civil Procedure 26(c) (2013), 167
Federal Rule of Civil Procedure 68 (2013), 288, 307
Federal Rule of Evidence 408 (2013), 165, 167, 169
Federal Rule of Evidence 501 (2013), 169
Fla. Sup. Ct. R.P.C. 4-2.1 (2013), 108
Florida Statutes Section 44-107(2) (2018), 147

Hawaii Rules of Professional Conduct Rule 2.1, Comment 5, 108

Massachusetts Supreme Judicial Court Rule 1: 18: Uniform Rules on Dispute Resolution Rule 5, 109
Mo. Sup. Ct. Rules, 17.02 (2013), 109
ABA MCPR EC 7-7, 112
Model Code of Professional Responsibility EC 7-8 (1980), 107
Model Rules of Prof'l Conduct 1.0 (2013), 118
Model Rules of Prof'l Conduct 1.2 (2013), 106–108, 116–117, 125–127
Model Rules of Prof'l Conduct 1.4 (2013), 107–108, 111–113, 123–126
Model Rules of Prof'l Conduct 1.6 (2013), 60, 64, 118–120, 127
Model Rules of Prof'l Conduct 2.1 (2013), 106–107, 109
Model Rules of Prof'l Conduct 3.2 (2013), 106–107, 124
Model Rules of Prof'l Conduct 3.3 (2013), 118–119
Model Rules of Prof'l Conduct 4.1 (2013), 55–56, 60–61, 64, 111, 119
Model Rules of Prof'l Conduct 4.1(b) (2013), 59–60, 117, 120, 127
Model Standards of Conduct for Mediators (2005), 137–142, 144–145, 156–160

Restatement (Second) of Contracts §161(b) (1979), 62
Restatement (Second) of Torts §551 (1977), 62

Sarbanes-Oxley Act, 15 U.S.C. §7201 (2002), 117

State of Mich. Standing Committee on Prof'l and Judicial Ethics, Opinion RI-255 (1996), 113

Tex. Lawyer's Creed, R. II.11 (2013), 109

U. S. Dist. Ct. Rules D.Mass., LR 16.1 (2013), 109

U.C.C. §2-313 (2001), 54

U.S. Bankr. Ct. R. S.D. Cal., LBR 7016-4 (1996), 109

U.S. Dist. Ct. for S. Dist. Texas Local Rule 16.4.B.1 (2014), 110

Uniform Mediation Act (2001), 148, 170, 175

Uniform Mediation Act §2(1) (2001), 130

Uniform Mediation Act §2(4) (2001), 178

Uniform Mediation Act §4(a) (2001), 177, 182

Uniform Mediation Act §4(b) (2001), 170, 177–182

Uniform Mediation Act §5 (2001), 172, 178, 182

Uniform Mediation Act §5(a) (2001), 178

Uniform Mediation Act §5(b) (2001), 181–183

Uniform Mediation Act §6 (2001), 183

Uniform Mediation Act §6(a) (2001), 173, 179–180, 183–184

Uniform Mediation Act §6(b) (2001), 174, 184–185

Uniform Mediation Act §6(c) (2001), 184–185

The Virginia State Bar Rules of Professional Conduct Rule 1.4, Comment 1, 109

Wyoming Statutes Annotated §1-43-104 (2019), 147

Other Sources

Farnsworth, Allan. *Contracts*. 4th ed. Aspen Publishers, 2004, 66

Fisher, Roger. William Ury and Bruce Patton, *Getting to Yes*, 3d ed. (2011), 3

Hackett, Frank Warren. *Reminiscences of the Geneva Tribunal of Arbitration 1872: The Alabama Claims* (Houghton Mifflin, 1911), 194

Henikoff, Jaime. Michael Moffitt. *Remodeling the Model Standards of Conduct for Mediators*, 2 Harv. Negot. L. Rev. 87 (1997), 142

Hinshaw, Art. *Regulating Mediators*, 21 Harv.Negot. L. Rev. 163 (2016), 146

Kovach, Kimberlee K. *Good Faith in Mediation–Requested, Recommended, or Required? A New Ethic*, 38 S. Tex. L. Rev. 575, 600 (1997), 48

Leff, Arthur A. *Unconscionability and the Code – The Emperor's New Clause*, 115 U. Pa. L. Rev. 485, 487 (1967), 233

Moffitt, Michael. *Settlement Malpractice*, 86U. Chicago L. Rev. 1825 (2019), 111

Riskin, Leonard. *Understanding Mediators' Orientations, Strategies, and Techniques: A Grid for the Perplexed*, 1 Harv. Negot. L. Rev. 7, 35 (1996), 133–134

Index

ABA. *See* American Bar Association
Active listening, interview and, 95–96
Adhesion contract, 226, 233–234, 245
ADR. *See* Court-ordered ADR
AFCC (Association of Family and Conciliation Courts), 144
Alternative Dispute Resolution Act of 1998 (ADR Act), 285, 291
Alternatives, defined, 3, 7
American Arbitration Association, 138, 198, 206, 230, 275
American Bar Association, 138, 170
  ABA Model Code of Professional Responsibility, 105
  ABA Model Rules of Professional Conduct. *See* Model Rules of Professional Conduct
  Model Standards of Conduct for Mediators, 137. *See also* Model Standards of Conduct for Mediators
Anchoring effect, 25, 30
Appeals of arbitrators' decisions, 200–205
  corruption, award procured by, 201–202
  exceeding authority of arbitrator, 202–203
  fraud, award procured by, 200–201
  manifest disregard standard, 205, 215–216
  partiality in arbitrators, 201–202, 214
  public policy, violation of, 204–205, 215
  sham hearing, 202
  undue means, award procured by, 200–201
  unintelligible decision, 203
  vacatur, grounds for, 200–203, 204
Arbitrability of dispute, 237–246
  breadth of arbitration clause, 239–240
  class actions, 243–246
  conditions precedent to arbitration, satisfaction of, 242–243
  examples/explanations, 247–264
  failure to follow procedures in agreement, 242–243
  gateway dispute, 242, 243, 255, 258
  procedural, 238, 242–243, 255–263
    intra-arbitration disputes, 242
    standards to apply, 243
    who decides, 243
  scope of arbitration agreement, 238–239
  substantive, 238–242, 255–264
    standards to apply, 239–240
    who decides, 240–242
  who decides, 240–242, 243
    ambiguity or silence on question, 240–241
    proceduralarbitrability, 243
    substantivearbitrability, 240–242
Arbitral awards
  challenging on nonstatutory grounds, 204–205
  challenging under FAA, 200–203
  confirmation of, 205–206
  corruption, effect of, 201–202
  enforcement of, 205–208
  fraud, effect of, 200–201
  international, 206–207
  judgments, entering as, 206
  preclusive effect of, 198–200
  undue means, effect of procuring by, 200–201
Arbitration
  appeals. *See* Appeals of arbitrators' decisions
  arbitrability. *See*Arbitrability of dispute
  awards. *See* Arbitral awards
  binding nature of, 188, 190, 191
  challenges to. *See*Arbitration agreement, challenges to
  chronology of, 190
  confidentiality in, 192
  as contractual substitute for litigation, 190–191
  courts, role of, 205–208
  defaults in, 197–198
  domestic disputes, 205–206
  enforceability of agreement to arbitrate. *See*Arbitration agreement, challenges to
  examples/explanations, 208–217
  historical background, 193–195
  international disputes, 207–208
  litigation compared, 187–191, 193
  mediation compared, 191–192

Arbitration (*continued*)
motion to compel, 197. *See also* Court-ordered ADR
nonbinding, 290–291
appearance by phone, 306–307
court-ordered, 290–291. *See also* Court-ordered ADR
objections to, nature of, 235–236
participation in, how courts compel, 195–200. *See also* Court-ordered ADR
preclusive effect of arbitral awards. *See* Arbitral awards
preemption, federal. *See* Preemption doctrine
of statutory claims, 227, 231
timeline, 190
Arbitration, state laws related to, 268–273
affecting all contracts, 269
choice of governing law, 273–276. *See also* Choice of law clauses
disfavoring arbitration clauses and some other subset of contracts, 271–272
disfavoring only arbitration clauses, 271–273
enforcing arbitration clauses, 269–270
only with modifications/restrictions, 270–271
not preempted by FAA, 269
preempted by FAA, 268–269
range of, 105–120
Arbitration agreement, challenges to
arbitrability of dispute. *See*Arbitrability of dispute
arbitration clause, challenge to, 223, 235–236
container agreement, challenge to, 221–222
delegation clause, challenge to, 223–224
enforceability of contract. *See* Contract, enforceability of
existence of contract. *See* Contract, existence of
generalized attacks, 231
Association for Conflict Resolution, Model Standards of Conduct for Mediators, 138. *See also* Model Standards of Conduct for Mediators
Association of Family and Conciliation Courts (AFCC), 144
Attorney client relationship, interview and, 91–93
Attorneys, ethical duties of. *See* Ethical duties of lawyers
Authority to contract, 227–228
Awards, arbitral. *See* Arbitral awards

Bargaining practices
competitive, 11
distributive, 11
hard, 11
"sharp," 67
Bargaining zone, 6. *See also* ZOPA
BATNA (best alternative to a negotiated agreement), 3–4
puffery and fraud in asserting, 55, 127
steps in calculation of, 3–4
Bottom lines, 4–5
Bush, Robert Baruch, 135

Capacity to contract, 227–228
Chance nodes, 27
Choice of law clauses, 273, 274–275
ambiguity about scope of coverage, 275–279
preemption doctrine and, 266–267. *See also* Preemption doctrine
state law specified as to arbitration, 274–275
state law specified only as to substance, 274
Civil Justice Reform Act of 1990, 285
Claim preclusion, 198–199
Class actions, 70, 243–246
waivers, 231, 234
Client confidentiality. *See* Confidentiality
Coercion, 66. *See also* Duress
Collateral estoppel, 198
Competitive bargaining, 11
Confidentiality, 68–74, 163–185
in arbitration, 191–192
clauses in agreements, 167–169
of client information, 34, 120
compromise and offers to compromise, 166
contractual clauses for protection of, 167–169
ethical duty of lawyer to maintain client confidences, 64, 116–120
evidentiary exclusions, 165–167
examples/explanations, 174–185
government, hiding settlement terms from, 69–70
interested parties in related disputes, hiding settlement terms from, 71–72
malpractice during course of, 173–174
mechanisms for protection of, 165–174
media, hiding settlement terms from, 73–74
offer of settlement, 165–167
open records laws, 68
positive/negative results of, 163–165
potential areas of trouble, 163–165
privilege, creation of, 165, 173–174

protective orders, 165, 167
public, hiding settlement terms from, 73–74
public policy violations, 169
related disputes, hiding settlement terms from interested parties in, 71–72
seal, filing settlement agreements under, 71
settlement offer, 165–167
sunshine laws, 68
Conflicts of interest, 137
Consent, informed, 141–142, 156–157
Container agreements
challenges to, 221–222
defined, 221
Contract, confidentiality, 167–169
Contract, enforceability of, 228–235
arbitration clause, fraud relating to, 229–230
duress, effect of, 232
examples/explanations, 247–264
formation of contract, fraud in, 229–230
fraudulently induced contract, 229–230
public policy objections, 230–232
unconscionability of contract, 232–235
who decides, 222–224
Contract, existence of, 224–228
acceptance, constructive, 227
acceptance, lack of, 225
capacity, authority, and legality, 227–228
consideration, adequacy of, 226–227
mutual assent, lack of, 225
offer and acceptance, lack of, 225
standards for deciding, 224–228
Contract, rescission for misbehavior, 65
Contrived ignorance, 52
Convention on Recognition and Enforcement of Foreign Arbitral Awards, 207
Cost gates, 27, 29
Court-ordered ADR, 283–307
arbitration, nonbinding, 291. *See also* Arbitration
attendance at, 293–294
authority for, sources of, 284–286
bad behavior in, 292–296
bad faith, sanctions for, 295, 297
boundaries of courts' authority, 286–289, 297–298
compelling particular nonbinding form of ADR, 289–291
confidentiality, maintaining, 295. *See also* Confidentiality
early neutral evaluation (ENE), 191
examples/explanations, 298–307
Federal Rules of Civil Procedure, 284
federal statutes, 285
good-faith participation, 292–297, 305
mediator reporting requirements, 195–296
good offer, effect of rejection of, 288–289
hard bargaining with nominal offer, 296
inherent powers of court, 285–286
limits on courts' authority, 286–289, 297–298
forcing party to make offer, no authority for, 287–288
forcing party to settle, no authority for, 287
forcing terms of offer, no authority for, 288–289
local rules, 285
mediation, 290
offer-of-judgment rule, 288–289, 303–304
participation, requirements of, 292–298
preparation for ADR process, 294
reasonable process, requirement of, 286
settlement authority of party, 294–295, 304–305
state ADR systems, 286
summary jury trials, 291–292, 303–304
turning down good offer, punishment for, 288–289
Credentialing of mediators, 143–144
organizational affiliation credentials, 143

Deception, 47. *See also* Falsity of statement; Fraud; Lying; Misrepresentation
Decision analysis, 26–45
anchoring risks, 25, 30
basic mechanisms in, 26–31
cash-flow implications of decision, 31–33
decision trees, 27–30
defined, 26
examples/explanations, 33–45
garbage in, garbage out, 30
ignoring impact of time, 30–31
ignoring nonmonetary interests, 30
ignoring value creation opportunities, 30
limits of, 30–31
money, time and the value of, 31–33
nonmonetary interests, ignoring, 30–31
structured settlements, 33
time and the value of money, 31–33
unreliability of data, 30
Decision nodes, 27, 30

Decision trees, 27–30
chance nodes, 27
cost gates, 27
decision nodes, 27
terminal nodes, 27
Delegation clauses, 223–224
Detrimental reliance, 52, 57–58. *See also* Fraud
Directive mediation, 133
Disciplinary actions for negotiator misbehavior, 65. *See also* Punishment; Sanctions
Dissembling, 55–57
Distributive bargaining, 11
Divorce mediation standards of practice, 144
Duress, 66, 232. *See also* Coercion
economic, 232
emotional, 232

Early neutral evaluation (ENE), 291
Economic duress, 232
Economies of scale, 8
Emotional duress, 232
Endowment effects, 24
ENE (early neutral evaluation), 291
Erie doctrine, 267
Estoppel, collateral, 198
Ethical duties of lawyers, 48. *See also* Model Rules of Professional Conduct
advising client of dispute resolution options, 106–111
sanctions for failure to advise, 110–111
candor of lawyer toward tribunal, 118–119
communicating settlement discussions/offers, 112–115
confidences of client, maintaining, 116–120. *See also* Confidentiality
examples/explanations, 120–127
fraud committed by client, 117, 119
mediation, confidential information in, 120. *See also* Confidentiality
settlement offers, communicating, 112–116
accuracy in communicating offers, 112
discretion given to lawyer by client, 114–115
sanctions for failure to communicate offer, 112–113
terrible offers, 113
unwise offer by client, 115–116
Ethics codes, 144–145
benefits for quality control, 144
for mediators, 144–145
Model Code of Professional Responsibility, 105
Model Rules of Professional Conduct. *See* Model Rules of Professional Conduct
Model Standards of Conduct for Mediators. *See* Model Standards of Conduct for Mediators
Evaluative mediation, 132–133, 148, 154. *See also* Mediation
broad and narrow, 133–134
likely processes, 136
mediator roles, 134, 136
negotiation challenges targeted, 136
primary goal, 136
primary mediation principle, 136
typical statements of mediator, 136
Express warranties, 54

FAA. *See* Federal Arbitration Act (FAA)
Facilitative mediation, 131–132, 148, 153. *See also* Mediation
broad and narrow, 133–134
likely processes, 136
mediator roles, 134, 136
negotiation challenges targeted, 136
primary goal, 136
primary mediation principle, 136
typical statements of mediator, 136
Falsity of statement, 53
fraud, 51–65. *See also* Fraud
lying, 51–53. *See also* Lying
misrepresentation, 53. *See also* Misrepresentation
puffery, 55–57. *See also* Puffery
Family mediation, standards of practice, 144–145
Federal Arbitration Act (FAA), 194–200. *See also* Preemption doctrine
challenging arbitral awards under, 200–203
compared to international law, 207–208
purpose of, 194
Federal preemption. *See* Preemption doctrine
Federal Rules of Civil Procedure
Rule 16, 284
Rule 23, 70
Rule 26, 167
Rule 68, 288, 303, 307
Federal Rules of Evidence, 165–166, 194
Rule 408, 168–167, 168
Rule 501, 169
Fiduciary relationships, omission of material fact as misrepresentation in, 61
Fixed-pie bias, 25–26

Folger, Joseph, 135
Fraud, 51–65
defined, 51, 119
detrimental reliance, 57–58
duty to correct, 62–64
elements of, 51, 229–230
knowledge, 52, 58–59
materiality, 53–54
misrepresentation, 53, 61, 117, 119, 127
negotiator's dilemma, 51
omission of information, 60–62
puffery, 55–57
sanctions for, 64–65
silence/confidentiality, 60–64
Fraud in the inducement, defined, 229, 264
Gateway dispute, 242, 255, 258
Getting to Yes (Fisher), 3

Golden Rule, 48, 50
Good faith
participation in court-ordered ADR, 292–298
mediator reporting requirements, 294–296
problem with requirement, 48–50
as standard for negotiators, 48–50

Haggling, 55
Hard bargaining, 11, 66

Ignorance, contrived, 52
Immunity of mediators
contractual waiver of liability, 146, 147
qualified, 146
quasi-judicial, 146
Impartiality of mediator, 159. *See also* Mediators
actual/perceived bias, 156
internal/external perceptions, 139, 142
maintaining neutral position, 131
Model Standards of Conduct, 137
prohibits dispensing of legal advice, 159
Informed consent
in mediation, 141–142, 156–157, 158–159
Integrative negotiation, 11
Interests
focus on, 2–3
shared, 7–8
interviewing through, 90–91
International arbitration awards, 207–208
International Chamber of Commerce, 198
International Institute for Conflict Prevention & Resolution, 144
Interview
attorney client relationship and, 91–93
interests and, 90–91
skills, 93–96
active listening, 95–96
facilitators & hindrances to gathering information, 96
questions, asking, 94–95
welcoming, 93–94
Issue preclusion, 198

Jurisdiction
diversity of citizenship, 267
subject matter, 267
Jury waivers, 282

Knowledge of falsity of statements, 52. *See also* Fraud

Lawyers, ethical duties of. *See* Ethical duties of lawyers
Legality of contract, 227–228
Litigation
arbitration compared, 193. *See also* Arbitration
motion to stay, 196, 198
timeline, 189
Logrolling, 10
Loss aversion, 24–25
Lying, 51–53, 229
duty to correct, 62–64
fraud. *See* Fraud
misrepresentation. *See* Misrepresentation
puffery. *See* Puffery
punishability of, 53, 58–59. *See also* Fraud
white lies, 54

Manifest disregard standard, 205, 215–217
Materiality of misrepresentation, 53–54
Media access to terms of settlement, 72–73
Mediation, 129–162
appearance by phone, 306–307
arbitration compared, 193
basic principles of, 137–142
confidentiality in. *See* Confidentiality
court-affiliated mediation program, 144
court-ordered, 290. *See also* Court-ordered ADR
defined, 129–130
directive, 133
divorce mediation, standards of practice, 144
enforcing settlement agreements, 297–298

Mediation (*continued*)
evaluative. *See* Evaluative mediation
examples/explanations, 149–162
facilitative. *See* Facilitative mediation
family mediation, standards of practice, 144
informality of, 139–140
informed consent, 141–142, 157–158
principles of, 142–143
private liability, 145–149
privilege in. *See* Privilege, in mediation
quality control, 142–149
Riskin's Grid, 133–135
self-determination, 135, 136, 137, 139–140, 142, 157
transformative. *See* Transformative mediation
understanding-based, 132
Mediation communication, defined, 170–171
Mediators
approaches of, 130–136
biases of, 25–26, 139
actual bias of, 139
breach of duty of care
causation, 148–149
damages, 148–149
certification of, 143–144
contractual waiver of liability, 147
credentialing of, 143–144
ethics codes, 144–145. *See also* Model Standards of Conduct for Mediators
good faith participation in court-ordered ADR reporting requirements, 293–296
immunity of, 146–147
impartiality of, 138–139, 142–143, 156–157
legal advice
provision of, 158–159
recommendation regarding, 159–160
liability, contractual waiver of, 147
neutrality of, 138–139, 142
partiality of
actual partiality or bias, 156
externally perceived, 139
internally perceived, 139
risk of perceived partiality or bias, 156
qualified immunity for, 146
quasi-judicial immunity for, 146
roles of, 130–136
standards of care, 147–148
standards of conduct, 137–138, 144–145. *See also* Model Standards of Conduct for Mediators
styles of, 130–136
waiver of liability, contractual, 147
Misbehavior of negotiator, 47–87. *See also* Fraud; Lying; Misrepresentation
coercion, 66
consequences of, 65
duress. *See* Duress
examples/explanations, 74–87
punishment for, 65. *See also* Sanctions
unconscionability. *See* Unconscionability, doctrine of
Misdirection, 55–57
Misrepresentation, 53. *See also* Fraud; Lying; Puffery
failure to act, 61
materiality of, 53–54
omission of material fact, 60–62
Mistake
duty to correct, 62–64
Model Code of Professional Responsibility, 105
Model Rule of Professional Conduct for the Lawyer as Third Party Neutral, 144
Model Rules of Professional Conduct
candor of lawyer toward tribunal, 118–119
confidentiality of client information, 64, 116–120
dispute resolution alternatives, duty to advise client of, 106–111
ethical duties, 47–48
fraud of client, duty of lawyer when, 117–119
misrepresentation, materiality of, 53–54. *See also* Misrepresentation
omission of information, 60–62
puffery, 55–57
settlement offers, duty to communicate, 112
Rule 1.2, 106, 116, 117, 127
Rule 1.4, 106
Rule 1.6, 60, 119
Rule 2.1, 106
Rule 3.2, 106
Rule 3.3, 119
Rule 4.1, 55, 60, 119–120, 127
Model Standards of Conduct for Mediators, 137. *See also* Mediators
conflicts of interest, 137
impartiality, 137, 138–139, 142, 156
informed consent, 141–142
scope of, 144–145
self-determination, 137, 139–140, 142
Motions
to compel arbitration, 197, 198–200
to stay litigation, 196, 198–200
Mutual gains negotiation, 11

Index

National Conference of Commissioners on Uniform State Laws, 170
Negotiation
- alternatives, defined, 3, 7
- bargaining zone, 6, 18
- BATNA, 3–4
- behavior in
  - bad behavior, 48–87
  - boundaries around, 47–48
- bottom lines, 4–5
- competitive bargaining, 11
- confidentiality in. *See* Confidentiality
- differences between negotiators
  - in capabilities, 10, 20
  - in predictions, 9, 21–22
  - in priorities, 10, 21
  - relative valuations, 21
  - in resources, 10, 20
  - in risk preference, 9, 22
  - in time frame, 9, 21
- distributive, 11
- economies of scale, 8, 20
- examples/explanations, 11–22
- good faith in, 48–50
- hard bargaining, 11, 66, 296
- integrative, 11
- interests, focus on, 2–3
- lying in, 51–23
- misbehavior in, 47–87
- models of, 10–11
- mutual gains, 11
- noncompetitive similarities, 7
- options, defined, 7
- positions, defined, 2
- principled, 10
- reservation values, 4–5, 15, 17
- shared interests, 7–8
- strategic/tactical decisions, 10–11
- value creation, 6–10
- ZOPA, 6, 17–20

Negotiator's dilemma, 51
Neutrality of mediator, 138–139, 142. *See also* Mediators; Partiality
New York Convention, 207
Nonbinding forms of ADR, 289–291
Noncompetitive similarities, shared interests of negotiators, 7–8

Offer-of-judgment rule, 288–289
Omission of fact, 60–62
- fiduciary relationships, effect of, 61

Open-meetings laws, 73
Open records laws, 68
Options, defined, 7
Overconfidence bias, 25

Partiality
- externally perceived, 139
- internally perceived, 139
- of mediator. *See*Impartiality of mediator; Mediators

Positions, defined, 2
Preemption doctrine, 247, 265–282
- background, 266–267
- choice of law clauses. *See* Choice of law clauses
- examples/explanations, 277–282
- federal arbitration law, 267–268
- state laws related to arbitration, categories of. *See* Arbitration, state laws related to

Preferences, risk, 21
Principled negotiation, 10
Privilege, in mediation
- consent of privilege holder to disclose information, 172–173
- creation of, 169–174
- defined, 169
- exceptions to, 173–174
- functioning of, 171
- waiver of, 172–173
- who holds, 170–172

Procedural unconscionability, 67–68. *See also* Substantive unconscionability
Protective orders, 167. *See also* Confidentiality
Psychological dynamics in negotiation, 24–26
- anchoring, 25
- endowment effects, 24
- loss aversion, 24–25
- overconfidence bias, 25
- reactive devaluation, 26
- zero-sum or fixed-pie bias, 25–26

Public access to terms of settlements, 72–74
Public policy doctrine, 230–232
Puffery, 55–57. *See also* Fraud; Lying; Misrepresentation
- mere, 56, 83, 127

Punishment
- disciplinary actions, 65
- good offer, turning down, 288–289
- for misbehavior, 65
- sanctions. *See* Sanctions

Reactive devaluation, 26
Relative valuations, 21

Reliance, detrimental. See Detrimental reliance
Reputation of negotiator
  importance of, 47
  misbehavior, consequences of, 65–68. See also Misbehavior of negotiator
Rescission of contract for misbehavior, 65
Reservation values, 4–5, 15, 17, 15–18
Res judicata, 198
Revised Uniform Arbitration Act (RUAA), 198, 270
Riskin, Leonard, 133
Riskin's Grid, 133–135
Risk preferences, 21

Sanctions
  for bad faith, in court-ordered ADR, 297–298
  for failure to advise client of dispute resolution options, 110–111
  for failure to communicate settlement offer, 112–113
  for misbehavior, 65–66. See also Misbehavior of negotiator
Sarbanes-Oxley Act, 117
Seal, filing settlement agreements under, 71–72
Self-determination, 136, 137, 139–140, 142, 157
  forms of, 139–140
Separability doctrine, 220–221, 223–224, 235–236, 263
Settlement offers, communicating, 112–116
  accuracy in communicating offers, 112
  discretion given to lawyer by client, 114–115
  sanctions for failure to communicate offer, 112–113
  terrible offers, 113
  unwise offer by client, 115–116
Settlements
  decisions, analysis of. See Decision analysis
  enforcing mediation agreements, 297–298
  structured, 33
  terms, hiding, 69–76
Silence
  regarding class actions, 245
  requirement of, 64
Similarities, noncompetitive, 7
Sophistication of parties, unconscionability of contract and, 67–68
Standards of Practice for Family and Divorce Mediation, 144
State laws
  on arbitration. See Arbitration, state laws related to
  preemption of. See Preemption doctrine
Statute of Frauds, 225
Structured settlements, 33
Substantive unconscionability, 67–68, 233–235. See also Procedural unconscionability
Summary jury trial
  court-ordered ADR, 291, 303–304
  regular trial compared, 291–292
Sunshine laws, 68, 69
Supremacy Clause, 266, 267

Terminal nodes, 27–28
Time value of money, 31–33, 42–43
Tort liability, for misbehavior, 65. See also Misbehavior of negotiator
Transformative mediation, 135–136, 154. See also Mediation
  likely processes, 136
  mediator roles, 136
  negotiation challenges targeted, 136
  primary goal, 136
  primary mediation principle, 136
  typical statements of mediator, 136
Tribunal, defined, 118–119

Unconscionability, doctrine of, 66–67, 232–235
  examples/explanations, 247–264
  proceduralunconscionability, 66–67, 233, 261–263
  substantiveunconscionability, 66–67, 233–235, 261–262
Uniform Arbitration Act (UAA), 198, 270
Uniform Mediation Act (UMA), 130, 148, 170, 175

Waivers, jury, 280–282
Warranties
  express, 54
  implied, 62
White lies, 54. See also Lying; Misrepresentation; Puffery

Zero-sum bias, 25–26
ZOPA (Zone of possible agreement)
  defined, 6, 17–20
  examples, 17–18, 41–42

www.ingramcontent.com/pod-product-compliance
Lightning Source LLC
LaVergne TN
LVHW080017210926
848481LV00011B/3048

* 9 7 9 8 8 8 6 1 4 2 1 5 0 *